Also by Khushwant Singh

FICTION

Train to Pakistan
I Shall Not Hear the Nightingale
Delhi: A Novel
The Company of Women
Burial at Sea
The Sunset Club
The Portrait of a Lady: Collected Stories

NON-FICTION

Truth, Love & a Little Malice: An Autobiography
Nature Watch
Indira Gandhi Returns
A History of the Sikhs
Ranjit Singh: Maharaja of the Punjab
The Freethinker's Prayer Book

TRANSLATIONS

Land of Five Rivers
Umrao Jan Ada (with M. A. Husaini)
Shikwa and Jawab-i-Shikwa
Celebrating the Best of Urdu Poetry (with Kamna Prasad)

unforgettable
fiction, non-fiction,
poetry & humour

KHUSHWANT SINGH

Edited by David Davidar and Mala Dayal
Introduction by David Davidar
Afterword by Mala Dayal

ALEPH

ALEPH

ALEPH BOOK COMPANY
An independent publishing firm
promoted by *Rupa Publications India*

Published in India in 2014 by
Aleph Book Company
7/16 Ansari Road, Daryaganj
New Delhi 110 002

ISBN: 978-93-83064-75-5

1 3 5 7 9 10 8 6 4 2

Printed and bound in India by Replika Press Pvt. Ltd.

For Naina,
Khushwant Singh's granddaughter, his pride and joy.

CONTENTS

The Uses & Abuses of Religion

Passage to Pakistan

Singular People

The Ferocity & Flamboyance of Nature

Sex on My Mind

A Merry Heart

Enthusiasms, Rants & Soliloquies

How to Live, How to Die

FICTION & POETRY

The Novels

The Portrait of a Lady & Other Stories

Toba Tek Singh: Fiction in Translation

A Passion for Poetry

A NOTE ABOUT THIS BOOK

99 is intended to be a lasting tribute to an iconic and much loved writer. Divided into fifteen sections, each corresponding to a genre Khushwant Singh worked in, this anthology showcases his finest fiction, journalism, essays, humour, translations, nature writing, travelogues, biographical and autobiographical works and historical writing. A collaborative effort, the initial selection was made by Mala Dayal, Naina Dayal, Ravi Singh and David Davidar. This was whittled down by Mala and David to the 99 pieces that appear in the book (one for every year of his life). The editors would like to thank (in alphabetical order) Aienla Ozukum, Bena Sareen, Chander Shekhar, Pujitha Krishnan and Simar Puneet for everything they have done for the book.

Khushwant Singh wrote many (and sometimes conflicting) versions of his favourite pieces—which is why the assiduous reader of anthologies bearing his name will often find essays with the same title differing from book to book. We have tried to be as forensic and accurate about our sourcing of all the material included in this volume. Where his original books are concerned this has been straightforward. We have chosen material that is representative of the books in question, obtained the necessary permissions from his publishers (who, without exception, have generously allowed us to use material from the books they have exclusive licenses in), and included them in the anthology. With pieces that have either appeared in many anthologies or have never been anthologized before, the process has been a little trickier given the multiple versions that have been published. Wherever possible, we have tried to track down and reprint the original article. Occasionally, we have had to edit a piece to make it cohere better, or cut out repetitions or, rarely, update it. (We have usually chosen not to update pieces in order to retain the flavour of the original composition.) All such editorial interventions are recorded in the notes at the back of the book.

99 can be read sequentially or can be dipped into at random. We hope you will take renewed pleasure in a piece you are familiar with or delight in one that you have never read before. Whether you are new to Khushwant Singh's work or a fan, we hope you will enjoy this book by one of our finest and most cherished writers.

INTRODUCTION

DAVID DAVIDAR

THE THREE LIVES OF KHUSHWANT SINGH

I

THE WRITER

He wrote every day of his life. For nearly seventy years. And fretted when he could not put down his daily quota of words on paper, for whatever reason. He tried to retire several times, especially when his wife died, but found he could not, writing had him too strongly in its grip. It helped that, after long years of practice, the words flowed easily. He wrote in long hand, with a ballpoint pen, on ruled, yellow legal pads, the kind that are sold in the Staples chain of stationery stores in North America. These were provided to him by friends and admirers. After the work was done, it was typed up on an old Remington typewriter by his secretary Lachman Das, who was the only one who could more or less decipher his untidy scrawl (Das often had to guess at what a word might be) and corrected by the author before being sent on to whoever the eventual recipient was. Khushwant Singh was legendary in journalistic circles for almost never missing a deadline. His final newspaper column was published a couple of weeks before his death.

For the last couple of decades, he worked in the living room of his apartment in Sujan Singh Park in Delhi. It is a room with high ceilings and two large windows that looks smaller than it actually is because it is cluttered with furniture and books—five chairs or sofas (besides his own); old-fashioned, glass-fronted bookshelves filled with hardcover books, most of them first editions; curtains with Urdu calligraphy on them; a glass-topped centre table, piled high with more books; other odds and ends of furniture; family photographs; a beautiful Italian wood sculpture of the head of Christ bought when he was a student; a couple of statues of the Buddha in an alcove; a framed Gauguin print on the wall; a valuable pen and ink sketch of a grouper by Günter Grass (bought cheap from the German Nobel Prize winner) on another wall; a television set (that was almost never turned on except to watch the news, National

Geographic programmes, tennis and cricket). It is a functional writer's room for the most part, with the tools of his trade ready to hand—books, pens, a telephone. His chair, to the right of the fireplace, was where he wrote, propping up his writing pads on a writing board, his feet resting comfortably on a moorha.

When he was at home in Delhi, he followed an unvarying routine. He rose early, between 4 and 5 a.m., with the help of two alarm clocks. 'One is the conventional type,' he wrote in a newspaper column, 'which goes off with an ear-splitting explosion of metal striking metal. The second is a Japanese speaking clock which starts with a short musical piece followed by a Jap speaking Ameringlish, "Good morning! It is five o'clock. Time to get up."' Once up, he would make ginseng tea for himself, and fill a bowl or platter with milk from the fridge, dilute and warm it with hot water, open his front door, and put it out for a dozen or so cats. Naina, his granddaughter, tells me that his favourite cat, Chanchal, a beautiful grey-and-white snob, who was born in his linen cupboard, would not deign to join the scrum, but would have to be fed separately. After the cats were fed, he would read the *Hindustan Times*, which was delivered early; he would pay particular attention to the obituaries and In Memoriams 'to find out which of my fellow citizens have left for their heavenly abode'. It was then time to turn on the radio to listen to 'Asa di var' from the Golden Temple and other Sikh hymns. Until his mid-eighties, the next step in his routine was to go off to the Gymkhana Club for a game of tennis. Back home, he would have a cold shower, even on winter days when the temperature plummeted (he believed it prevented him from catching a cold), read a few more papers over breakfast, after which he would get down to writing. If he had a heavy workload, he would put his phone off the hook and tell his staff to inform visitors that he was not at home. After a few hours of reading and writing, a light lunch (a bowl of soup or yogurt or curd rice) he would take a short nap, and then get back to writing. He would eventually knock off work in the evening. This extraordinary discipline led him to publish over twenty books. After he gave up a regular job in his seventies, the mainstay of his writing career was a newspaper column called 'With Malice Towards One and All' that he wrote for decades for the *Hindustan Times* and which was widely syndicated (another column entitled 'This Above All' appeared in the *Telegraph* and the *Tribune*)—it was arguably India's most popular newspaper column in its heyday. These columns were collected into dozens of anthologies by enterprising publishers, and swelled Khushwant Singh's oeuvre to over one hundred published works.

◆

I first met Khushwant Singh in 1985. At seventy, he was India's most famous magazine and newspaper editor, a world renowned historian and the author of *Train to Pakistan*, which I would rate as one of the ten finest novels published by an Indian writer in our time. I was twenty-six, with no profile whatsoever in any of the fields he had excelled in. It made no difference to the way he treated me. He greeted me with a faintly amused look. Over the next three decades I would never see that look fade from his eyes, except once, when he broke down and wept at the death of his wife. The Khushwant Singh gaze (of amused indifference) was that of a man who had stood up to everything the world could throw at him and had thrived; it was that of a man who refused to take himself seriously although he had been courted by presidents and kings (and beautiful women) for a quarter century; it was a distancing look that said 'this far and no further' (for a man who was almost constantly surrounded by admirers, sycophants and opportunistic users, he declared more than once that he was a loner who preferred his solitude).

At that first meeting, I remember being struck by the fact that he had driven himself in his ageing Fiat to Penguin India's modest first floor office in Gulmohar Park. His attire, a crumpled Pathan suit with fresh food stains, an untidily tied orange turban, and open-toed sandals, didn't seem to suggest the extraordinary wealth he was born into. (His father Sir Sobha Singh, one of Delhi's foremost builders, owned vast properties in Lutyens Delhi, and, as a young man, Khushwant Singh grew up in gigantic houses with numerous servants, and every luxury that money could buy). I mentioned being impressed by his modest comportment to his daughter Mala (the co-editor of this tribute volume). She said quietly: 'My father did not dress flashily and drove his own car because that was his style, but it was also because we were not wealthy.' I was astonished. But what about the fortune, estimated to be in the hundreds of crores of rupees, which Khushwant Singh and his family were reputed to be worth?

'No, we don't have a fortune,' Mala said. 'All the property and buildings that my father's family and my mother's father owned went into charitable trusts, or to other members of the family. Even when we were left something my father would insist we opt out because he said it would bring us nothing but grief. He had a horror of litigation. Once, when Rahul (her brother) was left a valuable house by our grandfather, my father simply tore up the will. We never ate out at five-star restaurants because we couldn't afford to.'

Did that explain Khushwant Singh's assertion that he'd never paid for any of his trips or junkets abroad or in India?

'Yes,' Mala said, 'my father lived off whatever he made from his writing. As he never cared much about negotiating a better price for his work, despite the fact that he was one of the most widely read columnists in the country, he was paid rather modestly.'

This was jaw-dropping stuff. I was aware of course that Khushwant Singh, by his own admission, had tried and abandoned more than one profession before settling on a career as a writer because he had loved literature as a boy and as a young man, but I'd always assumed that he was a wealthy dilettante dabbling in the writing trade because it was something he found fulfilling. To know that he wrote out of necessity as well gave me a deeper understanding of his anxiety to be a successful writer.

◆

In the early 1980s, just after he had won the Booker Prize for *Midnight's Children*, Salman Rushdie delivered a lecture (it was published as an essay entitled 'Outside the Whale') to a packed room in Bombay's President Hotel. It was a brilliant speech by a writer at the height of his powers, and one of his inspired coinages that I heard that evening remains with me to this day—'For every text, a context'. That is what I will try to do in this essay, provide the frame within which Khushwant Singh's writing should be placed and viewed.

His career as a writer began in Lahore. An indifferent student in Delhi, Lahore and England, he eventually took a law degree and began to practise, at his father's insistence, at the Lahore High Court. He hated the profession, and wasn't much of a success as a lawyer, although, as he writes in his autobiography, *Truth, Love & a Little Malice*, 'I have no doubt that, had I stuck to the law, I would have made it to the Bench and perhaps even to the Supreme Court... [However], I never regretted chucking up the law; my only regret was that I wasted five years studying it and another seven trying to make a living out of it.' As his legal career faltered, his interest in literature was rekindled; his love of great writing had been sparked off in school (thanks to an English teacher, Miss Budden, who read her charges exciting stories by Oscar Wilde and Sir Walter Scott rather than burden them with 'boring text books', and an Urdu tutor, Maulvi Shafiuddin Nayyar, who had initiated him into the splendour of Urdu poetry), and grown into a passion in college, where he had memorized poems and some of Shakespeare's plays, and had first tried to publish some of his own writing in the college magazine, *Ravi*—both his contributions were rejected.

In Lahore, as his legal career floundered, he began writing short stories, some of which were published in literary magazines. The decisive turning point in his life and career, the one that would turn him into one of the best-loved writers the subcontinent has produced in modern times, occurred in the 1940s. Khushwant was part of a literary circle which met frequently. At one such meeting, all the members were told to write short pieces on 'the values of life'. He says there was nothing original about what he wrote but it was well received.

As the literary circle continued to meet he began to realize (he writes in more than one piece) that he had a gift for storytelling that the others did not have. The writer might have thrilled to the talent that lay within him, but it would be a while yet before the world at large would recognize it. But meanwhile he had a wife to support, and he could not rely on his wealthy father's generosity indefinitely. He was also caught up in the cross-currents of history. The great violence and disruption of Partition hastened his departure from Lahore. And with it, his last connection to the legal profession. However, given the massive exodus of qualified people from India, there were plenty of other jobs to be had, and the young Khushwant decided to try to get a job with the Indian diplomatic service. A friend helped him land a position at India House in London, and he made his way back to the city he loved from the days he had spent in it as a student. The high commissioner at the time was V. K. Krishna Menon, and Khushwant soon found out that his relationship with him was going to be a tempestuous one. Fortunately, he was soon transferred to the High Commission in Canada. It was here that his writing career slowly began to take off. His short stories were published in magazines like *Canadian Forum*, *Saturday Night*, and *Harper's*. And, for the first time, in his mid-thirties, Khushwant Singh began to contemplate making a career out of his great passion.

But before he could do anything about it, he was transferred back to London to work for his old employer, Krishna Menon. Within a short time, the relationship soured and, emboldened by the publication of his first collection of short stories, *The Mark of Vishnu and Other Stories*, to excellent reviews, Khushwant decided that he was going to resign his position and become a full-time writer. His wife Kaval, a strong-willed and independent woman, whose support would play a large part in making him the man and professional he was, apparently did not object but to the extended family this seemed a decision that was foolish in the extreme. Undeterred, Khushwant made up his mind to subsist on his modest savings as he figured out his writing career.

Astonishingly, given his rather cavalier attitude to a regular job, he was quite strategic about the way in which he thought he could make a go of it in the writing world. Looking around, he thought he should write a short history of the Sikhs, given the paucity of works on the subject. His strategy paid off, and the book was widely noticed in England. Not that this impressed anyone when he returned home to Delhi. He writes in his autobiography, 'No one was impressed by the fact that I had a couple of books published in England. No one in the family wanted to read the reviews I had brought with me. All they wanted to know was how much I had earned in royalties. It was very little…I was described as a nikhattoo—a shirker, who does not earn his living. One day, Sir Shri Ram, whose home I often visited because of my wife's schooldays friendship with his son Bharat and Bharat's wife Sheila, asked me, "Do you do any kaam-vaam or do you live on your father's earnings?" These remarks stung me because they were true…'

Khushwant Singh decided he would have to leave Delhi if he was going to complete his first novel that he had begun while still in Europe. He went to Bhopal where his father had rented a house by a lake, and finished the novel in a month. He named it *Mano Majra*. It was typed by a friend, Tatty Bell, the wife of a diplomat at the British High Commission. When she handed the typescript back to the eager young novelist, her response was discouraging. 'It's no good! Nobody is going to publish it.' Downcast, Khushwant writes, 'I wanted to tear it up.' Fortunately, he was able to overcome the uneducated literary assessment of Ms Bell and sent the typescript to Grove Press, where it was accepted by the celebrated Barney Rosset, the publisher of Henry Miller and D. H. Lawrence. *Mano Majra* (which readers today will know as *Train to Pakistan*) would go on to win the Grove Press Award. Khushwant Singh the writer was on his way.

II

THE WRITER AS NOVELIST

The achievement of *Train to Pakistan*, which I re-read while working on this anthology, lies in what the renowned Czech-French novelist Milan Kundera described in *The Art of the Novel*: 'A novel examines not reality but existence. And existence is not what has occurred, existence is the realm of human possibilities, everything that man can become, everything he's capable of.' On the face of it, *Train to Pakistan* is a novel about Partition, the greatest tragedy to have been visited upon the subcontinent. If it had remained just that, it would have been just a few thousand more of the millions of words, both fiction and non-fiction, in many languages, that have been written about the event. What lifts it into the realm of great literature is the skilful way in which its author is an 'explorer of existence'.

Today, it is a cliché to say that the novel, a European invention, has had fresh life breathed into it by the Latin Americans, South Asians and Africans. But in this, as with many other things in his writing life, Khushwant was ahead of his time. While his peers were doggedly trying to fit the rhythm of subcontinental life into literary moulds devised in Europe, he was trying something original. He decided the novel's central characters—Juggut Singh, the small-time crook and farmer, Hukum Chand, the district magistrate, and Iqbal Singh, the idealistic communist—would represent an Eastern (more specifically an Indian) idea that he had been turning over in his mind—that every individual has within him or her the great Hindu trinity of Brahma (the Creator), Vishnu (the Preserver) and Shiva (the Destroyer) and, depending on the individual, one or the other aspects of the trinity would predominate.

Train to Pakistan has never been out of print since it was first published in 1956. It isn't hard to see why, because it hasn't dated. The story of Juggut Singh and Iqbal, Hukum Chand and Meet Singh, unlikely heroes in a world gone mad, has a timeless, universal quality to it, rather like Harper Lee's *To Kill a Mockingbird*. Both books detail man's inhumanity to man in precise, unsparing detail, and in prose that's sharp and glittering as a knife.

Khushwant Singh began to write the book in a small pensione by the side of Lago Elio on the Italian-Swiss border. He writes in his introduction to an omnibus edition of some of his novels: 'I had no idea how one wrote a novel. I did not think I had the stamina to write one. But I did have the theme. I had lived through the civil strife that engulfed the whole of northern India. Almost every other day of the spring to summer of 1947, we heard stories of massacres of Sikhs and Hindus in the villages of the Northwest Frontier Province and Rawalpindi and Campbellpur districts; and of thousands of refugees trekking eastwards to areas where Hindus and Sikhs were in preponderance. When communal violence broke out in Lahore there was hardly a night when we were not woken up by the sounds of gunfire and mobs yelling Allah-o-Akbar from one side and Har Har Mahadev and Sat Sri Akal from the other. The spreading communal violence did not affect our small circle of friends: Muslims, Hindus, Sikhs and Christians continued to meet as usual and enjoy their sundowners. Of course, we developed a sense of guilt. There was so much violence and wickedness going on around us and we did nothing about it except talk and drown our consciences in drink. It was after the partition of the country was over, after ten million people had been rendered homeless and one million slain, that I felt I had to purge myself of the guilt I bore by writing about it.'

◆

Khushwant Singh's second novel, *I Shall Not Hear the Nightingale*, was the one he considered his best. I am not so sure. Its plot is more complex, and there are more secondary narratives, and characters, including the first interesting female characters the novelist created, such as the temptress Champak, and Sabhrai, the magistrate's wife, but it lacks the clarity, concision (the quality novelists like Ernest Hemingway, George Orwell and V. S. Naipaul have described as the essential aspect of great writing) and sheer storytelling power of the novel that preceded it. You sense that here the writer is obsessed with technique and the need to be as literary as possible and these concerns take away from the novel. Written while he was on a UNESCO assignment in Paris (his last job that did not have to do with the written or spoken word), it is set against the backdrop of the Quit India Movement and tells the story of a conflicted family that the author says was based on his own family. Whatever the merits or demerits of the book (Mala and I agree that the title for one could have been better) it has one of the most arresting first chapters you will read in contemporary fiction.

And so we come to his ambitious, flawed (the author himself writes that 'he was not happy' with it) masterpiece, *Delhi*—this was the first book of his that I edited. A few years after we began working together, he invited me to his flat, and handed me a large sheaf of yellowing foolscap pages, the typescript of a novel that he had been working on for over twenty years. It was clear that the book needed to be extensively revised before it could be published. It was an exhilarating experience working with him; we had few arguments and he was quick to accept editorial suggestions that he felt had merit. I believe he had lived with the novel far too long to have the energy and enthusiasm to recast it completely, but whatever rewriting he was able to do gave the narrative the cohesiveness it lacked in parts. What it eventually turned out to be was a lasting memorial to Delhi, the city he loved and lived in. His imagining of it, down the ages, is still, in my view, superior to any of the other books written on the city. My father-in-law, the legendary bookseller K. D. Singh, another son of Delhi, felt it was the best book on Delhi he had ever read and sold.

The first three books did more than enough to cement Khushwant Singh's reputation as a novelist but there would be three more before he ended his career as a fiction writer. The first of these, *The Company of Women*, featured an ageing reprobate's sexual encounters with a series of women which the author published with a disclaimer: 'No characters in this exposé are real: they are the figments of my senile fantasies'. It did not fare well at the hands of critics but did well on the bestseller lists. His depictions of sex in this novel and in *Delhi* are among the most explicit erotic writing to be encountered in fiction by an Indian novelist.

◆

Writers who have had very long careers (V. S. Naipaul, Philip Roth, Gabriel García Márquez, R. K. Narayan come to mind) tend to write two kinds of novels towards the end of their careers. The first kind leans towards the philosophical and is full of ruminations about death and the afterlife; the second kind features a pared down narrative that dispenses with the sort of stuff the late great American novelist Elmore Leonard advised against (he suggested to would-be novelists that they 'try to leave out the part(s) that readers tend to skip'. By this he meant elaborate descriptions of people, places, the weather and so on). *Burial at Sea*, written when Khushwant was eighty-nine, tells the story of Victor Jai Bhagwan, who creates a business empire from scratch in the years following the country's achieving independence, in fast-moving prose. It is not one of his best efforts, and was regarded as such when it was published.

◆

The Sunset Club was Khushwant Singh's last novel. It was written when he was ninety-five years old and is full of wistful and erudite discourses about the glories of youth, the great disadvantages and small consolations of old age. The Sunset Club comprises three old men who meet every day, weather permitting, in Delhi's fabled Lodi Gardens, to talk and reminisce about times past and present. They are Pandit Preetam Sharma, a retired bureaucrat, Nawab Barkatullah Baig Dehlavi, a wealthy aristocrat, and Sardar Boota Singh, a journalist and bon vivant, and the author's alter ego. After their morning constitutional, the trio take their seats on what comes to be known as the 'Boorha Binch' (old men's bench)—a stone bench facing one of the most beautiful monuments in the park, the Bara Gumbad—'which is an exact replica of a young woman's bosom including the areola and the nipple'. Sardar Boota Singh, who has an endless repository of tawdry stories and jokes, as well as earthy opinions on every scandal that is featured in the media, entertains the group every day with his irreverent opinions. It has its moments, and is certainly more than just a curiosity, but I doubt it will last.

◆

When he was writing out of his skin, Khushwant Singh's short fiction was world class, easily on a par with other well-known writers of his generation from the subcontinent who dabbled in the genre, like R. K. Narayan and Raja Rao. In regard to his method and style, Khushwant had this to say: 'I believe that short stories should conform to tradition: in being short, having a good beginning, middle and end—preferably a surprise ending with some message to convey.' He said his role models were some of the masters of the form—Somerset Maugham, Dorothy Parker, Alberto

Moravia, Albert Camus, and, from the subcontinent, Munshi Premchand, Saadat Hasan Manto, and Intizar Husain. His early stories are, in my opinion, better than his later efforts. They have, as their hallmark, a tight narrative style, brevity, and often an O'Henry-esque twist at the end. They all move quickly, are studded with insights into human foibles and are written with lightness, accessibility and humour. His greatest story, 'Portrait of a Lady', is in the same league as O. V. Vijayan's 'After the Hanging', Saadat Hasan Manto's 'Toba Tek Singh', Premchand's 'Kafan' and R. K. Narayan's 'A Horse and Two Goats', which are among the finest examples of contemporary short fiction published anywhere in the world.

III

THE WRITER AS JOURNALIST

When Khushwant Singh became the editor of *The Illustrated Weekly of India* in 1969 he changed the world of magazine journalism in India forever. In its way, what he did with the *Weekly*, was as important as the change Tom Wolfe, Hunter S. Thompson and Gay Talese wrought in the world of American journalism, with the 'New Journalism'—which in the sixties and seventies was hailed as a seismic shift in the way news was reported and non-fiction stories were told.

Or let me put it differently. In regard to his impact on the media, Khushwant Singh was Barkha Dutt before Barkha Dutt, Arnab Goswami before Arnab Goswami, M. J. Akbar before M. J. Akbar, Shobhaa De (the magazine editor as opposed to Shobhaa De the novelist) before Shobhaa De and Vinod Mehta before Vinod Mehta. He was, in short, the granddaddy of them all, a man before his time.

When he took over as editor (a job he had already turned down once in order to write his history of the Sikhs), he was fifty-four years old, and knew very little about either journalism or editing. He had worked briefly for All India Radio, and had founded a government publication called *Yojana* which no one read, so he wasn't exactly a seasoned journalist or editor. He was exactly what the magazine needed.

At the time, the media scene in the country was dire. Besides the daily newspapers, there was no interesting television or radio, there was no internet, and the *Weekly* (owned by The Times of India Group), one of the few periodicals that existed, was dull, worthy and little read, although it was a favourite of maamis in Adyar, auntyjis in Karol Bagh and dentists everywhere. He wrote in a column, 'The *Weekly* was a mixture of unrelated articles. Some of it consisted of the tittle tattle at cocktail parties given by Parsi dowagers with outlandish names... A few pages were devoted to "They Were Married" and consisted of photographs of newly married couples from different parts of India, all looking very tight-lipped, glum and unhappy.' Apart from these it had a few pages devoted to children, syndicated features, and other material that was of scant interest to readers.

Its new editor had three clear objectives. He would inform, amuse and irritate. He decided that he would use the magazine 'to tell Indians about their own country', and that he would try and provoke and amuse his readers by publishing controversial or humorous articles.

Soon, changes began to appear throughout the magazine. Gone were the grim studio portraits of middle-class newly-weds; in their place were topless photographs of pretty tribal women or semi-clad foreigners on the beaches of Goa. Besides titillating readers with pictures of scantily clad women, he began writing about subjects that he personally found fascinating, such as gods and godmen (whom he exposed), 'the refined art of bottom pinching', and 'the joys of drink'. As with the subjects he chose to write about, so with the tone he adopted to write about them. He explained his approach in one of his columns: 'I have never taken anyone too seriously. I have always been a nosy person, forever probing into other people's lives. I love to gossip and have an insatiable appetite for scandal... I discovered I could exploit these negative traits to my benefit. Readers were amused by what I wrote and asked for more.' Circulation soared, and went from about 80,000 copies to a high of 400,000 copies.

Khushwant Singh became the most powerful editor in the country and was courted by political royalty, movie stars, sports heroes and celebrities of every stripe who would do anything to be featured in his magazine's pages. He lapped up the attention, but continued to be his own man for the most part. He also began to write some of the finest journalism of his career, using techniques that were being popularized at this time by practitioners of the New Journalism. Tom Wolfe described it in this way: 'The basic units of reporting are no longer who-what-when-where-why and how but whole scenes and stretches of dialogue. The New Journalism involves a depth of reporting and an attention to detail to the most minute facts and details most newspapermen, even the most experienced, have never dreamed of.' Some of Khushwant's work of this time, and a little later (pieces like 'The Hanging of Bhutto' and 'Indira Gandhi') are stellar examples of this kind of journalistic writing which tried to show readers, in the words of Wolfe, 'what actually happened'. As the *Weekly* grew and flourished, young journalists who would in time become stars in their own right (among them M. J. Akbar and Bachi Karkaria) joined its ranks. But the idyll wouldn't last forever.

In the first major stand that he took as editor, Khushwant Singh blundered. It was a mistake that would haunt him for decades. When Indira Gandhi, the then prime minister, declared a State of Emergency in 1975 that suspended civil liberties in the country, and imposed press censorship, Khushwant Singh offered the move his qualified support. He wrote in a much-discussed essay 'Why I Supported the Emergency' that he had an ambivalent attitude towards it. He supported the clamping down on law breakers (including Jayaprakash Narayan) but didn't approve of censorship of the press. But his public support of Mrs Gandhi's action after a cursory attempt at resistance affected him in more ways than one. He was now regarded as an Establishment stooge (in this he was not in a minority of one as several of the country's top editors behaved, if anything, even more supinely); more damagingly, as an unabashed supporter of Indira Gandhi and her son Sanjay Gandhi (whom he once described as 'a lovable goonda'), when Mrs Gandhi was voted out of power, he fell out of favour with his employers at the *Weekly*. Shortly thereafter he was fired, in what was widely regarded as a political move, just a week before he was due to retire. In one of the most famous episodes of his life, which he has mentioned more than once in his non-fiction, when he learned of his summary disposal, he 'picked up [his] umbrella, and walked out of *The Times of India* building'.

Back in Delhi, he began work on a novel, while attempting to (and largely succeeding) in putting his downfall behind him. He looked to Allama Iqbal's lines to inspire him:

In this world men of faith and self-confidence are like the sun,
They go down one side to come up on the other.

And he did rise again as a journalist and editor, going on to edit *The National Herald*, *New Delhi* magazine, and the *Hindustan Times*, but it was clear that his best days as a magazine and newspaper editor were behind him. However, being Khushwant Singh, he was far from done. Ahead lay a career as a public intellectual and India's most popular newspaper columnist.

◆

When he was the editor of the *Weekly*, the renowned cartoonist Mario Miranda created a logo for the Editor's Page. It showed a sardar seated cross-legged in silhouette with a bottle of Scotch and a pile of books by his side, and a pen and a long ribbon of paper in his hand. The illustration was encased in a light bulb. When he left the *Weekly* and became editor of the *Hindustan Times* the light bulb travelled with him to grace his editor's column; even after he quit the paper (he thinks this was because the mercurial Sanjay Gandhi or his mother did not like an article he had written) he continued to write a weekly column for it; it would become widely syndicated and propel him to the position of India's leading newspaper columnist. His columns were a mix of his take on political and other newsworthy items of the day, along with a dash of poetry or personal anecdotes, all written in his signature style (I will look at this in greater detail later in this piece). He said of his column writing: 'I have no pretensions of being a craftsman of letters. Having to meet a deadline did not allow me the time to wait for inspiration, indulge in witty turns of phrase or polish what I had written.'

Why did the column become so popular? Partly this was because of the lively interest of its author in current events, his astonishing erudition (he read constantly—often fifty or more books a year) that he wore lightly, his wit, his contrariness, but also because he treated the reader as an equal with whom he was having a constant, spirited dialogue. He writes in an article about how he approached his job as a columnist. 'One should never be pretentious…[one should] be honest and not show off by using difficult words. A writer's responsibility…is to inform your reader while you provoke or entertain him… Don't talk down to the reader; level with him.'

IV

THE WRITER AS HISTORIAN

Surprising as it may seem to those who feel his most singular achievements lay in journalism or in the writing of fiction, Khushwant Singh himself thought differently. 'The most fulfilling thing about my career,' he said in an interview with a magazine, 'was working on Sikh religion and history.' As we've seen, his first major coup as a writer was publishing a book on the Sikhs, which, in hindsight, he didn't feel was very good. Some years after this attempt, he decided he would write a magisterial history of the Sikhs for which he spent years doing research into the community around the world. Based as it was on original documents in Gurmukhi, Persian and English scattered in archives, libraries and private collections in India, Pakistan, Canada, the UK and the US, it was immediately acclaimed when it was published by Princeton University Press. Besides the quality of its research and insights into the community, it had the advantage of being readable, because it is universally acknowledged that the writing of most great Indian historians is dull and soporific. Khushwant Singh wrote in one of his columns about his attempt to breathe life into historical writing: 'A dry academic approach is the chief reason why our histories make such dull reading... The British conquest of Sindh is epitomized in the one-word message sent by Napier to the Governor-General: 'Peccavi'—I have sinned. The message may have been apocryphal; but it is stuff which sugar-coats history and makes it fascinating.'

Today, multiple reprints later, *A History of the Sikhs* exists in two volumes. The first volume starts with the founding of Sikhism towards the end of the fifteenth century by Guru Nanak, and ends with the death of the greatest ruler of the Punjab, Maharaja Ranjit Singh, in 1839. The second volume of his history brings the story of the Sikhs up to modern times. It is unlikely that this monumental work will be eclipsed anytime soon. Writes Khushwant in his autobiography, 'At the end of Volume II, I appended two words in Latin: Opus Exegii—My life's work is done. To write on Sikh religion and history was my life's ambition. Having done that I felt like one living on borrowed time, at peace with myself and the world. It did not bother me if I wrote nothing else.'

Besides his Sikh history, Khushwant Singh made exquisite translations of the Sikh hymns and wrote a popular biography of Maharaja Ranjit Singh. All of them continue to find new readers, and deepen his reputation as the pre-eminent chronicler of the Sikhs.

V
OTHER WRITINGS

At the height of his popularity, as I've said earlier, Khushwant Singh had over one hundred titles to his name. This, despite the fact that he only 'wrote' twenty-three books (this number fluctuates depending on the resource you consult as some of his translations, especially of the Sikh hymns, were published in more than one iteration)—six novels, the two-volume history of the Sikhs, his collected stories, the biography of Ranjit Singh, a book on nature, his brilliant autobiography and six books of translations of fiction and poetry, all of which are in print; besides these, he also published a book on Mrs Gandhi, a biography of an industrialist, and a couple of books on Punjab, which are now out of print. The other eighty odd books were anthologies of his columns, articles in the *Weekly* (and the other publications he worked for) as well as a series of books that simply collected the jokes that appeared as the tailpiece of his columns. It is a measure of his popularity that most of these books continue to sell.

◆

Great translators such as Richard Pevear and Larissa Volokhonsky, who have translated several of the Russian masters (Dostoevsky, Tolstoy, Gogol, Bulgakov and Chekhov among others) or Gregory Rabassa, who unveiled the genius of Gabriel García Márquez to readers in English, do not make literal translations of the work they are translating. Rather they recreate a supple, literary version of the work in question in the target language, using their considerable creativity and literary skills, to ensure the translated version shows off the excitement, stylistic flourishes and genius of the original work to best effect. In similar fashion, Khushwant Singh did a good job of recreating in English, the work of fiction writers and poets he admired from the languages he knew well—Urdu, Punjabi and Hindi. He began translating verse because of the dismal translations that existed of the poetry he admired. Readers of his column would be treated to snatches of poems he had translated. Today, most of these are collected in books such as *Celebrating the Best of Urdu Poetry* which features the work of remarkable poets like Ghalib, Zauq, Illahabadi, Faiz, Sauda and Meer. He also made an exceptionally fine translation of Iqbal's great poem

Shikwa, Jawab-i-Shikwa. Besides the poetry translations he was renowned for, he translated, arguably, the most famous Urdu novel of all time, Mirza Muhammad Hadi Ruswa's *Umrao Jan Ada* about the life and times of a famous courtesan, Umrao Jan; Rajinder Singh Bedi's novel, *I Take This Woman;* and some of the finest short fiction to be had in Hindi, Urdu and Punjabi, by writers like Saadat Hasan Manto, Premchand, Amrita Pritam, Khwaja Ahmad Abbas, and Kartar Singh Duggal.

◆

I must briefly mention his writings on nature and travel. A self-taught naturalist and conservationist, Khushwant wrote beautifully about nature. Take, for example, his exceptional essay on the monsoon, of which quite a few variants exist. In the one I'm quoting, he describes a dust storm that precedes the first monsoon showers:

> The temperature drops. The air becomes still. From the southern horizon a black wall begins to advance. Hundreds of kites and crows fly ahead. Can it be...? No! It is a dust storm. A fine powder begins to fall. A solid mass of locusts covers the sun. They devour whatever is left on the trees and in the fields. Then comes the storm itself. In furious sweeps it smacks open doors and windows, banging them forward and backward, smashing their glass panes. Thatched roofs and corrugated iron sheets are borne aloft into the sky like bits of paper. Trees are torn up by the roots and fall across power lines. The tangled wires electrocute people and set fire to houses. The storm carries the flames to other houses till there is a conflagration. All this happens in a few seconds. Before you can say 'Chakravarti Rajagopalachari', the gale is gone. The dust hanging in the air settles on your books, furniture and food; it gets in your eyes and ears and throat and nose.

He tells the charming story of how he first became interested in nature in his book *Nature Watch*. Apparently, as a young man in England, he once spent a summer with his friends, the Wints, in Oxford. 'For company, I had the Wint's three-year-old daughter, Allegra,' he writes. 'When Allegra returned from her nursery school, I gave her a sandwich and a glass of milk before we went out for a walk... Allegra, or Leggie as we called her, was a great chatterbox as well as an avid collector of wildflowers. Our return journey always took much longer as I had to pick whatever flower she wanted… A game she enjoyed was to stick flowers in my turban and beard. By the time we got home, I looked like a wild man of the woods. It was from little Allegra Wint that I learnt the names of many English wildflowers… Back home in Delhi I felt I was on alien territory as far as fauna and flora were concerned…when I returned I felt acutely conscious of this lacuna in my information as I could not identify more than a couple of dozen birds or trees. Getting to know about them was tedious but immensely rewarding.' Over the years he became a bit of an expert on nature. Most of his nature watching was done in his back garden but he would also make forays into the countryside 'armed with a pair of binoculars and Salim Ali's or Whistler's books on Indian birds'.

I've always wondered why Khushwant never wrote a proper travelogue, because he was obviously a travel writer of great gifts. He wrote short travel pieces throughout his career for magazines and newspapers such as 'The Haunted Simla Road' and 'Some Truths About Pakistan' that retain their freshness and beauty to this day. They have been collected into anthologies but it is a pity no one was able to persuade him to write the travel books I am sure he would have been capable of writing—it is a gap in his oeuvre.

VI

THE THREE LIVES OF KHUSHWANT SINGH

Some writers disappear into their work. Not Khushwant Singh. He was to be found everywhere in the books he wrote or translated, except perhaps the most scholarly. The great Colombian novelist, Gabriel García Márquez, who had a knack for the telling aphorism, once said to his biographer, Gerald Martin: 'All human beings have three lives—public, private and secret.' These three lives of Khushwant infused every aspect of his writing. They gave it its honesty, originality, humour, immediacy, accessibility, pugnacity and brilliance. Heightening the impact of the content was the fact that quite early on in his career he decided to write clear, simple prose, abjuring flowery phrases, clever wordplay, or pretentious words. It was a combination of all this that made it impossible to mistake his work, whether good or ordinary, for that of any other writer.

Mala tells a story about the writing of his autobiography, one of the top half a dozen books in the genre published by Indian writers in the modern era. It has the breadth and depth of learning, prickliness and unorthodox views of Nirad C. Chaudhuri's *Autobiography of an Unknown Indian*; the honesty and introspection of M. K. Gandhi's *The Story of My Experiments with Truth*; the sheer love of India and knowledge of its people and culture of Jawaharlal Nehru's *An Autobiography* and the forthrightness of Raj Thapar's *All These Years*.

She says that when he began writing it he handed her an early chapter that showed her mother in a somewhat negative way, and said bluntly that he intended to write the book in as honest and uninhibited a way as he could manage. If she didn't like it he would not continue, but if he was going to carry on, it would have to be done his way. Mala was unfazed. She'd been the one who had nagged him to write the book, and she said that she told him to write the book just the way he wanted to. 'It was important that the book was an honest portrayal of his life—as he saw it,' she said. In this Khushwant was fortunate—his family and closest friends backed him unhesitatingly, even as they were unafraid to criticize him. When she was alive, his wife was his foremost critic and sounding board, and when she passed away, two equally strong-minded people, his daughter, and his granddaughter, took her place. Laughing, Mala recalls the days she would give him a faux RSS salute and mutter 'Jai Ram ji ki' when he decided to propose the candidature of L. K. Advani, the veteran BJP politician, to fight the Lok Sabha elections.

◆

Let us then take a look at how exactly the three lives of Khushwant Singh marked his work. First, his public self. From the days of his *Weekly* editorship onwards, his was a voice that was heard in the corridors of power and the councils of the mighty. He did not hesitate to use it. Sometimes he got things wrong, as with the Emergency, but mostly his was a strong, unafraid voice which refused to be silenced. Broadly, he had four main areas of focus—religion, religious intolerance, probity in public life and Sikh politics. His greatest contribution to public life was probably his courageous defence of secularism, and the unending war he waged against religious fundamentalism until the very end, in his writings, in his speeches, in his interventions. He wrote once, in a column '[One of the regrets in my life] is that I could have played a bigger role in my battle against the fundoos... My columns have a vast readership and I should have written more against fundamentalists. My battle is against fundoos from all communities. I have spoken out against Muslim religious fundamentalists, against Hindu fundamentalists... Today [fundamentalists] burn books they do not like; they beat up journalists who write against them; they attack cinema houses showing films they do not approve of; they pervert texts from history books; they foul-mouth everyone who disagrees with them... If we love our country, we have to save it from communal forces.' For these beliefs, especially those he held against the brand of Sikh extremism promoted by Jarnail Singh Bhindranwale, he received death threats and assassins were dispatched to eliminate him. Khushwant refused to be cowed down.

His battle against religious zealotry did not mean he was an atheist or against religion. Perhaps his most famous public act of protest was when he returned to the government the high civilian award he had received, the Padma Bhushan, when the Indian army invaded the sacred precincts of the Golden Temple to flush out Sikh extremists on the orders of Mrs Gandhi.

One more story about the very public stance he took against sectarianism. I remember being at the launch function of a book by the journalist and politician, Chandan Mitra, at which L. K. Advani was the chief guest. This was in the years after the tragedy of the demolition of the Babri Masjid. When his turn came to speak, Khushwant growled at Mr Advani: 'I wanted to say in a public place that I am deeply ashamed of what you did and hold you responsible for destroying the secular fabric of the country... You have sowed the seeds of communal disharmony in the country and we are paying the price for it.'

◆

Khushwant Singh was probably India's most famous agnostic in his lifetime, although he knew more about religion than most believers. We have already noted his deep appreciation of the Sikh religion and scriptures, but he was also well-versed in the teachings of Islam, Judaism, Christianity, Hinduism, Buddhism and Jainism. He started out reading scripture in his twenties because he was struck by the beauty of some of the texts but only began a serious study of the great religions in the world in the sixties because he had to teach a course in comparative religion at Princeton University. Once hooked, it was something that he kept up with throughout his life. He could recite passages from the Quran, Gita, Bible and the Granth Sahib. And it is interesting that the two people he most admired were both people of faith—Mahatma Gandhi and Mother Teresa (after he wrote about her in the *Weekly* and *The New York Times* she sent him a short note of thanks which he said was one of his most valued possessions: 'I am told you do not believe in God. I send you God's blessings').

He wrote with sensitivity about the several faiths he was interested in, and his secular meditations on death, life, doubt, the afterlife (collected in books like *The Freethinker's Prayer Book* and *Agnostic Khushwant*) are better than those of most spiritual teachers. He despised religious charlatans and godmen who preyed on those in distress and in need of spiritual reassurance.

Besides his work on religious intolerance and religion, he was one of the country's most outspoken voices on free speech. Another of his pet bugbears was corruption, and he would frequently castigate dishonest politicians, government officials and industrialists in his columns.

◆

The private life of Khushwant Singh should be familiar to anyone who has read his autobiography or his journalism. He belonged to a close-knit family which he delighted in—his wife Kaval Malik, his son Rahul, his daughter Mala and son-in-law, Ravi Dayal (the distinguished publisher), his granddaughter, Naina, as well as assorted cats and a beloved Alsatian (Simba, about whom he wrote eloquently). Some of his best writing had its roots in his private self—articles, and sections of his autobiography that deal with his grandmother, father, mother; the wooing of his wife; the disappointments and small victories in his life that pertain to his family (the big triumphs were usually played out in public). Khushwant took an enormous amount of pleasure from the everyday acts of living with his family that he would then share with his readers. His granddaughter told me about one such episode. An Order of Injunction in the Delhi High Court restrained the publication of his autobiography after he was taken to court by the politician (and erstwhile friend) Maneka Gandhi for his comments about her in the book; it languished for six years before the high court allowed it to be published. To celebrate, Naina said, her grandfather dispatched her to buy the family some Kwality ice cream.

A simple man who enjoyed the simple pleasures of life that permeated his writing.

◆

And, finally, the secret life of Khushwant, the last major strand that invested his work. Most writers tend to hide or disguise their secret lives and fantasies. This was not true of Khushwant. He once wrote: 'If you write fearlessly and candidly you have to be prepared to pay the price. And there's no point writing if you're not honest... I've always written what I felt and believed to be true...there's no secret I kept to myself... At times this has upset people [but] I've never been bothered.' He wrote candidly about his marriage—'It wasn't a happy marriage'—and goes on to explain why. He talked about the affairs he'd had in one of his pieces on sex: 'I've been with many women over the years... I've had affairs that I have used as material for my writing. They contributed to the love-making scenes and passages in my stories and novels.' He was frank about his fantasies and was uninhibited about the failings of his body as he aged—rather like Philip Roth in his last couple of novels, but then the American writer is also one of those who has been unafraid to tap his secret life in his novels.

◆

Norman Mailer, the American novelist, whom Khushwant Singh met as a young man (he writes in typical fashion that he met many writers when he decided to become a writer himself, before he realized that you didn't become one by meeting your peers but by writing), had an excellent insight into writing style (which he mentioned in an interview to the *Paris Review*), which I believe explains why Khushwant became so popular with readers. We have already heard from the author himself about his technique and style, but what Mailer is talking about is what lies beneath mere technique: 'A really good style comes only when a man has become as good as he can be... A good style is a matter of rendering out of yourself all the cupidities, all the cripplings, all the velleities.' Or, in other words, if you are going to be a good writer learn how to truly be yourself (Mailer explains in the interview that he didn't mean 'becoming good' in the moral sense of the word) and then insinuate yourself into your writing. The fact that Khushwant let his three selves flow into his writing without dissimulation or coyness is what gave it its forcefulness, its bounce. That honesty drew readers in, enabled them to connect with the writer.

◆

He was so secure and comfortable with his own voice and style that in all the years that I knew him as his editor and his friend, he seemed not to mind what people thought of his writing. He wrote in one of his most famous essays, 'Seeing Oneself': 'I know that of the Indians or the Indian-born, Nirad Chaudhuri, V. S. Naipaul, Salman Rushdie, Amitav Ghosh and Vikram Seth handle the English language better than I. I also know I can, and have, written as well as any of the others— R. K. Narayan, Mulk Raj Anand, Manohar Malgonkar, Ruth Jhabvala, Nayantara Sahgal or Anita Desai. What is more, unlike most in the first or the second category, I have never laid claim to being a great writer.' This clear-headed view of his own work inoculated him against the criticism of others. Naina gives me an example of this: When the book he regarded as the crowning achievement of his life, *A History of the Sikhs*, was panned by Hew McLeod, an authority on the religion (and author of *Sikhism*) Khushwant took it well; moreover, he did not attack him when he got the opportunity, rather he reviewed McLeod's work positively.

Indeed, it could be said that his reaction to what others thought of his writing verged on indifference (I suspect that this was because doing the work, and doing it well, was what mattered, not the rewards). He was even less interested in how his books would fare after he was gone. He told one interviewer: 'How many of my books will be read fifty years after I am gone, I have no idea. And, quite frankly, I would not give a damn.'

VII

REQUIEM

The great ones shine the brightest at the moment of their passing. And so it was with Khushwant Singh. The outpouring of grief when he died on 20 March 2014 was unprecedented, no writer or journalist before him was mourned as he was. From the highest in the land to those who cast a more humble shadow, they spoke about how much he had meant to them, how deeply he had touched their hearts with his writing and his presence.

Before I began writing this tribute to the man I loved and admired, I wanted to take one last look at the room that he had worked in over the last decades of his life. Naina took me across. Outside, Delhi drowsed in the summer heat. Chauffeurs gossiped by parked cars, stray dogs lay panting in the thin shade of trees. Within, everything was more or less as I remembered it. As I looked at his empty chair, a line from one of my favourite novels, *The Great Gatsby*, came to me. 'In his blue gardens men and girls came and went like moths among the whisperings and the champagne and the stars.' I thought of the crowds who had assembled in this room almost every evening, to drink his whisky, and eat the delicious mushroom vol-au-vents that were made in his kitchen, and just be part of his force-field even for a little while.

What made Khushwant Khushwant? What was it that drew people to him, long after he had given up all his powerful positions, long after new stars had emerged on the media scene, long after his best work was behind him? I'd say two things. The first was his enormous zest for life, which stayed with him almost to the end. The passion for the world and everything in it burned so brightly in him that it made him irresistible. The second reason was his generosity. He gave so much of himself, both in his writing and in his life, that people couldn't get enough of him. Writers are not noted for this trait, but in this, as with many things about his personality, Khushwant was unique.

◆

Towards the end, as his body began to give way, as his thoughts turned towards death, he shut himself away and the evening soirees stopped. Miraculously, the column continued. He was, by now, a very old man. He grew frail, the blaze of his life dimmed. The only thing that remained to the very end was the amused look in his eye. It was the look of a man who was unafraid to die now that he had dealt with everything that he had been handed by life. When he went, in typical fashion, he gave even that away, by donating his eyes. To the end, he was singularly Khushwant Singh.

NON-FICTION

FAMILY

MATTERS

1

VILLAGE IN THE DESERT

It is safest to begin with the beginning.

Where I was born I have been told by people who were present at my birth. When I was born remains a matter of conjecture. I am told I was born in a tiny hamlet called Hadali, lost in the sand dunes of the Thar Desert some thirty kilometres west of the river Jhelum and somewhat the same distance southward of the Khewra Salt Range. Hadali is now deep inside Pakistan. At the time I was born, my father, Sobha Singh, was away in Delhi with his father, Sujan Singh. When the news was sent to him, he did not bother to put it down in his diary. I was his second son. At that time records of births and deaths were not kept in our villages. Unlike Hindus who noted down the time of birth of their offspring so that their horoscopes could be cast, we Sikhs had no faith in astrology, and therefore attached no importance to the time and place of nativity. Several years later, when he had to fill a form for our admission to Modern School in Delhi, my father gave my elder brother's and my date of birth out of his imagination. Mine was put down as 2 February 1915. Years later, my grandmother told me that I was born in Badroo—sometime in August. I decided to fix it in the middle of the month, to 15 August 1915, and made myself a Leo. Thirty-two years later, in 1947, 15 August became the birthday of independent India.

Sometime after I had been weaned, my father came to Hadali to take my mother and elder brother to Delhi, where he and his father had secured some building contracts. I was left with my grandmother. For the first few years of my life she was my sole companion and friend. Her name I later discovered was Lakshmi Bai. We called her Bhaabeejee. Like her, my mother also had a Hindu—Maharashtrian—name: Veeran Bai. The children knew her as Baybayjee.

I have hazy recollections of my childhood years in Hadali. The village consisted of about three hundred families, most of them Muslims of Baluch extraction. They were enormous men, mostly serving in the British Indian army, or having retired from it. A fair proportion of the viceroy's bodyguard came from Hadali. Till recently, a marble plaque on a wall alongside the railway station master's office stated that Hadali had provided proportionately more soldiers from its population for World War I than any other village in India. There were about fifty Hindu and Sikh families engaged in trade, shopkeeping and moneylending. My ancestors—I can

5

only trace them back to my great-grandfather, Inder Singh, and his father, Pyare Lal, who converted to Sikhism and became Sohel Singh—were tradesmen. They had camel caravans which took rock salt from the Khewra mines, and dates, the only fruit of our desert homeland, to sell in Lahore and Amritsar. They brought back textiles, kerosene oil, tea, sugar, spices and other items to sell in neighbouring towns and villages. Later, my grandfather and father got into the construction business. They laid a part of the small-gauge rail track and tunnels on the Kalka-Simla railway.

We were the most prosperous family of Hadali. We lived in a large brick-and-mud house with a spacious courtyard enclosing a buffalo shed and had a well of our own. The entrance was a massive wooden door that was rarely opened. It had a small aperture to let people in. A number of Hindus and Sikhs served us as clerks, and hired Muslim camel drivers took our wares to the markets. Many Muslim families were our debtors.

Our family's prosperity was ascribed to a legend. It is said that one year, when it rained heavily on the Salt Range, floodwaters swept down the rocky ridge, carrying with them a Muslim holy man named Shaida Peer who had climbed on to the thatched roof of his hut. By the time he floated down to Hadali, he had nothing on him except his loincloth. My grandfather, Sujan Singh, gave him clothes, made a hut for him near the Muslim graveyard and sent him food. Shaida Peer blessed him: 'I will give your two sons the keys of Delhi and Lahore. They will prosper.' And prosper they did—my father as a building contractor in Delhi; and his younger brother Ujjal Singh as one of pre-Partition Punjab's biggest landowners. He later became a Member of the Legislative Assembly and, after Independence, finance minister of Punjab and still later its governor. He ended his career as Governor of Tamil Nadu.

We Sikhs and Hindus of Hadali lived with the Muslims in an uneasy but peaceful relationship. Though we addressed their elders as uncles or aunts as they did ours, we rarely went to each other's homes except on marriages and deaths. We lived in slight awe of the Muslims because they were more numerous and much bigger built than us. Fortunately for us, they were split into different clans—Waddhals, Mastials, Awans, Janjuas, Noons and Tiwanas—and were often engaged in litigation over land, frequently murdering each other. We kept ourselves at a safe distance from them.

I recall passing their men striding down the village lanes. Most of them were over six feet tall and made as if of whipcord. They wore their well-oiled hair curling out behind their ears, stuck with small wooden or ivory combs. They normally twirled spindles with the fleece of sheep or camels to make yarn, or took their hooded falcons out for airing. Their women were also tall, slender and well proportioned. They could carry two pitchers full of water balanced on their heads, and one pitcher caught between the right arm and waist. Water splashed on their muslin shirts and ankle-length lungis, displaying the outlines of their taut, shapely, black-nippled breasts as well as their muscular, dimpled buttocks. They never looked up from the ground as they glided past, aware of men eating them up with their eyes. Though barely four years old, I became an inveterate voyeur.

Nothing very exciting happened in Hadali. Life had a soporific routine. My grandmother rose well before dawn to milk the buffaloes and put the milk in an earthen pot over smouldering embers of pats of buffalo dung. She went out into the open with neighbouring women to defecate. She pulled up a couple of buckets of water from the well and bathed herself under starlight as she mumbled the morning prayer, Japji. She spent the next half hour churning butter and buttermilk, reciting her prayers as she did so. Then she woke me up. I was allowed to defecate on the rooftop where the hot sun burnt up everything exposed to it. I washed myself. She combed my long hair and plaited it: being Sikhs we did not cut our hair. I got out my wooden takhti (slate) smeared over with yellow gaachnee (clay), my reed pen and earthen soot-inkpot. She got a bundle of stale chapatis left over from the previous evening's meal and wrapped them in her dupatta. We set out together for the Dharamsal-cum-school. Pye-dogs awaited us at our threshold. We took turns tearing up pieces of chapati and throwing them to the dogs. We kept a few in reserve for our return journey.

The Dharamsal was a short distance from our home. I was handed over to Bhai Hari Singh who was both granthi and teacher. I sat on the floor with other Hindu and Sikh boys and chanted multiplication tables in sing-song. My grandmother went to the large hall where three copies of the Granth Sahib were placed side by side on a low table. Beneath the table was an assortment of spectacles discarded by worshippers for the use of anyone they fitted. After chanting the tables, Bhai Hari Singh wrote the letters of the Gurmukhi alphabet on a board for us to copy. Though bent with age, he had a terrible temper. Any mistake he spotted on our wooden slates was rewarded with resounding kicks on our backsides. Mercifully, the lesson did not last more than an hour. My grandmother and I walked back, giving the village dogs all that remained of the chapatis. While she busied herself sweeping the floor, rolling up beds and cooking the midday meal, I went out to play hop-scotch or tip-cat (gullee-dundaa) with boys of my age.

What we did in the afternoons depended on the time of the year.

Desert winters could be very cold and the days very short. There was more to do and less time to do it in. But the real winter lasted barely forty days. After a brief spring, the long summer was upon us. It became hotter day by day with temperatures rising to 125° F. We hardly ever had any rain. Our tobas (ponds) were filled with brackish rainwater coming down the Salt Range. Some of it percolated into the wells. Only a few of these wells, which were brick-and-cement lined, yielded potable water fit for human consumption. For some reason brackish wells were referred to by the male gender as khaara khoo; those which yielded sweet water were known by the diminutive, feminine gender as mitthee khooee. Most of us had pale yellow teeth with a brown line running horizontally across the upper set. This was ascribed to the impure water we drank. No matter what time of year it was, my grandmother spent her afternoons plying the charkha while mumbling Guru Arjun's Sukhmani—the Psalm of Peace. My memories of my grandmother are closely linked with the hum of the spinning wheel and the murmur of prayers.

The long summer months were an ordeal. The hot sands burnt the soles of one's feet. Going from one house to another we had to hug the walls to walk in their shadows, deftly avoiding blobs of shit left by children who too had found the shadows the coolest places in which to defecate. We spent most of the day indoors gossiping, or drowsily fanning away flies. It was only late in the afternoon that camels and buffaloes were taken to the tobas for watering. The buffaloes were happiest wallowing in the stagnant ponds. Boys used them as jumping boards. At sunset the cattle were driven back, the buffaloes milked and hearths lit. The entire village became fragrant with the aroma of burning camel thorn and baking bread. Boys formed groups to go into the sand dunes to defecate. While we were at it, dung beetles gathered our turds into little marble-sized balls and rolled them to their holes in the sand. We had a unique way of cleansing ourselves. We sat on our bottoms in a line. At a given signal we raised our legs and propelled ourselves towards the winning post with our hands. By the end of the race, called gheesee, our bottoms were clean but full of sand. Later, in the night and during the early phases of the moon, we played kotla chapakee, our version of blind-man's buff. Full-moon nights on the sand dunes remain printed in my memory. We ran about chasing each other till summoned home for supper. The one threat that worked was that we might be kidnapped by dacoits. We were familiar with the names of notorious outlaws like Tora and Sultana who had spread terror in the countryside because of the number of murders and abductions they had committed.

Next to dacoits we most feared sand storms. We were used to

living with dust-raising winds and spiralling dust-devils, but haneyree or jhakkhar were something else. They came with such blinding fury that there was little we could do besides crouching on the ground with our heads between our knees to prevent sand getting into our nostrils, eyes and ears. There were times when so much sand was blown that the rail track was submerged under it, and no trains ran till it was cleared. But it purged the air of flies and insects, and for the following day or two the air would be cleaner and cooler.

After the evening meal we went to our rooftops to sleep. My grandmother, who had already said her evening prayer, Rehras, recited the last prayer of the day, Kirtan Sohila. She rubbed clotted cream on my back. If her gentle ministrations did not put me to sleep, she would tell me anecdotes from the lives of our Gurus. If I were still wide awake, she would point to the stars and reprimand me: 'Don't you see what time it is? Now chup' (shut up).

The nicest time in the summer was the early morning. A cool breeze blew over the desert, picking up the fragrances of roses and jasmine that grew in our courtyards. It was the time for half sleep and fantasizing. It was all too brief. The sun came up hot, bringing with it flies and the raucous caw-cawing of crows. The blissful half-hour that Urdu poets refer to as the baad-e-naseem (zephyr of early dawn) came to an end all too suddenly.

Little happened in Hadali to relieve the tedium of our daily routine. There was a murder or two every other year. But since murders were confined to the Muslims, we never got overexcited about them. Once a year there were tent-pegging competitions on the open ground near the railway station. Competitors lined up on their horses and, at a given signal, galloped towards the stakes waving their spears and yelling 'Allah Beli Ho' (Oh Allah is my best friend). After piercing the stakes they waved their spears triumphantly for all to see. They often raced passing railway trains and kept pace with them till their horses ran out of breath. I remember the first time a Sikh brought a bicycle to Hadali. He boasted that he would outrun any horse. Before a horseman could take up his challenge, we boys decided to take him on. Hadali had no metalled road and the cyclist was still wobbly on the wheels. He fared very poorly as his cycle got stuck in the sand. He became the laughing stock of the village and was thereafter mocked with the title 'Saikal Bahadur'—brave man of the bicycle.

I returned to Hadali three times after shifting to Delhi. The first time, to be initiated into reading the Granth Sahib. My elder brother, a cousin and I were made to read aloud the Japji in front of the congregation and asked to swear that we would read at least one hymn every day. None of us was able to keep our promise for very long. I went there next when practising law in Lahore. I drove to Hadali with a friend whose cousin was the manager of the salt mines. As we pulled up near the railway station tears welled up in my eyes. I resisted the urge to go down on my knees and kiss the earth. I walked up to the Dharamsal and to the house where I was born. A man who was risaldar in the viceroy's bodyguard recognized me and spread the news to the village. By the time I left, there was a crowd to see me off.

My last visit to Hadali was in the winter of 1987. The partition of India in 1947 had brought about a complete change in its population. Not a single Sikh or Hindu remained. Our homes were occupied by Muslim refugees from Haryana. Our family haveli was divided into three equal parts, each shared by Muslim refugees from Rohtak. A new generation of Hadalians who had never seen a Sikh were then in their forties. I was uncertain of the reception they would give me. My only contact with this generation was through meeting a few young soldiers taken captive in the Indo-Pakistan War of 1971 in the prisoner-of-war camp in Dhaka. I had sought them out and written to their parents that they were safe and in good health.

I drove from Lahore and reached Hadali early in the afternoon. Village elders awaited me on the roadside with garlands of silver and gold tassels with the words Khush Amdeed—welcome—inscribed on them in Urdu. I did not recognize any of the men whose hands I shook. I was escorted to the High School ground where a dais with the Pakistan flag over it had been put up. Over 2,000 Hadalians sat in rows on chairs and on the ground. Speeches in badly pronounced, florid Urdu were delivered acclaiming me as a son of Hadali. My heart was full of gratitude. I sensed that I was about to make an ass of myself; I did. I started off well. I spoke to them in the village dialect. I said that just as they looked forward to going on pilgrimage to Mecca and Medina, coming back to Hadali at the time of the Maghreb (evening prayer) of my life was my Haj (big pilgrimage) and my Umra (small pilgrimage). And as the Prophet on his return to Mecca as Victor had spent his first night wandering about the streets and praying beside the grave of his first wife, I would have liked nothing better than to be left alone to roam about the lanes of Hadali and rest my head on the threshold of the house in which I was born. Then I was overcome by emotion and broke down. They understood and forgave me. I was escorted to my former home with the entire village following me. Fireworks were let off; women standing on rooftops showered rose petals on me. Who was the author of the perfidious lie that Muslims and

Sikhs were sworn enemies? No animosity had soured relations between the Muslims, Hindus and Sikhs of Hadali. Muslims had left the Sikh-Hindu Dharamsal untouched because it had been a place of worship for their departed cousins.

The Rohtak families, living in what was once our home, had done up the haveli with coloured balloons and paper buntings. The elders of the village who once knew my father had a feast laid out in my honour. There was little that I saw of Hadali that I recognized. The sand dunes which had been the playgrounds of my childhood years were gone. A canal had greened the desert. The tobas had become swamps full of reeds. The marble plaque commemorating the services of the men who had fought in World War I had been removed. I left Hadali a little before sunset, aware that I would never return to it again.

2

WINNING MY FATHER'S APPROVAL

On my way back from the interview, which took place in Metcalfe House, I happened to pass through Sabzi Mandi. The street was blocked by what seemed to be some kind of fracas taking place ahead. I asked the driver to stop and went out to find out what it was. 'We've caught a couple of Muslim swine trying to take a cow for slaughter,' one of the crowd informed me. I pushed my way through the mob and came to the centre of the scene. There was a cow and three men—two Muslims and a Sikh—surrounded by men armed with steel rods and long knives. My arrival, clad in suit and tie, deterred them. 'What's going on?' I demanded angrily. 'These two fellows are butchers; this Sikh sold the cow to them,' I was informed. All three men were shaking with fear. The Muslims had been stripped naked and seen to be circumcised. The Sikh was to be beaten up and taught a lesson. I put my arms in front of the butchers and shouted back, 'No one is going to touch these men! I have seen enough of this during partition. It has to stop.'

The crowd turned nasty towards me. 'Do you understand that these men were going to butcher this cow? What kind of a Sikh are you?' I held my ground. 'I will not let you touch them. If anyone does, I'll have him arrested. I am a government official.' They were not impressed. But no one was willing to make the first move. I thought of a way out. 'Let's take them to the police station and see what we can do.' The crowd let me do what I wanted. I led the cow, and put my arms around the two butchers; the bloodthirsty mob followed in trams clanking madly at us to clear the way. We arrived at the Sabzi Mandi police station. I introduced myself to the inspector in charge, a Punjabi Hindu, and pleaded with him to take the butchers into custody. The Sikh had meanwhile slipped away into the crowd. 'They have committed no crime, why should I arrest them?' he demanded. 'To save their lives,' I pleaded. He was adamant. I threatened him with my status as an official. He could not care less. 'I don't care who you are or what the crowd will do to these fellows. They deserve what is coming to them.'

I resumed my march with the cow and the butchers through the crowded bazaar to Tis Hazari where there was a veterinary hospital. By the time I got there, the crowd had thinned. The vet was a white-bearded Sikh. I pleaded with him to take the cow into custody and to arrest the two men on the charge of cruelty to animals. He was adamant. 'I see no injury on the cow. And if they want to kill these snakes I am not going to stop them,' he said, walking away. I turned to address the few would-be killers who remained. 'Look, I will release the cow here and now and take these fellows to some place where I can teach them the lesson they deserve.' They agreed, they had had enough, their tempers had cooled. I let the cow loose. It ran across the open ground with its tail raised, kicking its hind legs in the sheer joy of being released from human bondage. I ordered the two butchers to get into my car. 'Where do you live?' I asked them.

'Daryaganj.'

'Don't you fellows realize how dangerous it is in these times to slaughter kine?'

'Janab, we had nothing to eat for two days. We pooled our resources to buy this cow. Now we are ruined.'

I dropped them at Daryaganj. They did not go to their homes. I saw them turn back to go and look for the cow they had bought.

I am not a brave man. I was amazed at the audacity I had shown in the face of danger. I asked the chauffeur to take me to Gurdwara Sisganj in Chandni Chowk. By now I had given up visiting places of worship. Sisganj marked the site of the execution of the ninth Guru, Tegh Bahadur. According to the legend, he had laid down his life to protect Hindus from persecution. It was the best place to go to for one who in his small way had saved the lives of two Muslims. At Sisganj I offered obeisance at the Guru's shrine, which is in an underground cell where the trunk of the banyan tree under which he was beheaded is preserved. I thanked the Guru for giving a coward like me the courage to uphold what I thought was a Sikh's duty. I broke down; tears of gratitude welled up in my eyes. As I left, my legs shook. I had come close to being murdered.

At home I narrated the incident with great pride. Far from being applauded I was called 'bewakoof' (a fool) and 'gadha' (a donkey) by my father's friend Sohan Singh of Rawalpindi who was staying with him. My mother was angry that I had put my life in jeopardy. My father kept silent. I knew I had the approval of the one man who mattered more to me than anyone else.

3

A GOOD WAY TO GO

I was in Bombay when my father died in Delhi. My relations with my parents were like those that exist in traditional Indian families. Rigid rules of courtesy were observed, but no confidences were exchanged. He did not have any favourite among his four sons. Perhaps I came closest to being one, but I had disappointed him by not being the conventional success he had hoped for. Like most fathers, he had a soft spot for his only daughter whom he plied with gifts and to whom he left an unencumbered estate bigger than the portions he gave his sons. My mother distinctly favoured her youngest son, Daljit. A bitter quarrel had arisen between my eldest and youngest brother. My mother never liked my eldest brother's wife and blatantly sided with Daljit. I knew nothing about my brothers' falling out over the division of property and dragging each other to court till my father wrote to me and asked me to come over. I was mortified to learn about the trivial issues they were wrangling over. My uncle, Ujjal Singh, had tried to arbitrate between the two and failed. I took over the unpleasant job. While Daljit appeared more amenable to reason on the surface, he broke his solemn promise given in writing to me by taking over a joint society when his eldest brother was away. I confronted him in front of my parents and angrily rebuked him of being a dagabaaz (betrayer). He broke down. He swore by his mother—he was always swearing by her—that he would not do it again. I tore up the proceedings of the meeting in which he had assumed control of the enterprise and succeeded in making a mutually acceptable partition between them.

Relations between my parents underwent a sea change over the years. For years he laid down the law with a heavy hand. As he began to get older and hard of hearing, his dependence on his wife increased. She began to tick him off for making people repeat whatever they had said—hain? kee kyaah?—and being clumsy. He dropped food on his tie and coat while eating. He no longer lost his temper but submitted meekly to being put in his place. Whenever I visited him, he asked me to read the papers to him and solicited my opinion on important events. He was never one for exercise: walking up and down his lawn was all he did to keep himself fit. He also observed no dietary rules. He had a large breakfast of cornflakes, eggs, sausages, toast and honey and tea. He had a couple of gins before lunch; for afternoon tea he took slices of cake, biscuits or Indian sweets. He took two to three Scotches before dinner and often brandy afterwards.

Dinner consisted of at least four or five courses: soup, fish, meat, vegetable and pudding. When travelling, he ate whatever was available on railway platforms. On his way to Mashobra by car he sampled the pickles at a dhaba four miles up the road from Kalka and ate pedas at Jablee. He never put on weight and remained slim to the last. He was a great one for taking pills—to whip up appetite, to digest what he had eaten. He had several operations—for kidney stones, cataract, piles and hernia. One thing he never missed was his sleep. No sooner did he put his head on the pillow than he was lost to the world. More than anything else, it was sound sleep that sustained him for ninety years.

It was sad to see him age and become frail. I made it a point to come to Delhi every fortnight and spend an hour with him in the mornings and either have my evening Scotch with him or get him over to dine with us. The last time I saw him alive, he looked frailer than ever, and was evidently aware that he did not have many days left. When I was taking my leave he asked me when I planned coming to Delhi next. I told him I would be back in a fortnight. 'Fortnight?' he asked. And said no more.

A week later my wife rang me to say he was not well and she was going over to see him. An hour later she rang again to say he was much better and she had had a drink with him. My mother and sister were with him. A few minutes later, she rang a third time to tell me he was dead. This was at 8.30 p.m. on 18 April 1978.

I was numbed. For a long time I sat still not knowing what to do. Then I rang up the Zakarias and asked Fatma if she could tell Rahul and put us on the early morning flight to Delhi. She never failed me in a crisis. A few minutes later the Zakarias came over to see me. After half an hour I asked them to leave me so that I could get some sleep.

I got no sleep that night. I kept going over events in my father's life. A self-made man, a generous father whom I had barely known as a person with human failings. I knew full well that if it had not been for his constant support, I would never have been able to write a single book.

Having once been the biggest builder of New Delhi, his death made the front pages of all the daily papers. There was a large turnout at his cremation and an even larger one filling the entire lawn of Sujan Singh Park at his last obsequial ceremony. I was asked by my brothers to make the final oration. Fortunately I was able to say my piece without breaking down.

Nishaan-e-mard-e-momin ba too goyam?
Choon marg aayad, tabassum bar lab-e-ost

(You ask me about the signs of a man of faith?
When death comes to him, he has a smile on his lips.)

(Allama Iqbal)

My father did better than face death with a smile; he had a glass of Scotch in his hand a few minutes before he laid himself on his deathbed.

4

DEATH OF A LADY

Of my parents, I felt more relaxed with my mother than with my father. None of her children were as scared of her as we were of our father. When we were small, she often threatened to slap us, but it never went beyond raising her hand and threatening 'maaraan chaat?' Nothing followed. She was frail, short, with little confidence in herself. Whatever little she may have had as a girl was squashed by her overbearing husband who would not trust her to run her home. He even prepared menus for his dinner parties—they hardly ever varied from tomato soup, fish, chicken, pilaf, followed by pudding—and he kept all the accounts except the dhobi's. There were other reasons for her willing subservience to her husband—her father and two brothers were in our employment; of her three sisters' husbands, two depended on my father's patronage. She had never been to school and only learnt Gurmukhi to be able to write letters and read the headlines of Punjabi newspapers. She didn't waste time on books and preferred to gossip with her sisters and maidservant, Bhajno, who was an inveterate carrier of tales against her sons' wives. However, when I was abroad I got more news from the few lines she wrote to me in Gurmukhi than the two pages of typescript my father dictated to his secretary. He wrote about the government, political wrangling and the budget; she wrote about births, liaisons, marriages and deaths. She often grumbled that she could not read or write English. Despite the instructors my father employed to teach her the language, she stubbornly refused to go beyond 'yes, no, good morning, good night, goodbye and thank you'.

When the Punjabi translation of my novel *Train to Pakistan* was published, I gave her the first copy. I did not expect her to read it. When I went to see her next morning, my father told me that she had been reading the novel late into the night and was down with a severe headache. I went to her bedroom. She was lying covered from head to foot in her shawl. I shook her by the shoulder and asked how she was feeling. She peeped out of the shawl with one eye and made a one-word comment: 'Beysharam!' (shameless creature).

My mother was somewhat of a hypochondriac. The only thing she really suffered from were migraine headaches. The attacks could be so severe that she had to stay in bed for two days and only felt better after she had thrown up a few times. But whenever she caught a cold she was sure it was her last moment. Whenever she felt a pain in any part of her body she was sure it was cancer. She had heard that cancer was incurable. Therefore what she had could be nothing except cancer. When my father died in his ninetieth year, she was in her eighties and in good health. Instead of being shattered by his going, as everyone expected, she came into her own as a very domineering materfamilias. Nobody dared to address her except as Lady Sobha Singh. Like Queen Victoria, she held court every day. At eleven she presided over the mid-morning coffee session; in the evening, over drinks and dinner. I persuaded her to have a little alcohol in the evenings. At first she consumed it surreptitiously. When bearers came round with tray loads of soft drinks for the ladies at parties she would tell them that her son was bringing her orange juice. I initially spiked her glass with a little gin, and then I introduced her to Scotch. Again she made a mild protest. 'What will people say! An old illiterate woman from a village drinking whisky?' She began to like her sundowner and became discerning enough to tell good Scotch from bad desi.

In her ninetieth year she began to sense that she did not have very much longer to live. She never said anything about it but started giving things away. My father's sweaters, his ebony walking stick with a silver knob, and his gold watch came to me; jewellery and a gold watch went to my sister; jewellery, watches, gold pens, gold buttons, and sovereigns were distributed amongst sons, daughters-in-law and their progeny. There was seldom a morning when I went to see her when she did not give me a shirt, a pair of socks or shoes that my father had worn. We knew that she meant to give these things away with her own hands.

Without there being anything specifically wrong with her, she began to wither away. Dr I. P. S. Kalra, who was married to my cousin, also a doctor, came to see her twice a day to take her blood pressure and temperature. She began to spend a longer time in bed. My sister slept in her bedroom to help her go to the bathroom. Then a night maid was hired to clean, sponge and help change her clothes. Her appearances at coffee sessions became rarer and rarer. But even when half conscious, she would send for her servant, Haria, and mumble 'Coffee'. He would assure her that visitors were being served coffee. Many times my telephone rang to tell me that she was sinking. We would hurry over. Dr Kalra would be there giving her a shot of something or the other. She then rallied round and we returned to our homes. One evening, when all her children, grandchildren and a number of great-grandchildren were there, she went into a coma from which she never recovered.

We spent many hours of many days sitting by her supine body, assured by the rise and fall of her sheet that she was still alive. More than once we asked Dr Kalra not to persist in injecting her with life-saving drugs and let her go in peace. He refused to listen to us and said that he was determined to keep her alive for as long as he could. Back in my flat, I dreaded the ringing telephone. The final call came on the afternoon of 9 March 1985. It was my sister's anguished voice crying, 'She's gone.'

By the time we got to her she looked peacefully asleep. Beside her pillow, incense spiralled upwards to the ceiling. My elder brother sat by her bedside reading out from a small prayer book. Others embraced each other in tears and sat in chairs in the garden, only to break down again and again as people came to condole. As in earlier happenings in the family, it was my younger brother, Brigadier Gurbux Singh, who took control of the situation. He made me draft the obituary notice, corrected it and sent it off to all the Delhi papers. He fixed the time of her cremation and the day the Akhand Path would commence and terminate with bhog and kirtan. He ordered us to return to our homes for the night. He, his wife and my sister would stay with the body. My elder brother sat by her making the japs over and over again throughout the night, as he had done years earlier by our father's body.

The next morning we took our mother's body to the same electric crematorium where we had earlier taken our father and uncle. My brother, Gurbux, took her ashes to Hardwar as he had our father's ashes and those of my grandmother, to be immersed in the Ganga. Thus ended the days of Veeran Bai, Lady Sobha Singh, my mother.

5

SIMBA

I returned home to Delhi. Once again I was without a job and with very little money in my pocket or in my bank account. All I had on the credit side was a collection of short stories which brought me some good notices but no money, a short and unsatisfactory short history of the Sikhs which was condemned by orthodox Sikhs, and a novel which brought me money which I had spent. And the manuscript of a second novel which had yet to be accepted by a publisher.

Among those who greeted me at home was a one-month old Alsatian pup presented by a friend of my father's to my daughter, Mala. To start with, he resented me as an intruder in his tight little human family consisting of my wife and our two children. He slept in the same upstairs bedroom in my father's house and used the roof of the porch as his lavatory. Till then he had no name. I decided to name him Simba after the marmalade cat we had abandoned in Paris. As with most Alsatians, Simba was a one-person dog. He belonged to my daughter, my wife fed him, took him to the vet for his shots and for any ailment he had, but he adopted me as his master. He was as human a dog as I have ever known and shared our joys as he did our sorrows. By the time we moved into our own ground-floor apartment in Sujan Singh Park, he had got over his frisky puppiness and had grown into a powerful full-sized German shepherd. He still shared our bedroom, where he had his own cot. And for his sake more than ours we had an air conditioner put in the room. Often at night he would sniff into my ears and ask me to make room for him. I did. He would heave himself on to the bed with a deep sigh of gratitude, and take over more than half of my bed for the rest of the night.

We would talk to him. If we pretended to cry, he would sniff soothingly in our ears and join us wailing: *booo, ooo, ooo*. If he was naughty, we would order him to the corner. He stayed there with his head down in penitence until we said, 'Okay, now you can come back.'

Simba developed a special relationship with Mala's ayah, the seventy-five-year-old Mayee. 'Vey Shambia!' she would greet him as she opened the door to let Simba out into the garden. She waited for him to do his business in the garden before going to the neighbouring gurdwara to say her prayers. He knew he was not allowed inside the gurdwara and sat outside guarding her slippers. Just as the morning prayer was about to end, he would take one of her slippers in his mouth, trot home and hide it under a bed. Mayee would follow him pleading. 'Vey Shambia! Where have you hidden my slipper?' He followed her from room to room wagging his tail till she found the missing slipper.

Simba was always impatient for his evening walk. He would put his head in my lap and look appealingly at me: 'Isn't it time?' his eyes asked. 'Not yet,' I would reply. Then he would bring his leash and put it at my feet. 'Now?' I would tell him not to be so impatient. Next he brought my walking stick and dropped it on the book I was reading. 'Surely now!' There was no escape. He whined and trembled with excitement as we left. As he jumped onto the rear seat of the car his whining became louder. He liked to put his head out of the window and bark challenges to every dog, cow or bull we passed on the road. He had to be let off at the entrance of the Lodi Gardens. He raced the car, stopping briefly to defecate, and resumed the race to the parking lot. At that time there used to be some hares at the park. He would sniff them out of the hedges and then go in hot pursuit, yelping as he tried to catch up with them. They were too fast and dodged him. But he became quite adept at hunting squirrels. He learnt that they ran to the nearest tree and ran around its bole to avoid pursuit. He would steal up to the tree and then go for them. In the open ground, they had no escape. However much I reprimanded him and even beat him, he could not resist killing harmless squirrels.

On Saturday evenings he could sense from the picnic basket being packed that the next day would be devoted largely to him. Long before dawn he would start whimpering with excitement and wake everyone up. It was difficult to control him in the car. When we got to the open countryside near Surajkund, or Tilpat, we had to let him out to prevent him from jumping out of the car. He would chase herds of cows and scatter them over the fields. Once he nearly got his face bashed in by the rear kick of a cow. And once he almost killed a goat.

Three to four hours in the open countryside chasing hares, deer or peafowl made him happily tired. It was a drowsy, sleepy Simba we brought back from our Sunday morning picnics. He was not so impatient now for his evening walk.

He was, again, restless for his after dinner stroll around Khan Market, where we went to get paan. He would stop by the ice cream man and plead with us to buy him one. He was passionately fond of ice cream. He was also very possessive. Once somebody had two lovely pups for sale under a tree in the market. He resented our paying attention to them. Whenever we stopped by the tree, he would savagely bite its bole. Everyone in and around Sujan Singh Park knew Simba. We came to be known by the children of the locality as Simba's parents.

Simba was also feared. Once when going out with my wife and daughter in the Lodi Gardens, a cyclist slapped my daughter on her back and sped on. My wife screamed, 'Simba get him!' Simba chased the man, knocked him off his bicycle and stood over him baring his fangs. The poor fellow folded the palms of his hands and pleaded for forgiveness. Another time, as I was stepping out of my flat after dinner, I heard a girl shout for help. Two young lads were trying to molest her. I ran towards her with Simba at my heels. The boys tried to run away. I ordered Simba to get them. He ran and brought one fellow down on the ground. He was a big fellow and much stronger than I. But with Simba at my side, I had no hesitation in slapping the man many times across his face and roundly abusing him, calling him a goonda and a badmaash. He asked to be forgiven and swore he would never make passes at women again.

We always took Simba with us to Mashobra or Kasauli. He was happiest in the mountains. I often put him on the leash to make him pull us up steep inclines. He liked Kasauli more than Shimla because of its troops of rhesus monkeys and langurs. He waged unceasing warfare against them, and against hill crows which flocked round when he was having his evening meal.

Most dogs have a sixth sense. Our Simba had seventh and eighth senses as well. I will mention only one incident to prove it. My wife and I had to go abroad for a couple of months. Our children were in boarding schools. We decided to give our servants leave and lock up our flat. Simba was to be housed with Prem Kirpal: the two were on very friendly terms, as Prem was always with us on our Sunday outings and a regular visitor to our home. He happily agreed to take Simba. Being a senior government official, he had a bungalow on Canning Lane with a large garden. Simba had been there many times and sensed that we meant to leave him there. He did not seem to mind very much.

My wife returned to Delhi a few days before me. She went to Canning Lane to fetch Simba. He greeted her joyfully but refused to get into her car. Prem was very pleased at his success in winning Simba's affections. My wife reluctantly gave in. 'If he is happy with you, he can stay here,' she said. Apparently they mentioned the day I was due to return, and Simba heard them. The evening before I returned to Delhi, Simba walked all the way from Canning Lane to Sujan Singh Park and scratched at the door with his paws to announce his arrival. He knew I was coming next morning. Prem was more dejected at Simba leaving him than he would have been had I stolen his mistress.

Simba aged gracefully. The hair about his mouth turned white. He developed cataracts in his eyes. Sometimes he got feverish: there were times when my wife spent whole nights with his head on her lap, stroking his head. He was then well over thirteen years old. When I got a three-month teaching assignment at Swarthmore College, we had to leave him in the care of his real mistress, my daughter Mala. She had to take him to the vet almost every day. He didn't get any better. His legs began to give in. She sent us a cable 'Return immediately, Simba seriously ill.' The next day we received another cable from Mala: 'Simba passed away peacefully.'

Apparently, the vet advised Mala that Simba was in pain, his legs were paralysed and he couldn't last much longer. With her permission he gave him a lethal dose of something that put him to sleep. If I had to talk of my close friendships, Simba would be amongst the top in my list. We never kept another dog. One can't replace friends.

6

BILLO

My granddaughter Naina found a kitten lying on the road. It had been bitten and mauled by a dog and left for dead. It was in a state of shock. She brought it home and nursed it for several weeks, cradling it in her arms like a new-born baby. Its face had been cut and one eye damaged seemingly beyond repair.

Slowly the kitten recovered. Its wound healed and its damaged eye recovered its golden sparkle. But it was scared to go out of the flat because of the dogs. Since my granddaughter had to be at the university for several hours of the day, it attached itself to her maidservant, Kamla.

During the day, it remained close to Kamla and when my granddaughter came back, it shuttled between the two, purring as it snuggled in their laps. When neither of its two foster mothers were at home, it sat in my ailing wife's lap and purred loudly to give her comfort. It refused to respond to my overtures.

When I put it in my lap, it would stop purring and become impatient to get away. It hurt my pride, because I was convinced all animals liked me as much as I liked them. I didn't know whether it was female or male—a billee or a billa, so I named it 'Billo'. Cats do not respond to names; neither did Billo.

Billo grew into a full-sized cat and spent most of its time in my apartment without coming too close to me except when I was having my meals. Then, it would try to grab whatever it could lay its paws or mouth on and run away. It would look under sofas and chairs, examine all my bookshelves and artefacts and was particularly intrigued by the TV set.

Early one morning, when without switching on the lights I switched on the TV, I noticed a long tail dangling in front of the screen. It was Billo, seated on the top surveying the room. As the sound came on, it went round the set looking for its source. Then it stared at the pictures and pawed the screen to make sure the flattened images were of real people.

For many days the TV set became its favourite perch. Then one day as I was watching Discovery Channel, its hackles went up as a tiger appeared on the screen. The tiger roared and Billo fled for its life. Since then, it has not been near the TV set.

Not all people like cats. Some have even gone to the extent of wanting to pass laws to prevent them from wandering about. The classic example is of the state of Illinois considering a bill to ban their prowling about.

When it came for approval to Adlai Stevenson, governor of the state, he wrote a dissenting note; 'I cannot agree that it should be the declared public policy of Illinois that a cat visiting a neighbour's yard or crossing the highway is a public nuisance. It is in the nature of cats to do a certain amount of unescorted roaming—to escort a cat on a leash is against the nature of the owners.

'Moreover, cats perform a useful service, particularly in the rural areas. The problem of the cat versus the bird or the rat is as old as time. If we attempt to resolve it by legislation, who knows but what we may be called upon to take sides on besides the age-old problems of dog versus cat, bird versus bird, or even bird versus worm. In my opinion, the state of Illinois and its local government bodies already have enough to do without trying to control feline delinquency.'

There must have been something in my character which Billo did not like. Perhaps like Maneka Gandhi and a few others of her kind, Billo decided I was not very nice.

7

FAMILY MATTERS

'Nana, are you really a womanizer?' my sixteen-year-old granddaughter asked me one morning. My wife and daughter were present.

How does a seventy-seven-year old grandfather answer so direct a question put to him by his teenaged grandchild? 'Of course I am!' I replied. 'Don't you see all the pretty women who come to see me: Sadia, Kamna, Jayalalitha, Syeda, Prema, Kum Kum, Mrinal, Masooma?'

'That's not the same thing,' she replied, looking very knowledgeable.

What had provoked the question was an incident that took place in her English class at school. They had a new teacher who did not know much about her students' parentage and my granddaughter had in any case never told anyone about me! Only her closest friend, who sat next to her in class, knew about our relationship. The lesson that morning was my short story, 'The Portrait of a Lady', about my grandmother. The teacher thought it best to tell her students something about the author before she dealt his work. She told them that the writer of the story was the worst stereotype of a Sardarji's image in the popular mind: loud-mouthed, aggressive, a philanderer, drunkard and womanizer. The girls took it down in their notebooks. My granddaughter and her friend giggled merrily. By the next morning, the teacher had discovered that one of her students was my granddaughter. She adopted a different tone. She lauded my virtues as a writer of great sensibility, concise in the use of words, and so on. My granddaughter and her friend had more reason to giggle as they sensed their teacher painfully trying to make up for the faux pas she had committed the day before.

I cannot blame the teacher too much because that is my popular image: of a drunkard and a womanizer. I can't even blame people who visualize me inebriated, with my arms round bosomy women. I am chiefly responsible for painting myself in those lurid colours. Unfortunately, it is not a true portrayal. I am not a drunkard; I have never been drunk even once in the over fifty years I have been drinking. And though some women have come into my life as they do into the lives of most men, I have never made unwelcome passes at them, nor have I been snubbed or slapped for taking undue liberties with any. As a matter of fact, though I am nothing to look at, it is women who have sought my company more than I have sought theirs. I am a good listener and very liberal with my compliments. These two traits account for the limited popularity I enjoy with the opposite sex.

My daily routine, which has varied only a little over the years due to changing whereabouts and my preoccupations at the time, has been much the same for the last ten years that I have been living in Delhi. I get up between 4 and 5 a.m. It is usually closer to 4 a.m. and never beyond 5 as two alarm clocks make sure I sleep no more. One is the conventional type which goes off with an ear-splitting explosion of metal striking metal. The second is a Japanese speaking clock which starts with a short musical piece followed by a Jap speaking Ameringlish, 'Good morning! It is five o' clock. Time to get up.' Five minutes later, it comes on again to remind me: 'It is five minutes after five. Time for you to get going.' And five minutes after that yet another reminder: 'It is now ten minutes after five. Please hurry!'

I do. I go into my study, switch on the kettle, get milk out of the fridge, a packet of ginseng from a pewter box. I fill a platter with chilled milk and dilute it with hot water; I make two mugs of tea for my security guards (they've been with me for over five years) and one with ginseng for myself. As I open my front door, a dozen cats of different sizes and colours charge at me. I put the platter of milk on the floor—about six manage to get their heads in to sip; others stay at a respectful distance. I give the mugs of tea to my guards and am rewarded with a copy of the *Hindustan Times* which is delivered to me free of charge around 4 a.m. because I edited it for three years (1980-1983). I scan the headlines while I sip my ginseng. I look up Obituaries and In Memoriams on Page 4 to find out which of my fellow citizens have left for their heavenly abode. I switch on my transistor and listen to 'Asa di var' from the Golden Temple or hymns on the national service while I change into my tennis clothes.

In summer, I am at the Gymkhana Club tennis courts at 6 a.m. (in winter it is 7 a.m.). My tennis has deteriorated with time. I no longer play it with the vigour I did some years ago; my sporting companions suffer me because I am their best supplier of imported tennis balls. I now rarely play more than one set. Back home, I have a quick shower—I believe in taking a cold shower on the coldest of days as a preventer of colds—and get down to reading other papers while I have my breakfast of two toasts and tea. About the only time I waste is when I'm solving crossword puzzles. Then I get down to my reading and writing. I have to fight off telephone calls and visitors. Sometimes I simply put the phone off the hook and tell my security guards to tell visitors I am not at home. I never see anyone who has not made a prior appointment. This is not snobbery but self-preservation. To me, time is sacred. And fleeting. There is so much to read, write, see and do. And so little time to fit it all in.

I have a very light lunch—a bowl of soup or yoghurt, germinated cereals or thayir saadam followed by half an hour of siesta. Then back to reading and writing and fighting off the telephone. I receive an average of ten to twenty letters a day and make it a point to answer each one. Often, it is no more than a line or two on a postcard. I regard not answering letters a gross discourtesy. Dealing with correspondence wastes a lot of my time as there are quite a few people who write very long letters, and far too frequently. They write in English, Hindi, Urdu and Punjabi. I often receive abusive letters as well as love letters from girls I have never met.

I take a couple of hours' break to go for a swim in the Golf Club open-air pool. They let me in before others and I usually have it all to myself to do thirty to forty lengths. I do not enjoy it any more than I do my tennis but feel I must persist in taking exercise to keep myself fit for mental work: mens sana in corpore sano—a healthy mind needs a healthy body. I always take a book with me to read after I've had my swim. I have to dodge people who want to talk to me.

Come evening and I look forward to my Scotch. After all that exercise and the frugal meals, I feel it warming its way down my entrails. Left to myself, I would like to drink alone while listening to music or watching TV. But I am rarely left alone, and usually have quite a mehfil to drink with me. I rarely go to cocktail receptions given by Delhi's diplomatic community, except when my stock of Scotch is low and then too, for just long enough to take my quota of three large Scotches and get back home.

Many stories of my rudeness have been circulated. They are true. I prescribe the time for my drink and dinner and walk out if my host does not observe it. In my own home, I have dinner parties at least twice a week. I make sure my guests arrive on time. And ask them to leave before 9 p.m. They do…and are quite happy to have an early evening. I watch the English news on Doordarshan and take a crossword puzzle to put me to sleep. I also have a collection of books of dirty jokes by my bedside which I dip into before my siesta and night's sleep. By now I know all the dirty jokes there are in the world. I enjoy dirty jokes.

Now consider how much time I have to indulge in drinking or womanizing! My drinking never lasts more than forty minutes. And as I have said before, not once in my life have I been drunk—high, yes; garrulous, yes; amorous, yes. But never out of control, staggering or talking bullshit. I have even less time to indulge in women. And when I have, as when I am in Bombay, Calcutta, Madras, Hyderabad or abroad, I have a gunman with a bayonet fixed on his rifle outside my hotel door. That can dampen the ardour of any Casanova and turn any nymphomaniac frigid.

The picture of my present-day life would be incomplete if I did not tell you something about my wife. Most people who don't know me or my family are under the impression that she doesn't exist, or is tucked away in some village like the wives of many of our netas. This is a grievous error as my wife is quite a formidable character who rules the home with as firm a hand as Indira Gandhi ruled India. Unlike the mod girls of today who bob their hair, wear T-shirts, jeans and speak chi-chi Hindish but tamely surrender their right to choose husbands to their parents when it comes to being married, my wife made her own choice over fifty years ago.

I soon learnt that I could not take my wife for granted. If she did not like any of my friends, she told them so to their face in no uncertain terms. She is a stronger woman than any I have known. Her mother was very upset when she discovered she drank whisky. One evening she stormed into the room, picked up her glass and threw it on the marble floor. The glass did not break but slithered across the floor, spilling its contents. My wife quickly picked it up and refilled it. 'I am an adult and a married woman. You have no right to dictate to me,' she told her mother. When her mother was ill with cancer, she asked her to promise that she would say her prayers regularly. Despite my pleas to say 'yes' to her dying mother, she refused to do so. 'I will not make a promise that I know I will not keep.' She nursed her mother for many months, sitting with her head in her lap and pressing it all through the nights. She was with her when she died. She took her bath and went to the Coffee House to have her breakfast. When some friends asked her about her mother's health she replied, 'She is okay.' She then came home and told the servants that she would not receive any visitors who came to condole with her. She did not shed a tear. She did not go to her mother's funeral or any religious ceremonies that followed. On the other hand, when our dog Simba (he was really a member of the family) fell ill, she sat all night stroking him. When he died at the ripe old age of fourteen (ninety by human reckoning), she was heartbroken.

The rigid discipline of time maintained in our home is entirely due to her. I have only recently taught myself how to speed the departure of long-winded visitors. She has always given them short shrift. No one drops in on us without prior warning. If any relation breezes in, in the morning, she ignores their presence and continues with her housework and decides the menu for the day. We eat the most gourmet food—French, Chinese, Italian, South Indian and occasionally Punjabi. She has two shelves full of cookery books which she consults before discussing the menu with our cook, Chandan, who has been with us for over thirty years, or she continues to teach the servants' children and help them with their homework. We don't accept lunch or tea invitations nor invite people for them. When we have people for dinner, no matter who they are—cabinet ministers, ambassadors, or whoever—they are reminded to be punctual and told that we do not expect our guests to stay after 9 p.m. Once the German ambassador and his wife came over. The meal was finished at 8.30 p.m. Liqueurs were served. It was 8.45 p.m. The ambassador took out his cigar and asked my wife, 'I know, Mrs Singh, that you like your guests to leave before 9 p.m. but can I have my cigar before we go?' My wife promptly replied, 'I am sure, Mr Ambassador, you will enjoy it more in your car.' He laughed and stood up, 'I get it.' And departed without any rancour.

I have a lot of pretty girls visiting me. They are dead scared of my wife and know they have to keep on her good side to continue dropping in. All of them take great care never to offend her.

Why do so few people know about my wife? She is allergic to photographers and pressmen. All you have to do is take out your camera, tape recorder or pen, and she will order you out of the house. The allergy runs in the females of the family. My daughter and granddaughter react the same way.

From all this I may sound like a virtuous old man rather than the dirty old one of the popular image. Neither is true.

MY
BELOVED
COUNTRY

WHY I AM AN INDIAN

Why am I an Indian? I did not have any choice: I was born one. If the good Lord had consulted me on the subject I might have chosen a country more affluent, less crowded, less censorious in matters of food and drink, unconcerned with personal equations and free of religious bigotry.

Am I proud of being an Indian? I can't really answer this one. I can scarcely take credit for the achievements of my forefathers. And I have little to be proud of what we are doing today. On balance, I would say, 'No, I am not proud of being an Indian.'

'Why don't you get out and settle in some other country?' Once again, I have very little choice. All the countries I might like to live in have restricted quotas for emigrants. Most of them are white and have a prejudice against coloured people. In any case I feel more relaxed and at home in India.

I dislike many things in my country, mostly the government. I know the government is not the same thing as the country, but it never stops trying to appear in that garb. This is where I belong and this is where I intend to live and die. Of course I like going abroad. Living is easier, the wine and food are better, the women more forthcoming—it's more fun. However, I soon get tired of all those things and want to get back to my dung-heap and be among my loud-mouthed, sweaty, smelly countrymen. I am like my kinsmen in Africa and England and elsewhere. My head tells me it's better to live abroad, my belly tells me it is more fulfilling to be in 'phoren', but my heart tells me 'get back to India'. Each time I return home, and drive through the stench of bare-bottomed defecators that line the road from Santa Cruz airport to the city, I ask myself:

Breathes there the man with soul so dead
Who never to himself hath said
This is my own, my native land?

I can scarcely breathe, but I yell, 'Yeah, this is my native land. I don't like it, but I love it.'

'Are you an Indian first and a Punjabi or Sikh second? Or is it the other way round?' I don't like the way these questions are framed and if I am denied my Punjabiness or my community tradition, I would refuse to call myself Indian. I am Indian, Punjabi and Sikh. And even so I have a patriotic kinship with one who says 'I am Indian, Hindu and Haryanvi' or 'I am Indian, Moplah Muslim and Malayali'. I want to retain my religious and linguistic identity without making them exclusive in any way.

I am convinced that our guaranteed diversity is our strength as a nation. As soon as you try to obliterate regional language in favour of one 'national' language or religion, in the name of one Indian credo, you will destroy the unity of the country. Twice was our Indianness challenged. In 1962 by the Chinese; in 1965 by the Pakistanis. Then, despite our many differences of language, religion and faith, we rose as one to defend our country. In the ultimate analysis, it is the consciousness of frontiers that makes a nation. We have proved that we are one nation.

What then is this talk about Indianizing people who are already Indian? And has anyone any right to arrogate to himself the right to decide who is and who is not a good Indian?

9

THE GHOSTS OF KASAULI

Some years ago, I bought three etchings of Kasauli drawn sometime between 1839 and 1857 from an antiquarian in London. Kasauli was one of the string of hill cantonments like Dagshai and Sabathu built after the death of Maharaja Ranjit Singh in anticipation of wars against the Sikhs. By the time the Mutiny broke out in the summer of 1857, these cantonments had English, Gorkha, Dogra and Sikh troops billeted in them and Sanawar school was under construction to provide educational facilities to sons of Tommies and Anglo-Indians.

The etchings are most revealing. One shows what later became the Kasauli bazaar: a single wayside chaikhana with a tonga standing on a kucha road. In the background is a mountain then known as Tapp's Nose (Tapp was a commissioner with a long snout): the hill is now known as Monkey Point. The other picture is of a solitary chapel standing on top of a pine-forested hill with the caption 'Lawrence Asylum, Sanawar'. It was Henry Lawrence who authorized the asylum to be expanded into a school.

Captain Hodson, who was then under suspension on charges of corruption, was given the job of constructing the school buildings while awaiting trial by court martial. The Mutiny came to his rescue. He was ordered to raise a cavalry of Sikhs, later known as Hodson's Horse, and proceed to Delhi where the East India Company's forces were besieging the city. After the fall of Delhi, Captain Hodson and his Sikh cavalry took King Bahadur Shah, his queen, Mumtaz Mahal, and their son prisoner from Humayun's tomb. The next day he took the king's three older sons from the mausoleum and shot them dead while nearing Delhi Gate.

The third etching is of a fir- and rhododendron-covered hillside, which I have not been able to locate. In all the etchings the town is spelt as Kussowlie.

Before the Kalka-Simla road and railway were laid, the only route from the plains to Simla was the dusty road passing through Kasauli to Dharampur and Sabathu on to Simla. The only mode of transport was the tonga, while caravans of mules carried the baggage. Rudyard Kipling writes about this in his poem 'An Old Song':

So long as 'neath the Kalka hills
The tonga horn shall ring
So long as down the Solon dip

The hard-held ponies swing,
So long as Tara Devi sees
The lights of Simla town,
So long as pleasure calls us up,
Or duty drives us down,
If you love me as I love you,
What pair as happy as we two?

The Kalka-Simla small gauge and the metalled road going right up to the Tibetan border left Kasauli, as it were, isolated by the wayside. As the years went by, people came to regard it as an unimportant little cantonment, a sanatorium for the convalescence of those stricken by consumption or bitten by mad dogs, as it had the only Pasteur Institute in India producing the anti-rabies serum. It had one small hotel, Alasia-Bestozo, run by an Italian, where British soldiers came to guzzle beer and ogle his busty señora and her nubile daughters. Officers had their own Kasauli Club on the Upper Mall with tennis courts, a squash court, billiards and bridge rooms, a library and dance floor. Its cellars were stocked with French vintage wines. Needless to say, both the hotel and the club were 'for whites only'. There was one Anglican and a couple of Catholic churches. Indian Christians had their own place of worship.

I first went to Kasauli sometime in the 1920s with a party of boys from Modern School. We were put up in Shantikunj, a large house on the Lower Mall belonging to the founder of the school, Lala Raghubir Singh. An unwritten apartheid was strictly observed. White sahibs lived in houses on the Upper Mall: the only natives who ventured on these heights were domestic servants or coolies. Indian houses were on the lower reaches or outside cantonment limits. It was only on the road leading to the bazaar and the cantonment cinema (again, for whites only) that we saw sahibs or their mems drinking in the garden of Alasia-Bestozo or outside their churches on Sunday mornings.

I went to Shantikunj several times on successive summer vacations. It was a long way away from the bazaar but close to Kasauli's two best-known features, Monkey Point and a cypress-shaded grove at its base with a small column like those on which sundials are placed. It was, in fact, a tombstone, after which the place was known as Ladies' Grave. We often climbed up Monkey Hill and on clear afternoons got a splendid panoramic view of Kalka and the plains of the Punjab with the Sutlej meandering through. We rested in the grove to cool ourselves after the arduous climb and descent. It had to be accomplished before sunset because Ladies' Grave was known to be haunted by the ghosts of the girls buried there.

Kasauli had its own ghosts. One was of a British Tommy who had been hanged there for the murder of a fellow solider. His ghost was said to march up and down the Lower Mall in full uniform, carrying his rifle with bayonet fixed on his shoulder. Different stories were current about the ghosts of Ladies' Grave. The most common one was that two sisters had tried to go up Monkey Point on horseback and had fallen to their death. On moonlit nights the girls, who were avid tennis players, were known to play against each other in the grove. What I discovered from the district gazetteer turned out to be less romantic. The two had died in a cholera epidemic, had been cremated and their ashes buried at the base of Monkey Point. We boys often took bets to see who would dare to go to Ladies' Grave at night. Only one, my elder brother, won the bet.

Kasauli's social life underwent a dramatic change during World War II. There were hardly any white men left in the station. Most of the houses were occupied by their memsahibs and babalogs. They were lonely and somewhat frightened of being isolated, and so began to mix with the Indians. Kasauli Club, too, accepted a few Indians, like the deputy commissioner and the brigadier in charge of the station. By the time the war ended, most white-owned houses were for sale and were bought by Indians, mainly Sardars, at ridiculously low prices. The only whites that remained were the three Rivett sisters, all spinsters, and a colonel who had retired after World War I and made Kasauli his home.

By 1947 the colonel was a frail, crusty old bachelor in his late eighties, very short-sighted and with a failing memory. He had been a member of the Kasauli Club since its inception but rarely visited it. He took his afternoon walk on the Upper Mall which separates the clubhouse from the tennis courts. He was a familiar figure in his deer-stalker hat and knickerbockers. His Pathan servant, almost as old as him, always followed him to see that his master did not fall or lose his way. It was several months after Independence that the aged colonel noticed that something odd had happened to the Club. He stopped by the tennis courts and saw Indian men and women playing. He went up to the squash court and saw two Sardars battling against each other. Then he went to the Club office where he had been in the past to pay his subscription. The clerk who knew him well stood up and asked if he could be of any service. The colonel gave a one-sentence reply: 'Too many natives about the place!'

10

THE ROMANCE OF NEW DELHI

Once upon a time there was a boy who dreamed of great buildings. He made friends with a blind man whose ambition in life was to design a church. One evening the blind man told his young friend of his concept of the perfect cathedral. The boy got out his sketchbook and began to draw according to the specifications dictated by the blind man. The blind man's wife came in while this was going on. She put her finger to her forehead to indicate that her husband had a screw loose and should not be taken seriously. Then she went over to the boy. She was amazed to see the sketch of a magnificent cathedral.

We do not know who the blind man was, but the young boy who drew the picture of the cathedral from dictation rose to be the greatest architect of his time, Edwin Landseer Lutyens, the builder of New Delhi.

Lutyens was forty-two when he was called upon to design the city. His wife, Lady Emily, was the daughter of Lord Lytton. This aristocratic connection had, in no small measure, helped Lutyens in his professional career. It also helped him in securing the assignment of building New Delhi. But above all, it was the man's innate genius and confidence that he was the master of his destiny that paved the way to success. On a casket that he had designed as an engagement present for his fiancée, he had inscribed his motto: 'As faith wills, fate fulfils.'

On 12 December 1911, King George and Queen Mary laid the foundation stones of the new capital on a hurriedly chosen site north of the old city of Shahjahanabad.

There was an outcry against the project. European business houses established in Calcutta were vociferous in their protests. Lord Curzon decried it as wasteful expenditure; later so did Mahatma Gandhi when he came to India. The age-old superstition about Delhi being 'the graveyard of dynasties' was revived. Didn't seven cities lie in ruins about Shahjahanabad? The viceroy, Lord Hardinge, was strong enough to brush aside these objections. A committee, under the chairmanship of Captain Swinton of the London County Council, was appointed to examine the site and the Royal Institute of British Architects was asked to suggest names of architects to design the city.

The Royal Institute recommended Edwin Lutyens. The government not only accepted the nomination but also Lutyens's own recommendation of a colleague—Herbert Baker, a man he had befriended in his student

38

days and who had also designed buildings in South Africa.

In the summer of 1912 Lutyens arrived in India with the Swinton Committee. The committee was unanimous in condemning the site selected earlier and in recommending another south of Delhi with its centre on a low-lying rocky escarpment known as Raisina Hill. There was plenty of barren land available at low cost. There was also the ridge to give the main buildings the necessary elevation and provide building material. Lord Hardinge agreed with the suggestion. One night, under cover of darkness, the two foundation stones so solemnly laid by Their Majesties amid the pomp and splendour of princely India were uprooted and conveyed by bullock cart ten miles south to be planted in the wilderness of cactus, acacia and camel thorn.

Lord Hardinge was strongly of the opinion that the chief buildings—the viceregal lodge, the secretariats and the parliament—should be in the traditional Indian style. He was reinforced in his opinion by the king who had been deeply impressed by Mughal architecture. Both Lutyens and Baker were taken round to see India's famous buildings—the Buddhist stupas of Sarnath and Sanchi, the temples in south India, the Taj Mahal at Agra, the palaces of Bikaner and Mandu. Lutyens was fascinated by some of the buildings he saw but totally rejected Indian style. 'Personally I do not believe there is any real Indian architecture or any great tradition', he wrote. 'These are just spurts by various mushroom dynasties.' His colleague agreed that despite its charm, Indian architecture did not have 'the constructive and geometric qualities necessary to embody the idea of law and order which has been produced out of chaos by British administration'. However, in the rough sketches, they made concessions to their patron's views by adapting some features of old Indian buildings, e.g., the sun-breaker (chajja), the latticed window (jali), the umbrella dome (chhattri). In Baker's words, the blueprints had 'the eternal beauty of classical architecture with appropriate features of Indian architecture grafted on it'. It was left to Lutyens to get the viceroy and the king to agree. Lutyens was gifted with a honeyed tongue and had no difficulty in winning over Lady Hardinge to his point of view. The vicereine persuaded the viceroy who readily approved of the first sketches. Lutyens and Baker worked them out in greater detail on their voyage back to England. Lutyens presented them to the king at a dinner at Buckingham Palace and had no difficulty in getting royal approval.

Lutyens and Baker divided their work evenly. Lutyens took over the plan of the general outlay of the city with two big buildings, the Viceregal Palace and the War Memorial arch. Baker designed the two secretariats and the Parliament. There were other public buildings and bungalows for officers, clerks' quarters etc., which were also equally shared. Assisting them was a string of talented juniors—Greaves, Shoosmith, Walter George and Medd. The execution of the plans was entrusted to the Public Works Department (PWD), then under Sir Hugh Keeling, the chief engineer. Keeling was also assisted by men who rose to become chief engineers—Sir Alexander Rouse and later Sir Teja Singh Malik who became the first Indian incumbent of the post.

The going was not easy. Lord Hardinge's initial enthusiasm waned as Lutyens's estimates for the projected city mounted. Then Hardinge soured of India altogether. Terrorists tried to murder him—and almost succeeded. He became peevish and began to find fault with everything, particularly the magnitude of Lutyens's plans. Lutyens hit back. 'The viceroy thinks only of what the place will be like in three years' time—300 is what I think of.' Lutyens turned his courtly charm on the vicereine. For some time Lady Hardinge became the chief patroness of the nebulous city. Once when she pulled up Lutyens for wilfully disobeying her instructions, he promised to make amends by washing her feet with his tears and drying them with his hair... 'It is true I have very little hair,' he added, 'but then you have such very little feet.' He was readily forgiven.

Lady Hardinge's patronage did not last long. Her son was wounded in Flanders. The over-anxious mother lost her health and died before her son succumbed to his injuries. Preoccupation with the war and the absence of viceregal enthusiasm put the plans for the building of New Delhi in cold storage. Only Lutyens and Baker continued to dream of the city they would raise on Raisina Hill. Herbert Baker records how, one evening, he and two of his friends stood on the ridge looking down at 'the deserted cities of dreary and disconsolate tombs' and wondered how the new city would rise. The sky was overcast and it rained intermittently. Suddenly, the clouds lifted and the sun broke through. 'A brilliant rainbow formed a perfect arch on what was destined to be a great vista, where Lutyens's memorial arch now stands. We acclaimed it as a good omen.'

As soon as the blueprints for New Delhi were ready, the troubles began—and they came in the proverbial battalions. Lutyens and Baker fell out. The main dispute was over the question of the level of the Viceregal Palace vis-à-vis the secretariats. Lutyens wanted the ruler of the country to be housed at a higher level than his civil servants. Baker wanted the acropolis—as the secretariats and the palace buildings had come to be known—to be on the same level to conform to the prevailing notions of democracy. Baker won. Lutyens next desired the road between the secretariats to be at a sharp gradient so that the Viceregal Palace was distinctly visible from a distance. Baker disagreed. And Baker won again.

99: Khushwant Singh

Lutyens became peevish and fought the 'battle of the gradient' to the bitter end. The two architects were not on speaking terms for many years.

The supply of raw material presented another problem. The architects had planned to quarry the ridge to make an amphitheatre and use the stone so dug up for other buildings. The quartzite on the ridge was found unsuitable; the plan to build an open-air amphitheatre was abandoned. It was decided to quarry Vindhyan stone used by the Mughals: white and buff stone from Dholpur; red from Bharatpur; marble from Makrana, Alwar, Jaisalmer, Baroda and Ajmer. To get Badarpur sand and rubble, a fifteen-mile light railway (Imperial Delhi Railway) with five miles of siding was made. Transportation costs upset all estimates. Lutyens's rough guess of ten million came closest to the mark. But even Lutyens did not expect that instead of four to five years, New Delhi would take almost sixteen to look like a city.

Lutyens's puckish sense of humour sustained his enthusiasm in those trying times. Once the Duke of Connaught asked him why he had hung bells from the tops of columns. Lutyens replied, 'Did you never hear, Sir, of the Mogul superstition that the ringing of bells proclaimed the end of a dynasty? That is why my bells are made of stone.' Another time at a press conference a journalist asked him, 'What is the place of women in architecture?' Lutyens replied, 'As the wives of architects.'

Slowly a new city began to rise on the escarpment. By 1922 most of the stone had been delivered to the site. The stone yard at New Delhi was the biggest in the world; 3,500 stone masons worked in its sheds. Brick-kilns went up in the suburbs. The quantity of brick consumed was astronomical—700 million. Lutyens took interest in every detail. The most important was the planting of trees. W. R. Mustoe of the horticultural department established a nursery with 500 varieties of trees at Safdarjung. Most of them were indigenous; some were imported from Australia or East Africa. As soon as the roads had been marked, trees were planted. They began to rise with the public buildings and bungalows. Lutyens chose wood for viceregal furnishings and instructed cabinetmakers. Likewise carpets, pictures and murals were made under his instructions. All this was done with the cooperation of a succession of viceroys and civil servants.

The last day of the year 1929 was set as the target date for the completion of the three major buildings on the acropolis and the India Gate (bearing the names of 13,516 of 70,000 Indians killed in the Great War). For many months, work went on round the clock.

The formal inauguration of New Delhi took place in January 1931. The kind of tragedy that had soured Hardinge against India was repeated. An attempt was made by terrorists to blow up the train in which Lord Irwin was coming to New Delhi. Fortunately, the viceroy was unhurt and unshaken. He went through the inaugural ceremonies with British sangfroid. Lutyens records his entry into the Viceregal Palace: 'The ceremony proceeded. Then HE went up the stairway to the great portico, where I and others were presented to him. At a given signal the doors were opened (there was no key, as there was no lock). They went into the House, and for the first time in 17 years the House was closed on me.'

Lutyens was also present at the first official banquet given by the viceroy. He believed this was to be his last visit to the place. He later confessed to a friend, 'I had not the nerve to say goodbye to Irwin. I just walked out, and I kissed the wall of the House.'

This was, however, not Lutyens's last visit. He was consulted many times for inscriptions that should go on some of the monuments. Could Lutyens suggest what should be inscribed on the Jaipur Column? asked Lord Irwin. This was too good an opportunity for Lutyens to miss. 'No dogs must be allowed on the ramp,' he wrote back. While the viceroy was still digesting the quip, Lutyens forwarded a more serious suggestion:

Endow your thought with faith
Your deed with courage
Your life with sacrifice
So all men may know
The greatness of India.

Lord Irwin distilled from this the more concise version used:

In thought faith; in word wisdom
In deed courage; in life service
So may India be great.

The inscription on the thrones was suggested by the talented painter-wife of the engineer Shoosmith. It was taken from Proverbs: Wisdom resteth in the heart of him that hath understanding.

Lutyens's last visit to the city he had designed was in the autumn of October 1938. Lord Linlithgow invited him to repair the damage done by the wilful Lady Willingdon: she had the furniture and fittings of the palace changed to her favourite colour, mauve, and she had many of Mustoe's trees in the Mughal gardens uprooted and replaced by rows of cypress. Lutyens was very upset and did the best he could to restore the old design. But he could do nothing to the stadium built in Willingdon's regime. The stadium blocked Purana Qila from view.

Much has been said and written on the architecture of New Delhi. Most of the criticism has been levelled against Baker's buildings. Lutyens's work has been universally acclaimed. And of Lutyens's buildings, the Rashtrapati Bhavan of today is a veritable masterpiece. Captain Swinton, who had first seen the barren escarpment and then the completed building exulted, 'There has now risen before us in all its majesty, the Viceroy's House—one looks, one accepts, one marvels.'

As one mounts up the central vista between the two secretariats the first thing that catches the visitor's eye are slabs of yellow sandstone fixed in alcoves bearing the names of the architects, engineers and builders of the acropolis. On the builders' tablet five names are listed in the following order: Sobha Singh, Dharam Singh Sethi, Basakha Singh, Seth Haroon, Nawab Ali. Some of the other major buildings of New Delhi also have the names of the men who conceived them and were contracted to build them placed on tablets. There is, however, no record of the 30,000 workers who came from all parts of northern India to hew rock, mix mortar and carry brick and cement to its ultimate destination.

The largest group of unskilled workers came from Rajasthan. It was the Bagris, as they were known, who, more than any others, built New Delhi. They were paid at the rate of eight annas for the man and six for the woman per day. (Wheat sold at four rupees for a maund.) They lived in coolie camps where drinking water was supplied, latrines provided and medical attention given free of charge. Throughout the decade and a half of building operations, there was never a labour strike. The other group of unskilled workers were the Bandhanis from the Punjab. They hauled loads too heavy for the frailer Rajasthani. There were also a variety of skilled craftsmen in marble and stone. The sangtarash (stonecutters) came from Agra, Mirzapur and Bharatpur and were largely descendants of people who had built the monuments for the Mughals. Slabs of stone, gravel and sand were transported by the Imperial Delhi Railway from Bada Badarpur near Tughlaqabad right into what is today Vijay Chowk. Where the All India Radio is today were a series of enormous corrugated iron sheds where electrically propelled saws cut stone into proper dimensions. For many years the citizens of New Delhi were awakened by the deafening roar of the ara-masheen. The artistic designs on stone were executed under the direction of a Scottish master mason, Cairns.

The fortunes of the families who took on the contracts for building would provide a writer rich material for a novel. With rare exceptions, these pioneer builders were men of little or no education, no experience of building and of modest means. By the time New Delhi was half-built, they had taught themselves a brand of pidgin English, learnt the tricks of the building trade and, due to the sudden boost in the value of land, had become millionaires. One expression of this windfall was palatial mansions of stone and marble; another was indulgence towards their progeny. Many scions of these nouveau riche families remained as unlettered as their sires. But they were infinitely better dressed and owned the latest models of cars. And while their fathers sweated out their guts on Raisina Hill, they patronized the muses of song and dance in the red-light area of Chawri Bazaar.

The first to arrive on the scene were the Sindhis—Rai Bahadur Fateh Chand of Sukkar built the Old Secretariat near Metcalfe House. He was not able to participate in the building of New Delhi, but another Sindhi, Khan Bahadur Seth Haroon, shared in the building of Rashtrapati Bhavan. A third Sindhi, Lachman Das, took a lion's share in the building of Parliament House. He became legendary for his honesty. He did not use cheap material; he was punctilious in the payment of his labour. He did not even cheat on income tax. It was the tax which finally broke him. Lachman Das retired to Hardwar where he died in the saffron robes of a sadhu.

The Punjabis wrested the initiative from the Sindhis. The first in the field was Narain Singh, a peasant from Sangrur (Jind). He was responsible for the arrangements for the Royal Durbar. Most of the roads and officers' bungalows were built by him. He also prepared the foundations of Rashtrapati Bhavan. He was made a Rai Bahadur. Of his many sons, the most successful is Ranjit Singh who not only multiplied the family fortunes by adding sugar to his building interests but also acquired real estate (including the Imperial Hotel) and became a Member of Parliament. Dharam Singh Sethi, at one time a canal overseer and then a minor partner in the building firm of Ram Singh Kabuli and Co., rose to be one of the wealthiest builders of his time. He had virtual monopoly of the supply of stone and marble. Dharam Singh lived in a palatial house on Jantar Mantar Road, which is now the office of the All India Congress Committee (AICC). He left most of his millions to the Guru Nanak Vidya Bhandar Trust which to this day maintains innumerable schools and gurdwaras. Dharam Singh died of cancer in distant Vienna. Basakha Singh of village Muchhal (district Amritsar) also started as an overseer. He built the entire North Block of the secretariat and many officers' bungalows. Besides these men there were two Punjabi Muslims—Khan Bahadur Akbar Ali of Jhelum who built the National Archives, and Nawab Ali of Rohtak who had a big share in the laying out of the Mughal Gardens.

Without question the first place in the list of New Delhi's many building contractors belongs to Sujan Singh (of Sujan Singh Park) and his illustrious son, Sobha Singh. The family was, by comparison with other contractors, rich and experienced. Besides owning land in Shahpur district, they had a large camel transportation business in western Punjab. They had built some of Punjab's railways and laid most of the Kalka-Simla line. The family came to Delhi before the First World War. After a few insignificant ventures in cotton and textile they went in for building in a big way. The lion's share of the building of New Delhi was taken by Sobha Singh. Amongst the many buildings that are his handiwork are South Block, the Court of Rashtrapati Bhavan, Vijay Chowk, India Gate, Baroda House, All India Radio, the National Museum and innumerable bungalows, chummeries and clerks' quarters. Sobha Singh shared with Lutyens and Baker a vision of the shape of things to come. When Raisina was a jungle of barren rock and kikar trees he bought large tracts of land at open auction. Some plots in what is now Karol Bagh were acquired at two annas a square yard. The highest he paid was two rupees per square yard for land in today's Connaught Circus. Like his other colleagues, Sobha Singh taught himself English, became president of the New Delhi Municipal Committee and member of the Council of States. He was later knighted by the British Government.

The building contractors of New Delhi were a close-knit fraternity. Despite the differences of religion, language and background there was much coming and going between them. Very seldom did they quarrel—profits made quarrels unnecessary. When they first came to Raisina they lived in a row of shacks along what is now Old Mill Road (it was Herbert Baker's modesty which saved it from being named Baker Street). En bloc they moved to more expansive houses on Jantar Mantar Road where they spent the next two decades. As the city grew, they dispersed to different parts of it. And one after the other, they were gathered to their forefathers.

11

BOMBAY RHAPSODY

Bombay, you will be told, is the only city India has, in the sense that the word city is understood in the West. Other Indian metropolises like Calcutta, Madras and Delhi are like oversized villages. It is true that Bombay has many more high-rise buildings than any other Indian city: when you approach it by sea it looks like a miniature New York. It has other things to justify its city status: it is congested, it has traffic jams at all hours of the day, it is highly polluted and many parts of it stink. Arthur Koestler compared his arrival at Santa Cruz airport to having a baby's soiled diaper flung in his face. Bombay discharges the sewage of its ten million or more inhabitants into the sea so close to the shore that a good bit of it is carried back to the land with incoming tides: used condoms can be picked up in the shallows. The stench of human shit prevails over some parts of the seafront. Since it has very few public conveniences, its bazaars smell of stale urine. Twice a year, early in spring and autumn, fish along the coast die in their millions and the acrid smell of rotting fish is overpowering. Bombay has no parks or gardens worth speaking of: only a few small parklets where people go round and round narrow paths like animals in cages. Usually the only place where one can take a walk of sorts is Marine Drive, running from the Chowpatty sands to Nariman Point. This has a dual highway crowded with speeding cars and buses on one side, and massive cement-concrete tripods along the sea walk to prevent it from making further inroads. The tripods are placed at convenient angles, which make it easy for the citizens to rest their feet, let down their trousers or pull up their dhotis to defecate. Nevertheless, Bombaywalas throng to Marine Drive in their thousands morning and evening to jostle their way through masses of humanity. Old people sit on benches placed en route to take in the sea air and gossip. Marine Drive is Bombay's pride and joy. After sunset, as the street lights are switched on, they gape at it in amazement and call it a queen's diamond necklace.

However, there are some points in favour of Bombay. It has a heterogeneous mix of races, religions and linguistic groups. They mind their own business and do not bother with their neighbours, nor are they unduly concerned if they are happily married, divorced, having affairs or living in sin. People of diverse ethnic and religious backgrounds get on reasonably well. Till 1982, Bombay did not have many communal riots, but it would be wrong to conclude that the different communities have affection for each other. Every community thinks it is better than the others and behind their backs uses derogatory expressions to describe them. Parsis regard themselves as a cut above everyone else. They are indeed the most prosperous, and have given to Bombay more than other community. They are conscious of their superiority and look down on the rest as ghatees—coastal trash. Others regard Parsis as effete, senile bawajis, most of whom are highly eccentric and on the verge òf lunacy. Since they are very voluble, they are also known as kagha khaus—crow eaters. Then we have Gujaratis, largely in trade, commerce and industry. Their language, Gujarati, is more widely spoken than Marathi, the language of the more numerous Maharashtrians. The Gujaratis are generally peace-loving, law-abiding and vegetarian. Behind their backs they are referred to as Gujjus. Bombay has a variety of Muslims who, though they have little to do with each other, get together when there is anti-Muslim violence. Besides the major divisions of Sunni and Shia, there are Ismailis (of two kinds), Bohras (of two kinds), and Memons (Cutchee and Halai). They are lumped together as mian bhais. There is also a sizeable community of Christians, both Catholic and Protestant, known to the rest as makapaos —bread eaters (from pao, Portuguese for bread). The latest arrivals are Sindhis and Punjabis. Slowly but surely they have captured a sizeable chunk of the city business and real estate and are consequently eyed with suspicion as grabbers. But Bombay's outsiders outnumber the self-styled insiders who call themselves 'sons of the soil' and insist on calling Bombay by its original name Mumbai, after its patron goddess, Maha Amba. No educated Indian calls it anything other than Bombay.

Bombay is much the richest city of India. More than half of India's income tax comes from this one city. Bombay is also India's most corrupt city: more than half of the black money in circulation is generated in Bombay. It has more millionaires than the other three metropolitan cities put together. It attracts an endless stream of outsiders who hope to make their fortunes here. It also probably has more prostitutes and call girls than any other city in the world. Bombay's rich live very well: in large air-cooled apartments facing the sea, with rooftop gardens and bathing pools. A Sindhi multi-millionaire has a glass-bottomed pool above his bar-cum-sitting room. Whenever he has parties, he hires young girls to bathe in the nude so that his guests can watch them from below while they sip their Scotch. Bombay provides the best food in India: Mughlai, European, Chinese and vegetarian. It has more good, cheap restaurants than any other Indian city. All said and done, Bombay is the most enjoyable city in India—if you can find a place to live in.

12

THE VENUS OF CHURCHGATE

For the first few months after taking over the editorship of *The Illustrated Weekly of India*, I lived as a paying guest of a young Parsi couple in a flat in Churchgate. I did not know many people, so had very little of a social life. I walked to the office every morning and walked back every evening as I refused to use the car and chauffeur provided for me.

Among the earliest friends I made was A. G. Noorani who combined practising law with journalism. He was, and is, a bachelor. We began to spend our evenings together. We would go for a stroll along Marine Drive and return to my flat.

I had my evening ration of Scotch; Noorani, who was, and is, a teetotaller, had a glass of aerated water. Then we set off to try out different restaurants in the neighbourhood. After dinner we tried different paanwalas and bade each other good night. This routine was upset with the onset of the monsoon in Bombay. That's when I ran into the lady about whom I write. There was a break in the downpour. I was alone as I stepped out of a restaurant. A gas station and a few shops were on my way home. I stopped there to buy myself a paan and chatted with a bhelpuriwala and asked him how his business was during the rains. 'Not very well,' he admitted. 'Magar iski kismat jaag jatee hai (her fortune increases),' he added pointing to a woman sitting on the steps of a shop nearby. 'What I can't sell, I give to her. She is a beggar. Thori paagal hai (she is a little mad).' I looked at the woman devouring bhelpuri.

An uncommonly attractive girl, she was in her mid-twenties. Fair, beautifully proportioned, uncombed hair wildly scattered about her face, a dirty white dhoti untidily draped around her body. I gazed at her for quite some time and wondered what an attractive young woman was doing alone in this vice-ridden city. I fantasized about her long into the night.

Thereafter I made it a point to buy my after-dinner paan from the same paanwala by the gas station, exchange a few words with the bhelpuriwala as I ogled the beggar maid on the steps of the closed shop. I often saw her talking to herself. I tried to buy bhelpuri to give to the girl, but the stall owner rejected my offer. He had plenty of leftovers, and feeding the girl was his monopoly.

One evening while I was at dinner, the clouds burst in all their fury and the roads around Churchgate were flooded. I tucked my trousers up to my knees, took my sandals in my hands, unfurled my umbrella to save my turban and waded through the swirling muddy water.

Both the paanwala and the bhelpuriwala had shut shop and gone home. I saw the beggar girl stretched out on the marble steps, barely an inch above the stream of rainwater running past her. She couldn't have had anything to eat that night. I was sorely tempted to give her some money but was not sure how she would react.

I walked home thinking about her, and again thought about her late into the night.

It poured all through the night. As I woke up to look out of the window that overlooked the maidan with the Rajabhai clock tower on the other side, the rain was still coming down in sheets. The maidan was flooded. I saw the shadowy figure of a woman walking across the maidan with a tin in her hand. I saw her hike her wet dhoti and start splashing water between her buttocks. I trained my field glasses on her. She turned to see whether anyone was around. Having reassured herself that she wasn't being watched, she took off her dhoti and stood stark naked in the pouring rain. It was my beggar woman. She poured dirty water on her body, rubbed her bosom, waist, arms and legs. The 'bath' over, she put the wet dhoti back on her and sloshed her way back towards Churchgate station.

The vision of Venus arising out of the sea in the form of a beggar maid of Bombay haunted me for the many days that I was away in Delhi. When I returned to Bombay I made it a point to go to Churchgate for my after-dinner stroll. The paanwala and the bhelpuriwala were there. But not the beggar. I asked the bhelpuriwala what had happened to the girl. His eyes filled with tears and his voice choked as he replied: 'Saaley bharwey utha ke lay gaye (the bloody pimps abducted her).'

13

IN MADRAS

The first thing anyone would like to know about any place they are about to visit is the origin of its name. Why was Chennai known as Madras for three centuries (and before that Fort St George)? I looked up my copy of *Hobson-Jobson*. It gives several explanations. After Fort St George, established as a British Cantonment, the town that grew up around it came to be known as Madrasapatnam, after some Muslim madrasa school. Then 'patnam' was dropped and it became Madras.

I was expecting to see a bit of rain in Madras. There was not a drop. It was hot, humid and still. Gulmohars were in flower just like they are in Delhi before the monsoon sets in. Like Delhi in mid-summer, electric power went off without prior warning and taps went dry. No great problem for me, as I was staying in an old mansion with high ceilings and thick walls. When my mouth was full of toothpaste and not a trickle of water came out of the tap, I rinsed my mouth with Campa Cola. There was plenty of that about as my hostess Surjit Kaur's son (Sunny) ran the fizz plant. Fluoride toothpaste and cola make a pleasant mouthwash.

No other city of India (not even Mumbai) is as film-struck as Chennai. The people who live there worship their screen idols as they worship their deities. They used to worship M. G. Ramachandran and Sivaji Ganesan; they worship Jayalalithaa and even Karunanidhi, who is no beauty. Whichever way you turn in Chennai, you see huge cut-outs of their living gods doing namaskaram to you. All along Marina Beach is a row of statues of men they once worshipped. It is also a city of temples, Kanjeevaram saris, incense and fragrant jasmine, with which their women adorn their heavily oiled hair. It is the city of *The Hindu*, the most readable and reliable journal of the country and the only paper to have its own Indian-made crossword puzzle: other papers take them from England or America. It has produced our best Bharatanatyam dancers: Rukmini Devi, Yamini Krishnamurthy, Malavika Sarukkai and singers like M. S. Subbulakshmi. Also some of our best tennis players, the Krishnans and the Amritraj brothers.

Lunch at the Madras Club, the oldest and swankiest in town, was a non-starter. My hostess assured me it had the best chef in town and I could invite any friends I liked. Rajmohan Gandhi was one; dimpled and ever-smiling Geeta (Padmanabhan), a doctor, was the other. She warned me not to go barefoot to the club (she had seen me always shoeless in the hotel at Goa). We drove into the stately club portico and walked through its spacious Victorian lounge into the dining room. A black-coated and necktied waiter scanned me from turban to toe and announced. 'Not allowed, sir. You have to wear socks and shoes. Also must have collar in your shirt. Club rules.' I was the only defaulter in the party. 'I told you so,' reprimanded Geeta. 'I am not barefooted,' I protested, 'I have sandals.' They were not good enough. We were turned back. In this very club when Rajaji (Rajmohan's grandfather) and prohibition ruled, I had been surreptitiously served Scotch in metal tumblers.

'Very conservative city, Madras,' remarked Rajmohan Gandhi. 'They don't like changing.' Too true.

14

BLOWING UP CALCUTTA

In the days of Gurudev Tagore, Rathi Babu, Nandalal Bose and Jamini Roy, I was of the opinion that there were no people who were as cultured as my Bengali countrymen. And their women were the easiest on the eye. As the years passed, my enthusiasm for everything Bengali began to wane. This was entirely due to repeated exposures to Calcutta. I saw it decline from a grand metropolis to an unkempt, unwashed city with more people than was good for its health. Soon it became, as Kipling had described it, a 'packed and pestilential town' with death hanging over it like dirty smog. I began to dislike it and avoided going there. In the last two years, my dislike for Calcutta has turned to dread; I am frightened of the city and its denizens. Every time I walk down the corridor of Grand Hotel and come face to face with the solid wall of humanity flowing down Chowringhee, I want to run back to my room. I have to muster all my courage to plunge into the smelly human stream, suffer jostling and buffeting, then stumble over uneven, broken pavements, avoid slimy ooze that is always there, dodge incoming, overloaded buses and cabs which bear down on me from all sides. I have developed all the phobias associated with filth and squalor, most of all claustrophobia—fear of crowds. No crowd in the world is more hostile than those in Calcutta. If a car brushes against a pedestrian, a mob will collect, rock it till it turns over, and set it on fire. I still believe Bengalis have more going for them than other Indians and their women have the longest, loveliest hair and the largest, loveliest eyes. But I cannot understand why they have Calcutta. And if they can't do without it, why don't they do something about it like, for instance, blow it up?

15

THE MAGIC OF SIKKIM

The confluence of the Rangpo and the Teesta marks the boundaries of Bengal; follow the rivers as they pass through Siliguri into an expanse of paddy fields and fishponds aglitter with water lilies and hyacinths, flecked with egrets and herons—all very green, clean, fresh and utterly-butterly enchanting. Then, from open country, you enter forests of stately teak and sal, loud with the hum of cicadas. The Himalayas rise before you like a massive, moss-covered wall of black granite.

You cross the Mahananda and go along the mightier Teesta. The road climbs steeply along the mountainside till the river looks like a khaki snake coursing through a narrow gorge a thousand feet below; next, the road dips and you can feel the river current lap the tyres of your car. It is a spectacle not to be missed. Then you come to the sangam of the Teesta and the Rangpo.

The first Sikkimese town, Rangpo, is named after the hill torrent. A large hoarding bids you 'Welcome to Sikkim' with a promise of good things to come. A Black Cat to bring you good luck; Himalayan Peak for a glimpse of the Kanchenjunga; Old Gold for prosperity; and Shangrila for heavenly peace. All these are names of spirits distilled at Rangpo by Jimmy Contractor who, in twenty years, has built up a business that fills his pockets with a few lakhs every year and gives the state half a crore in excise and taxes. Raise your glasses to the enterprising bawaji and proceed on your way!

ABLAZE WITH COLOUR

From Rangpo the road continues its eccentric up-and-down course through forest farmsteads, terraced fields, rivulets and waterfalls. The number of stragglers, trucks and jeeps increases and names of places have a Tibetan ring—Rangpo, Singtam, Tadong. Coral and African tulips, rusty shield bearers, dhatura and the yucca cactus; pretty villas ablaze with canna, gladioli and hibiscus, with peacock swallowtail and brimstone butterflies flitting about. And all at once Gangtok hoves into view.

From the hill on which stands the Institute of Tibetology you go into Deorali with its litter of liquor shops, dhabas, chaikhanas, sweetmeat stalls and bania stores. A yellow four-storeyed building, Elephant Mansion (property of the ex-Chogyal), stands guard over Deorali. You pass rows of trucks, gas stations and suddenly, on your right, rise tiers of the bazaar, one on top of the other. You pass Tenzing and Tenzing (another of the ex-Chogyal's concerns), the Secretariat (also the ex-Chogyal's property rented to the Government) and an English-medium school followed by two signboards. One enjoins you to pray and to come unto Jesus; the other is of the Divine through love. Then come the Hotel Paradise and the Himalayan Restaurant promising spiritual solace through whisky, rum and juniper gin. Noticeboards read: 'We trust in God; but terms strictly cash.' You know you are in Gangtok.

PIGS AND TAPE-RECORDERS
Gangtok looks like Simla, Mussoorie or neighbouring Darjeeling; the same mountainous landscape, the same kind of bazaars and houses. But it is a much smaller town. Its total population is under 15,000 souls. It has two main bazaars almost entirely run by Marwaris, UP bhaiyyas, Biharis and Punjabis. There is one open-air market, Lall, where every Sunday peasants bring farm produce: vegetables, poultry, pigs and yak cheese. (You can also buy smuggled watches, tape recorders, cameras and synthetic fabrics).

There are two cinema houses, five schools and one intermediate college—running night classes. A large hospital, a tiny Legislative Assembly Hall (it has only thirty-two members), a community centre and a cottage industries emporium. The rest consists of villas, large and small, police and army barracks and a few playgrounds.

Gangtok is a small capital of a small state. Four races co-exist and co-mingle: Lepchas, Bhotiyas, Nepalis and Indians. Lepchas, who are the original Adivasis, form a bare 13 per cent and the Bhotiyas 14 per cent of the people. The rest are Nepalis. The Indians, who are less than 1 per cent of the population, are entirely confined to towns but monopolize most of the trade.

The vast majority of the populace are Buddhist or Hindu but there are some Muslims and Christians as well. Religious differences do not matter a tinker's cuss in Sikkim. Nor do the ethnic. The erstwhile ruling family of Sikkim are Bhotiyas; the present chief minister, Kazi Lhendup Dorji, is a Lepcha.

The name 'Sikkim' has an amusing genesis. It is believed that in days gone by a Nepali princess given in marriage to a Lepcha chieftain described her groom's abode as her new home—Su Him. In course of time Su Him became Sikkim. I have not been able to trace the origin of the name Gangtok.

♦

I turn in early. Eight hours of travel is more than enough to tire out an ageing man. I open my window, which looks northwards towards Tibet. 'At 5 a.m. you can see Kanchenjunga,' the photographer Shiv Kumar had promised me. My bed is placed in such a way that I can see the northern panorama without raising my head from the pillow.

The notes of a bugle rouse me from my slumber. It is pitch-dark. I switch on the table lamp and discover it is 4.30 a.m. An hour later it turns grey. I can see nothing but mist and rain. I can hear nothing but the dawn chorus of birds and orders of command in Anglo-Hindi. 'Platoon saavdhan! Platoon kandhey shastra!' Gradually the mist raises its veil. I see jawans of the Central Reserve Police parading up and down a soggy football ground below me. By the time I get dressed I see them playing hockey and football on the same ground with the rain pelting down on them.

Ranjit Mukherjee, manager of the Nor-Khill Hotel, joins me for breakfast. He tells me the name of the hotel means 'surrounded by jewels'. The twenty-four-room hotel has poor occupancy—the long monsoon season inhibits travel; only during autumn and winter does the Nor-Khill fill up.

'But the country is so beautiful,' I protest. 'People should come pouring in.' 'We Indians are not venturesome,' replies Mukherjee ruefully. 'And, at the moment, there are few facilities for tourists.' But what about a haversack and a portable tent? In a hospitable country which has so much to offer, that is all a young person needs to carry. And leech-repelling lotion. There is a pestilence of these blood-suckers everywhere.

The rain thins down to a drizzle. I decide to take a look at Gangtok. I pass children going to school. Pink-cheeked boys full of robust good health. Girls in clean baku dresses daintily tripping along. Are they Lepchas, Bhotiyas or Nepalis? It is difficult for a stranger to tell. All he can vouch for is that they are an attractive lot with clean, unblemished skin, slanting eyes, high cheekbones and bewitching smiles. I stroll through the bazaar. It has not much to offer but it is cleaner than Indian bazaars (which is not saying very much). No odour of urine or shit, no slop or garbage thrown out of windows. The Sikkimese are tidier and more disciplined than us (which again is not saying much). And there are fewer beggars—a fair proportion of them Indians. I saunter through a medley of songs by the Mangeshkar sisters, Kishore Kumar, Mohammad Rafi and past the two cinema houses. Very reluctantly I admit to myself that the most powerful medium for national integration is Hindi cinema. Long live Lata and Asha, Rajesh, Amitabh, Shatrughan, Sharmila, Jaya, Neetu, Chintu, Dimpu, Rekha, Raakhee, and Helen! Long live all the hams!

My first assignment is a courtesy call on His Excellency the first

Governor of Sikkim, Mr B.B. Lall. He is indeed a courteous man. He was two years my junior in Delhi but considerably senior in mental development. He walked into the ICS and now governs this most sensitive of our frontier states. He is a widower, a teetotaller and cautious in speech. He looks uneasily at my notebook and pencil. I push them away. Thereafter he explodes with laughter at all my PJs (phlat jokes). He gives away nothing except cups of coffee and a thimbleful of Sikkimese liquor that makes my head reel. We talk of orchids, butterflies, Kanchenjunga and our college days. It is all in the past tense. I spend an hour with him without getting much copy. He was born to be a diplomat.

BOOKS AND NOSTALGIA

The ex-Chogyal, on whom I call in the afternoon, proves to be more communicative. He receives me in his study. I present him with the traditional scarf, which he promptly thrusts back into my hands. I look around. Every wall of the room is lined with books from floor to ceiling. They are in English, ranging from rare travelogues, books on flora, fauna down to *Lolita*. Much of the floor space is also littered with books. 'These are my American wife's collections,' he explains. 'She even turned my garage into a library,' he says, pointing to an extension.

The ex-Chogyal has aged in the last year, become more fidgety, the nervous tic on his face has become more pronounced and he is drinking more. He is an unhappy man. He has been stripped of his titles but his present and future status remain undefined: New Delhi is taking its time and keeping him guessing. He complains that he is hard up and has had to retrench most of his staff. There is little doubt that he has less money now.

The number of his supporters have also dwindled. (Of the thirty-two members of the state legislature, only one supports him). His fate is no worse than that of our other maharajas. He, like them, finds it hard to reconcile himself to the deprivation of titles and wealth he acquired by the accident of birth. The inexorable march of events has left him straggling behind—lonely, disillusioned and sad. I wish New Delhi would settle his future and with generosity.

His eldest son is a strapping, handsome youngster reading science in Trinity College, Cambridge. He has taken two years off to be with his father. He is an excellent football player and much more truculent than his sire. He still flies the old Sikkimese flag on his car. I wish he were reading modern history instead of science.

In the evening I call upon the chief minister, Kazi Lhendup Dorji. I pass the Assembly Chamber. It is past 6 p.m. but it is still in session discussing the Budget. Armed constables of the CRPF guard the building. They are also in evidence outside ministers' bungalows. The Kazi sahib has not returned, but the Kazini sahiba is very much at home.

THE KAZINI

Here is a woman the likes of whom I have never encountered before. It is difficult to tell her age. She may be sixty getting on to seventy. She has the vitality of a girl in her twenties. She is a tall, powerfully built woman who must have been a beauty in her younger days. I wasn't able to discover whether she was born Belgian, domiciled Scots or Scots married Belgian. She speaks excellent French and her English has no trace of the Scottish accent. She speaks both languages plus Hindi and Nepali with fluency, animation and embarrassing candour.

She has been married before (how many times is the subject of popular gossip in Gangtok), but has been the Kazini for the last twenty years. She played an important role in the Sikkimese National Movement and is today the power behind the throne—i.e., the chief minister. I have not met anyone who better deserves to be chosen 'Woman of the Year' for International Women's Year.

'What about the Chogyal?' I ask her. 'Good man, badly advised,' she replies. 'Won't read the writing on the wall. Folie de grandeur instilled into him by his stupid Indian advisers and Sikkimese sycophants. But it is wrong to keep him in limbo. The Government of India must tell him what his status is to be.' She illustrated her point by narrating an amusing dialogue she had with him. 'I am the Chogyal, I am half-sacred,' the Chogyal is reported to have said. 'Which half?' demanded the Kazini.

NOT A COLONY

The Kazini is outspokenly critical of the ham-handed way Indian officials behave, the ambivalent loyalties and aloofness of Indian traders and OSDs (Officers on Special Duty) who refuse to learn the language or identify themselves with the Sikkimese and their aspirations. 'They just make their pile and go away,' she says.

At the same time she is passionately pro-Indian. 'We are the twenty-second state: we must be treated as a part of India and not as a colony,' she says over and over again.

One can see why the Dorjis have hit it off so well. She is volatile, emotional, explosive and tactlessly outspoken; he is quiet, phlegmatic and cautious in the choice of his words. In Gangtok you will hear many amusing anecdotes of how at some place or the other the Kazini stormed and ranted at this or that not being done. The Kazi sahib whispered to the same people to let his wife blow off steam and not to be perturbed. They make an ideal foil to each other and, in a subtle way, help each other to get things done.

Kazi Lhendup Dorji is a Lepcha—one of the original inhabitants of Sikkim. He, like most other well-to-do Sikkimese, was schooled in Darjeeling. He has no university degrees and feels more at home with Nepali or Hindi than with English. He has considerable experience of men and things that matter. He is a prosperous businessman and owns some property.

But most of the Kazi's life was spent in voluntary exile in nearby Kurseong from where he organized the Sikkim Congress to press for land reforms (Sikkimese landowners made exorbitant demands on labourers) and a fair share of power for the Nepalis who formed the overwhelming proportion of the population. He strongly opposed the autocratic regime of the Chogyals and advocated a democratic system based on 'one man one vote'.

The Kazi was the chief instrument of the Sikkimese demand for integration with India as its twenty-second state. The popularity of his party can be gauged from the fact that in the last general election it won thirty-one out of thirty-two seats in the Legislature; and, recently, both the Rajya Sabha and the Lok Sabha seats allotted to Sikkim. As in other states of the union, he has to accommodate other pressure groups within his party; he has a cabinet of seven members—drawn from the Nepalis, Bhotiyas and Lepchas.

I was fortunate enough to meet all the people who today control the destinies of Sikkim. This was on the last evening of my brief sojourn there. I had been well briefed (and 'oiled' with Scotch) by Khorana, the Commissioner of Police. There is no serious law-and-order problem in the state. But no one ever knows when disgruntled elements can get together to create disturbances and whip up anti-Indian feeling. That is why a company of 2,000 CRPF men are discreetly scattered about the state to guard roads, bridges, administrators and even trouble spots in the bazaar.

BIGWIG STAGS

It is at the CRPF Mess that I meet them. It is a stag affair with all the stags who matter in friendly conviviality over glasses of orange juice (Sikkim grows lots of oranges and cans them). HE the Governor is there, as are the Kazi sahib and his seven-member cabinet, and Indian officials on deputation to advise the Sikkimese on matters of finance, development and land laws. And, of course, the intelligence and security personnel.

The Chinese are dangerously close to Sikkim at Nathu La, about thirty kilometres away, within hollering distance. Since there is no Hindi-Chini bhai-bhaism, one can presume that their watch of Sikkim extends beyond their frontiers, beyond the pickets where jawans of our army face them. So we have our CRPF to lend muscle to the Sikkim police in times of internal trouble and to supplement the army in the event of any hanky-panky by foreign elements. But right now the atmosphere is as peaceful as it could be. The backslapping and carefree laughter at the party was most reassuring.

On my last day I rise well before dawn in the hope of catching a glimpse of Kanchenjunga. I am out of luck. Once again the sky is overcast and a heavy mist blots out the mountains. I walk down from Gangtok—five miles of breathtaking scenery of green hills, sparkling streams—and enchanting, lovable people.

Next time I must come in winter when the skies are blue and the snows whiter.

16

GANGA MAI

It becomes increasingly difficult for someone like me who yells at the top of his voice about not believing in any religion to explain why I go to Hardwar once or twice a year to witness the aarti of the river Ganga which takes place every evening at sunset.

I neither offer any prayers nor subscribe to expenses of aartis. I am simply a spectator, a tamashbeen. I never tire of seeing this spectacle of worship of the river with the blowing of conch shells, clanging of brass gongs, waving of oil lamps over the fast moving stream to the chanting of 'Om Jai Gangay Mata'.

I do not see it as a Hindu religious practice but a pagan ritual performed by our Aryan forefathers many times removed. They worshipped elements of nature: mountains, rivers, lakes, seas, trees and animals. I do not worship any of them but stand in awe of their majesty. I do not worship the Ganga; I have a close personal relationship with her—she is my mother, sister, sweetheart, wife and daughter, all rolled into one. Do I make sense? Perhaps not. But that is how it is.

However, on a recent visit I did pray to Ganga Mai. As the temple bells, gongs and chanting were ending and the thousands of oil lamps burning out, I joined both the palms of my hands and said to her, 'Ma Ganga, you know I have never asked you for any favours. I promise never to ask you for any again. But promise to grant this one if it is within your powers to do so.

'It is not for me but for my country through which you flow from the snowy Himalayas to the silvery sea. I do not think there is anything mahaan about it but main us desh ka vaasee hoon jis desh mein Ganga behti hai (I belong to the land through which you flow). It has been soiled by preachers of hate and violence. Come into a mighty flood, sweep all these evil elements into the sea and repurify my motherland.'

I don't know if Ganga Mai heard my silent prayer. She looked dark and forbidding. If she grants me my prayer, I will return to Har Ki Pauri to thank her. If she dismisses me as a crackpot, I will still return to her banks to reproach her. Our relationship is no saudey-bazee kind of give-and-take. She is the only one in my country I truly love. Whether or not she returns my love does not bother me.

17

THE HAUNTED SIMLA ROAD

Many years ago the bells of St Crispins woke up the people of Mashobra on Sunday mornings. We threw open our windows and let the chimes flood into the room along with the sunlight. We watched the English folk coming from the hotels and houses for service. It was the only day in the week they were up before the local inhabitants. All morning, visitors continued to pour in from Simla in rickshaws, on horseback and on foot. At evensong when the religious were at prayer once more, the road to Simla echoed with the songs and laughter of people returning to the city.

The bells of St Crispins do not toll any more. The lychgate is padlocked and there is mildew on the golden letters of the church notice board. The haunts of the English holiday-makers, 'Wild Flower Hall' and 'Gables', have not had their shutters up since they were put down in the autumn of 1947. The only white people around are a couple of elderly missionary ladies who walk about briskly, stopping occasionally to inspect a wild flower, inhale the crisp mountain air, holding their arms stiff at their sides with beatific expressions on their upturned faces. There is a young English writer in khaki shorts and sandals getting the feel of the country at the country liquor shop. Sometimes Italian priests from the monastery of San Damiano stray into the bazaar to buy provisions.

Apart from the people little else has changed. There is the deckle-edged snow line beyond the peaks of Shali in the north, and the vast plains of Hindustan towards the south; one can see the Sutlej winding its silvery serpentine course through the orange haze. There are the dense forests of deodar, fir and mountain hemlocks. There are the terraced fields with clusters of villages in their midst—and flat roofs with corn drying on them. All day long the lammergeyers circle in the deep blue of the sky or sit on crags amongst the rhododendrons, sunning themselves with their wings stretched out. Barbets call in the valleys and the cicadas drown the distant roar of the stream with their chirpings. Convoys of mules bell their way endlessly into the Himalayas with the muleteer's plaintive flute receding in the distance. A hill woman's song rises above all other sounds and for one ecstatic minute fills the hills and valleys with its long melodious monotone. It ends abruptly and there again are the barbet, cicada, mule bells, the flute and the roar of the stream.

There are things that make you pause and wonder whether the British have really left. Houses which look like English country homes are still unoccupied and give the impression that they await their departed masters. Local inhabitants never tire of gassing about memsahibs who did their shopping in the bazaar. Even now the bania will slip into quoting prices for the pound instead of the seer or kilogram. An asthmatic old Sinhalese who made jams and pickles for hotel residents still refers wheezily to England as home and presses his syrupy rhubarb wines on his listeners with a toothless 'doch an doris'. One comes across names and pierced hearts on trunks of trees that tell tales of romance which lichen and moss have not obliterated. Then there is the cuckoo—the English cuckoo—with its two distinct notes which people say was imported by an Englishman in a fit of nostalgia.

In the evening when the mules are tethered and muleteers sip tea or smoke their hookahs, they tell of the many foreigners who had lived in and around Mashobra. The eccentric American missionary who converted the whole of the apple-growing valley of Kotgarh to Christianity and then converted them back to Hinduism; of an ayah who still haunts the house in which she was murdered by her master's wife; of the people who had simply abandoned homes they had built and lived in for many years because they could not be bothered to come back from England; of phantom rickshaws and phantom ladies riding side-saddle on phantom horses.

It is a long walk back from Mashobra to Simla. The road is deserted after sunset and only the lights of the city scattered in profusion on Jacko Hill keep your spirits up. On the right is the Koti Valley with its stream glistening like quicksilver and the soft glow of oil lamps that come on unnoticed in distant farmsteads. There is something which makes you keep looking back over your shoulder. You hear the stamp of rickshaw-pullers' feet and whiffs of perfume and cigar smoke steal mysteriously across the moon-flecked road—and your heart is too full for words.

THE
SIKHS

WRITING SIKH HISTORY

THE SIKH HOMELAND

RANJIT SINGH, MAHARAJA OF THE PUNJAB

THE SIKHS

A RIOT OF PASSAGE

BARA MAH

18

WRITING SIKH HISTORY

For one who is not a trained historian, the three big problems are the paucity of original documents, the method of interpreting those that are discovered, and finally, having to decide whether or not their contents are 'history'. I will illustrate these points with my experience of four years of research in Sikh history. I have no training as a historian and some of my observations may appear naive. But as I have had to telescope learning history and writing it into one piece, I am in a position to question the material on which many histories are based and suggest reasons why histories of India tend invariably to be 'periodized' and make desperately dull reading.

The history of the Sikhs is assumed to begin with Guru Nanak who was born in 1469 and died seventy years later in 1539. He did not attain prominence till he proclaimed his faith in the year 1500. Thereafter he spent so much of his time wandering over Asia—from Assam to Basra, from Tibet to Ceylon—that no one was able to keep pace with him. On some of his travels he was accompanied by a Muslim minstrel called Mardana, at others by a peasant named Bala or people of whom nothing is known besides their names.

Guru Nanak made no record of his journeys and only very few of his hymns refer to actual incidents. More frequently incidents were fabricated to make a setting for his hymns. Mardana wrote nothing except a few verses which were later incorporated into the Adi Granth. Other companions of Nanak were completely illiterate. The chief source for the life of the Guru is a biography—Janam Sakhi—said to have been dictated by Bala. This Janam Sakhi has caused Sikh historians endless trouble. It is in rustic dialect and crammed with fairy tales, which the most devout shudder to accept. Fifty years ago, the late Bhai Vir Singh subjected Bala's Janam Sakhi to a searching analysis and proved beyond doubt that it was spurious and that we could not be even sure whether there was any such person as Bala who was a companion to the Guru.

There is little doubt that some of the miracles associated with Nanak were the stock-in-trade miracles ascribed to the Bhakti and Sufi saints of the time. The cobra shading the infant avatar with its hood, and the disappearance of the body of the Guru while his Hindu and Muslim disciples clamoured for its possession appear in the life of Kabir. The parable of returning a bowl of milk with a jasmine in it (to indicate that even if the world is full of goodness as the bowl is full of milk there is still room for fragrance in it) is ascribed to many Sufi divines. It was an age of plagiarism in which writings, incidents, miracles—everything—was freely borrowed without acknowledgement. What then are we left with in reconstructing the life of the founder Guru? There are many other Janam Sakhis—all based on that of 'Bala' or something which closely resembled 'Bala's'.

SOURCE MATERIALS

The only authentic material historians are left with are relics at places the Guru visited (inscribed stones have been found in East Bengal, Assam and one near Basra), his own compositions and the writings of contemporary scholars relating to incidents of common experience. Thus we know that at the time of Nanak, the reigning dynasty was the Lodi and that the local zamindar of Talwandi was one Rai Bular. But we do not know whether the Guru was really imprisoned by Babar who then repented his misdeeds (as Sikh historians claim) because the *Tuzuk-i-Babari* has no reference to this meeting (perhaps Nanak was not then as famous a saint as he became later). Basically this is all the material that a biographer can really trust; the rest is inference and conjecture.

By the time Guru Nanak died, his movement was well and properly launched. It attracted the attention of Mughal subedars and the official Waqa-i-Navis began to send in regular reports. This was more so after the execution of the fifth Guru, Arjun (1606) when the Sikhs began to transform themselves from a pacifist to a militant sect. The succeeding Gurus had their own bards who recorded important events. These two sources provide two opposite versions from which a discerning and honest historian can get a reasonably accurate picture of the period. This phenomenon, however, ends with the Gurus. After the death of Guru Gobind (1708) the historian is left with only one source, the official anti-Sikh one because the Sikhs themselves abandoned the pen for the sword.

The rise and fall of Banda (1708-1716) and the struggles of the Sikh misls against Mughal subedars and Ahmed Shah Abdali who invaded the Punjab nine times between 1747-1765 are largely based on Afghan and Mughal accounts. Non-Muslim historians usually extract compliments to the Sikhs (which are rare) and delete derogatory references; abusive epithets invariably used for the Sikhs were 'black-faced' or 'bearded dogs'. As the Sikh misldars elevated themselves from common freebooters to chieftains, they acquired their own bards and news writers. Thereafter we get a mass of family histories—many of which were utilized by Griffin to compile his voluminous *Chiefs and Families of Note in the Punjab*.

With the advent of Ranjit Singh, the source material becomes enormous. Accounts by European travellers; political correspondence between the Durbar and the East India Company; Mughal, Gurkha, Rajput, Afghan and Maratha news writers' reports; and, of course, the detailed entries of court historians like Sohan Lal Suri whose *Umdat-ut-Tawarikh* even records the maharaja's bowel movements. Thereafter, the problem is not the paucity of material, but the method of treatment.

EARLY HISTORIANS
During the eighteenth and the early nineteenth centuries, Sikhs produced historians of their own. Ratan Singh Bhangu, Gyani Gyan Singh and Santokh Singh wrote detailed accounts of their co-religionists and, to compensate for the diatribes of Muslim historians, denounced everything Islamic whether Mughal or Afghan and glorified the achievements of the Khalsa. The pattern set by these men was followed by two later historians, Karam Singh and Baba Prem Singh of Hoti Mardan to whom the present generation of Sikhs owe most of their knowledge of the misls, Ranjit Singh and wars with the British. None of these writers pretended to be objective, and strictly followed the traditional pattern of reducing history to the biographies of successive rulers. Economic conditions (apart from an occasional reference to the cost of food grains), class conflicts and social phenomena rarely obtrude in their narratives.

Sikh history in the sense in which history is used in modern times has been written by half a dozen men. Professor Indubhushan Banerjee subjected Macauliffe's six tomes of the religion of the Sikhs to a critical analysis and condensed them into two extremely compact and readable volumes entitled: *Evolution of the Khalsa.* He did not go to any original sources nor add to the existent knowledge on Sikhism. The same could be said of Dr Gokul Chand Narang's *Transformation of Sikhism* which is an excellent piece of interpretative history—a forensic marshalling of well-known facts to sustain a thesis on the factors which transformed the quietist followers of Nanak to the aggressive and hirsute Khalsa of Gobind. Dr N. K. Sinha of Calcutta University broke fresh—though not very fertile—ground with his study of the rise of the misls and a short biography of Ranjit Singh. (By strange oversight he ended his narrative eight years before the death of the maharaja. Did Sinha mean to immortalize the Lion of the Punjab?)

SIGNIFICANT WORKS
The Punjab has produced three distinguished historians of the Sikhs—all of whom have added enormously to our information on the community.

Dr Sita Ram Kohli was the first to examine the records of the Khalsa Durbar, which, but for him, would have been lost forever. His biography of Ranjit Singh, unfortunately only available in Hindi and Gurmukhi, is infinitely more detailed, accurate and objective than the sketchy works of Griffin and Sinha. Dr Kohli also completed an equally detailed account of the fall of the Sikh kingdom.

Dr Hari Ram Gupta's research on the misl period has been the most exhaustive done so far on any period of Sikh history by anyone. His three volumes are based on hitherto untapped Persian material and have undoubtedly been the basis of some of the work by Dr Sinha and the team comprising the late Professor Teja Singh and Dr Ganda Singh. Dr Gupta's otherwise invaluable work becomes somewhat prosaic because of his reluctance to propound a theme or draw conclusions. But that may well be his view of what history should be.

The most eminent and respected contemporary Sikh historian is Dr Ganda Singh of Patiala. He has written a large number of books both in English and Gurmukhi of which three are recognized as classics—*Banda Singh Bahadur*, *Ahmed Shah Durrani* and an account of the Kuka movement. In all of them, battles and dynasties assume great importance. Dr Ganda Singh's dates are usually in triplicate—Vikrami, Hijri and the Christian era—along with the precise quarters of the moon.

NO THEMATIC CONTENT

Following the style current in academic circles of the Punjab, all the three historians make a deliberate effort to make their histories many-sided by inserting separate chapters under such headings as 'Judicial system', 'Revenue system', 'Army', etc. Little or no attempt is made to knit these into one story or pull out the one string on which events are strung as beads on a rosary. No one, for instance, has yet propounded the most obvious theme that the rise of Sikhism was the rise of Punjabi consciousness, culminating in the formation of a Punjabi State. The absence of the thematic approach is chiefly responsible for this strange fact that these historians write finis to Sikh history on the annexation of the Punjab in 1849. Captain Joseph Darey Cunningham's history of the Sikhs brings the account up to the end of the First Anglo-Sikh War in 1845.

It is a strange phenomenon that no historian has thought it fit to complete the story by writing of the last 150 years. Undoubtedly what has daunted them is the fact that since they look upon the kingdom of Ranjit Singh as a Sikh kingdom its fall is considered as the end of Sikh history. This is far from the truth as not only did more than half the Sikhs (the Malwais of the Cis-Sutlej region) have nothing to do with the

Sikh kingdom but the so-called Sikh kingdom itself was so thoroughly Punjabi, with Muslim and Hindu ministers and generals, that labelling it 'Sikh' is almost a libel on Ranjit Singh's secularism.

THE ABSORPTION

After the end of the 'Sikh' kingdom the history of the Sikhs is so completely mingled with that of the other communities that it becomes as difficult to separate it as it would be to separate one strand from a hank of hair. But the thread has a distinct historical role and personality. Just as from its inception Sikhism was an expression of militant Hinduism as well as Punjabi nationalism, so too, after its nationalist role had been played, its history became one of resistance to the absorptive tendencies of resurgent Hinduism and to find a raison d'etre for its separate existence.

During my research, I came across an incident in the Second Anglo-Sikh War (1848-1849) which caused me some amusement as well as gave me food for thought. In the spring of 1849 Diwan Mulraj, the Governor of Multan, had resigned his post. Kahan Singh Man was nominated by the English Resident to replace him. Two English officers, Vans Agnew and Lt. Anderson, along with troops of the Durbar infantry and cavalry, had been sent with Kahan Singh to take possession of the fort. After the ceremonial handing over of the place, when the Durbar party was returning to its encampment, a mutinous soldier angered by the order to salute the ferringees lunged at Vans Agnew with his spear and wounded him. The disbanded Multani soldiery rallied round Vans Agnew's assailant and later in the afternoon looted the Durbar camp and carried off all provisions.

Mulraj, who was forced to become the leader of the rebellion, was presented with part of the loot. It consisted of bottles of whisky, brandy and beer. There were also hermetically sealed lead boxes. The stores were spread out in front of the Diwan for the benefit of the courtiers. The bottles were uncorked and passed round for scrutiny. The courtiers sniffed at the contents and passed the brandy and Scotch as fit for human consumption. Beer did not have a familiar smell; its pale yellow colour made it particularly suspect and it was poured out into the gutter as maila pani. The hermetically sealed boxes were the subject of much debate. The majority were of the opinion that it was a new kind of shrapnel and the best thing to do was to use it against the enemy. Next morning, Mulraj's guns opened up against the Durbar English encampment, which was without food, and pelted it with bully beef, shrimps, sardines, lobsters and other delicacies.

THE DRY APPROACH

Did this incident qualify for inclusion in a book of history? Many scholars had undoubtedly examined the records before me but no one had made use of it because they considered it too trivial. Some had extracted what they considered material of 'historic' importance, e.g., Mulraj's court was familiar with hard liquor but not beer; that by the middle of the nineteenth century the English knew how to make airtight boxes; that tin had not yet been introduced as a container and lead was used despite the danger of lead-poisoning—and so on. This sort of dry academic approach is the chief reason why our histories make such dull reading.

The British conquest of Sindh is epitomized in the one-word message sent by Napier to the Governor-General: 'Peccavi (I have sinned)'. The message may have been apocryphal; but it is the stuff which sugar-coats history and makes it fascinating.

19

THE SIKH HOMELAND

The Punjab has a geographical unity distinct from the neighbouring countries and the rest of India. It is shaped like a scalene triangle balanced on its sharpest angle. The shortest side is in the north and is composed of the massive Himalayas, which separate it from the Tibetan plateau. The western side is bounded by the river Indus from the point it enters the plains to another point 1,650 miles downstream, where it meets the confluence of the Punjab's rivers at a place appropriately named Panjnad—the five streams. Westwards of the Indus runs a chain of rugged mountains, the Hindu Kush and the Sulaiman, pierced by several passes like the Khyber and the Bolan, which have served as inlets for the people of the countries which lie beyond, Afghanistan and Baluchistan. The eastern boundary of the Punjab's triangle is not clearly marked, but from a point near Karnal where the Jumna plunges southeastwards a jagged line can be drawn up to Panjnad, which will demarcate the state from the rest of Hindustan and the Sindh desert.

The Punjab, except for the salt range in its centre, is an extensive plain sloping gently down from the mountains in the north and the west towards the desert in the south. Across this monotonously flat land flow six large rivers: the Indus, Jhelum, Chenab, Ravi, Beas, and the Sutlej. In the intra-fluvial tracts or doabs between these rivers and in the western half of the tract between the Sutlej and the Jumna live people who speak the Punjabi language and describe themselves as the people of the Punjab. The homeland of the vast majority of the Sikhs is in the doabs between the Chenab and the Jumna.

THE NAME: PUNJAB
When the Aryans came to India there were seven rivers in the Punjab, so they named it Sapta Sindhva, the land of the seven seas. The Persians took the name from the Aryans and called it the Hafta Hindva. Sometime later, after the seventh river, the Sarasvati, had dried up, people began to exclude the Indus from the count (since it marked only the western boundary of the province) and renamed it after the remaining five rivers as Pentopotamia or the panj-ab, the land of the five waters.

PEOPLE OF THE PUNJAB
The ethnic pattern of the Punjab has changed with every new conquest.

71

At the time of the birth of Nanak (AD 1469) it was somewhat as follows:

In the northwest stretching along both sides of the Indus were Pathans and Baluchis—the former on the upper and the latter on the lower reaches of the river. These people, like their neighbours (Gakkhars, Awans, Janjuas, and others who settled between the Indus and the Jhelum) were divided into innumerable warring tribes, jealously preserving their traditions and way of life but united in their fierce loyalty to the Islamic faith. On the northern fringe of the country in a narrow belt running along the foothills of the Himalayas were the domains of Hindu princes who had fled the plains in front of the Muslim onslaughts. In this submontane region intersected by mountain streams and deep ravines, made impassable by entangled bushes of lantana, vasica, and ipomoea they built chains of forts which defended them from further inroads of Muslim invaders. Here they burnt incense to their gods and preserved their inegalitarian society in which the Brahmins and Kshatriyas exploited the lesser castes. In the rest of the Punjab, consisting of the vast champaign stretching to the Jumna and beyond, the countryside was inhabited by Jats and Rajput agricultural tribes, the cities by the trading Banias, Mahajans, Suds and Aroras. In all cities, towns and villages there were the dark and somewhat negroid descendants of the aboriginals who were considered beyond the pale of the caste system, forced to do the dirtiest work and then condemned as untouchables. In addition to all these were nomadic tribes of gypsies wandering across the plains in their donkey caravans with their hunting dogs and herds of sheep and goats.

BIRTH OF PUNJABI NATIONALISM

The Punjab, being the main gateway into India, was fated to be the perpetual field of battle and the first home of all the conquerors. Few invaders, if any, brought wives with them, and most of those who settled in their conquered domains acquired local women. Thus the blood of many conquering races came to mingle, and many alien languages—Arabic, Persian, Pushto and Turkish—came to be spoken in the land. Thus, too, was the animism of the aboriginal subjected to the Vedantic, Jain and Buddhist religions of the Aryans, and to the Islamic faith of the Arabs, Turks, Mongols, Persians and Afghans. Out of this mixture of blood and speech were born the Punjabi people and their language. There also grew a sense of expectancy that out of the many faiths of their ancestors would be born a new faith for the people of the Punjab.

By the end of the fifteenth century, the different races who had come together in the Punjab had lost the nostalgic memories of the lands of their birth and begun to develop an attachment to the land of their adoption. The chief factor in the growth of Punjabi consciousness was the evolution of one common tongue from a babel of languages. Although the Punjabis were sharply divided into Muslims and Hindus, attempts had been made to bring about a rapprochement between the two faiths and a certain desire to live and let live had grown among the people. It was left to Guru Nanak and his nine successors to harness the spirit of tolerance and give it a positive content in the shape of Punjabi nationalism.

It is significant that the spirit of Punjabi nationalism first manifested itself in Majha, the heart of the Punjab, and among a people who were deeply rooted in the soil. Although the founders and many of the leaders of the movement were not agriculturists, its backbone was the Jat peasantry of the central plains.

There are as many conjectures about the etymology of the word Jat as there are of the origin of the race. It is now generally accepted that the Jats who made the northern plains of India their home were of Aryan stock. They brought with them certain institutions, the most important being the panchayat, an elected body of five elders, to which they pledged their allegiance. Every Jat village was a small republic made up of people of kindred blood who were as conscious of absolute equality between themselves as they were of their superiority over men of other castes who earned their livelihood as weavers, potters, cobblers or scavengers. The relationship of a Jat village with the state was that of a semi-autonomous unit paying a fixed sum of revenue. Few governments tried to assert more authority, and those which did soon discovered that sending out armed militia against fortified villages was not very profitable. The Jat's spirit of freedom and equality refused to submit to Brahmanical Hinduism and in its turn drew the censure of the privileged Brahmins of the Gangetic plains who pronounced that 'no Aryan should stay in the Punjab for even two days' because the Punjabis refused to obey the priests. The upper caste Hindu's denigration of the Jat did not in the least lower the Jat in his own eyes nor elevate the Brahmin or the Kshatriya in the Jat's estimation. On the contrary, he assumed a somewhat condescending attitude towards the Brahmin, whom he considered little better than a soothsayer or a beggar, and the Kshatriya, who disdained earning an honest living and was proud of being a mercenary. The Jat was born the worker and the warrior. He tilled his land with his sword girded round his waist. He fought more battles for the defence of his homestead than the Kshatriya for, unlike the martial Kshatriya, the Jat seldom fled from his village when the invaders came. And if the Jat was maltreated or if his women were molested by the conqueror on his way to Hindustan, he settled his score by looting the invaders' caravans on their return journey and freeing the women he was taking back. The Punjabi Jat developed an attitude of indifference to worldly possessions and an instinct for gambling with his life against the odds. At the same time he became conscious of his role in the defence of Hindustan. His brand of patriotism was at once hostile towards the foreigner and benign, even contemptuous, towards his own countrymen whose fate depended so much on his courage and fortitude.

20

RANJIT SINGH, MAHARAJA OF THE PUNJAB

A calligraphist who had spent many years making a copy of the Quran and had failed to get any of the Muslim princes of Hindustan to give him an adequate price for his labours turned up at Lahore to try and sell it to the foreign minister, Fakeer Azizuddin. The Fakeer praised the work but expressed his inability to pay for it. The discussion was overheard by Ranjit Singh, who summoned the calligraphist to his presence. The Maharaja respectfully pressed the holy book against his forehead and then scrutinized the writing with his single eye. He was impressed with the excellence of the work and bought the Quran for his private collection. Sometime later Fakeer Azizuddin asked him why he had paid such a high price for a book for which he, as a Sikh, would have no use. Ranjit Singh replied: 'God intended me to look upon all religions with one eye; that is why he took away the light from the other.'

The story is apocryphal. But it continues to be told by Punjabis to this day because it has the answer to the question why Ranjit Singh was able to unite Punjabi Mussalmans, Hindus and Sikhs and create the one and only independent kingdom in the history of the Punjab. Another anecdote, equally apocryphal and even more popular, illustrates the second reason why Ranjit Singh succeeded in the face of heavy odds: his single-minded pursuit of power. It is said that once his Muslim wife, Mohran, remarked on his ugliness—he was dark, pitted with smallpox and blind of one eye ('exactly like an old mouse with grey whiskers and one eye'—Emily Eden)—'Where was your Highness when God was distributing beauty?'

'I had gone to find myself a kingdom,' replied the monarch.

Ranjit Singh has been poorly served by his biographers. Hindu and Sikh admirers deified him as a virtuous man and a selfless patriot. This academic apotheosis reduced a full-blooded man and an astute politician to an anaemic saint and a simple-minded nationalist. Muslim historians were unduly harsh in describing him as an avaricious freebooter. English writers, who took their material largely from Muslim sources, portrayed him as a cunning man (the cliché often used is 'wily Oriental') devoid of moral considerations, whose only redeeming feature was his friendship with the English. They were not only not averse to picking up any gossip they could (every Oriental court has always been a whispering gallery of rumours) but also gave them currency by incorporating them in works of history. In recent years monographs on different aspects of Ranjit Singh's government have been produced under the auspices of departments of history in some Indian universities. These are mostly catalogues of known facts put in chronological order without any attempt to explain them in terms of historical movements. This method of treatment makes the meteoric collapse of his kingdom appear as a freak of history instead of as the culmination of an important historical movement. Just as a tide seems deceptively still to those who watch it from the shore, so did the swift undercurrent of Punjabi nationalism pass unnoticed by people who did not fathom the depths beneath the swell on which the Sikhs led by Ranjit Singh rode to power. In the same way, the fall of the Sikh kingdom was not simply due to misfortune in the field of battle but, as a wave spends itself on the sands when its driving force is gone, it was the petering out of a movement whose life force was spent and which had lost its leader.

Ranjit Singh was neither a selfless patriot nor an avaricious freebooter. He was neither a model of virtue nor a lascivious sensualist. Above all, he was too warm and lively a character to have his life story told in a lifeless catalogue of facts, figures and footnotes. As a political figure Ranjit Singh was in every way as remarkable a man as his two famous contemporaries, Napoleon Bonaparte of France and Mohammed Ali of Egypt. He rose from the status of petty chieftain to become the most powerful Indian ruler of his time. He was the first Indian in a thousand years to stem the tides of invasions from whence they had come across the northwest frontiers of Hindustan. Although he dispossessed hundreds of feudal landholders to consolidate his kingdom, he succeeded in winning their affections and converting them into faithful courtiers. In the history of the world, it would be hard to find another despot who never took life in cold blood yet built as large an empire as Ranjit's. He persuaded the turbulent Sikhs and Mussalmans of the Punjab to become the willing instruments of an expansionist policy that brought the Kashmiris and the Pathans of the Northwest Frontier under his subjection and extended his sphere of influence from the borders of China and Afghanistan in the north to the deserts of Sindh in the south. His success was undoubtedly due to his ability to arouse the nascent sense of nationalism amongst his people and make them conscious that more important than being Muslim, Hindu or Sikh was the fact of being Punjabi. His Sikh and Hindu troops subdued the Sikh and Hindu rajas of the Punjab. His Mussalman najibs rejected the appeals of their Hindustani, Afghan and Pathan co-religionists to crusade against the 'infidel' and instead helped to liquidate the crusaders. The year Ranjit Singh died, it was his Muslim troops led by Colonel Sheikh Basawan that forced the Khyber Pass and carried Ranjit's colours through the streets of Kabul in the victory parade.

And a couple of years later Zorawar Singh, a Dogra Hindu, planted the Sikh flag in the heart of Tibet. These events were the high watermark of Punjabi imperialism which had carried Ranjit Singh to the heights of power and which subsided soon after his death.

21

THE SIKHS

On 13 April 1999, the Khalsa will be 300 years old and Sikhism, from which it emerged, will be over 500 years old. Sikhism was, and is, a pacifist creed started by Guru Nanak (1469-1539) and developed by four succeeding Gurus whose writings were compiled in an anthology, the Adi Granth, by the fifth Guru, Arjun, around AD 1600. The Adi Granth comprises over 6,000 hymns composed by five Gurus (mainly those of the compiler Guru Arjun) and includes compositions of Hindu and Muslim saints as well as some bards.

In the final version, the one compiled by Guru Gobind Singh, he inserted hymns composed by his father Guru Tegh Bahadur. Guru Gobind compiled an anthology of his own, the Dasam Granth. While the Adi (first) Granth is essentially a distillation of the Vedanta in Punjabi, the Dasam (tenth) Granth is a compilation of tales of valour of Hindu goddesses, some composed by the Guru himself, others by bards of his court. It is not accorded the same status as the Adi Granth. Thus we have two parallel scriptures, one extolling the virtues of peaceful submission, the other of combating oppression with force. The martyrdom of two Gurus changed the course of Sikh history. Guru Arjun succumbed to torture in Lahore jail in 1606; his son and sixth Guru, Har Gobind, took up arms. Tegh Bahadur was executed in Delhi in 1675; his son Gobind Rai (later Singh) converted a sizeable chunk of hitherto peace-loving Sikhs into the militant fraternity called the Khalsa or the 'pure'.

As a consequence of these historic changes, we have several brands of Sikhs. There are Hindus who believe in Sikhism, visit gurdwaras, have a Granth Sahib in their homes and perform rituals according to Sikh rites. A large section of them are from Sindh, mainly Amils. Then there are Sahaj-dharis (slow adopters) who don't wear the external forms of the Khalsa viz. unshorn hair and beard. The majority of Sikhs are Khalsa who undergo baptism (pahul), take vows to observe the five Ks—kesh, kangha, kachha, karha and kirpan—and add the suffix Singh, and if female, Kaur, to their names.

Those Khalsa who cut off their hair and shave their beards are regarded as patits (renegades) but still see themselves as Sikhs. The matter becomes more complex as, while all the above categories of Sikhs revere only ten Gurus and the Granth Sahib as their living embodiment, there are two sects—Nirankaris and Namdharis—who have living Gurus but nevertheless describe themselves as Sikhs.

Transition from one Sikh sect to the other, indeed from Hinduism to Sikhism, is without many hassles. Inter-marriage is not uncommon. The relationship between Hindus and Sikhs has always been roti-beti ka rishta (breaking bread together and giving daughters in marriage) or nauh-maas da rishta (as fingernail is to the flesh). In this situation, the Khalsa find themselves losing ground, as an increasing number of their youth cut their hair and shave their beards to become no different from Hindus believing in Sikhism, while the number of Hindus accepting baptism to become Khalsas is becoming rarer.

When the Khalsa was in the ascendant politically, their numbers rose steadily. After they lost their kingdom in 1849, their population began to decline. Fortunately for them, the British came to their aid by giving them preferential treatment in services like the army and the police; separate electorates; and reservation of seats in elected bodies like municipalities, legislatures and the central assembly.

With independence, such privileges were abolished and the economic benefits that came with being Khalsa disappeared.

In growing numbers, young Sikhs began to abandon the external symbols of the Khalsa. This was more noticeable among Sikhs settled in foreign countries. Wherever they were in large numbers and formed compact social groups—as in some East African countries and Singapore— social pressures kept the younger generation from reneging on their ancestral faith; where they were scattered in small numbers as in England, Canada and the US, a second generation emigrant conforming to Khalsa traditions became a rarity. The same phenomenon is visible among the educated elite who live in Indian cities and are exposed to Western influences. Young Sikh boys question the necessity of keeping long hair and growing beards to be religious. The only rational answer is that it gives them a sense of belonging to the Khalsa Panth. Many don't find that convincing enough and become like Hindus performing Sikh rituals and prayer. The real danger to the Khalsa has always been, as it is today, the absorptive capacity of Hinduism. An English scholar correctly described it as the boa constrictor of the Indian jungles: it can swallow religions which come in contact with it, with a special taste for its own offspring.

The real challenge facing the Khalsa Panth will be to find ways and means to arrest, possibly reverse, the process of disintegration. Perhaps the most important issue to be considered by scholars of Sikh theology will be to convince people that there is a continuous and unbroken line between the teachings of Guru Nanak and the first five Gurus enshrined in the Adi Granth and the militant tradition begun by the sixth Guru and brought to culmination by the tenth and last Guru, Gobind Singh with the establishment of the Khalsa Panth.

The roots of Sikhism lie deep in the Bhakti form of Hinduism. Guru Nanak picked what he felt were its salient features: belief in one God who is undefinable, unborn, immortal, omniscient, all-pervading and the epitome of Truth; belief in the institution of the Guru as the guide in matters spiritual; unity of mankind without the distinction of caste; rejection of idol worship and meaningless ritual; sanctity of the sangat (congregation), which was expected to break bread together at the Guru ka Langar; the gentle way of sahaj to approach God while fulfilling domestic obligations; hymn singing (kirtan); emphasis on work as a moral obligation. A slogan ascribed to Guru Nanak is 'kirat karo, vand chhako, naam japo' (work, share what you earn, take the name of the Lord). There's little doubt that Nanak felt he had a new message that needed to be conveyed after him as he nominated his closest disciple Angad to be his successor in preference to his two sons. Angad, likewise, nominated his disciple Amar Das to succeed him. Thereafter, guruship remained among members of the same family, the Sodhis.

The compilation of the Adi Granth around AD 1604 was a landmark in the evolution of Sikhism. Though an eclectic work with compositions of Hindu and Muslim saints, it echoes the Vedanta through most of its nearly 6,000 hymns. There is a new breed of Sikh scholars who bend backwards to prove Sikhism has taken little or nothing from Hinduism. All they need to be told is that of the 15,028 names of God that appear in the Adi Granth, Hari occurs over 8,000 times, Ram 2,533 times, followed by Prabhu, Gopal Govind, Parbrahm and other Hindu nomenclature for the Divine. The purely Sikh coinage 'Wahe Guru' appears only sixteen times.

There can be little doubt that the martyrdom of Guru Arjun in 1606 resulted in a radical change in the community's outlook. Though its creed remained wedded to the Adi Granth, it was ready to defend itself by the use of arms. Guru Arjun's son, the sixth Guru, Har Gobind, raised a cavalry of horsemen. He built the Akal Takht facing the Harmandir Sahib (Golden Temple) as the seat of temporal power and came to be designated Miri Piri Da Malik (lord of temporal and spiritual power). For some years he was imprisoned in Gwalior Fort. The final transition came after the execution of the ninth Guru, Tegh Bahadur, in 1675. His son, Guru Gobind, justified the transition in a letter, Zafarnamah, said to have been addressed to Emperor Aurangzeb: 'When all other means have failed it is righteous to draw the sword'. Guru Gobind's concept of God underwent a martial metamorphosis. In his Akal Ustat (Praise of the Timeless God) he wrote:

Eternal God, thou art our shield,
The dagger, knife, the sword we wield.
To us Protector there is given
The timeless, deathless Lord of Heaven;
To us All-steel's unvanquished might,
To us All-time's resistless flight;
But chiefly Thou, Protector brave
All-steel, wilt Thine own servant save
(Translated by M. A. Macauliffe)

In his ode to Goddess Chandi, Guru Gobind asked Lord Shiva to grant him the most fitting end to a warrior's life:

O Lord, these boons of Thee I ask,
Let me never shun a righteous task,
Let me be fearless when I go to battle,
Give me faith that victory will be mine,
Give me power to sing Thy praise,
And when comes the time to end my life,
Let me fall in mighty strife.

Though not very successful in the campaigns he fought, he fired his followers with martial fervour. 'I will teach the sparrow to hunt the hawk, one man to fight 1,25,000 (sava lakh).' He made the downtrodden feel they were God's chosen people—Wahe Guru ji da khalsa—and would be ever victorious—Wahe Guru ji di fateh.

The Guru succeeded in creating a new breed of intrepid warriors imbued with a do-or-die spirit. Within a few years of his death, disciple Banda Bairagi overran the region around Sirhind and laid to waste large domains of the Mughal kingdom. Even after the capture and execution of hundreds of Banda's followers, bands of Sikh horsemen harried Nadir Shah's forces and forced his successor Ahmed Shah Abdali, who blew up the Harmandir Sahib twice, to retreat. When Sikhs became rulers of the Punjab, Maharaja Ranjit Singh realized the value of having troops of Nihangs whom he threw into battles against Ghazis waging jihad against him. The determination never to give in came to be deeply rooted in the Sikh psyche; even in adversity they were exhorted to remain in buoyant spirits—charhdi kala. With it came the conviction that destiny was in their hands. At the end of each congregational prayer, comes the chant 'Raj Karega Khalsa' (the Khalsa will rule). No one will be able to resist them. Those who confront them will be routed. Those who seek their protection will be saved.

The Green Revolution in the production of wheat and rice was largely the achievement of Sikh farmers. Its epicentre was the Punjab Agricultural University at Ludhiana set up in 1962. Within a few years the production of crops per acre was doubled, then trebled. Simultaneous with the Green Revolution came the opening up of the Middle East and the Western countries to emigrants. Since the turn of the century, small Sikh communities had existed in Canada, the US, England, Australia and countries on the East African coast. Taking advantage of their status as citizens of the Commonwealth, thousands of Sikhs who emigrated to the UK, Canada and Australia acquired British citizenship. Others, who could, went to the United States. Many found employment in the Arab countries of the Gulf and the Middle East. The remittances they sent home helped their families wipe out old debts, buy more land and build new houses. The well-to-do Sikh farmer never had it as good as he did in the 1960s and 1970s.

The halcyon years of the Green Revolution and foreign remittances did not last long. After the orgy of prosperity came the hangover of overindulgence. Young Sikhs coming out of school and colleges found there was not enough for them to do on the land; they couldn't go abroad because of restrictions put on emigrants by foreign countries and there was hardly any industry in Punjab that could absorb them. As the number of landless increased, so did the numbers of uneducated unemployed. They were willing to lend their ears to Marxists as well as to preachers of religious fundamentalism. The latter proved to be more persuasive.

Sikh religious revival coincided with the Green Revolution. The man who started it was Giani Zail Singh. His motives were entirely political, viz., to get the better of the Akalis who had monopolized the propagation of Sikhism. Zail Singh, chief minister for five years (1972-1977), utilized every opportunity to give a Sikh orientation to government: official functions began with an ardas; kirtan darbars were organized on a provincial scale; the new university set up in Amritsar was named after Guru Nanak; a new township was named after one of Guru Gobind's sons. The most ludicrous was his discovery of horses said to be descendants of the stallion ridden by Guru Gobind. They were led down a 400-kilometre road, renamed Guru Gobind Singh Marg, running from Anandpur to Patiala—villagers reverentially collected their droppings to take home. It was Zail Singh more than anyone else who supported the rustic preacher Jarnail Singh Bhindranwale, who had earned a name for himself for bringing back into the Khalsa fold thousands of young Sikhs who had strayed from the path of orthodoxy. He exhorted Sikhs to become shastradhari (bearers of arms), added firearms (revolvers and rifles) to the kirpan and replaced horses with motorcycles. He was no orator but his uncouth village vocabulary was full of disparaging references to Hindus as 'dhotian vale, topian vale'; he referred to Mrs Gandhi as 'Panditan di dhee'—daughter of a Brahmin. He acquired the charisma of an acerbic-tongued saint-warrior. Special targets of his ire were Sant Nirankaris who recognized a living guru, an anathema to orthodox Sikhs. Bhindranwale's followers (he himself was not among them) clashed with the Nirankaris on 13 April 1978, Baisakhi day—seventeen lost their lives. Two years later (24 April 1980) Baba Gurbachan Singh, head of the Nirankari sect, and his bodyguard were gunned down in Delhi. Bhai Ranjit Singh was convicted of the crime and sentenced to fourteen years imprisonment. While in jail, he was nominated jathedar of the Akal Takht by Gurcharan Singh Tohra, president of the Shiromani Gurdwara Parbandhak Committee.

Bhindranwale's followers spread terror in the state by killing eminent Hindus like Lala Jagat Narain, founder-owner of the Hind Samachar group of newspapers (his son Ramesh Chandra too was killed later). Thereafter, hardly a day went by when gangs owing allegiance to Bhindranwale did not kill between ten to twenty Hindus and Sikhs opposed to his ideology. When Bhindranwale was arrested from his Chowk Mehta residence, it was at a date and time of his own choosing (Zail Singh was then union home minister and enjoyed the support of Mrs Gandhi's son, Sanjay). When he was released, he felt he would be safer in the Golden Temple complex than in Chowk Mehta. He took up residence in the Akal Takht and began to fortify it.

Killings, bank robberies, extortions, hijacking of planes continued apace. Bhindranwale discovered the easiest way of preventing the absorption of the Khalsa into Hinduism was to create a gulf between Sikhs and Hindus. For a while he succeeded in splitting the two communities: Punjabi Hindus who were alienated from their Sikh brethren answered abuse with abuse and the desecration of Hindu temples with the desecration of gurdwaras. Attempts to resolve disputes with the government failed and Mrs Gandhi decided to settle Bhindranwale's hash once and for all. She persuaded Zail Singh, now President of the Republic, to put Punjab under military rule. Then without informing him, she ordered the army to storm the Golden Temple. She chose to do so on 5 June 1984, the anniversary of the martyrdom of the founder of the temple, Guru Arjun, when thousands of pilgrims were present. In the action that took place over two nights and days, there were heavy casualties on both sides; hundreds of innocent worshippers were killed in the crossfire, the Akal Takht was wrecked, the entrance to the central shrine damaged and the shrine itself pocked with bullet marks. Amongst the dead was Bhindranwale. Operation Blue Star, as it was called, shocked the entire community, including a substantial number of those who strongly disapproved of Bhindranwale. Army operations to wipe out Bhindranwale's supporters in the state, though ruthless, did not produce results. The Khalsa does not have a spirit of forgiveness. On 31 October 1984, two of Mrs Gandhi's Sikh bodyguards killed her in her garden. The ruling coterie decided 'to teach the Sikhs a lesson'. In many towns and cities of northern India, scores of gurdwaras and Sikh properties were destroyed and thousands of Sikhs burnt alive by frenzied mobs instigated by members of the Congress. The police looked on as bemused spectators. Far from being suppressed, Sikh terrorism picked up and over a dozen gangs—some trained and armed by Pakistan—spread terror in the state. It took the government over a year to realize that strong-arm tactics wouldn't work with the Sikhs. Dialogue was reopened with Akali leaders. By then Punjabis had had their fill of violence by the terrorists and the Punjab police and were longing for peace. On 23 July 1985, a comprehensive pact covering all points of dispute was signed by Sant Longowal, representing the Akalis, with Prime Minister Rajiv Gandhi. After ten years of violence, in which over 10,000 lives were lost, peace was finally restored to the state. The elections that followed gave the Akalis a decisive victory.

22

A RIOT OF PASSAGE

There are two anniversaries so deeply etched in my mind that every year they come around I recollect with pain what happened on those two days. One is 31 October, when Mrs Gandhi was gunned down by her two Sikh security guards. The other is the following day, when the 'aftermath' consummated itself: frenzied Hindu mobs, driven by hate and revenge, killed nearly 10,000 innocent Sikhs across north India down to Karnataka. Four years later, Mrs Gandhi's assassins, Satwant Singh and Kehar Singh, paid the penalty for their crime by being hanged to death in Tihar jail. The killers of 10,000 Sikhs remain unpunished. The conclusion is clear: in secular India there is one law for the Hindu majority, another for Muslims, Christians and Sikhs who are in the minority.

31 October 1984: The sequence of events remains as vivid as ever. Around 11 a.m. I heard of Mrs Gandhi being shot in her house and taken to hospital. By the afternoon, I heard on the BBC that she was dead. For a couple of hours, life in Delhi came to a standstill. Then all hell broke loose—mobs yelling 'khoon ka badla khoon se lenge' (we'll avenge blood with blood) roamed the streets. Ordinary Sikhs going about their lives were waylaid and roughed up. In the evening, I saw a cloud of black smoke billowing up from Connaught Circus: Sikh-owned shops had been set on fire. An hour later, mobs were smashing up taxis owned by Sikhs right opposite my apartment. Sikh-owned shops in Khan Market were being looted. Over hundred policemen armed with lathis lined the middle of the road and did nothing. At midnight, truckloads of men armed with cans of petrol attacked the gurdwara behind my back garden, beat up the granthi and set fire to the shrine. I was bewildered and did not know what to do. Early next morning, I rang up President Zail Singh. He would not come to the phone. His secretary told me that the president advised me to move into the home of a Hindu friend till the trouble was over. The newly-appointed prime minister, Rajiv Gandhi, was busy receiving guests arriving for his mother's funeral; Home Minister Narasimha Rao did not budge from his office; the Lieutenant Governor of Delhi had no orders to put down the rioters. Seventy-two gurdwaras were torched and thousands of Sikh houses looted. The next few days, TV and radio sets were available for less than half their price.

Mid-morning, a Swedish diplomat came and took me and my wife to his home in the diplomatic enclave. My aged mother had been taken by

Romesh Thapar to his home. Our family lawyer, Anant Bir Singh, who lived close to my mother, cut off his long hair and shaved his beard to avoid being recognized as a Sikh. I watched Mrs Gandhi's cremation on TV in the home of my Swedish protector. I felt like a Jew must have in Nazi Germany. I was a refugee in my own homeland because I was a Sikh.

What I found most distressing was the attitude of many of my Hindu friends. Only two couples made a point to call on me after I returned home. They were Sri S. Mulgaonkar and his wife and Arun Shourie and his wife Anita. As for the others, the less said the better. Girilal Jain, editor of *The Times of India*, rationalized the violence: the Hindu cup of patience, he wrote, had become full to the brim. N. C. Menon, who succeeded me as editor of the *Hindustan Times*, wrote of how Sikhs had 'clawed their way to prosperity' and well-nigh had it coming to them. Some spread gossip of how Sikhs had poisoned Delhi's drinking water, how they had attacked trains and slaughtered Hindu passengers. At the Gymkhana Club, where I played tennis every morning, one man said I had no right to complain after what Sikhs had done to Hindus in Punjab. At a party, another gloated, 'Khoob mazaa chakhaya' (We gave them a taste of their own medicine). Word had gone round: 'Teach the Sikhs a lesson'.

Did the Sikhs deserve to be taught a lesson? I pondered over the matter for many days and many hours and reluctantly admitted that Hindus had some justification for their anger against Sikhs. The starting point was the emergence of Jarnail Singh Bhindranwale as a leader. He used vituperative language against the Hindus. He exhorted every Sikh to kill thirty-two Hindus to solve the Hindu-Sikh problem. Anyone who opposed him was put on his hit list and some eliminated. More depressing to me was that no one spoke out openly against him. He had a wily patron in Giani Zail Singh who had him released when he was charged as an accomplice in the murder of Jagat Narain. Akali leaders supported him. Some like Badal and Barnala, who used to tie their beards to their chins, let them down in deference to his wishes. So did many Sikh civil servants. They lauded him as the saviour of the Khalsa Panth and called him Sant. I am proud to say I was the only one who wrote against him and attacked him as a hate-monger. I was on his hit list and continued to be on that of his followers—for fifteen long years—and was given police protection, which I never asked for.

Bhindranwale, with the tacit connivance of Akali leaders like Gurcharan Singh Tohra, turned the Golden Temple into an armed fortress of Sikh defiance. He provided the Indian government the excuse to send the army into the temple complex. I warned the government, in Parliament and through my articles, against using the army to get hold of Bhindranwale and his followers as the consequences would be grave. And so they were. Operation Blue Star was a blunder of Himalayan proportions. Bhindranwale was killed but hailed as a martyr. Over 5,000 men and women lost their lives in the exchange of fire. The Akal Takht was wrecked.

Symbolic protests did not take long coming. I was part of it; I surrendered the Padma Bhushan awarded to me. Among the people who condemned my action was Vinod Mehta, then editor of *The Observer*. He wrote that when it came to choosing between being an Indian or a Sikh, I had chosen to be a Sikh. I stopped contributing to his paper. I had never believed that I had to be one or the other. I was both an Indian and a Sikh and proud of being so. I might well have asked Mehta in return, 'Are you a Hindu or an Indian?' Hindus do not have to prove their nationality; only Muslims, Christians and Sikhs are required to give evidence of their patriotism.

Anti-Sikh violence gave a boost to the demand for a separate Sikh state and Khalistan-inspired terrorism in Punjab and abroad. Amongst the worst was the blowing up of Air India's *Kanishka* (23 June 1985); all its 329 passengers and crew, including over thirty Sikhs, lost their lives. Sant Harchand Singh Longowal, who signed the Rajiv-Longowal accord (24 July 1985), was murdered while praying in a gurdwara just three weeks later. General A. S. Vaidya, who was chief of staff when Operation Blue Star took place, was gunned down in Pune in August 1986. The killings went on unabated for almost ten years during which over 25,000 were killed. Terrorists ran a parallel government in districts adjoining Pakistan, which also provided them arms training and escape routes.

The Golden Temple had again become a sanctuary for criminals. This time, the Punjab police, led by K. P. S. Gill, was able to get the better of the terrorists, with the loss of only two lives, in what came to be known as Operation Black Thunder (13-18 May 1988). The terrorist movement petered out as the terrorists turned gangsters and took to extortion and robbery. The peasantry turned its back on them. About the last action of Khalistani terrorists was the murder of Chief Minister Beant Singh, who was blown up along with twelve others by a suicide bomber on 31 August 1995, at Chandigarh.

It is not surprising that with this legacy of ill-will and bloodshed a sense of alienation grew among the Sikhs. It was reinforced by the reluctance of successive governments at the Centre to bring the perpetrators of the anti-Sikh pogrom of 31 October and 1 November 1984 to justice. A growing number of non-Sikhs have also come to the conclusion that grave injustice has been done to the Sikhs. Several non-official commissions of inquiry—including one headed by retired Supreme Court Chief Justice S. M. Sikri, comprising retired ambassadors and senior civil servants—have categorically named the guilty. However, all that the government has done is to appoint one commission of inquiry after another to look into charges of minor relevance to the issue without taking any action.

I have to concede that the attitude of the BJP government led by Atal Behari Vajpayee and L. K. Advani towards the Sikhs has been more positive than that of the Congress, many of whose leaders were involved in the 1984 anti-Sikh violence. Some of it may be due to its alliance with the principal Sikh political party, the Akalis, led by Parkash Singh Badal. It also gives them a valid excuse to criticize the Congress leadership. Nevertheless, I welcomed the Congress party's return to power in the Centre because it also promises a fairer deal to other minorities like the Muslims and Christians. And I make no secret of my rejoicing over the choice of Manmohan Singh, the first Sikh to become prime minister of India and he in his turn selecting another Sikh, Montek Singh Ahluwalia, to head the Planning Commission.

The dark months of alienation are over; the new dawn promises blue skies and sunshine for the minorities with only one black cloud remaining to be blown away—a fair deal to families of victims of the anti-Sikh violence of 1984. It was the most horrendous crime committed on a mass scale since we became an independent nation. Its perpetrators must be punished because unpunished crimes generate more criminals.

23

BARA MAH

Composing verses on the twelve months of the year was once common amongst Indian poets. It gave them the opportunity to describe nature and human moods, and moralize at the same time. Several exist in the Punjabi language, of which Guru Nanak's is the most highly rated. It is believed to be amongst the last of the Guru's compositions.

CHET (MARCH-APRIL)
Chet basant bhala bhavar suhavde

> *It is the month of Chet*
> *It is spring. All is seemly,*
> *The beauteous bumble-bees*
> *The woodlands in flower;*
> *But there is a sorrow in my soul*
> *For away is the Lord my Master*

> *If the husband comes not home, how can a wife*
> *Find peace of mind?*
> *Sorrows of separation waste away her body.*

> *The koel calls in the mango grove,*
> *Her notes are full of joy*
> *But there is sorrow in my soul.*

> *The bumble-bee hovers about the blossoming bough*
> *(A messenger of life and hope)*
> *But O Mother of mine, 'tis like death to me*
> *For there is sorrow in my soul.*
> *How shall I banish sorrow and find blessed peace?*
> *Sayeth Nanak: When the Lord her Master comes home to her*
> *Then is spring seemly because she is fulfilled.*

VAISAKH (APRIL-MAY)
Vaisakh bhala sakha ves kare

> *Beauteous Vaisakh, when the bough adorns itself anew*

89

The wife awaits the coming of her Lord
Her eyes fixed on the door.
'My love, who alone can help me cross
The turbulent waters of life,
Have compassion for me and come home,
Without thee I am as worthless as a shell.
Love, look thou upon me with favour
And let our eyes mingle
Then I will become priceless beyond compare.'

Nanak asks: 'Whither seekest thou the Lord?
Whom awaitest thou?
Thou hast not far to go, for the Lord
Is within thee, thou art His mansion.
If thy body and soul yearn for the Lord,
The Lord shall love thee
And Vaisakh will beautiful be.'

JETH (MAY-JUNE)
Mah jeth bhala pritam kyon bisrai

Why forget the beloved Lord in the good month of Jeth?
The earth shimmers in the summer's heat
The wife makes obeisance and prays
Let me find favour in Thine eyes O Lord,
Thou art great and good
Truth manifest and unshakable,
Of attachments art Thou free.
And I, lowly, humble, helpless.
How shall I approach Thee?
How find the haven of peace?

In the month of Jeth, says Nanak,
She who knoweth the Lord
Becometh like the Lord
She knoweth Him
By treading the path of virtue.

ASADH (JUNE-JULY)
Asadh bhala suraj gagan tapai

In Asadh the sun scorches.
Skies are hot
The earth burns like an oven
Waters give up their vapours.
It burns and scorches relentlessly
Thus the land fails not
To fulfil its destiny.

The sun's chariot passes the mountain tops;
Long shadows stretch across the land
And the cicada calls from the glades.
The beloved seeks the cool of the evening.
If the comfort she seeks be in falsehood,
There will be sorrow in store for her.
If it be in truth,
Hers will be a life of joy everlasting.

My life and its ending depend on the will of the Lord.
To Him says Nanak, I surrendered my soul.

SAVAN (JULY-AUGUST)
Savan saras mana ghan varsai rut ae

O my heart, rejoice! It's Savan
The season of nimbus clouds and rain,
My body and soul yearn for my Lord.
But my Lord is gone to foreign lands.
If He return not, I shall die pining for Him.

The lightning strikes terror in my heart.
I stand all alone in my courtyard,
In solitude and in sorrow.
O Mother of mine, I stand on the brink of death.
Without the Lord I have neither hunger nor sleep
I cannot suffer the clothes on my body.

Nanak says, she alone is the true wife
Who loses herself in the Lord.

BHADON (AUGUST-SEPTEMBER)
Bhadon bharam bhuli bhar joban pachtani

> In the month of Bhadon
> I lose myself in a maze of falsehood
> I waste my wanton youth.
> River and land are one endless expanse of water
> For it is the monsoon, the season of merry-making.
> It rains,
> The nights are dark,
> What comfort is it to the wife left alone?
> Frogs croak
> Peacocks scream
> The papeeha calls 'peeoh, peeoh'.
> The fangs of serpents that crawl,
> The stings of mosquitoes that fly
> Are full of venom.
> The seas have burst their bounds in the ecstasy
> Of fulfilment.
> Without the Lord I alone am bereft of joy,
> Whither shall I go?
>
> Says Nanak, ask the guru the way
> He knoweth the path which leads to the Lord.

ASAN (SEPTEMBER-OCTOBER)
Asan au pira sa dhan jhur mui

> It's the month of Asan
> O Master come to me
> I waste and I shall die. If the Master wills,
> I shall meet Him.
> If He wills not,
> In a deep well shall I be lost.
>
> I strayed on to the paths of falsehood
> And the Master forsook me.
> Age hath greyed my locks
> I have left many winters behind.
> But the fires of hell still lie ahead.
> Whither shall I turn?

99: Khushwant Singh

The bough remaineth ever green
For the sap that moveth within day and night,
Night and day, reneweth life.
If the name of the Lord courseth in thy veins,
Life and hope will forever be green.
That which cooketh slowly cooketh best.

It is Asan, says Nanak,
It is trysting time, O Lord,
And we have waited long.

KATAK (OCTOBER-NOVEMBER)
Katak kirat paiya jo prabh bhaia

In the month Katak
Will I get my due.
What pleases the Lord
Is all I merit.
The lamp of wisdom burneth steadily
If the oil that feeds it
Be reality.
If the oil that feeds the lamp
Be love,
The beloved will meet the Lord and be fulfilled.

Full of faults, she dies not
Nor gains release
It's death after virtuous life.
That doth the Lord please.

Those who are granted the worship of Thy name
Merge in Thee, for Thou art then
Their aim and end in life.

Nanak says: Lord, till Thou grant vision
And burst the bonds of superstition,
One watch of day will drag on like half a year.

MAGHAR (NOVEMBER-DECEMBER)
Maghar mah bhala hari gun ank samave

The month of Maghar is bliss

For her who is lost in the Lord.
She singeth songs of joy and fulfilment.
Why not love the Lord who is eternal?

He who is eternal, wise, omniscient is also the master of destiny.
The world is agitated because it hath lost faith in Him.
She that hath knowledge and contemplates
Loses herself in Him.
She loveth the Lord, the Lord loveth her.

In song and dance and verse, let it be the name of Lord Rama
And sorrows will fly away.
Nanak says, only she is loved by her Lord
Who prayeth, not only with her lips
But worships Him with her soul.

POKH (DECEMBER-JANUARY)
Pokh tukhar pade van trin ras sokhai

As in the month of Pokh
Winter's frost doth freeze
The sap in tree and bush, so does
The absence of the Lord
Kill the body and the mind.
O Lord, why earnest not Thou?

I praise though the guru's Word
Him that gives life to all the world,
His light shines in all life born
Of egg or womb or sweat or seed.
Merciful God and master! Thy vision grant
And grant me salvation.

Nanak says, only she mingles with Him
Who loves the Lord, the giver of life.

MAGH (JANUARY-FEBRUARY)
Magh punit bhai tirath antar jania

In the month of Magh
I made my ablution,

The Lord entered my being.
I made pilgrimage within myself and was purified.
I met Him.
He found me good
And let me lose myself in Him.

'Beloved! If Thou findest me fair
My pilgrimage is made,
My ablution done.
More than the sacred waters
Of Ganga, Yamuna and Triveni mingled at the Sangam,
More than the seven seas.
All these and charity, alms-giving and prayer,
Are the knowledge of eternity that is the Lord.'
Nanak says, Magh is the essence of ambrosia
For him who hath worshipped the great giver of life.
Hath done more than bathe in the sixty and eight places of pilgrimage.

PHALGUN (FEBRUARY-MARCH)
Phalgun man rahsi prem subhaya ea

In the month of Phalgun
She whose heart is full of love
Is ever in full bloom.
Day and night she is in spiritual exaltation
She is in bliss because she hath no love of self.

Only those that love Thee
Conquer love of self.
Be kind to me
And make my home Thy abode.
Many a lovely garment did I wear.
The Master willed not and
His palace doors were barred to me.
When He wanted me I went
With garlands and strings of jewels and raiments of finery.

O Nanak, a bride welcomed in the Master's mansion
Hath found her true Lord and Love.

THE USES & ABUSES OF RELIGION

ON RELIGION

GURUS AND GODMEN

THE BOY GOD

CARNAGE IN GUJARAT

A FUNDAMENTAL PROBLEM

24

ON RELIGION

I have lived a reasonably contented life, and it will be easy to go. Sometimes, however, I wish I knew where to. I am not a man of faith. Since I do not believe in paradise or the possibility of rebirth, I have no idea where I will be after I die. It is like staring into an endless dark void. Paul Valery put it very well: 'Death speaks to us in a very deep voice but has nothing to say.'

For many years I dreaded death. To cure myself of the phobia, I would go to the cremation ground at Delhi's Nigambodh Ghat and watch corpses burn to ashes and bone. It was cathartic. It cleansed me of petty vanities and anxieties and I returned home at peace with myself. But it did not help me overcome my fear. Now I am no longer afraid of dying—in fact, the end will be welcome, as long as it is swift and painless. I have made my peace with the great void. But I still don't know where I will be after I breathe my last.

People who have religion seem to derive comfort from the belief that they will meet their Maker after they die, or that they will be reborn in some form. The more self-righteous among them are convinced that they will ascend straight to heaven. As an agnostic, I have no such comfort. So be it. I have no regrets.

As a child I liked the rituals of my faith. I was a good boy, my grandmother's favourite, because I could recite my morning and evening prayers by rote and sing a shabad or two in the village gurdwara. I barely understood the words, but that did not seem to matter because few of my elders understood or made any attempt to understand what they recited every day. By the time I was fifteen or sixteen, I had begun to question ritual and religious dogma. At Delhi's newly opened Modern School, I was learning how science, technology and the liberal arts were transforming the Western world. There was nothing scientific or liberal about religion as I saw it practised around me. But I did not want to invite trouble at home and kept my doubts to myself. At the age of seventeen, I underwent the ceremony of sipping amrit (holy water) and became a member of the Khalsa Panth, the fraternity of the pure.

In college, my conviction that religion was irrational and encouraged superstition and ignorance grew stronger. I also saw how it generated more prejudice and hatred than love and friendship. In Sikhism, for instance, the abhorrent practice of untouchability is forbidden, but I saw almost all my elders discriminate against converts from the 'low' castes. I also found it ironic that the followers of Guru Nanak, the founder of the Sikh faith who proclaimed God to be nirankaar (formless) and forbade the worship of idols, treated the Guru Granth Sahib, the compilation of Nanak's and other Gurus' writings, as an idol worthy of worship. They draped it in silk and brocade, roused it in the morning (prakash) and put it to rest in the evenings (santokh). It wasn't among the Sikhs alone that I noticed rituals which made a travesty of their faith—Hindus, Muslims and Christians were all alike in this. I gradually gave up on organized religion. Yet, I continued to retain the outward emblems of the Khalsa because it gave me a sense of belonging and social security, as it does to this day.

It also took me some time to free myself of the habit of prayer. I gave it up off and on, but returned to it when in physical pain or fear or under emotional stress. When my relations with my wife once came to breaking point and she told me that she meant to leave me, I spent the whole night at Gurdwara Bangla Sahib, praying for strength to face the crisis. Many a time in Tokyo, when I got up at three in the morning to work on the translations of the hymns of Guru Nanak, I felt the hand of the Guru on my shoulder. Though I knew it was make-believe, I found it very comforting.

Eventually, I lost the habit of prayer as well. However, my interest in the Sikh faith and scriptures remained. I also became interested in the sacred texts of other major religions: Christianity, Hinduism, Islam, Judaism, Jainism, Buddhism, Zoroastrianism and the Baha'i faith. I studied the world's religions and met gurus, babas and matas with the curiosity of a dispassionate observer. I even taught comparative religion for a period in the 1960s, at the universities of Princeton and Hawaii. I did this as a complete agnostic, because by my thirties I had stopped believing that there was a God. Nothing since has convinced me otherwise.

The most endearing attempt to make a believer of me was made by a little girl some twenty-five years ago. I had written an article in *The Indian Express* spelling out my views on God and religion. Soon after, I received a letter from Supriya, the twelve-year-old daughter of the then editor of the paper, Rajmohan Gandhi. 'Dear Uncle,' she wrote, 'I read your article in Daddy's paper. So you don't believe in God? You are wrong! Let me tell you, God exists. He visits our garden every day. He talks to my Mummy and my Daddy. He also talks to me and my little brother. So there!' I was charmed and wrote back: 'Dear Supriya, I am glad to hear that God visits your garden every day. And that He talks to your Mummy, Daddy, you and your brother. But He does not talk to me. Please send me His telephone number.' Supriya did not reply. Three years later I met her parents in Delhi. They told me ruefully, 'Supriya no longer believes in God.' I was delighted that I had won a convert in the great-grandchild of two great believers in God—Mahatma Gandhi and C. Rajagopalachari.

Many people have argued with me about the existence of God, trying to prove me wrong. I have always responded with simple logic: there is not a shred of credible evidence to support what they say. Despite the occasional claims by mystics, the truth is that no one has seen God. No one has been able to define God besides investing him with innumerable fantastic attributes: He is the creator, preserver and destroyer; benevolent and helpful; wrathful as well as just. He is everything and he is also, as the Upanishads say, neti, neti—not this, not this. The truth is that no one has a clue. It is more honest to admit that we don't know rather than accept fairy tales about God having created the world in six days or in the blink of an eye.

The Voltairian argument that if there is a watch there must then be a watchmaker has never made sense to me. I have met a few watchmakers, I have never met God. If God created the universe, who created God? If an all-powerful, all-seeing God does exist, why is there injustice and suffering in the world? Even those who believe in God have little justification for describing Him as omnipotent and just. Whatever evidence we have is to the contrary. Some children are born with severe physical and mental disabilities; God-fearing parents who never harmed anyone in their lives are punished by the loss of their innocent children; the gentlest people suffer terribly while thieves and murderers prosper. I cannot accept a God who is selective in granting his grace, or who is blind. And a 'Mighty Avenger' who must be constantly appeased is no God at all.

Even as a concept, God fails. Belief in God has little bearing on making a person good or bad. In our country alone, for every Mother Teresa and Baba Amte, there are thousands who have killed and raped in the name of their gods, as was done during Partition on both sides of the border, in Delhi in 1984 and in Gujarat in 2002. The masterminds of the 1984 and 2002 pogroms are ministers and party leaders. Neither the law nor God has made them pay for their crimes.

Rejecting the idea of God and giving up on the basics of religion was not easy. It required searching within myself and questioning beliefs on which I had been nurtured. And once I had done it, how would I fill the vacuum? How could one explain the universe, life on earth and the laws of nature? Reason and logic helped me demolish much that I had been brought up on, but they did not give me all the answers I was looking for. So began the quest for a personal religion. Iqbal echoed my sentiments:

Dhoondta phirta hoon main, ai Iqbal, apney aap ko
Aap hi goya musaafir, aap hi manzil hoon main.

(O Iqbal, I go about everywhere looking for myself
As if I was the wayfarer as well as the destination.)

Over some years, I came up with a religion of my own. It had very simple rules: ahimsa—non-violence—above all; work as worship; honesty (even about one's dishonesties); helping people in need; silent charity; and respecting and preserving the natural world. I may have failed to live by these rules sometimes, but I have tried to do so to the best of my ability. My role models have never been the pious who contemplate God and the universe in the seclusion of caves or by the banks of holy rivers. Rather, they are people who work among the poor and the handicapped. Mother Teresa, Bhagat Puran Singh, Ela Bhatt and Baba Amte are worth more than a hundred Shankaracharyas, Chinmayanandas and other godmen put together. They are our true saints, not those who merely pray and meditate or give long sermons to the gullible. I do not dismiss prayer altogether—one does not have to believe in God to concede that prayer has power. But all that it does is comfort the person saying the prayer. To change the world, you need to get out of your temples and do some useful work. I am more than ready to respect any baba, sant or maulvi if he joins the man breaking stones to build a road.

All my life I have also believed that since we have only one life to live, it is our duty to live well and be happy. Renunciation does not impress me. It is self-righteous and anti-life—as Rumi said, 'People who renounce desire turn suddenly into hypocrites.' For all its imperfections, life is a great gift, and I have tried to get as much out of it as I could. I have feasted my eyes and senses on all that is beautiful in the world: its mountains and lakes, seashores and deserts; the break of the monsoon and the scent of wet earth; good food from all parts of the world, vintage wines and the finest Scotch whisky; Western classical music and shabad-kirtan; the fragrance of flowers and herbs and the shade of mighty trees; birdsong at the break of dawn; classic literature; and beautiful, spirited women, preferably with the gift of gossip. To quote the English poet and journalist, Arthur St. John Adcock:

Come, let us go a-roaming!
The world is all our own,
And half its paths are still untrod,
And half its joys unknown.

I would sum up my faith in a time-worn cliché: a good life is the only religion. A life of giving happiness and also finding it for oneself.

25

GURUS AND GODMEN

The climate of India has always been one that produces prophets and messiahs. Every age has had its quota of men and women claiming kinship with God; some even claiming to be His human reincarnations. Neither the march of science nor the spread of Marxist atheism has made the slightest impact on the widespread belief in the spiritual powers and missions of these gods in human form.

There are many self-styled bhagwans, swamis, rishis, maharishis, acharyas, sants and gurus with large followings. It is not possible to make an estimate of the numbers of followers because wildly exaggerated claims are made by each one of them. But it can be assumed that most religious Hindus and Sikhs (together making 85 per cent of the population of India) and some Muslims, Christians and Parsis as well, pay homage to some living saint or the other whom they regard as God incarnate.

◆

All over India, one comes across pictures of a wizened old man sitting on a slab of stone with one leg on the other. This is Sai Baba of Shirdi, a latter-day Saint Christopher of India. Miniature shrines with Sai Baba figurines can be seen in niches in the bazaars, hung on tree trunks and draped with fresh marigold garlands. Cab drivers have Sai Baba medallions on their dashboards; lots of people wear them on their necklace.

Eight years after Shirdi Sai Baba died, his spirit entered the body of a young boy, Satyanarayana Raju, of the village of Puttaparthi. He began to perform miracles and was soon acclaimed as the incarnation of the Shirdi Sai Baba.

Sathya Sai Baba has a bigger following than any of the contemporary godmen of India. Wherever he goes, people flock to him in their hundreds of thousands to get his darshan. In the cities, his arrival snarls traffic for many hours. Next to Indira Gandhi, he is the biggest draw.

Sathya Sai Baba sports a shock of curly hair which sits on his head like a black halo. He drapes his body from his shoulders to his feet in a flaming saffron robe. He performs miracles with a wave of his hand: from the air he produces vibhuti, wristwatches (made not in heaven but in Switzerland), rosaries and rings with his pictures.

Sathya Sai Baba has brought solace to many people. The late Dr K. M. Munshi, one-time minister of the central government, described him as a 'God-possessed individual who plants the seed of faith in men—a seed which, when it blossoms, will liberate men from greed, hate and fear.'

Another miracle-man who has a startling resemblance to Sathya Sai Baba, with the same beehive mop of hair and wearing the same body-length saffron robe is the thirty-seven-year-old Bhagwan Sri Neelakantha Tathaji. When I went to pay my respects to him he 'materialized' sacred ash and a brown berry out of the air.

I asked him how he came to acquire these supernatural powers. He did not remember the precise moment when the divine spirit entered his bodily frame but other people noticed strange phenomena about him. When he put his hand on the forehead of a man down with fever, the fever left him. When he touched the gangrenous leg of a man on his way to the hospital to have it amputated, the gangrene disappeared. A devotee sitting beside me whispered in my ear: 'My heart had stopped beating: I was dead. The Baba gave me a second life. Can't you see he is divine? Look, there is a light round his head!' I looked. Did I see a halo round the Baba's head?

The number of saintly men and women are beyond enumeration. Every district has its quota of living saints to whom people turn for advice on spiritual and worldly matters. Men ask them about business affairs, barren women for blessings of motherhood, young men for help in their examinations, sick people for charms against sickness. And everyone will come for their darshan. Of the living saints among the most famous is Anandamayi Ma. Prime Minister Indira Gandhi has visited her on many occasions. The seventy-six-year-old Anandamayi Ma (Mother of Bliss) is a phenomenon. Although she has a number of ashrams (some with schools attached to them) in different parts of India where her devotees live and meditate, the only solace most of them get is from her darshan. She has no message for the world. Anandamayi was born in village Kheora, now in Bangladesh, in 1896. Her real name was Nirmala Sundari Devi. Her parents were Brahmins and, when Nirmala was thirteen, she was given in marriage to a Brahmin boy, Ramani Mohan Chakravarty. It would appear that the marriage was never consummated. Nirmala Devi was a wayward child subject to prolonged periods of depression when she would stop speaking (one period lasted three years.) She wandered about the countryside alone. She had seizures and foamed from the mouth. But she was a beautiful child who grew into a beautiful woman. It was in Dhaka that a clerk working in a government office discovered that Nirmala Devi was in fact a reincarnation of the goddess Kali, consort of Shiva. This clerk was of the same age as Nirmala Devi. In his biography, *Mother As Revealed To Me,* he describes how from the seventeenth year, various supernatural phenomena began to be manifest in her. Her body would go into convulsions, adopting yogic postures, and she would chant the names of gods and goddesses. The clerk was a Matribhakta (worshipper of God in the form of a mother). He proclaimed her to be the universal mother and gave her the name of Anandamayi Ma. Bhaiji (brother) as her clerk-devotee came to be known, served Anandamayi for twelve years till he died of consumption at the age of forty. Arthur Koestler in his *The Lotus and the Robot* described Bhaiji uncharitably as something of a tragic clown.

'Who are you? What are you?' Bhaiji is said to have asked Anandamayi Ma soon after he had attached himself to her. 'What a childish question to ask!' retorted Anandamayi Ma. 'What I was before, I am now, and shall be hereafter. I am, whatever you or anybody may think I am. The yearnings (of the seekers of truth) have brought this body. You have all wanted it and so you have found it. That is all you need to know. So play with this doll for some time. Further questions will be fruitless.'

'These words of yours, Mother, do not satisfy my yearning,' insisted Bhaiji. Hearing this she spoke with slight vehemence, 'Say, say, whatever you desire,' and immediately a dazzling flood of heavenly light shone forth from Her face. Bhaiji records that he was 'struck dumb with awe and wonder... All my doubts were laid at rest.' However, he tried to test her by placing a live ember on her foot. It burnt, developed into a blister and suppurated. When medicines failed, Bhaiji sucked the pus out of her lotus feet with his own mouth.

Anandamayi Ma still refers to herself as 'the doll' or 'the body'. She allows her devotees to bathe and dress her. She does not eat with her own hands; her female devotees take turns to place food in her mouth.

Anandamayi Ma's following also runs into the hundreds of thousands. The majority of them are women. Amongst them there is the usual sprinkling of foreigners.

The Mother is a lady of few words. She smiles silently most of the time; sometimes she giggles like a little girl, plays with her toes and abruptly orders supplicants to go away. Nevertheless the crowds flock to her, sit in rapt silence with their eyes shut, imbibing the aura of sanctity that pervades the place. One of the women closest to her is the daughter of a wealthy Sikh landowner. She left her husband a few days after her marriage without consummating it and has served Anandamayi Ma faithfully for the last thirty years. 'What have you got out of all this?' I asked her. She answered my question in one word, 'Everything.'

26

THE BOY GOD

The Delhi headquarters of the Divine Light Mission is like a fortress: an eight-foot-high wall with an iron-grilled gate encloses a courtyard and a complex of buildings consisting of offices, reception rooms, kitchen, refectory, dormitories, a temple and the residential suite of the Balyogeshwar, the Child God.

'God is great, but greater is guru because He reveals God,' runs the legend on the poster adorning the gatekeeper's shack. I enter my name, address, profession and purpose in the visitor's book. The gatekeeper asks me to wait and takes the book indoors for scrutiny.

A stocky man with a shawl wrapped about his shoulders emerges and introduces himself as the personal private secretary of Shri Guru Maharaj Ji, the title by which devotees refer to Balyogeshwar. He leads me through an office where three American girls in white saris sit on the floor hammering away on their typewriters. The reception room is furnished with sofas and chairs. An armchair with multi-coloured cushions is set apart from the others. There is a projector on one side, a portable screen facing it on the other. In a niche above the sofa on which I am told to sit are two large pictures of the Balyogeshwar. One bears the message, 'Maharaj Ji, Light of Lights'; the other poses the question: 'Do you know the aim of life?'

Balyogeshwar's private secretary goes out and comes back. He tells me that Shri Guru Maharaj Ji is busy. There has been a spot of trouble with the customs. On the guru's return from a world tour last November, accompanied by 400 foreign devotees, a large amount of US currency and goods were seized from the entourage.

While thumbing through the pages of *And It Is Divine*, I ask the private secretary how he came to join the mission and what it has meant to him.

'I belonged to a family of Brahmin priests attached to the court of the maharajas of Kashmir. Although I was brought up in a religious atmosphere, I did not find any satisfaction in temple rituals and chanting of mantras. I was looking for a guru who could give me real knowledge. Someone gave me the address of an ashram in Hardwar. Although I was only sixteen when I arrived there, I knew I had found the one I had been seeking. This was our present Maharaj Ji's father. I attached myself to His lotus feet and served him till the day he left his body on 19 July

1966. Now I serve the new Guru Maharaj Ji. I have dedicated my life to the mission.'

At thirty-two, Sampurnanand is the senior-most in the hierarchy of the Divine Light Mission. Apart from being personal secretary to the Balyogeshwar, he is a Mahatma in his own right. Though celibacy is not compulsory, Mahatma Sampurnanand, and almost a thousand others who have likewise dedicated their lives to the spread of Divine Light, keep themselves free of family entanglements.

'What is your estimate of the following of your mission?' I ask.

'In the world? About four million spread over sixty-three countries. It is catching on like wildfire.'

'And so it should,' remarks another, taking up the thread. 'I have been with the holy family since I was this much,' he says, lowering the palm of his hand to knee level. 'I was at Prem Nagar Ashram in Hardwar when our Guru Maharaj Ji was born on 10 December 1957. I remember his father saying: "This child will be the world's greatest saint. There has never been one so great as he; there never will be." This is Bihari Singh who has been a chauffeur of the family. It is hard to tell his age as his hair and moustache are dyed jet black and his eyes sparkle with enthusiasm. More people slip in and sit quietly on the floor. Amongst them are some white foreigners. Before I can talk to them, all eyes turn expectantly towards the door. Two men hold the curtains on either side. Balyogeshwar makes his entrance.

The name given to him on birth was Pratap Singh Rawat. When he succeeded his father as head of the Divine Light Mission, he came to be known both as Balyogeshwar and Shri Guru Maharaj Ji. He is a little over fifteen. He is the youngest of a family of five consisting of three brothers and a married sister. His late father, generally regarded as the founder of the Mission, is alluded to by his full title: Yogiraj (King of Yogis) Param Sant (first and supreme saint) Satgurudev (true worshipful teacher) Shri Hansji Maharaj. Balyogeshwar's mother is addressed as Shri Mataji (revered holy mother). She is a buxom, good-looking woman with a chocolate brown complexion and high cheek bones. She blushes as easily as she smiles. Her rows of sparkling teeth are outdone in their lustre only by the diamonds in her nose and ears. Balyogeshwar resembles his mother. He has the same dark brown, smooth, mahogany skin; the same mongoloid features with slanting eyes and a tendency to fatness. He looks like a brown cherub. His hair is well oiled. He wears a black waistcoat over a starched white shirt, white pyjamas and, believe it or not, ankle-high cowboy boots. As he enters, the devotees go down on their knees and press their foreheads to the floor. He takes the cushioned armchair.

He looks uncomfortable, fidgets and eyes me with suspicion. He has had his fill of journalists questioning him about his trouble with customs. 'I came for your darshan,' I say in Hindi. 'I read in American and English papers that your tour was a great success.' He smiles. His narrow eyes close when he does so. 'Will you be going abroad again?' The smile freezes; the look of suspicion comes back. I realize I have committed a faux pas; the police have impounded his passport. I quickly make amends. 'I believe your English disciples gave you a Rolls-Royce.' He smiles again. I cash in on the changed mood. 'I've read a lot about your holiness; but I haven't discovered why your father chose you instead of your elder brothers to be his successor.'

'I can tell you that,' he replies, leaning back in his armchair. 'I was only eight when the late Maharaj Ji left His body. I was at school in Dehra Dun. The chauffeur came to fetch me. I went home. Everyone was weeping. I was just sitting there not weeping. Something began to happen to me. I began to feel that I am not this body; that I could not move these lips.' He points to his lips.

'I always thought that the soul would leave by the mouth but my mouth was shut. Still I felt I was leaving my body and my soul was everywhere going out. And this voice came to me saying: "You are He, you are the one to continue." He pauses and looks around to see what impact his words have made on his audience. They are listening with rapt attention. Some have shut their eyes as if meditating. Somebody pushes a tape-recorder closer towards his feet. He continues: 'I puzzled over this voice. Thirteen days later when I was going to immerse my father's ashes in the Ganga, the voice came again: "You are He. You are the one to go and give this to the world." I didn't want to be Satguru. I would have been satisfied to be a mischievous little boy. But the late Maharaj Ji had left a letter in which He sent his love to his oldest three sons and obeisance to His youngest. So they crowned me with the crown of Rama and Krishna and put the saffron mark of succession on my forehead.'

A few days later Balyogeshwar spoke at a condolence meeting. He said, 'Dear Children of God, why are you weeping? The Perfect Master never dies. Maharaj Ji is here amongst you now. Recognize Him, obey Him and worship Him.'

It is obvious he has told this story many times. His words are well-chosen. His Hindi is impeccable. His manner of delivery and the gestures he makes are those of an accomplished orator. He pauses to heighten expectation before he delivers the punch line. He tells me how on 8 November 1970, before a million devotees gathered in Delhi, he announced his plan to take the message to foreign lands and thus 'explode the peace bombs'.

Though his eyes are focused on me, he is addressing everyone in the room, and perhaps an unseen multitude beyond.

'Why do people come to you? What do they get from you?' I ask him.

'Why do people come to me?' he asks, repeating my question. 'They come to me because they are unhappy, restless. They want peace. What do they get from me? They get this knowledge that I have.'

'Knowledge? What knowledge? Do you give them the guru mantra?'

'I give them the Maha mantra,' he says emphatically. 'I tell them of the true aim of human life. It is not to eat, drink and be merry; it is realization, the true realization of God.'

'Surely, it is for everyone to make his own equation with himself and with God. Why must a person have a guru?'

'Why must a person have a guru? Because without a guru no one can achieve salvation.' Seeing that I am a Sikh, he quotes the Sikh scriptures to me: 'Were a hundred moons to rise and a thousand suns as well, without the guru, the world would still be in utter darkness.' He likes to illustrate his points with parables. He breaks into English: 'Divine knowledge is like money in a bank. It is my money. I have the cheque book. But only after I write on that cheque and sign it can you draw the money, see?'

His English is not very good. He speaks with an American accent with the query 'see?' at the end of the sentence. 'There is this special technique I have, Raja Yoga—yoga of the mind, not of the body which is Hatha Yoga. The yoga of the mind that I teach, Krishna taught in his sermon in the Gita, see?'

'One of your posters says the guru is greater than God. This would be considered blasphemous by Jews, Christians, Muslims and many others.'

'The guru is the only one who can open the third eye through which a person can see Divine Light. The guru is the only one who can give the word. It is the same word which the Bible speaks of: In the beginning was the Word, and the Word was with God, and the Word was God.' Having said that he quickly corrects himself, 'I am not God; I am only His servant.'

The dialogue becomes a little confusing. At one time he says the preacher is more important than the Bible, apparently equating the preacher with the guru; then retracts the statement and says that the function of the guru is exactly what the word means. It is composed of two syllables: 'gu' meaning dark and 'ru' meaning light, therefore one who dispels darkness and gives light.

Balyogeshwar has coined a number of acronyms to serve as aide-memoires for his disciples. He sums up his mission as DODREL—he is the Dispeller of Darkness, Revealer of Light. Even GOD has been mnemonicized as Generator, Operator, Destroyer. When I draw his attention to the fact that this is precisely the Hindu concept of God as the trinity composed of Brahma, Vishnu and Shiva, he repeats his own variation of the theme, 'Generator, Operator, Destroyer.'

'The world is turning against God,' I tell him. 'In Russia and other Communist countries they have abolished religion.'

'The world is not so much turning against God as towards materialism,' he corrects me. 'One may deny God but no one can abolish Him. It is like refusing to see that a man has two legs, a goat has four. Really, these materialistic things can give us very little satisfaction. Suppose I want to sit on a chair and I am not getting a chair, I am frustrated. As soon as I get a chair, I will feel some satisfaction of the mind. But then I will need a table, then a pad over it, then pen and ink, then my name on that pad, and so on goes the extension of the mind. The mind has such strong vibrations that they are multiplied. What we have to do is to put a divisional sign. We have to divide our desires by two. Half to complete the needs of the body, the other half to give to the Supreme Master for the realization of God. For that realization...'

'I am agnostic,' I interrupt him. 'I don't believe or disbelieve in God. I simply say "I don't know". What is more, I don't think whether there is or isn't a God is very important in human affairs. There are many people like me.'

'Are you not seeking for something?' he asks.

'No.'

'Then why are you here?' he asks pointing his finger at me.

'Because I am curious.'

'Curious? Curiosity is a vacuum. You have a vacuum in your mind and want to fill it. That's why you have come to see me.' He snaps his fingers triumphantly. I maintain my ground. 'No! Curiosity is my profession. I am a journalist. I have come to see you to find out what you have to say and what your followers get out of you.'

An uneasy silence pervades the room. One of the foreigners breaks in. 'I, too, was an agnostic once. But I knew I was missing something. Then I came to the Guru Maharaj Ji and He gave me this knowledge.'

'What knowledge?' I ask the young man and turn to the Balyogeshwar for the answer.

'Let him answer that,' replies Balyogeshwar.

Bob Misheler is a thin, pale, flaxen haired, grey-eyed youth who was teaching yoga in Denver. He tells me of his disappointment with the

Protestant faith and how agnosticism had left a void in his heart. It was only when he met the Guru Maharaj Ji and was given knowledge that he found a sense of fulfilment.

I don't understand what the word knowledge means to these people. It sounds like a trinket; you don't have it, then you have it.

I turn to the other young man. He is Gary Girard, from Los Angeles. He was Jewish. 'My search brought me to India,' he says. 'I became a sadhu and walked barefoot on dusty roads along the Ganga from one place of pilgrimage to another. I did not find what I was looking for. Then I met Guru Maharaj Ji. He gave me this knowledge.'

The knowledge continues to elude me. So does the quest. I thank Balyogeshwar for sparing an hour for me. He stands up. His devotees make obeisance. He smiles, nods a farewell and walks out.

27

CARNAGE IN GUJARAT

There are many things in common between the mass violence against the Sikhs in 1984 and the massacre of Muslims in Gujarat in 2002. If we had done the right thing in 1984, we would not have the same kind of thing repeated in 2002. Let me elucidate.

When Prime Minister Indira Gandhi was assassinated by her Sikh bodyguards, a strong anti-Sikh sentiment was prevalent because of the unpunished crimes committed by Bhindranwale's followers against Hindus. It only needed a spark to ignite a blazing fire of vengefulness. The government should have been prepared to douse the flames of hatred before they became an inferno. Far from being ready to put it down, the government became a party to it. Word came from one among the topmost of leaders: 'Teach the Sikhs a lesson'.

It was inevitable that if murderers could get away so lightly in Delhi, they could get away with such crimes elsewhere in India. So they did in Gujarat. As in Delhi, so in Gujarat the administration, police and the law courts became subservient to the wishes of the rulers and let the mobs run riot.

After reading the affidavit of Sanjiv Bhatt, a senior police officer in Gujarat, stating that Chief Minister Narendra Modi had exhorted Hindus to teach Muslims a lesson for what some of their fellow Muslims had done to the Sabarmati Express at Godhra railway station in which sixty-eight Hindu kar sevaks returning from Ayodhya were burnt alive, one can easily understand why Sonia Gandhi, President of the Indian National Congress, had called him 'maut ka saudagar' (merchant of death).

◆

The ghastly carnage in Gujarat in 2002 reminds us that the scourge of communal hatred is not new. I would like to quote from a document from another time. Summing up his report for the Maharashtra government after the riots in Bhiwandi and Jalgaon in 1970, Judge Madon wrote:

> It was a lonely, arduous and weary journey through a land of hatred and violence, of prejudice and perjury. The encounters on the way were with men without compassion, lusting for the blood of their fellow men, with politicians who trafficked in communal hatred and religious fanaticism, with local leaders who sought power by sowing

disunity and bitterness, with police officers and policemen who were unworthy of their uniform, with investigating officers without honour and without scruples, with men committed to falsehood and wedded to fraud and with dealers in mayhem and murder.

He could have been writing about Narendra Modi's Gujarat. But at least the Maharashtra government under S.B. Chavan accepted Judge Madon's damning report with all its recommendations. Modi's government dismissed the report of the National Human Rights Commission as incorrect and biased. The central government's attitude was no different. Cabinet ministers like Arun Jaitley shamelessly supported Modi's stand. To them it was mere propaganda by 'pseudo-secularists'.

What can one expect from an administration that has openly sided with murderers? It is clear that the attack on the train at Godhra was pre-planned. Far from putting the perpetrators down with an iron hand, the government colluded with the mischief-makers as its police and its chief minister were imbued with the spirit of badla (revenge). It is also clear that the revenge was so vicious and effective because it was also pre-planned. There have been credible reports that within hours of the Godhra massacre, armed mobs were out in different parts of Gujarat with detailed lists of Muslim homes and establishments. Several hundred Muslims were hacked to death or burnt alive, women raped, homes and shops looted and burnt down.

◆

It is ironic that the highest incidence of violence against Muslims and Christians has taken place in Gujarat, the home state of Bapu Gandhi. It has been going on for years. Before the 2002 riots, Christian missionaries were being attacked in the tribal districts of the state. There were reports of violence and intimidation coming in almost every day. We will see more of that.

Since the late 1990s, newspaper reports have put the blame for this communalization squarely on neo-fascist members of the Sangh Parivar: the RSS, Vishwa Hindu Parishad, Bajrang Dal and Shiv Sena, with the collusion of the BJP government. Reports of the Minorities Commission substantiate what has appeared in the national press. For those interested, photographic evidence of destroyed churches, dargahs, Muslim homes and shops is available. Among the most ludicrous is the state-sponsored attempt to wipe out remnants of Muslim presence. I first saw this in 1998. Gujarat's capital, Ahmedabad, was built by a Muslim ruler in the middle ages. I noticed that milestones on the main highway leading to the city had dropped Ahmed from its name and made it into Amdavad. How did Gujarat become the laboratory of Hindutva? It did not happen overnight. The Sangh and its sympathizers began poisoning Gujarat not long after Independence. Even the Congress took advantage of the slowly vitiating atmosphere to divide Gujarati society for electoral gains, unwittingly helping the RSS. The 1969 Ahmedabad riots were the first triumph of the RSS in Gujarat. Its fortunes began rising after that.

I went to Ahmedabad in 1970, five months after the riots. I quote from the article I wrote after my return:

I had constituted myself into a one-man commission of inquiry to find out all I could in three days and pass on my verdict to my readers. My object was not to discover what had happened...but why it happened. And, even more, what the people of Ahmedabad thought about it today and what they would do tomorrow if some incident again strained relations between the city's 90 per cent Hindus and 10 per cent Muslims.

I start my investigation by visiting the temple of Jagannath... I detect no sign of damage. To make sure I ask (a) priest. He tells me to look outside. I go outside and look. Above the entrance is a glass pane to cover an effigy of a mahant. The pane is splintered in three places. I approach a band of ash-smeared sadhus lolling under the shade of a banyan tree and ask them if anything else had been damaged... They express themselves in unholy language.

I walked around the bazaar and come to the dargah where it is said to have begun—with the herd of temple cows stampeding into pilgrims going to some Urs. The dargah gate is barred. A posse of constabulary guard the entrance. I ask the caretaker seated outside if this is the right place. He looks at me suspiciously. For an answer he spits a blob of phlegm on the pavement. The sub-inspector of police gives me a dirty look. I do not like policemen. I move on.

I go to the Sindhi Bazaar. It is a cluster of cubicles made of plywood and tin. Row upon row of mini-shops cluttered with bales of cloth and hung with multicoloured saris. The place looks as inflammable as an Indian Oil petrol carrier. I was told that the bazaar had gone up in smoke. I can well believe it. But I see no sign of damage. Sindhis are an enterprising race; they must have rebuilt it and resumed business. I accept one of the many invitations hurled at me to buy something... I pay for a dhoti to buy some information...I get an earful of hate.

I hire a scooter. From the Arabic numerals 786 painted on

the meter I know the faith of the driver. A scooter is not the best mode of transport for a friendly dialogue. I yell my comment on the 'bad days'. The driver turns back, 'You take me for a sucker? I know on which side you are!' He doesn't say so with his tongue but with his doleful eyes.

I try paanwalas, chanawalas, fruit vendors. The result is the same. If they talk, they are Hindus. If they do not, they are Muslims. Both speech and silence are pregnant with hate…

I remind myself of my mission. It is not to probe into the dead past but to gauge the prevailing mood and so forecast the future. But the yesterdays of September are always with me. I drive out of Ahmedabad along the Sabarmati. I pass a mound of debris. A half-broken minaret reveals its identity. I pass graves with their gravestones smashed. And my temper mounts and tears come to my eyes. What species of monstrous swine were those who spared neither places of worship nor the peace of the dead?

At the end of my visit I told the then Mayor of Ahmedabad about what I had seen and heard. 'It is all over,' he assured me. 'It will not happen again.' I hoped he was right. But I was not so sure.

Of course it did happen again, more than once, and most tragically in February 2002. Those deep divisions I saw over thirty years before this latest atrocity were not allowed to heal. The Sanghwalas were never interested in bringing communities together. In Gujarat, a border state, they have terrorized and alienated the state's Muslim population. History will judge them for the damage they have caused, but that will happen in the future. Meanwhile, with a triumphant Modi as their mentor, they will repeat the Gujarat experiment all over India, unless we stop them.

28

A FUNDAMENTAL PROBLEM

Wherever people of different races, religions, languages and cultures have co-existed, instead of amity and cooperation there is tension. And if land, property or business is involved, tension often explodes into violence. This is why no matter what the canards spread by those who would like to lull us into a false sense of complacency, we should always expose them. Whenever we hear that communalism is not a threat to the country we should expose it for the untruth it is. The other canard is that there were no communal riots before the British introduced their policy of divide and rule. In fact, Hindu-Muslim tensions have existed since Islam came to India. And before Islam there were conflicts between Hindus and Jains, Hindus and Buddhists, Dravidians and Aryans.

It is wrong and counter-productive to pretend that communalism is something the Sangh Parivar invented in India. The Sangh's genius was in creating a monster out of existing prejudices. The Congress, especially under Indira Gandhi, played its own dirty role. The BJP is only more dangerous because of its brazenness. It is more dangerous because it uses democracy to camouflage its fascist agenda. But everybody has blood on their hands. Every religious or ethnic group in India can and has been incited to kill and plunder. The most gruesome example of this was what happened at Nellie in Assam in 1983. There, over 3,000 men, women and children were slain in one long orgy of killing. Bangladeshi refugees killed Bengalis and Assamese, Assamese and Bengalis killed each other, tribals killed non-tribals, Muslims killed Hindus and Christians, and Christians killed Hindus. In short, it was just about everyone killing everyone else.

It would be naive to believe that communalism can be banished simply by voting the BJP out of power. The problem is much larger, and though it has assumed diabolical proportions today because of the BJP's politics, it has been around for a long time.

◆

Over two thousand years ago, Buddhism was on the ascendant in India. Emperor Ashoka was the most famous convert to Buddhism. When Brahminical Hinduism gained favour again with ruling dynasties, especially in the ninth and tenth centuries, Buddhists were persecuted and their places of worship demolished. Later, during the reign of many Muslim rulers, Hindus were discriminated against and their temples destroyed.

The British followed a policy of divide and rule, but in India it was never difficult to divide. There were Hindu-Muslim riots every now and then and that suited the British fine as long as there was no threat to their empire. The Christians, naturally, felt more secure during British rule. But there was no religious persecution. The discrimination was based on race.

With Independence came Partition and the worst communal violence in India's history. I was a witness to that madness, and I thought the nation was coming to an end. In the first week of August 1947, I was in Lahore. In the second half of the same month I was in Delhi. I did not know which country I belonged to—India or Pakistan. I was born in what is now a village in Pakistan. I expected to live the rest of my life in Lahore. I sympathized with Muslims who wanted a separate state of their own, and had reconciled myself to living and prospering in that Muslim state. I was not given the choice.

For some time the shock of having been deprived of my home and belongings and the tragedy of civil strife that took thousands of lives and left millions homeless was forgotten in the euphoria of our newly won independence. When the moment passed, the truth slowly dawned on me. Was this the kind of independence we were looking forward to? Faiz Ahmed Faiz's lines written in August 1947 came to mind:

Yeh daagh daagh ujaala, yeh shab guzeeda seher
Voh jis ka intizaar tha ham ko, yeh voh seher to nahin;
Yeh voh seher to nahin jis kee aarzoo lay kar
Chaley thhey yaar ke mil jaaegee kaheen na kaheen
Falak kay dasht mein taaron kee aakhree manzil.

(This dawn dappled with shades of twilight;
This is not the dawn for which we waited all night;
This is not the dawn that we had hoped for
When we comrades set out on our march in the hope
That somewhere in the vast wilderness of the sky
We will find our final destination beyond the stars.)

I was luckier than most of the millions of refugees who had trekked out of Pakistan, having lost everything they owned, and many of whose relations had been murdered or their womenfolk kidnapped and raped. I had my parents' home to come to. And I soon got a job with the Ministry of External Affairs. But memories of the Partition massacres continued to haunt me.

◆

Independent India began limping back to health. I thought we had seen the worst and hoped that the one thing that would never happen again was Hindu-Muslim rioting, especially now that the British with their malevolent and bumbling politics were gone. I hoped we would evolve a common Indian identity overriding religious, linguistic and caste divisions. I hoped that the massive bloodletting of Partition would have taken all the venom of communal hatred out of our bodies.

Alas! After a lull of a few years, the communal virus erupted again in different parts of the country. Commissions of inquiry have stated in categorical terms that in all Hindu-Muslim riots after Independence, over 75 per cent of casualties—in terms of life and property—were Muslim. I have little faith in the impartiality of our police in quelling communal violence but I had hoped for a better performance from the majority community. It has failed in its duty and politicians have taken advantage of this.

From the time Indira Gandhi became prime minister religion began to encroach on the political domain. Religion- and community-based political parties began to exploit religious and communal sentiments to gain political leverage. They succeeded beyond their own wildest dreams. We have come to such a pass that it would not be an exaggeration to describe Indian secularism as only notional—naam kay vaastey. During British rule communal violence was limited to Hindu-Muslim confrontations on religious holidays like Holi, Eid-ul Zuha, the Ganapati festival. Riots occurred in a few riot-prone towns. Today, riots take place between Hindus and Muslims, Hindus and Sikhs, Hindus and Christians, caste-Hindus and Harijans, tribals and non-tribals, Bengalis and Assamese, Maharashtrians and Kannadigas. The entire country has become riot-prone. Everyone's hand rises against his neighbour because everyone wants what his neighbour has—his land, his job, or his business. Racial, religious and linguistic differences provide the excuse to do so. The instigation usually comes from the educated middle class of tradesmen (incidentally, the constituency of the BJP) and politicians (except perhaps the communists); their instruments are lumpen elements and the educated-unemployed—Gujarat showed us in 2002 how the dispossessed can be swayed by a dangerous cocktail of passionate rhetoric, attractive lies, and plain hard cash.

For anyone interested in understanding the persistence of communal feelings among Indians and the tragic results of letting them grow unchecked or encouraging them, Punjab makes for a good case study. I use Punjab as an example because it is home to the community I know best. Also because, through history, Punjab has suffered more than any other Indian state due to religious conflict.

The Punjabis of today are what they are because of the legacy their forefathers left them. They had to face invasions by tribesmen of Central Asia and beyond. Recorded in history are the invasions by Greeks under Alexander. From AD 1000 onwards, came invaders like Ghazni, Ghori, and the conquering dynasties—the Tughlaqs, the Lodis and then the Mughals. When the Mughal empire began to totter, came Nadir Shah and his Afghan successor, Ahmed Shah Abdali, who invaded India nine times in quick succession, laying bare the countryside and Delhi. Punjabis bore the brunt of these invasions and the humiliations which followed in their wake. It took centuries of periodic depredations for the people of Punjab to realize that they must stand together in order to be able to resist and, if possible, repel invaders.

Although by this time more than half of the people of the region had converted to Islam, they were willing to join hands with Hindus and Sikhs. An important factor in this was the new Sikh religion, born of the need to bring the Hindu and Muslim communities together. The new faith borrowed elements from both Hinduism and Islam—an edifice built as it were with Hindu bricks and Muslim mortar. The founder of Sikhism, Guru Nanak (1469-1539), came to be acclaimed by both communities.

The spirit of Punjabi nationality, Punjabiyat, was thus born. It did not, of course, resolve all conflict. Sikhs, in fact, soon found themselves the target of Mughal anger. The Mughal empire was naturally concerned by the growing popularity of the Sikh Gurus, whom they saw as leaders of a cult with political ambitions. Punjab was too important a region for them. The Sikh Gurus and their followers were persecuted. The reason was clearly more political than religious. The fifth Guru, Arjun, was executed by the Muslim rulers in Lahore. With this began the transformation of the Sikhs into a militant sect. Under the last Guru, Gobind Singh, whose father, Guru Tegh Bahadur, was executed in Delhi, this transformation was completed.

There was tension between the Hindu Brahmin order and the Sikhs too. Many of Guru Nanak's teachings went against entrenched Hindu beliefs and attitudes, like idol-worship, religious ritual and the caste system. Hindu rulers of the hill kingdoms in and around Punjab perceived the Sikhs, sometimes rightly, as a threat and often colluded with Mughal forces in their campaigns against them. Sikh historians maintain that among the tormentors of Guru Arjun was a Hindu banker whose daughter's hand Arjun had refused to accept for his son. There are also historical records that say that Guru Gobind Singh's sons, who were captured and killed by Mughal forces, were betrayed by their Brahmin servant.

Despite this, there was no serious rift between Muslims, Hindus and Sikhs in Punjab. The spirit of Punjabi nationalism survived. It took the genius of Maharaja Ranjit Singh to harness this emotion and create a truly Punjabi kingdom. Among his principal advisers were Muslims, Hindus and Sikhs. Likewise, his army, trained by Europeans, comprised all three: his artillery was commanded by General Elahi Baksh, his cavalry consisted mainly of Sikh horsemen, his infantry was a mix of Hindus, Sikhs, Muslims and Gurkhas. General Diwan Chand captured the fort of Multan for him. Hari Singh Nalwa and Akali Phula Singh reduced the turbulent tribesmen of the northwest frontier to submission. Punjabi Muslims fought shoulder to shoulder with their Punjabi brethren against Muslim Pathans and Afghans. It was a remarkable achievement. When he died, his Muslim and Hindu troops and officers upheld his legacy. It is significant that the only person to make an attempt on Ranjit Singh's life was a Sikh.

The British annexed the Sikh kingdom in 1849. They successfully split the three communities apart by giving preferential treatment to Punjabi Muslims and Sikhs (only the Khalsas) at the expense of the Punjabi Hindus. Special electorates and reservation of seats in elected bodies were given to Muslim and Sikhs in excess of their numbers. Punjabi Mussalmans and Khalsa Sikhs were declared 'martial races' for recruitment to the army or the police; only one small Hindu caste, the Mohyal Brahmins, qualified as martial. The seeds of division sowed by the British sprouted and split the three communities.

As the freedom movement picked up all over India, Punjabis lagged behind. Initially, the Punjab Congress consisted largely of urban Hindus. After the Akali agitation of the 1920s, Sikhs began to join it in larger numbers. With a few notable exceptions like Dr Alam and Saifuddin Kitchlew, Punjabi Muslims kept aloof. This was roughly the situation on the eve of Independence. Punjabi Muslims wanted the partition of the country and an independent state, Pakistan. Punjabi Hindus and Sikhs opposed it and were expelled. Punjab paid a very heavy price for Partition. Almost ten million people lost their lands, homes and belongings, while almost a million lost their lives in the communal strife that came with it.

India was able to accommodate five million Hindu and Sikh Punjabi refugees. Sikh farmers took over the small-holdings of the Muslims who had fled east Punjab. These Sikh refugees had left behind large agricultural land irrigated by canals. What they got was no more than thirty acres irrigated by well water. They made the arid wastes of Ganganagar district of Rajasthan and swamplands of the Terai the most prosperous regions of India. In East Punjab, which came in the Indian share, a few years after the setting up of the Punjab Agricultural University in 1962, the average yield of wheat and rice was three times the yield of all of Pakistan. More remarkable was the fact that while Hindu and Sikh refugees who migrated from Pakistan were readily and painlessly integrated as Indians, Muslim refugees who migrated from India to Pakistan are still referred to as Mohajirs and locals do not intermingle with them. Yet more remarkable was the fact that though migrating Punjabis were reduced to penury, it was rare to see a Punjabi beg for alms.

Despite the prosperity, post-Partition Punjab has a wounded history. There came the serious rift between Hindus and Sikhs. When Sikhs demanded a Punjabi-speaking state, many Punjabi Hindus were persuaded by Hindu communal groups to declare to census officials that their mother tongue was Hindi. Sikhs who clamoured for the new state in reality wanted a Sikh-majority state and used the linguistic argument as a sugar-coating. But logic was on their side and after prolonged agitation, their demand was conceded. Himachal and Haryana were separated from old Punjab and a purely Punjabi-speaking state came into being. Sixty per cent of the Punjabi-speaking population of present-day Punjab is Sikh, 40 per cent Hindu.

Hindu-Sikh tensions continued to bedevil the Punjab and came to a head in 1984 with the assault on the Golden Temple to rid the world of Jarnail Singh Bhindranwale, the assassination of Indira Gandhi and the massacre of Sikhs.

◆

As I never tire of saying, what the Congress began, the BJP perfected. Before Gujarat, the worst example of police connivance with terrorism was witnessed during the two days following the assassination of Mrs Gandhi.

What could have been put down with a firm hand in a few hours was deliberately allowed to go on for seventy-two hours. Far from condemning it, in his first public oration as prime minister, Rajiv Gandhi explained it away: 'When a big tree falls, the earth around it shakes.' The conduct of the Congress in the elections that followed was equally reprehensible. Its posters had a distinctly anti-Sikh bias. The Congress party won its landslide victory on a wave of anti-Sikh sentiment generated by it.

But 1984 was not the only case of communal violence during Congress rule. The record of Congress governments in the states ruled by it has been generally abysmal. The cold-blooded shooting down of over seventy Muslim peasants in Hashimpura, anti-Muslim riots in Ahmedabad, in Bhiwandi and Jalgaon, in the towns of Madhya Pradesh, and in Bhagalpur, give the lie to the Congress's secular credentials.

One should not judge political parties by the labels they wear on their lapels or by the high-sounding manifestos issued by them, but by their actions. I will concede that Muslims have never had it as bad as when the BJP is in power. But they were never allowed to flourish under Congress rule either. Indira Gandhi and then Rajiv used the Muslim community as a vote bank. They weren't interested in their future as Indian citizens. They ensured that, like the Dalits, Indian Muslims remained poor and insecure, so they could be fooled into seeing the Congress as their only saviour.

By encouraging regressive mullahs and orthodox leaders and treating Indian Muslims as a homogenous mass, the Congress consigned the whole community to an intellectual and social ghetto. The Muslim closed his mind, he withdrew into himself as a tortoise withdraws into its shell. This helped the BJP demonize the community.

◆

The country's attitude towards its Muslims citizens is not a political but a national problem. We did not do enough after 1947 to rehabilitate them into the national mainstream. The non-Muslim has always had it deeply embedded in his mind that Muslims are bigots, fanatics and treacherous. We were brought up on the tales of heroism of Prithviraj Chauhan, Maharana Pratap, Guru Gobind Singh and Chhatrapati Shivaji. All our heroes were non-Muslims who had fought Muslims. Not one in our pantheon was Muslim. Akbar was just a token figure. We were exposed to evidence of what Muslim conquerors had done: desecrated our temples, massacred our citizenry and imposed humiliating taxes on them. Although all this ended with British rule, we continued to harbour distrust towards the Muslims. The more liberal kept up the façade of friendship with some, but rarely did we learn to relax in their company and speak our minds. They were not a part of the Indian mainstream. Jinnah did not have to invent the two-nation theory; it was there for anyone who had eyes to see.

The Sangh and the BJP have capitalized on these old prejudices about Muslims. Ironically, these so-called nationalists in saffron have been doing exactly what the British did to rule over us. They will do anything in their power to keep the Muslims in ghettos, so that they remain the 'other'. The lies they try to sell us include the one that says polygamous Muslims are multiplying at an alarming rate and soon Hindus will become a minority. We believe them, though census results clearly show that the rate of growth of the Hindu population has always been higher. They tell us that all Muslim rulers followed a policy of genocide against their Hindu subjects, when it is a proven fact of history in India that more Muslim blood was shed by Muslims than by Hindus. They tell us that today's Muslims resent not being the rulers of India and are intolerant and prone to violence. The fact is that in almost every communal confrontation since Independence, Muslim loss of life and property has been almost ten times that of the Hindus.

The Hindu right have also targeted the Christians. Their numbers too, we are told, are increasing exponentially because of conversions. Many of us assume this is true. Find out for yourselves—the Christian population in India has in fact gone down. And why don't the Sanghwalas acknowledge that the missionaries have done more good for the country than they ever will? Christian missionaries do not limit themselves to preaching but put their beliefs into practice by opening schools, colleges and hospitals all over the country that are among the very best in India. In every natural calamity that visits our country, Christian relief workers are usually the first to arrive on the scene to aid the stricken. Everywhere they work among the sick and diseased whom our society discards.

It is being insinuated that Christian institutions increased their activities encouraged by the fact that Sonia Gandhi is a Catholic. This is absolute rubbish. Ever since she married Rajiv, she threw in her lot with her husband's community and, besides paying homage to Mother Teresa, as millions of non-Christians did, kept aloof from religious organizations. She chose India as her home and brought up her children as Hindus though she had every right to bring them up as Christians.

Similar fancies and false arguments have been spread by the likes of Arun Shourie and Prafull Goradia in their books and columns. They are intelligent, well-read men. If they give us selective information and plain lies instead of proven facts, they do so with some purpose. Whipping up hatred among the majority community, emphasizing differences and creating grievances will win them elections.

Arthur Koestler in his *Suicide of a Nation* summed it up beautifully: 'Throughout the ages, painters and writers of fantastic tales have been fond of creating chimaeras (a monster with a lion's head, goat's torso and a serpent's tail). My own favourite brain-child is the mimophant. He is a phenomenon most of us have met in life: a hybrid who combines the delicate frailness of the mimosa, crumbling at a touch when his own feelings are hurt, with the thick-skinned robustness of the elephant trampling over the feelings of others.' To me, the Shouries and Goradias are classic mimophants. They will ruin the country.

We have helped them by not confronting our long history of prejudice. Every Indian community has kept itself apart from the others. It is time for us to accept this fact. The traditional approach to defuse communal tension was the Ram-Rahim or the Ishwar-Allah teyro naam approach, preaching that all religions emphasize love between humans. It worked when we had people like Mahatma Gandhi around because he symbolized in his own person the spirit of Allah and Ishwar. Unfortunately, it does not work any more. C. Rajagopalachari used to say that God was our best policeman. It is true that a truly religious man has no hatred in him. But such men have become a rarity while those who display their religiosity by emphasizing differences between religions have become a common phenomenon. Most of us have double standards of judgement: we are unable to see the shortcomings of our own religions but are more than eager to see the fatuous in other people's faiths. The Ram-Rahim approach is just a smokescreen.

Once we have seen the villain in ourselves, we will have taken the first step towards securing our future.

◆

In her novel, *In Times of Siege*, Githa Hariharan quotes a German pastor, Reverend Martin Niemöller, who was persecuted by the Nazis:

In Germany, they first came for the communists, and I did not speak up because I was not a communist.
Then they came for the Jews and I did not speak up because I was not a Jew.
Then they came for the trade unionists, and I did not speak up because I was not a trade unionist.
Then they came for the homosexuals, and I did not speak up because I was not a homosexual.
Then they came for the Catholics, and I did not speak up because I was Protestant.
Then they came for me...but by that time there was no one left to speak up.

In my defence, I can say with a clean conscience that I did raise my voice against religious fundamentalism and fanaticism whenever it surfaced. I condemned Jarnail Singh Bhindranwale when he made hateful utterances against Hindus. I was on his hit list and that of the Khalistanis and had to be guarded for fifteen years. Disillusioned with the Congress, I had proposed the name of L. K. Advani as MP from New Delhi in 1989, but have never spared him after he launched his notorious rath yatra from Somnath to Ayodhya. Once I confronted him at an open public meeting and told him to his face, 'You sowed the dragon seeds of hatred in this country which led to the breaking of the Babri Masjid.' Now in response to my columns I get hate mail from Hindu fundamentalists. Not a week goes by without my receiving a letter or postcard describing me as a disgrace to Sikhism and India, or a Pakistani agent—'Pakistan randi ki aulad' (born of a Pakistani whore). And much more that is unprintably obscene. It washes over me like water off a duck's back. I have not given up, nor will I give up because I feel I owe it to my country to fight these forces of evil for as long as I can.

Enough of heroics. I am not cast in a hero's mould. I am a coward, but I do speak my mind when it comes to the real enemies of my country. That is the least I can do. For a long time I was searching for an appropriate word to describe religious fundamentalists. At last I have found it in Githa Hariharan's novel. She calls them 'fundoos' and defines them perfectly:

> A nickname, *fundoos*, rolls off Meena's tongue with ease. A nickname for a pet, a pet enemy. The familiar garden-variety hatemonger, inescapable because he has taken root in your own backyard. Fundoo, fundamentalist. Fascist. Obscurantist. Terrorist. And the made-in-India brand, the communalist—a deceptively innocuous-sounding name for professional other-community haters.

The 'fundoos' may rule over us while paying lip service to secularism—or not even that but I still hope that revulsion against them will build up and they will eventually be thrown into the garbage can of history, where they belong. It is the duty of every sane Indian to put them there.

PASSAGE
TO
PAKISTAN

MUHAMMAD ALI JINNAH

LAST DAYS IN LAHORE

GENERAL TIKKA KHAN

SOME TRUTHS ABOUT PAKISTAN

THE HANGING OF BHUTTO

29

MUHAMMAD ALI JINNAH

Muhammad Ali Jinnah knew my father. In fact, when Partition was taking place, he had sent word to my father that I should stay put in Lahore, and that he would appoint me a judge in the Lahore High Court. He also attended my wedding reception.

To understand Jinnah's role as an ambassador of Hindu-Muslim unity, a title conferred on him by Sarojini Naidu, one needs to know his background. He was born in Bombay into an Ismaili Khoja family, regarded by orthodox Muslims as 'beliefless'. They were traders and merchants who had more dealings with Parsis and Hindus than with fellow Muslims. In 1897, he converted to the Shia faith. What the conversion entailed is not clear because he never conformed to any religious trends. In 1892, he proceeded to England to study law at Lincoln's Inn. During the four years he was in England, he made it a point to go to the Houses of Parliament to listen to debates. He was deeply impressed by the speeches made by Dadabhai Naoroji, the first Indian to be elected to the House of Commons, and John Morley. Both men were liberals. Jinnah accepted them as his role models and liberalism as his political creed. Back home in Bombay, he befriended Sir Pherozeshah Mehta, Gopal Krishna Gokhale and Badruddin Tyabji. He was determined to pursue the careers of law and politics. He regarded both as gentlemanly professions. Although he married a Parsi girl, Ruttie, many years younger than him, his professional occupations left him little time to discharge his domestic obligations. He was also dour, unsmiling, tense and a chain-smoker. After some years, Ruttie left him taking their daughter, Dina (the mother of Nusli Wadia of Bombay Dyeing), with her.

Jinnah was quite clear about the role of Indian politicians. They must never mix religion with politics: one was a private matter, the other public service. Political differences should be settled by debate and not taken to the streets to create mob hysteria. The right to vote should be restricted to the educated taxpayer and not be extended to the illiterate and those who do not contribute to the cost of administration. Primary education should be compulsory. What is truly amazing is that he found many takers for his ideas and was acceptable to the Indian National Congress as well as the Muslim League. For some years, he straddled both parties and was accepted by them as their spokesperson. He used his diplomatic skill to reconcile the Muslim League's demands and persuaded the Congress to accept them:

separate electorates with weightage for Muslims in states where they were in a minority, and Muslim hegemony in Sindh, Punjab, the NWFP and Bengal, where they formed a majority. He succeeded in bringing about political unity between Hindus and Muslims so that they could jointly pressurize their British rulers to hand over the governance of the country to Indians. In a speech at the Muslim League Conference in Lucknow in 1917, he urged Muslims not to look upon the Hindu majority as a bogey, saying: 'This is a bogey which is put before you by your enemies to frighten you, to scare you away from the cooperation with the Hindus which is essential for the establishment of self-government.' Unlike most other Indian politicians, he was not overwhelmed by English governors and viceroys: he spoke his mind to them without mincing his words. He carried on verbal warfare with Lord Willingdon, Governor of Bombay and then Viceroy of India. In short, he was, for a time, India's top political leader, till Mahatma Gandhi arrived on the scene. Gandhi not only infused religion into politics but also took politics to the streets through his call for non-cooperation and boycott of government-run institutions, including schools. Jinnah found this distasteful and difficult to digest. Gandhi also showed a marked preference for Jawaharlal Nehru as the future leader of the country. Gradually, Jinnah was pushed off the centre stage of Indian politics to become more and more a leader of the Muslims.

In any event, Jinnah was elected to the Legislative Council from a Muslim constituency. He was among the Muslim delegates at the Round Table Conference in London. He stayed on in England for a few years and toyed with the idea of fighting elections to the House of Commons. No party was willing to accept him as its candidate. It was not surprising. As *The Manchester Guardian* summed him up: 'The Hindus thought he was a Muslim communalist, the Muslims took him to be pro-Hindu, the princes declared him to be too democratic, the British considered him a rabid extremist—with the result that he was everywhere but nowhere. None wanted him.' Reluctantly, Jinnah returned to Bombay to resume his legal practice and his political career, now as a spokesperson of Muslim interests.

30

LAST DAYS IN LAHORE

It was one day in mid-June 1947. Hot, still and silent. People were rudely shaken out of their siestas by shouts and exploding crackers. Since March, their nights had been disturbed by sporadic gunfire and mobs yelling in the streets, hurling slogans like missiles. From one end Muslims armed with knives and lathis shouted 'Naara-e-Takbeer' followed by full-throated 'Allah-o-Akbars'. From the other end came the reply: 'Har Har Mahadev' and 'Boley So Nihal, Sat Sri Akal'. Stones were thrown, words of abuse exchanged, and unwary pedestrians stabbed to death. The police fired to disperse mobs, a few people were killed before peace was restored. Next morning, the papers reported the casualties like Muslims vs The Rest cricket scores. The score was invariably in favour of Muslims. The chief reason for Muslims having the upper hand was that the umpires were Muslims. Over 80 per cent of Punjab Police was Muslim; the state government was Muslim-dominated. It was the same story all over western Punjab. Hindus and Sikhs had begun pulling out of Muslim-dominated towns to Lahore. And finding Lahore equally unsafe, trudged on to Amritsar and towns of eastern Punjab where Hindus and Sikhs outnumbered Muslims.

That June afternoon of 1947 remains etched in my mind. I had returned from the high court when I heard the uproar. I ran up to the roof of my apartment. The sun burned down fiercely over the city. From the centre billowed a huge cloud of dense, black smoke. I did not have to make guesses; the Hindu-Sikh mohalla of Shahalmi was going up in flames. Muslim goondas had broken the back of non-Muslim resistance. After Shahalmi, the fight went out of the Hindus and Sikhs of Lahore. We remained mute spectators to Muslim League supporters marching in disciplined phalanxes chanting: 'Pakistan ka naara kya/ La-ilaha-il-lal-lah'.

The turmoil had little impact on the well-to-do who lived around Lawrence Gardens (today's Bagh-e-Jinnah), and on either side of the canal which ran along the eastern end of Lahore. We went about in our cars to our offices, spent evenings playing tennis at the Cosmopolitan or the Gymkhana Club, had dinner parties where Scotch which cost Rs 11 per bottle flowed like the waters of the Ravi. In elite residential areas, the old bonhomie of Hindu-Muslim bhai bhai-ism continued. We placed a lot of faith in the Unionist government of Khizar Hayat Tiwana who had Hindus and Sikhs in his cabinet and was strongly opposed to a separate Muslim state. League leaders turned their ire on him. Processionists chanted: 'Taazi khabar, mar gaya khizar'. Then he threw in the sponge. Overnight he became the hero of Muslim sloganeers: 'Taazi khabar aayee hai/khizar hamara bhai hai'.

The juggernaut gathered speed. Hindus and Sikhs began to sell properties and slip out towards eastern Punjab. We were within walking distance of Mozang, a centre of Muslim goondas. I did not see anyone being killed but, unknown to me, escaped being murdered myself. I had gone to fight a case in Abbottabad. I decided to walk down to Taxila to catch a train to Lahore. I was surprised to see the road deserted. Suddenly a lorryload of Sikh soldiers pulled up and a lieutenant ordered me to get in. 'Are you crazy?' he shouted. 'They have killed all Sikhs in neighbouring villages and you are out as if on an evening stroll.' At Taxila station, I noticed the train halt at a signal. Sikhs were dragged out and killed. At Badami Bagh, there was another massacre. Locked in my first-class bogey, I neither saw nor heard anything. At Lahore, my friend Manzur Qadir was on the platform to take me home.

By July 1947, stories of violence against Muslims in east Punjab circulated in Lahore, and a trickle of Muslim refugees flew westwards. This further roused Muslim fury. The last time I went to the high court I saw a dozen Sikh students of National College in handcuffs. They were charged with the murder of two Muslims on Grand Trunk Road, which passed in front of their college. Among them was Ganga Singh Dhillon, later pioneer of the demand for Khalistan. They were produced before Justice Teja Singh, the only Sikh judge. He freed them on bail. That had become the pattern of justice.

A week before Independence, Chris Everett, head of the CID in Punjab who had studied Law with me in London, advised me to get out of Lahore. Escorted by six Baluch constables, my wife and I took a train to Kalka to join our two children, who had been sent ahead to their grandparents in Kasauli. By arrangement, I met Manzur Qadir coming down from Simla and handed him the keys of my house.

Then I drove down to Delhi. There wasn't a soul on the 200-mile stretch. I arrived in Delhi on 13 August 1947. The next night I was among the crowd outside Parliament House chanting 'Bharat Mata ki Jai'.

31

GENERAL TIKKA KHAN

The Bangladesh War had just ended, and I was as eager to be the first Indian journalist to interview General Tikka Khan as he was determined to have nothing to do with any Indian. He was angry that he had been dubbed by the Indian press as the 'Butcher of Bengal' and was smarting under the ignominious defeat inflicted by the Indian Army on Pakistan. He did not acknowledge my letter asking for an interview; it was my friend Manzur Qadir who interceded on my behalf and persuaded him to talk to me as 'a friend of Pakistan'.

General Tikka Khan received me courteously in his bungalow. He was a short, stocky man with a dour expression—he looked more like a bank clerk than a soldier. With him was his orderly, a huge man in a Pathan-style skull cap with a stiffly-starched turban. As I looked around, I noticed the paraphernalia usual in the homes of army top brass—regimental insignias, trophies and photographs in silver frames. On the mantelpiece and the walls were quotations from the Quran, including one that I was able to decipher. I kept it to myself as I felt it might come in handy in my dialogue with the general.

Tikka Khan was a bitter man. He maintained that stories published in the Indian and foreign press, of mass killings and gang rapes committed by Pakistanis, were untrue. 'We are a God-fearing people, my soldiers were a disciplined body of men. They didn't go about shooting innocent Bengalis and molesting their women. It is you Indians who spread these lies and had British newspapers publish these calumnies against us,' he said, looking directly into my eyes.

I made a mild protest. I told him that I had visited Bangladesh soon after the war and heard stories of atrocities committed by Pakistani troops and officers from the mouths of Bangladeshi Muslims. 'They could not all be lies,' I said. 'And I saw the enormous anger against Pakistanis. But for the Indian troops to protect them, Pakistani prisoners of war would have been lynched by Bangladeshi mobs.'

'There might have been a few incidents,' the general finally conceded. 'There are some black sheep in every herd. And you know how prone Bengalis are to exaggerating everything!' He then quoted an Urdu couplet:

Shauq-e-tool-o-peych iss zulmat qaidey mein hai agar
Bangaali ki baat sun aur Bangaalan ke baal dekh

(If you like to add length to a story, put a twist in its tail
Hear a Bengali talk (endlessly) and gaze upon his woman's long hair)

I found this very amusing and put it down in my notebook, fodder to tease my Bengali friends with.

I asked the general why Pakistan had put up such a miserable performance on the field of battle.

'It was not a fair fight,' he replied. 'First, you cut off air contact between West and East Pakistan. Then your men infiltrated deep inside East Pakistan, long before we were compelled to declare war. All these stories of the Mukti Bahini were propaganda. The Mukti Bahini were Indian soldiers trained for guerrilla warfare; there were very few Bengalis in it to start with. You armed them, your officers led and directed them. Our troops had to face the enemy in front as well as in their rear.'

The orderly volunteered his opinion: 'Awaam humare khilaaf ho gaya tha' (the people had turned against us.)

The general did not approve of his orderly expressing an opinion and raised his hands to silence him. But I cashed in on the pronouncement. 'That is exactly what I have been saying. What can an army do if the entire populace of a country rises against it?'

'It was Indian propaganda,' maintained the general.

I did not have very much more to ask him. I pointed to the quotation from the Quran on the mantelpiece and, feigning innocence, asked, 'What does it mean?'

The general read it out loudly: 'Nasr min Allah Fateh-un qareeb. It means: Allah grants victory to those whose cause is just.'

'General sahib, Allah in His wisdom granted us victory because our cause was just.'

For the first time during the interview, the general smiled. 'Sardar sahib, I suspect you knew what the quotation meant.'

I admitted I did and took my leave.

32

SOME TRUTHS ABOUT PAKISTAN

The Pakistan International Airlines flight from Bombay to Karachi flies into the setting sun. An hour later you can see the lights of Karachi scattered below. It seems as if a bare fifteen minutes have passed since the handsomely statuesque Zeenat Peerani had wished us an Assalam alaikum and promised that 'if God willed (inshallah) we shall be in Karachi by 7.30 p.m'. And now she is telling us to refasten our seat belts for landing.

The hour has contracted into a few minutes because the gentleman beside me is Mr Abbas Mirza, a bon viveur, bursting with goodwill and Sardarji jokes. PIA treats him like royalty. Zeenat is particularly attentive to him. She gives him a double Scotch on the rocks and lots of smiles; all I get is tepid champagne and a flash of the diamond on her nose ring.

'You must be Punjabi,' I interrupt the dialogue, hoping she will take it as a compliment. 'No, I am not,' she snaps and continues talking to Mirza. I persist: 'Peerani, Peerani—then you must be a Kutchi Memon.' The second pass also misfires. 'No, I am not,' she replies firmly and withdraws her graceful presence to order us in a very pucca British accent to refrain from smoking and remain seated till the aircraft comes to a halt.

'Old boy!' exclaims Abbas Mirza (we were on 'old boy' terms now), 'if you must know, she is an Aga Khani Khoja. But what you really want to find out is not her sect but her address and telephone number in Karachi, don't you?'

I protest: 'Tauba! Tauba! What would an ageing Sikh want to do with a pretty Pakistani air hostess?'

Abbas Mirza has a mischievous smile on his face. 'I don't know about an ageing Sikh,' he replies, 'but I can tell you what an ageing Mussalman would like to do.' Within an hour the Pakistani Muslim Abbas Mirza and I, an Indian Sikh, have become brothers. Mirza's favourite takia kalam for anyone he likes is 'down to earth'. He finds me very earthy. I find him very likeable. This two-nation theory that the Pakistanis swear by is a lot of hogwash. And they know it.

BEGUM PARA'S AMPLE EMBRACE
Karachi airport gets bigger every year. And yet too small to cope with the increasing load of traffic. This time, as the cliché goes, the confusion is worse confounded. Thirty-five thousand Pakistani hajis are returning from Mecca and a part of the airport had burnt down a few days ago.

135

Airport officials rescue me from the milling mob of pilgrims and escort me to the air-conditioned luxury of a VIP lounge. A few minutes later I find myself in the embrace of Begum Para and her lovely sixteen-year-old daughter, Lubna. An hour later we are in the Midway Hotel.

A Sikh continues to be a curiosity in Pakistan. A Sikh accompanied by a film star like Begum Para is a sight no one can miss. And the two with half a bottle of Scotch inside them are a grand spectacle. We make quite a display in the crowded dining room. Para is nostalgic about Bombay. She breaks down and cries. Then she hears about the eminence achieved by her niece, Meenoo, alias Rukhsana Sultana Sahiba, and the success of her brother-in-law Dilip Kumar's *Bairaag* and roars happily. To complete the performance, as we get up to leave, she misses her step and twists her ankle: she howls like a child. I rub her damaged foot. A crowd gathers around—not solicitous but curious. They recognize Begum Para. But what is this weird-looking foreigner doing with her?

'WHAT IS SHE TO YOU?'

As I am turning in, there is a knock on my door. A young sub-inspector of police strides in uninvited and makes himself comfortable on the sofa. He lights a cigarette and demands: 'What is your name?' I tell him. He is not impressed. 'What do you do?' I tell him about the *Weekly* and its circulation. He is not impressed. 'Who was the lady with you?' I tell him. He knows but wants to know more. 'What is she to you?'

My temper flares up. 'That is none of your business. I've been invited to Pakistan by your prime minister (which is not strictly true). I am seeing him tomorrow in Islamabad. If you do not get out this instant I will report you to the authorities.' It works like a pin stuck into the fellow's bottom. He leaps up from the chair and salutes. 'Aap koi minister-vinister hain?' I wish him a very curt adaab arz and slam the door behind him.

At 5 a.m. the bearer brings tea. I greet him: 'Assalam alaikum.' He replies: 'Sat Sri Akal.'

At six I am back at the airport. The crowd and the chaos! Lots of policemen armed with rifles and pistols sauntering about and gossiping. I join a mini-queue and find myself wedged in between bearded hajis loaded with bedding rolls and steel trunks. Alongside us is a parallel line of Europeans with another quota of hajis—fore and aft. Neither queue moves forward as people who know people go behind the counter and get checked in.

I try to rouse an old greybeard to protest. 'Why are you getting so worked up, Sardarji?' he admonishes me in avuncular tones. 'We will all be on the same plane. They won't get there any quicker.' I hold my peace.

But a foreign lady who is ahead of me does not. Somebody's bedding roll tumbles and knocks against her legs. She gives it a vicious kick. It rolls away. A swarthy young Pathan rolls it back on to her legs. She gives it another kick backwards. This time the Pathan pushes the bedding roll with his hands, walks up to the white lady and with his hands demonstrates what he will do to her posterior if she dares to kick his belongings. She now holds her peace.

WE AREN'T THE WORST
At long last I manage to check in. We are an hour and a half behind schedule. I am cheered by the thought that there is at least one country where discipline is worse than in my own.

Breakfast is brought in trolleys. It should be hot. It is not. I swear not to be so critical of Indian Airlines in the future. Coffee and tea follow. They are piping hot. I retract my promise and decide to tell Indian Airlines of the better services on PIA. In India the non-smoking section is in the front; in Pak planes it is in the rear. In Indian Airlines they take the non-smoking rule seriously, in the Pakistani airline they don't give a damn. No sooner is the 'No Smoking' sign switched off than half a dozen men in the non-smoking section light their cigarettes. The steward admonishes them. The hajis obey. The sahib log ignore the steward. He pretends he can't see them.

We arrive in Islamabad on a cold, grey morning. People are in overcoats or have shawls wrapped about their shoulders. The Murree hills are capped under dark clouds. O. P. Khanna, Press Counsellor of our Embassy, greets me. We ride in a large Mercedes-Benz to the Hotel Intercontinental in Rawalpindi.

A pile of documents await me. I am one of 200 delegates from thirty-eight countries of the world invited to participate in the centenary celebrations of the birth of Qaid-i-Azam Muhammad Ali Jinnah. Amongst the gifts is a Jinnah medallion, a marble inkpot and tray (courtesy PIA) and a Jinnah cap with the request that I should wear it at the inaugural ceremony.

I take a quick look at the room. It is like any other in any five-star hotel in the world. I notice that the toilet paper and matchboxes called 'Double Happiness' are of Chinese manufacture. Indian toilet paper is a little rough but our matches could certainly outmatch the Chinese. Why don't they buy from us?

I decide to have a look at the venue of the Congress. My hotel is in Pindi; the conference is to meet eleven miles away in Islamabad. (Rawalpindi has hotels but no conference facilities. Islamabad has conference facilities but no hotels. With the petrol they have wasted to-ing and fro-ing between two cities they could have raised a third one.)

A TOUCH OF CLASS
The inaugural session of the Qaid Congress is held in Parliament House. As the clock on the wall registers 4 p.m., the Speaker announces, 'Gentlemen, the prime minister!' Zulfiqar Ali Bhutto, followed by Hafizuddin Pirzada and Vice-Chancellor Dani, makes his entrance. The three men take the throne seats on the dais beneath a massive portrait of the Qaid. Bhutto is a strikingly handsome man; so is Pirzada, sporting his Jinnah cap at a slightly rakish angle.

Their speeches are mercifully short, well phrased, well delivered, but not particularly exciting. Also, Mr Bhutto's references to the 'wrongs' committed by the majority community (Hindus) in pre-Partition India against the Muslims strikes a jarring note in my ears. How long will history continue to cast its baleful shadow on both our countries?

RELIGIOUS ARROGANCE
Another thing that makes for discord between us is the appeal to religion which one constantly hears in Pakistan. Pakistanis, particularly the Punjabis, are incredibly warm-hearted and effusive in their expression of friendship. And though most of the upper class is indifferent to the tenets of Islam (there is no shortage of liquour in this Islamic state), they never cease harping on the fact that they are Muslims. It makes me feel as if being non-Muslim was a misfortune visited by Allah on kafirs like me. In the next four days I am often exposed to this combination of racial and religious arrogance. I tell my Pakistani friends how I feel.

The prime minister has hosted a dinner for the delegates. 'Will he give me a drink before the meal?' I ask everyone I meet. Everyone says: 'Not on the Qaid's centenary.' It's no use telling them that the Qaid never bothered about such silly things. My drooping spirits are sustained by flattery (I sign several autograph albums) and the warm embraces of old friends.

There is Hamida Khuhro, daughter of M.A. Khuhro, once CM of Sindh; Shaukat Hayat Khan, friend of my college days; and S.N. Qutb, who spent many years in Delhi. There is General Tikka Khan and General Akbar Khan who, as General Tariq, led the tribal invasion of Kashmir in 1947-1948. And there is the poet Faiz Ahmed Faiz, Sir Penderel Moon, H. V. Hodson, once editor of *The Sunday Times*, and Ian Stephens, once editor of *The Statesman*. While I am embracing one, I am talking to the other.

Mr Bhutto arrives with Pirzada and an ADC. He shakes a few selected hands. I am one of those he shakes hands with. A few minutes later enters a posse of towering Pathans bearing trays full of Scotch and soda. What more does one want of life than sweet words, celebrities and good Scotch to quench one's thirst. And no sooner have I had my first gulp than the ADC informs me that the PM would like to talk to me.

I like Bhutto sahib and sense he does not dislike me. I ask for an interview. He replies: 'Here I am. Ask me what you want.' I plead I do not have the questions in my head and there is too much liquor in my belly. He smiles. 'Okay, I'll tell the ADC to give you time. Also come to the National Assembly and hear what I have to say. But aren't you happy at the turn of Indo-Pak relations?'

I say: 'I am delighted. The friendlier the better. I have always believed that friendship between us is more important than friendship with other nations. But why can't we step up the pace? I know from experience that the people in both countries are willing to fall into each other's arms. Why keep them back?'

He replies: 'In such matters it is wise to go slow. Ayub tried to force the pace at Tashkent and see what happened! We have plenty of time to build relations slowly but surely. On our side we have no inhibitions about India.'

'India has no inhibitions about Pakistan,' I state with equal confidence.

'If you see your PM, convey my best wishes to her. You can repeat my invitation to her to visit us in Pakistan. I have asked her many times but she has not responded. I have two reasons to invite her: one because of the enormous respect I had for her father. The other is personal. I feel it would help me with my own people. On my side I had done all I could to generate a feeling of goodwill. You will recall that when your Emergency was declared, we made absolutely no comment. Even though Piloo Mody, who is one of my closest friends, was arrested, I said nothing which would embarrass her judgement and did not want to jeopardize the relations between our two countries.'

QAID CONGRESS
There are Bangladeshis, Malays, Sinhalese, Koreans, Arabs, Africans, Americans, Englishmen, Iranians—and of course a large number of Pakistanis. Three Indians were invited: only one made it. I wonder if the papers are going to be objective and academic or an exercise in hagiology. The opening speech by M. A. H. Ispahani, the industrial magnate, a close friend of the Qaid and later Pakistan's ambassador in England and India, ends with an impassioned declaration: 'I have lived in Pakistan, I will die

for Pakistan.' I can guess what will follow. And it does.

The only assessments which, despite the eulogy for the Qaid, could be described as objective are read by the white participants: Sir Penderel Moon, H. V. Hodson and, above all, Betty Unterberger who makes a lively and witty résumé of the American press reporting on Mr Jinnah and Pakistan.

The papers of Pakistani scholars are full of the 'machinations' of the 'majority community' (Hindus) and reassertions of the two-nation theory which compelled the Qaid to demand a sovereign state for the Muslims. They overlook or explain away the most significant speech that the Qaid made to the Pakistan Constituent Assembly in 1947.

I quote the relevant passage which refutes the two-nation humbug:

> If you work in cooperation, forgetting the past, burying the hatchet, you are bound to succeed, if you change your past and work together in a spirit that every one of you, no matter to what community he belongs, is first, second and last a citizen of this state with equal rights, privileges and obligations, there will be no end to the progress you will make…we are starting with this fundamental principle that we are all citizens and equal citizens of one state. You may belong to any religion or creed or caste—that has nothing to do with the business of the state. I think we should keep that in front as our ideal and you will find that in course of time Hindus would cease to be Hindus and Muslims would cease to be Muslims, not in the religious sense, because that is the personal faith of each individual, but in the political sense as citizens of the state.

There is enough evidence to prove that Mr Jinnah never wanted nor foresaw the exchange of population that followed Partition. He wanted India and Pakistan to be like Norway and Sweden. He retained his house in Bombay for several months hoping to come back to it every year.

I am in a fix. I am notorious for my bias in favour of Pakistan and am proud of it. But my pro-Pak leanings come from the conviction that friendship with Pakistan must take top priority in India's international dealings because an inimical Pakistan not only retards progress in both our countries but also slows the pace of integration of Indian Muslims into the Indian mainstream. I am convinced that we can win the goodwill of Pakistan by showing more understanding of their problems and anxieties, by showing more respect to the memory of people like their Qaid-i-Azam who means the same to them as Mahatma Gandhi to us. I never accepted the two-nation theory but strongly supported the rights of Muslims in defined areas to self-determination—i.e., Pakistan. I am convinced I am right and those who disagree with me are utterly wrong.

I have paid the price for airing my views by being dubbed by stupid people as a Pakistani agent.

WE WISH YOU PEACE

The paper I read is a kind of résumé of my views on the genesis of Pakistan and the aftermath in India. I say that going to Pakistan means to me what going on haj means to a Muslim (applause). I pay tribute to the Qaid whom I had met a few times and whose ability and integrity I had rated as high as Gandhiji's and Nehru's (applause). I say that there was no one in India who questioned the sovereign status of Pakistan and did not wish it peace and prosperity (applause). I end with the affirmation: 'We never have, nor do today, nor ever will accept your two-nation theory. But this does not prevent us from wishing Pakistan Zindabad.'

They are kind to me, pay me many compliments—then proceed to lambast me. 'If you do not accept the two-nation theory, you do not accept Pakistan,' says one speaker after another.

One point I make in my speech is the progressive improvement in Hindu-Muslim relations and the increasing employment of Muslims in all sectors of our industry. Never since Independence has the lot of Indian Muslims been better than it is today. I give the credit to those to whom credit is due; it was the blood of Gandhiji and the sweat of Nehru which fertilized the soil in which the seeds of communal harmony were planted. I tell them about our Muslim presidents, Muslim chief ministers of states where Muslims formed no more than 5 per cent of the population, of Muslim generals and captains of industry; of joint Muslim-Sikh celebrations of Eid and the Guru's birthday and so on.

Not to be outdone, a Hindu member of the Pakistani Parliament affirms that the lot of non-Muslim minorities (3 per cent of the population) is better than that of the Muslims in India. And he too reels off names of Hindus, Christians and Parsis in Pakistan's diplomatic and civil services. I am delighted.

A DAY IN PARLIAMENT

The next evening I attend the joint session of the two Houses of the Pakistani Parliament. The contrast with our Parliament strikes me very forcefully. The majority of the Pakistani parliamentarians are younger (thirty to fifty years old) than ours; most of them are immaculately dressed in European clothes and are wearing Jinnah caps. And most speak in English with the affected accents heard in Oxbridge debating societies.

Except for Maulana Kausar Niazi and Shaukat Hayat Khan (a new entrant in the ruling PPP), the only people clad in the traditional salwar kameez and sporting turbans and beards are the handful of members of the Opposition—mainly from Baluchistan and the Northwest Frontier Province. And, of course, there are eight women members in saris, only distinguishable from Hindu ladies by the absence of bindis on their foreheads. Parliamentary tributes are also heavily loaded against the 'Hindu-dominated Congress' and 'the so-called nationalistic Muslims'.

A lighter side is provided by the Speaker's interruption. After twelve members have quoted Iqbal...

Hazaron saal nargis apni beynoori peh roti hai
Badi mushkil sey hota hain chaman mein deedavar paida.

(A thousand years does the narcissus lament her sightlessness
It takes an age before a lover of beauty in the garden is born.)

...the Speaker tells the members to omit the quotation from their speeches as it would be taken as read.

The prime minister, as is his wont, makes a dramatic entry as the session is about to conclude. His tribute to the Qaid is well prepared in the style of Nehru's famous 'tryst with destiny' speech. But despite his superior oratory he does not have the same felicitous choice of words. Although he had the same kind of education in a prestigious university (Oxford), he did not spend as long a time in jail as did Nehru (nine years) to turn that education into a creative faculty.

'YOU TOO ARE MY BROTHER'
A telling comment on the two-nation theory is made by the comely Aliya Khan who is quite the lioness of Karachi's Urdu literary circles. She produced a handful of silver rings she had got from Iran for her friends and relatives. One is to be given to her brother in India. Another to the poet Ali Sardar Jafri and a third to the novelist Krishan Chander. She then slips one on my finger and says, 'You too are my brother.'

My only encounter with any member of Pakistan's minority communities is with the managing director of Murree Breweries, Mr Bhandara. I am not sure of his identity and ask him, 'Are you a bawaji?' He looks somewhat nonplussed and asks me in perfect Punjabi, 'Bawaji kee honda?' There are upwards of 5,000 Parsis in Pakistan—and, predictably, all very prosperous.

I leave Islamabad in the mid-morning. Ambassador Bajpai deposits me in the safe custody of an airport official with the request that I be locked up in the VIP lounge till my flight is called. I prefer to mingle with the crowd and am rewarded with free cups of tea and 7-Ups by strangers who want nothing of me except to take good wishes to their friends in India.

Islamabad to Lahore is a one-hour flight by a twin-engined Fokker Friendship. We fly over towns I had known well in the days of my youth—and over Nankana Sahib and the Ravi to Lahore. And once more into the embraces of my friends Mohammed Anwar, Rehman and Manzur Qadir's family, which is as close to me as my own. The Qadirs live in the house that once was mine.

THE LAST DAYS OF MANZUR QADIR

The chief object of my coming to Lahore is to catch up with the last days of Manzur Qadir's illness and death. He was my closest and dearest friend and the most dominant influence in my life. I felt my knowledge of him would be incomplete unless I had read the last chapter of his biography. I asked his wife Asghari Qadir, and son Basharat, to talk to me about my friend and his last days.

Manzur Qadir was a man of contradictions. He showed little promise as a student; he became much the most outstanding lawyer of Pakistan. Next to law, his favourite reading was the Old Testament and the Quran. Nevertheless he remained an agnostic until he was facing death, when he turned to his religion, Islam.

He was an uncommonly good poet and wrote some of the wittiest, bawdiest verse known in the Urdu language. At the same time he was extremely conservative, correct in his speech and deportment. Although born a Punjabi he rarely spoke the language and preferred to converse in Hindustani, which he did with uncommon elegance. He was long-winded but never a bore; a teetotaller who effervesced like vintage champagne.

The dominant traits of his character were kindliness—he never said a hurtful word about anyone. And integrity, which surpassed belief. Income tax authorities were constantly refunding tax he had paid in excess. He did not give a damn about money. It was commonly said, 'God may lie, but not Manzur Qadir.' Though godless he had more goodness in him than a clutch of saints.

The respect and admiration he commanded amongst his friends was unparalleled. Some years after Partition a group of us were discussing G. D. Khosla's *Stern Reckoning*. The book, as the title signifies, justified the killings that took place in East Punjab in the wake of Partition as legitimate retribution. We were attacking Khosla's partisan approach; he and his wife were arguing back. Suddenly a friend asked Khosla, 'Would you present a copy of this book to Manzur?' Khosla pondered for a while and replied, 'No, not to him.' That ended the argument. We came to judge the right or wrong of our actions by how Manzur Qadir would react. He was the human touchstone of our moral pretensions.

Manzur Qadir had no interest in politics and seldom bothered to read newspapers. His ignorance of world affairs was abysmal. Once, in London, we happened to see a newsreel of Dr Sun Yat-Sen. He asked me who this Sen was. When I expressed my amazement at his lack of information, he retorted testily; 'Hoga koee sala Bangali daktar!' Later in the evening, when I narrated the incident to his daughter Shireen, she chided her father. He made me swear I wouldn't tell anyone about it. I didn't till I read in the papers that President Ayub Khan had made him foreign minister of Pakistan. I sent him a telegram of congratulations, 'Greetings from Dr Sun Yat-Sen, the Bengali doctor.'

He told me how he had become foreign minister. He had criticized Ayub Khan's dictatorship at a meeting. That evening an army jeep came to fetch him. Believing that he was being arrested he said goodbye to his family. He was driven to the president's residence. Said Ayub Khan: 'It is no good criticizing me and my government unless you are willing to take the responsibility for what you say.' Manzur Qadir returned home as foreign minister.

True to his character, Manzur never canvassed for any job nor showed the slightest eagerness to hold on to power. He strove with none, for none was worth his strife. He allowed himself to be outmanoeuvred by unscrupulous politicians. After four years as foreign minister, during which he made a desperate bid to improve relations with India, he quit the job with no regrets. He was forced to become chief justice and, when he desired to throw that up, persuaded to take up briefs on behalf of the government. He was engaged as government counsel in all the important conspiracy cases and represented his country before international tribunals. Whether it was Iskander Mirza or Ayub Khan, Yahya Khan or Bhutto, no ruler of Pakistan could do without Manzur Qadir.

During his last days, emissions of blood and transfusions had made him very weak and he could not even pick up a book. When his friends came to visit him in hospital, he would ask them to read to him. Sometimes it was Hali's 'Musaddas' or Iqbal's 'Shikwa'. Then it was 'Ayat-ul-Kursi' from the Quran:

No slumber can seize Him
Nor sleep. His are all things
In the heavens and on earth.
Who is there can intercede
In His Presence except

As He permitteth? He knoweth
What (appeareth to His creatures as)
Before or After
Or Behind them.

◆

It is not the peal of church bells but the call of the muezzin which rouses me from slumber—for the rest it could be Christmas morning in London. Lahore is a lot like it—cold, frosty and misty. A Sui gas fire which has burnt all night (this natural gas is cheap and plentiful) in the main rooms fills them with a bright orange glow. I join Begum Qadir by the fire for a cup of 'bed tea'. Pakistani tea is an insipid affair tasting like sugared hot water with a dash of milk (when visiting Pakistan the presents you should take are tea, cardamoms, betel leaves and jharoos).

THE PILGRIMAGE
Mohammed Anwar arrives in his cream-coloured Mercedes-Benz. We drive out into the grey dawn towards Bahawalpur Road. I recognize a few old landmarks and then am lost in a maze of graveyards and mosques. We finally locate the object of my pilgrimage to Lahore. A small, dusty enclosure contains the graves of people I had known, revered and loved: Sir Abdul and Lady Qadir, Mohammed Saleem (the great tennis player and criminal lawyer) and beside him the latest inmate, my friend, Manzur Qadir. I scatter rose petals on his grave and garland his tombstone. The epitaph is taken from Iqbal's dialogue between the poet and the taper:

Main to jalti hoon keh muzmir hai meri fitrat men soz
Too ferozaan hai keh parvanon ko ho sauda tera

(I burn because it is in my nature to burn and give light;
You burn and give light to enter into a contract with the moth.)

Basharat Qadir has transposed the lines to form a more fitting tribute to his great sire.

Too ferozaan hai keh muzmir hai teri fitrat men soz

(You are alight because it is in your nature to be bright)

I read and re-read the epitaph till the tears in my eyes blur my vision. I drop a few on my friend's grave and bid him and Pakistan farewell.

33

THE HANGING OF BHUTTO

The first thing they did was to confiscate the Scotch I had brought with me; the second was to take me in their embrace and say 'Khush amdeed'—welcome to Pakistan. The customs official who did so explained with relentless Punjabi logic: 'Law is law and friendship is friendship.'

The experience at Lahore airport was symbolic of the atmosphere that prevailed in Pakistan the week preceding the execution of Bhutto. Whatever he may have done—and that is fiercely debated—and whatever be the consequences of hanging him, hang he must because no one is above the law and the law found him guilty of murder.

There was a third thing about Pakistan that occurred to me even before I put foot on its soil, viz., the contrast with India. As the 'fasten your seat belts' sign came on and the Fokker Friendship descended from the azure sky through the dusty haze, and the landscape became clearer, I realized how little it had changed. We flew over several villages. They looked exactly as they did in 1947: a shapeless huddle of flat-roofed mud homes with usually only one building made of brick and plaster and fresh with a new coat of paint, white or green. And this one building was then as it was now invariably a mosque. As the plane touched down, the air-hostess announced the temperature at Lahore and told us to correct our watches. It occurred to me that while Pakistani time was thirty minutes behind ours Pakistan was thirty years behind us in every field of development: agricultural, industrial, educational and social. It did not make sense because they were the same people as we, man to man they were physically fitter than us, and being more united by faith and speaking one language they had fewer problems than us. To start with they had forged ahead of us, and then for some inexplicable reason slowed down and stagnated.

Of course, we were lucky in having long years of stability under Jawaharlal Nehru and Indira Gandhi while they were changing rulers every other year. Nehru put us on the right path, building an industrial base and at the same time developing our villages by linking them with roads, digging tubewells and electrifying them. The Pakistanis concentrated their energies on improving their cities where the rich upper classes live. Lahore is a good example of lopsided priorities. While the villages surrounding it remained untouched, the city had its roads widened to provide for chariot-sized limousines of foreign make: Mercedes-Benzes, Volvos, Toyotas

146

(one fellow is said to have paid over eight lakhs for a second-hand car of Italian make). More parks for the Brown sahibs' babalog, big bungalows like those in which the rich and the corrupt Indians of the cities live. The bazaars sell much the same kind of junk as ours; only their textiles are fancier than ours. They have many more music shops selling tapes. One bookstore I visited, Ferozesons, is bigger than any we have in India. Almost everything is more expensive than in India. And despite the harsh penalties imposed by the Nizam-e-Mustafa, liquor is easily available but at exorbitant prices. The one item we share in equal measure is corruption; it is as much on the up and up in Pakistan as it is in India.

To me, more important than whether or not Zia would hang Bhutto was to find out whether or not the Pakistanis believed that Bhutto deserved to be hanged. From the few people I met in the first four days of my stay in Lahore and Islamabad I gathered that most Pakistanis believed that not only was Bhutto guilty of the murder of Nawab Kasuri, but of many other diabolical crimes for which he had not been brought to book. These included assassination of political opponents, torture, humiliation (buggery of a son in the presence of his father, abduction and raping of unmarried girls, etc.). However a large proportion were equally convinced that though he had brought about a reign of terror, the prosecution had failed to prove his hand in the murder of Kasuri and if the constitution of the courts had not been what it was, or if Bhutto had been tried under Islamic law, the outcome would have been different. But no sooner was Bhutto executed than opinion swung in Bhutto's favour.

I was at a disadvantage in Lahore as most of my friends had suffered at Bhutto's hands and their families were bitter about it. My closest friend, the late Manzur Qadir, had been put out of President Ayub's cabinet because Bhutto (himself a gay liver and a hard drinker) had published pamphlets denouncing the teetotal, god-fearing Manzur as a non-believer. Manzur was the chief defence counsel in prosecutions launched by Bhutto against his political adversaries. After Manzur died, Mohammed Anwar took over the defence of Bhutto's victims. He organized the Lahore High Court Association to protest against Bhutto's high-handedness. He was beaten up by the police and jailed for fifteen days. He died soon after. My first call of duty was to pay homage at his grave. I strewed jasmine flowers and read the epitaph from Iqbal's 'Shikwa':

Qaid-i-Mausam se tabeeat rahi azad uskee
Kash! gulshan mein samajhta koee faryad uskee

(He remained free of the shackles of the changing seasons
Alas! there was no one in the garden to listen to his pleadings.)

The epitaph was a deserved tribute to Anwar's character. He was not anti-Bhutto but anti-tyrant. Anwar had often told me that Bhutto was not only a wicked man but also bordering on insane.

The baton passed from Anwar's hands to those of M. A. Rehman who led the prosecution's case against Bhutto and four men of the Federal Security Force (Bhutto's private army) in the murder of Nawab Kasuri on the night of 10–11 November 1974. It was in Rehman's home that I met the murdered Nawab's son, Ahmed Raza, the man Bhutto really wanted eliminated. Ahmed Raza has had a charmed life; he escaped as many as eighteen attempts to kill him. Bhutto emphatically denied that he ever wanted Ahmed Raza killed and dismissed him with lofty disdain as 'a mere nobody'. Ahmed Raza is a man of substance; he was a student leader, one of the founder members of Bhutto's Pakistan People's Party (PPP), a member of the Pakistan National Assembly, and the leader of the anti-Bhutto faction of the same party. He was not a nobody but a somebody who had become a thorn (maybe not a big one) in Bhutto's side. Behind his back Ahmed Raza was known as a bhaunka—the barker—and also as a chota Bhutto. He was in the witness box for eight days, five hours every day. The defence was unable to break his testimony in the cross-examination.

The pro-Bhutto element which was substantial and as vehement in his defence usually avoided getting into arguments about its leader's involvement in Nawab Kasuri's murder. Instead they emphasized Bhutto's unique status as the only leader of world stature that Pakistan had produced since M. A. Jinnah (he was the Qaid-i-Azam, the great leader; Bhutto was the Qaid-i-Awam, the leader of the people.) When the anti-Bhuttoists condemned him as the architect of the destruction of Pakistan by forcing East Pakistan to break away and for his inept handling of the Baluchistan and Northwest Frontier Province (NWFP) dissidents, the pro-Bhuttoists were equally vehement about how he alone had saved whatever remained of Pakistan after the disastrous defeat at the hands of India in December 1971, the man who led a vanquished nation to deal on an equal level with victorious India at the Simla conference, the man who liberated the 93,000 prisoners of war (POWs) from Indian camps, and so on.

Between the two contending points of view there was no meeting ground. To one lot Bhutto was a villain; to the other a hero. The only point everyone agreed upon was that Bhutto was also a playboy: flamboyant in his dress, lavish with the use of public money, lascivious in his relations with women. (He had three wives: the first, Begum Ameer, was a cousin fifteen years older than himself; the second, an Iranian divorcee Nusrat, who bore him four children; the third, a Bihari sex-bomb, who divorced her Bengali husband to share Bhutto's bed and now lives in London.) He was not very discreet in his liaisons. As a cabinet minister he was caught in flagrante delicto with the wife of a visiting head of state. General Ayub reprimanded him but, like an indulgent father, did not throw him out. He had cause to regret his paternal benignity. It was also common knowledge that Bhutto was a sadist. He beat his wife Nusrat often enough to compel her to wear long-sleeved blouses to hide the marks of injuries and at least once drove her to such despair as to take an overdose of sleeping tablets. He was at once an aristocratic wadhera (landlord) and a gentleman in the European mould, and a guttersnipe using language worthy of an urban hoodlum. Many people told me that when he lost his temper, which was often, he used epithets like haramzada (bastard), sooer ka baccha (son of a pig) and madarchod (mother-fucker).

Yet another point on which both the pro- and the anti-Bhutto elements were agreed was that if Bhutto had been released and allowed to contest the elections, he would have swept the polls. How then can an outsider make an assessment?

General Zia had given me an appointment for the evening of 4 April. I arrived in Rawalpindi two days earlier. Our Press Counsellor O. P. Khanna drove me round the Central Jail where Bhutto was housed. It is a fortress-like square structure situated between the airport and the President's House once occupied by Bhutto. The place bristled with barbed wire, soldiers and armed police. It was cold enough, and the thought of an unshaven Zulfie squatting on the damp floor of a dark dingy cell awaiting the hangman sent a shiver down my spine. Hadn't he said that when he died, the Himalayas would shed tears? And so it seemed. By the time we got to Islamabad (fifteen kilometres from Rawalpindi), a fine drizzle was coming down.

There were over a hundred foreign journalists and newsreel cameramen in the Holiday Inn. They were hunched over cups of black coffee like vultures on the parapet of some abattoir. The presiding genius was Mark Tully of the BBC. Where and how he picked up news of what Zulfie was doing in his cell, who saw him at what time and what they said to each other, remains a mystery. But the first thing everyone said after good morning or hello was, 'Did you hear Mark Tully on the BBC?' General Zia's bureaucrats hated him, the staff of the Holiday Inn loved him; we journalists envied him.

I had nothing much to do. So Khanna and I went off to see *Khak aur Khoon* a much-lauded film on the Partition theme produced by a government agency. I was sorely disappointed at its crudely propagandist approach to the great tragedy. All the angels were on the side of the god-fearing Muslims; almost all the devils on the side of the Hindus and Sikhs. It exploited the stereotype notion of the cunning Hindu Bania with Rashtriya Swayamsevak Sangh (RSS) sympathies paying the simple-minded Sikh to murder Muslims. I only saw half the film—but that was bad enough. I was told the second half was much worse. Apparently, our Embassy had lodged a protest against this wilful falsification of history and the harmful effects it would have on the minds of young Pakistanis. In an already depressing atmosphere, this film made me even more depressed.

That evening, in the house of the Lambahs, a young couple in the Indian Embassy, roused my spirits. There were lots of Pakistani journalists with their wives and girlfriends. Warm, friendly and a good-looking bunch they were too. The topic of conversation was restricted: one question and two answers. Will Zia hang Bhutto? Answers: Yes, he will. Or, no, he won't. Most agreed that General Zia need not have put himself in the predicament he found himself in: where there was neither room to move nor to stand—Na jai raftan, na pai mandan.

ONE DAY BEFORE THE HANGING
The chill rain and wind blew all morning. In the afternoon I called on Abdul Hafeez Pirzada at Piracha House, once occupied by Nusrat and Benazir Bhutto. Their pictures were on the walls. Pirzada, who was a minister in Bhutto's cabinet, was convinced that Bhutto would not be hanged. Mumtaz Bhutto, Zulfie's cousin, came in looking dishevelled and out of sorts. He had waited half an hour in the rain at the jail gates and had not been let in.

Shankar Bajpai, the Indian ambassador in Islamabad, returned from briefing Delhi on the situation in Pakistan. I recalled that a year ago he had told me that General Zia would hang Bhutto. He had not changed his opinion. It was heartening to discover that the diplomatic corps in Islamabad regarded Bajpai and his team the best informed on Pakistani affairs. When I told him about my conversation with Pirzada, he brushed it away with a wave of his hand and repeated, 'They will hang him for sure; when I cannot tell...' I tried to solicit the views of Lady Vicky Noon and Miandad Aurangzeb, Wali of Swat and his wife Begum Naseem, daughter of the late General Ayub Khan. Like seasoned diplomats they parried my questions.

4 APRIL 1979
I rose at 5 a.m. The sky was an azure blue, the Margalla Hills looked washed and green. 'What a beautiful morning!' I said to myself, 'Allah is in His heaven and all is right with Pakistan.' Was it? I heard the sputter

of motorcycles. Fifty men in air force grey-and-white spats took their places in front of the hotel. They were followed by jeeps loaded with soldiers. The hotel was surrounded on all sides. I sent for coffee. I asked the waiter if he had any news. He said that he had heard that the jail and the airport had been cordoned off at night and people were saying that the worst had happened. He added the words 'Bahut ziatee hooee' (too much) and 'zulum hua'. Neither the English nor the Urdu papers mentioned anything on the subject. Had Zulfie been taken to Lahore for the final act? I rang up Bajpai. As usual he knew. He had heard over the Voice of America (it had beaten the BBC) that Bhutto had been executed at 2 a.m. in Rawalpindi. But he had no confirmation. I was chilled to the bone.

I went down to the dining room to join the vultures' club. It was true. Zulfie was dead. His body had been flown to be interred in the family graveyard in village Naudero near Larkana. By then a new story was in circulation viz., that the Chinese Air Force had come to plead with General Zia to let them take Zulfie away to be confined for life in China but the general had jumped the gun by hanging him. The men in uniform outside the hotel were to escort the Chinese back to the airport.

Khanna and I drove to Rawalpindi to see if anything was happening. All seemed normal—if you can describe streets bristling with soldiers and policemen as normal. Most shops were open, people were going about their business. But there was an atmosphere of fear and sullen resentment: supplements of *Jang* announcing the execution were selling fast; people lowered their voices when they talked; not even hawkers cried out their wares. I saw four men being led away in handcuffs: they may have been thieves.

There was some action in the afternoon. As the prayers ended people formed a procession: burqa-clad women in front, the men behind them. They raised slogans: 'Zia kutta! Hai! Hai!' and 'Zulfikar Ali Bhutto, zindabad!' Four policewomen who faced the women protesters were brushed aside. Policemen retreated before the marchers: Pakistani men have an exaggerated respect for the burqa-clad which they do not have for the unveiled. Tear gas bombs exploded, the marchers broke ranks and fled. Some men were apprehended (not Mumtaz Bhutto or Pirzada), offices of *Jang* were put to the flames. An American cameraman had his leg blown off. An army captain riding a motorcycle was knocked down and almost beaten to death by the mob. That was all.

My friend Rehman called me from Lahore. He said nothing had happened in the city. The BBC news reported otherwise. Suneet Aiyar called from Karachi and said nothing had happened in Karachi. The BBC report said otherwise.

My appointment with General Zia scheduled for that evening was cancelled. That was understandable. But the order that no journalists were to leave Islamabad to visit other cities was hard to accept. The pitch had been queered by *Nawa-i-Waqt* stating that the BBC and All India Radio were, between them, causing all the mischief in Pakistan.

THE DAY AFTER

The next day at a luncheon given for me by the *Pakistan Times* there were over forty journalists present. It was strange that the same people who for months had talked of little besides what Zia would do to Bhutto now talked of the weather. My statement, that Zia had committed a political blunder and Bhutto's ghost would haunt Pakistan for many years to come, elicited no response whatsoever.

They did not stop me from leaving Islamabad. The Pak Airways plane was packed. I arrived in Karachi on Friday, 8 April. They expected demonstrations after jumma prayers. At my request our consul-general, Mani Shankar Aiyar, and his Sikh wife Suneet, drove me round the city. All shops were shut because Friday is a public holiday. But we passed many open spaces where boys were playing cricket or hockey. We passed the grand Memon Masjid and the huge single-domed air-conditioned mosque. The congregations had dispersed and everything was peaceful—as peaceful as the grave. I was told that Karachi had never been for Bhutto.

At Karachi I met Sardar Sherbaz Khan Mazari, leader of the PDF in Baluchistan, Khuhro who had once been chief minister of Sindh, and Pesh Imam, secretary-general of Air Marshal Asghar Khan's Tehrik-e-Istiqlal party. The fate of poor Zulfie did not exercise their minds very much. Mazari was concerned with the repression of the Baluchis by Bhutto. The Khuhros (particularly their Cambridge-educated daughter Hamida) with how the Sindhis had suffered at the hands of the Urdu-speaking mulhajareen (refugee settlers), a body pejoratively described as tiligars (starlings—because they chitter so much) from Uttar Pradesh and Bihar and the arrogant, bullying Punjabis. Pesh Imam felt that the PPP had disintegrated, the people disenchanted with backward looking mullahs of the numerous jamats and the future beckoned the Tehrik. The few journalists I met in Karachi dismissed the Tehrik as of no consequence.

The breakdown of Pakistan's political parties almost sounded feudal. The PDF, in power in Baluchistan and the NWFP, is dominated by baronial landlords, the jamats by the Muslim clergy and the Tehrik by men in the professions. The only doubtful factor is Bhutto's PPP. Now that Zulfie has become a martyr, his widow Nusrat or daughter Benazir may emerge as leaders invoking the spirit of their dead man.

◆

The curtain rose for the final act in the drama of Zulfikar Ali Bhutto's life at 8.30 a.m. on 18 March 1978. The scene was the main courtroom of the High Court of Lahore. It is a large hall divided into three by two sets of wooden railings. On the northern end sitting at a higher level were five judges in their wigs and black gowns. Facing them in the main body of the hall were members of the High Court Bar including counsels for the prosecution and the defence likewise attired in black. Behind them separated by another railing were members of the public. And on the western wing, alongside the judges and the lawyers, stood the five accused with an armed police escort behind them. Chief amongst them was Zulfikar Ali Bhutto, impeccably dressed in a light spring suit and sporting a tie.

No prior notice had been given of this day of judgement. The lawyers engaged in the case had been rung up by the registrar in the early hours and asked to be present in the main room. The accused were brought in from Kot Lakhpat jail in the Black Maria under heavy escort. Word had however got round and the courtroom was packed.

All eyes were turned on acting chief justice, Mushtaq Hussain. He read a summary of the unanimous verdict of the five judges in the case of the murder of Nawab Mohammed Raza Kasuri on the night of 10–11 November 1974 at Lahore. All the accused had pleaded not guilty. Four had presented their defence. Only one, Zulfikar Ali Bhutto, had refused to take part in the proceedings.

Justice Mushtaq Hussain finished reading the findings of the panel of judges and proceeded to pass the sentence 'to be hanged by the neck till you are dead'.

All eyes turned from the judges to the accused—mainly to Zulfikar Ali Bhutto. He heard the sentence without flinching and simply turned his face away from the judges. He was lost in his own thoughts. 'You could see that he was stunned,' said one of the lawyers, 'but he showed no sign of fear or anger, it seemed as if he had not heard the judge. Or believed it was some kind of grim charade he was witnessing.'

There were no slogans of any kind, no expression of approval or disgust. Neither Bhutto's wife Nusrat nor his daughter Benazir was in court. And armed police were all over the place.

Lawyers representing the four other accused went over to them for consultation; Bhutto, having boycotted the high court proceedings, had no one to talk to him and remained lost in himself for some time.

Back in Kot Lakhpat jail, six rooms had been reserved for Bhutto. He went straight to his bedroom and flopped on it fully dressed. He had his eyes fixed on the ceiling. 'He lay there for an hour or more without moving,' says a warder. 'Only when I approached him and asked him if he would like to eat something, I noticed he had been crying. He did not answer me.'

At 11 a.m. the lawyer Yahya Bakhtiar came to visit him. The two men embraced each other and broke down: 'Is this the end?' asked Bhutto. 'No,' replied Bakhtiar emphatically. 'We shall appeal against the sentence.' They talked for quite some time. Bhutto's spirits were revived and he was more himself.

According to jail rules, prisoners condemned to death have to be lodged in specially designed cells on which constant watch can be maintained to prevent inmates from taking their own lives. Only in the morning and evening are they let out for half an hour to take tehlaee (exercise).

At 5 p.m. Bhutto was removed to a condemned cell—but at his insistence he was allowed to wear his own clothes, keep his own bed and chair and eat his own food. He was given writing material and got all the magazines and newspapers he desired. The mood of depression descended on him again and according to a jail warder, 'He lay on his bed like a dead rat.' This lasted for a couple of days.

It seems that the appeals of clemency from different heads of state published in the papers revived his sagging spirits. He began to believe that the chorus of protests from all parts of the world would deter the courts and rulers of Pakistan from doing him harm and all the exercise was to break his morale. He resolved to show no sign of cracking under the strain.

Yahya Bakhtiar filed the appeal in the Supreme Court. Since the court was located in Rawalpindi, in mid-May, Bhutto and his co-accused were transferred to the jail in Rawalpindi—ironically alongside the very mansion from which only a few months earlier he had ruled Pakistan. A set of four rooms normally reserved for women convicted of murder were prepared for him. He had a bedroom, a study, a bathroom and a kitchen—all to himself. Once again jail regulations were overlooked in order to make the distinguished prisoner comfortable. He was given a niwar bed instead of a hospital-type steel bed, a rubber-foam mattress, his own blankets, and a fan and light with the switchboard within his reach. He was also furnished with a table, chair, table-lamp, books and magazines. His food and his Havana cigars came from his home. He wore his own clothes (he had two suitcases full of them) and used his own shaving kit. He was allowed an hour everyday with his counsel and could take his half-hour of tehlaee at times of his own choosing. Since winters in Rawalpindi are sharp, he was provided with electric heaters. His wife and daughter joined him for tea in the afternoon. Very often, Benazir lay on the same bed with her father and the two talked in whispers to avoid being overheard by the ever-present warders and to ensure their dialogue was not recorded by bugging devices.

On 6 February 1979 the Supreme Court dismissed Bhutto's appeal. He was not present in court. The news was conveyed by the jail superintendent. His only comment was: 'This is very sad,' followed by a question, 'Was it unanimous?' The superintendent without checking replied, 'Yes.' Bhutto remarked, 'That is very surprising.'

When the news reached Nusrat Bhutto at Sihala (fifteen miles from Pindi) where she was under house arrest, she got into a car, broke through the police cordon and stormed up to the jail gates. She was allowed to meet her husband. She collapsed in her husband's arms. When she came to, the first question he asked her was, 'Was it unanimous?' Nusrat told him that of the seven judges of the Supreme Court three had given him the benefit of the doubt. 'Don't worry!' he assured her. 'We will go in for a review.'

Once the death sentence had been confirmed, the jail authorities decided to treat Bhutto as they treated other convicts under sentence of death. They took away his shaving kit, removed the niwar bed (niwar can be used to hang oneself) and stopped home food. Bhutto refused to eat jail food and refused to lie on the hospital bed. Instead, he spread the rubber foam mattress on the floor: it was to be his bed till the last day. By the afternoon, the government relented and let him have home-cooked food.

◆

On 24 March 1979 the Supreme Court rejected the review petition. The last ray of hope was extinguished. Yahya Bakhtiar's role as Bhutto's lawyer was over but he requested the court to let him see Bhutto. The prosecution represented by M. A. Rehman made no objection. Outside the courtroom Yahya Bakhtiar told waiting pressmen that there were grounds for a second review petition. Meanwhile, the superintendent of the jail wrote a formal memorandum to Bhutto informing him of the confirmation of the death sentence and telling him that he had seven days to make a petition for mercy. When he took it to Bhutto and asked him to sign on the carbon copy, he refused to do so and dismissed him brusquely, 'Yes, yes, I know all about it.'

The next day (25 March 1979) the Lahore High Court issued a 'Black' warrant to the five convicted men, specifying that they were liable to be executed after 4 April 1979. The exact date was kept a secret.

Bhutto was allowed to receive as many relatives and friends as he wished to receive. His first wife, Begum Ameer, uncles, cousins including Mumtaz Bhutto, and erstwhile cabinet colleague, Hafeez Pirzada, were amongst the many who came to see him. All visitors were searched and no one was allowed inside the cell; a six-foot-wide table was placed in front of the iron grill to prevent physical contact (or the passing of cyanide or other poison).

One night Bhutto sent for the deputy superintendent of the jail and asked him to send for Hafeez Pirzada. Bhutto made no specific request to Pirzada to appeal for mercy but the words he used, 'Marna bahut mushkil hota hai' (Dying is not easy), and the fact that Pirzada did in fact file a petition after his last meeting on 1 April 1979 indicates that Bhutto, without relenting from his determination never to beg for his life, still hoped that somehow, someone would make General Zia hold his hand. While leaving the jail Pirzada was asked by pressmen whether Bhutto had made an appeal for mercy. He replied, 'No, he has not. But I will do so.'

Pirzada appealed to President Zia to spare Bhutto's life. His appeal was widely published but there was no comment from the President's office.

The decision to execute Bhutto on 4 April was taken two days earlier (2 April). Rules required that executions take place at 5.30 a.m. (or 6 a.m. in winter)—but the hour was fixed at 2 a.m. to avoid demonstrations and give time to have the body flown to Larkana and interred in the family graveyard in village Naudero. Meanwhile, the hangman Tara Masih was brought from Bahawalpur to Lahore. There was speculation that the condemned man might be taken to Kot Lakhpat jail to be executed.

On 3 April 1979, Nusrat and Benazir Bhutto were brought from Sihala to Rawalpindi jail at 11 a.m. They demanded to be told whether or not this was to be their last meeting. They received an evasive reply: 'Aap yeh hee samajh le' (You may take it as so). When the wife and daughter told Bhutto of it, he sent for the jail superintendent and received confirmation that as far as mulakaats (meetings) were concerned this was to be the aakhree (last). The exact hour when the hanging would take place was not divulged.

Nusrat and Benazir spent three hours with Bhutto talking across the table. For once Bhutto was indiscreet and gave instructions about some papers which he had secreted away behind the walls in his Larkana house. Within four hours the house was searched and the papers recovered.

♦

There are heart-rending accounts of this last meeting between Bhutto and his wife and daughter. Benazir's request to let her embrace her father or at least touch his feet before going was firmly turned down. A silver salver in which tea was served to Bhutto was handed back to her with the words 'Ab sahib ko iskee zaroorat nahin padegee (The sahib will not be needing this any more).' It was obvious that the hour of doom was near. Nusrat and Benazir left the jail around 2.30 p.m. and demanded to be taken to see President Zia-ul-Haq. The superintendent rang up the president's house and was told to tell the ladies to put whatever they wanted to say on paper.

At 4 p.m. a magistrate arrived with writing material and asked Bhutto to write his last will which he would attest for him. Bhutto spent an hour or more writing out his last message. No one will ever know what he wrote because with his own cigar lighter he burnt the paper to ashes.

At 6 p.m. he asked for hot water and his shaving set, saying, 'I don't want to die looking like a mullah.' And after he had erased the growth on his chin he looked into the mirror and remarked in self-mockery, 'Now I look like a third-world leader.'

A maulvi arrived with a tasbih (rosary) and a musalla (prayer mat) to assist Bhutto in his last prayers. Bhutto put the rosary round his neck but told the maulvi to remove the prayer mat and himself as he did not need anyone's assistance to meet his Maker. Then the bravado went out of him. He lay down on the mattress and went into a kind of coma. As the time of execution drew near other inmates of the jail were woken up and ordered to chant verses from the holy Quran. Only Bhutto remained impervious to the goings-on. At 1.30 a.m. jail officials accompanied by a magistrate and doctor arrived to take him out on his last journey to the scaffold. The superintendent shook him and said 'Bhutto sahib, janey ka waqt aa gaya hai (It is time to go).' There are different versions of what followed. According to one, Bhutto was roused and as soon as he saw the men with handcuffs, he panicked. He tried various ploys to play for time: he wanted to take a bath, write his will, have a cup of tea. But all were firmly but politely denied to him. According to the second version, he refused to be woken up. The superintendent feared that he had taken his own life and sent for the doctor. The doctor felt his pulse, heard his heartbeat through his stethoscope and opened his eyelids to make sure that he was alive. In either case, he was unable or unwilling to get up and had to be put on a stretcher. Since he was supine his hands were cuffed in front instead of behind him as prescribed for condemned men on their last journey.

Extensive precautions had been taken against possible attempts to storm the jail: names of the Palestine Liberation Organization and even some foreign governments were whispered as likely to make a desperate bid to save Bhutto. Precautions taken included look-outs for parachutists and hostile helicopters. Consequently, a very large number of defence personnel were present in the jail at the time. It is estimated that upwards of 250 men saw the execution with their own eyes.

◆

The scaffold is quite a distance from the condemned cell. The party with Bhutto on the stretcher arrived at the foot of the gallows at about 1.45 a.m. As the stretcher was put down and the superintendent approached Bhutto, he suddenly sat up. He mumbled some words which were interpreted as, 'Nusrat will be left alone'. When the handcuffs were unlocked and his hands tied behind him, he is reported to have protested that the knot was too tight. Then without assistance he went up the steps to the gallows. Before Tara Masih put the black hood over his face, Bhutto's lips moved. According to one version, he mumbled 'Finish it!' According to another, his lips moved but no sound came from them. The trap was sprung exactly at 2 a.m. and the dapper, flamboyant Zulfie, once President and Prime Minister of Pakistan and next to Jinnah, its most popular leader (Qaid-i-Awam), plunged to his doom.

At the time of his death, Bhutto was dressed in salwar kameez which he had elevated to the status of an awami suit. He had a gold Zenith watch on his wrist and a gold ring with three diamonds on his finger. After Hayat Mohammed, a humble servitor in a Pindi mosque, had bathed his corpse and draped it in a shroud, somebody noticed that the diamond-studded ring was missing. The superintendent immediately arrested Tara Masih and Hayat Mohammed and ordered them to be searched. The ring was found in the pocket of the hangman, Tara Masih. Both the watch and the ring were handed over to Benazir Bhutto the next morning.

The body was flown to Larkana and then taken to Naudero. Bhutto's first wife, Begum Ameer, his uncles, aunts and other relatives were allowed to see the dead man's face. It was serene and calm as if in deep slumber with no visible marks of injury save a gash in the neck. (There is no truth in the story that men who are hanged have their necks elongated and their eyes and tongues hang out.)

Bhutto's execution will wipe out memories of his evil deeds and highlight some of the good he did for his country. He is already being acclaimed as a martyr. There are reports of people going to his grave to offer fateha for the peace of his soul. Many are reported to kiss the grave, pick up the dust about the grave and smear it on their foreheads.

In every hamlet, village, town and city stretching from the Khyber to Karachi, groups gather to offer ghaibana namaz-i-janaza (funeral prayers in the absence of the body). Bhutto's ghost has already emerged from its tomb; it will not be long before it turns the illusory dreams of power of the ruling generals into a nightmare.

SINGULAR
PEOPLE

MAHATMA GANDHI

PANDIT NEHRU

INDIRA GANDHI

SANJAY GANDHI

KRISHNA MENON

MOTHER TERESA

MADHAV SADASHIV GOLWALKAR

AMRITA SHER-GIL

NIRAD C. CHAUDHURI

R. K. NARAYAN

DOM MORAES

SIR VIDIA

34

MAHATMA GANDHI
(1869–1948)

In the study in my cottage in Kasauli, I have pictures of the people I admire most—one of them is Mahatma Gandhi. I admire Bapu Gandhi more than any other man. Of all the other prophets of the past we have no knowledge. Almost everything about them is myth or miracle. With Gandhi, we know—he walked among us not long ago and there are many people alive, like me, who have seen him. He was always in the public eye. He bared himself; no one was more honest.

I don't accept his foibles. He took a vow of celibacy in his prime, but without consulting his wife, which I think was grossly unfair. He would sleep naked beside young girls to test his brahmacharya. He could be very odd. But his insistence on truth at all times made him a Mahatma. And the principle of ahimsa: not to hurt anyone. Ahimsa and honesty should be the basis of all religion, of every life.

I have been a regular drinker all my adult life. I celebrate sex and cannot say that I have never lied. I have not hurt anyone physically, but I think I have caused hurt with my words and actions. And sometimes there is no forgiveness in me. But I consider myself a Gandhian. Whenever I feel unsure of anything, I try to imagine what Gandhi would have done, and that is what I do.

If only Mahatma Gandhi were alive today, the whole situation of the country would have been different. I don't believe the likes of Anna Hazare can do a thing about corruption in India—his fasting is to no avail. Only Mahatma Gandhi would have been able to arouse mass consciousness to halt the tide of corruption and chaos spreading around us today.

I became a Gandhi bhakta at a young age. I first saw Bapu when I was six or seven years old, when I was studying at Modern School. He had come on a visit. All of us children—there were very few students in the school in those days—sat on the ground in the front row. Bapu bent down and tugged my uniform playfully.

'Beta, yeh kapda kahaan ka hai?' he asked. (Where is this cloth from?)
'Vilayati,' I said with pride. (It was from abroad.)

He told me gently, 'Yeh apne desh ka hota toh acchha hota, nahin?' (It would have been good had this been from our country, wouldn't it?)

Soon after, I started wearing khadi. My mother used to spin khaddar, so it was easy. I continued wearing khaddar for many years. Before I went to London to attend university, I took some khaddar to our tailor because I had been told I would need a proper English suit. The tailor laughed and told my father, who asked me to stop being a khotta (donkey).

◆

Mahatma Gandhi was the one person who seemed to comprehend the grave consequences of the Partition. He did not take part in any of the Independence celebrations. When anti-Pakistan feelings were at fever pitch and the Indian government refused to honour its pledge to pay Pakistan Rs 55 crores, the Mahatma went on a fast and forced the government to abide by its word. He knew he was asking for trouble but did not give it a second thought. A calumny was spread about his having agreed to the partition of India along communal lines. He told his secretary Pyarelal: 'Today I find myself alone. Even the Sardar [Patel] and Jawaharlal Nehru think that my reading of the situation is wrong and peace is sure to return if the partition is agreed upon... I shall perhaps not be alive to witness it, but should the evil I apprehend overtake India and her independence be imperilled, let it not be said that Gandhi was party to India's vivisection.'

◆

I was in London when Mahatma Gandhi was assassinated in Delhi on 30 January 1948. I had taken leave to pack my belongings to proceed to Canada. My wife and I had been invited to lunch by Sir Malcolm Darling, the retired income tax commissioner who lived in a basement flat near Victoria station. As we came out into the cold windy day after lunch, I noted scribbled in hand on a placard by a newspaper stall the message: 'Gandhi assassinated'. I did not believe it could be our Bapu. Who could kill a saintly man who had harmed no one? I asked the stall holder. He had tears in his eyes as he handed me a copy of The *Evening Standard*. 'Yes, mate, some bloody villain's got him,' he said. Tears also welled up in my eyes. I was only able to read the headlines. Instead of going on to the shipping office to confirm our passage, we made our way to India House to be with our people. Oil lamps had been lit at the base of Gandhi's portrait. The smell of aromatic incense pervaded the place. Men and women sat on the floor chanting Gandhi's favourite hymns. 'Vaishnav jan toh tainey kaheeye jo peed paraie jaane rey'—Know him only as a man of God who feels the suffering of others; and 'Ishwar Allah terey naam, sab ko sanmati dey Bhagwan'—Ishwar and Allah are but names of the same God, may His blessings be on us.

Bapu was pretty certain that he would not be allowed to live. At a prayer meeting on 16 June 1947, he said, 'I shall consider myself brave if I am killed and if I still pray to God for my assassin.' As he had anticipated, the assassin finally got him the following year. He went with the name of Ram on his lips—a glorious end to a glorious life.

35

PANDIT NEHRU
(1889–1964)

Pandit Jawaharlal Nehru, it must be said, fully answered the poet Allama Iqbal's requirements of a Meer-e-Kaarvaan—leader of the caravan:

Nigah buland, sukhan dilnawaz, jaan par soz
Yahi hain rakht-e-safar Meer-e-Kaarvaan ke liye

(Lofty vision, winning speech and a warm personality
This is all the baggage the leader of a caravan needs on his journey.)

Nehru should have been the role model for the prime ministers of India. He was above prejudices of any kind: racial, religious or of caste. He was an agnostic and firmly believed that religion played a very negative role in Indian society. What I admired most about him was his secularism. He was a visionary and an exemplary leader; the father of Indian constitutional democracy, of universal adult franchise, the five-year plans and giving equal rights to women, among other things. He was better educated than any of his successors, with the exception of Manmohan Singh, and spent nine long years in jail reading, writing and thinking about the country's future.

But being human, Nehru had his human failings. He was not above political chicanery. Having accepted the Cabinet Mission Plan to hand over power to a united India, he reneged on his undertaking when he realized that Jinnah might end up becoming prime minister. Nehru had blind spots too. He refused to believe that India's exploding population needed to be contained. He refused to see the gathering strength of Muslim separatism, which led to the formation of Pakistan. He failed to come to terms with Pakistan and was chiefly responsible for the mess we made in Jammu and Kashmir. He was also given to nepotism and favouritism. And his love affairs with Shraddha Mata and Lady Mountbatten are well-known. I have been often asked whether the central character of my novel *Burial at Sea* was based on Nehru—you could say that the inspiration for the character was Nehru.

I first met Nehru in London, when I was a press officer at the Indian Embassy, and my first impression of him was that he was short-tempered. He could also be ill-mannered. I once had to host a lunch so that the editors of leading British newspapers could meet him. Halfway through the meal, Nehru fell silent. When questions were put to him, he looked up at the ceiling and did not reply. He then proceeded to light a cigarette while others were still eating. To make matters worse, Krishna Menon fell asleep. It was a disastrous attempt at public relations.

Another time, Nehru arrived in London past midnight. I asked him whether he would like me to accompany him to his hotel. 'Don't be silly,' he said. 'Go home and sleep.' The next morning, one of the papers carried a photo of him with Lady Mountbatten opening the door in her negligee. The photographer had taken the chance of catching them, if not in flagrante delicto, at least in preparation of it, and got his scoop. The huge caption read: 'Lady Mountbatten's Midnight Visitor'. Nehru was furious. On another occasion, he had taken Lady Mountbatten for a quiet dinner at a Greek restaurant. Once again, the following morning's papers carried photographs of them sitting close to each other. Our prime minister's liaison with Lady Edwina had assumed scandalous proportions, and I knew I was in trouble.

I arrived at the office to find a note from Krishna Menon on my table, saying that the prime minister wished to see me immediately.

I gently knocked on the prime minister's door and went in. He was busy going through some files.

'Yes?' he said, raising his head.

'Sir, you sent for me. '

'I sent for you? Who are you?'

'I am your PRO in London, sir,' I replied.

He looked me up and down. 'You have a strange notion of publicity,' he said curtly.

I thought it best to remain silent.

36

INDIRA GANDHI
(1917–1984)

Indira Gandhi has had more ups and downs in her sixty-three years than any other woman: her childhood and adolescence overshadowed by giants, her middle years blighted by insinuations that she had inherited a domain she did not deserve; then suddenly pedestalled to supreme heights, worshipped by the masses as a goddess reincarnated, execrated by the elite as the female incarnation of the devil and a fascist dictator. In a handful she inspires dread, in the remaining millions she raises hope as the nation's redeemer. These are different facets of this one woman. Age has not withered her nor custom staled her infinite variety.

Friends who are under the impression that I know Indira Gandhi well often ask me: 'What is she really like as a person?' My answer, based on scraps of information picked up from people who see her everyday and from my own observations, run somewhat as follows: She is very likeable if you are on her right side. Icily aloof if you are not. For those on her right side she can produce a smile which will dissolve a stone statue. For those who have incurred her displeasure she can be the reincarnation of Durga: few people have developed the technique of snubbing into as fine an art as she. An Indira-snub will rankle for years. And woe betide anyone who tries to appear familiar or spreads canards about being close to her. She is close to no one except herself. And next to herself she is closest to her younger son, Sanjay, only because they share a common interest in politics. The elder, Rajiv, does not share this interest and therefore sees less of her than his brother. Almost as if to compensate for the uneven distribution of closeness between her sons, she is closer to Rajiv's wife, Sonia, who has no interest in politics than to Sanjay's wife, Maneka, who is totally absorbed in it. She is inordinately fond of her grandchildren. Her seven-person family (an eighth is on the way) is as closely-knit as any traditional Hindu joint family. Whatever tensions they have are resolved without a whisper being heard outside. She sets no store by friendship and has therefore never bothered to cultivate any. She suffers expressions of friendship for what they are worth and is a little perturbed when those who had protested their friendship turn against her. Her circle of acquaintances embraces the entire world.

Indira Gandhi has no set routine because she is hardly ever in the same place for more than a few days at a stretch. When she is in residence in Delhi, she rises well before dawn. Since she keeps her bedroom bolted from the inside, even members of the household do not know what she does in the first two hours of the morning. As her bedroom is crammed with books, it can be presumed she reads, writes letters and works on speeches she has to make that day. She is very punctilious about her health and spends fifteen to twenty minutes, morning and evening, doing yogic asanas. The secret of her physical vitality and freedom from tension in a tension-ridden life lies in the half-hour in the care of her body. The newspapers are brought in with morning tea at 6 a.m. She does no more than scan the headlines. She has neither time nor patience to read magazines and has some kind of inhibition against reading anything about herself. She picks up news, comments and political gossip from the hundreds of people who see her every day. Very frequently she has one of her secretaries read out important clippings to her while she is working on her files. One thing she does not like to miss is arranging flowers brought in by the mali. Flower arrangement has always been her passion.

The family try to be together at meals. This is not very easy as their daily schedules are as different as their culinary tastes. They manage to combine both at the breakfast table. Thereafter begin the day's hectic activities. By the time Indira Gandhi emerges on to the front verandah, a couple of hundred people who have been let in are scattered about the lawns and under the flowing chorisia tree facing the house. Several hundred others await their turn outside the gates. She receives a few in her sparsely furnished sitting room. It has a couple of sofas and four armchairs. One of these in a corner is designated as 'madam's chair'—no one else might sit in it. Above her head on the wall is a photograph of her father by Karsh. A long glass-topped table bears a bowl of flowers and an ash tray. Presiding over the room from above the fireplace is a long, rectangular green and white painting of a young boy playing the flute with a dove perched on his shoulders. This is by the Mexican artist, Rafael Navarro. There is a smaller painting of Gandhiji and Tagore by Jamini Roy; two etchings in sepia: one of Amber Fort and the other of the tomb of Muhammad Tughlaq by an unknown English artist. It is in the same drawing room that her inner cabinet of advisers and small delegations meet her. Between these confabulations she comes out to greet the assembled crowd, to be garlanded and photographed with them. On an average between 500 to 2,000 people have themselves photographed with her every day. She is said to have wistfully remarked: 'I have become one of the sights of Delhi.' In recent months, flower sellers, ice cream vendors and chaatwalas have established themselves outside 12, Willingdon Crescent to cater to the crowds that come to see her.

The morning ends with lunch with the family. It is usually a dal-chawal-roti affair served in thalis and seldom eaten in one go. In between courses, Indira Gandhi darts in and out of the room to dispose of a visitor, give instructions to her secretary, R. K. Dhawan. Most of Indira Gandhi's diet consists of small savouries. Of Indian cuisines her favourite is the Gujarati khakhra. She is not vegetarian but often, for reasons best known to her, abstains from fish, fowl, and flesh for months on end. She has no siesta and resumes the tedium of receiving visitors and disposing of files till the late hours of the evening. The evening meal is usually light and European—often cooked Italian style. Visitors and meetings continue late into the night. It is rarely that Indira Gandhi can switch off her bedside reading lamp before midnight. Usually it is between 1 and 2 a.m.—and not infrequently at 3 a.m.

'I have never met anyone who has this enormous capacity for work as Indiraji,' says R. K. Dhawan. 'After retiring at 3 a.m. she is up by six and in the office at eight attending to her files and correspondence. None of the chief ministers and governors who accompanied her on her state visits could stand the pace she set and were exhausted in a couple of days. Madam...never. After her visit they needed a few days off to recover. In the eighteen years I have been with her, I have never known her to complain of overwork. She once told me "tiredness is a state of mind; if you think you are tired, you get tired. If you don't think about it you never tire".'

Indira Gandhi drives herself to the utmost of her capacity, often doing two things at the same time. While she is reading a file she will get one of her secretaries to read out the news or brief her on a totally unrelated topic; her eyes scan the print, her ears take in the speech, her mind comprehends both. She is a great stickler for detail. Not only does she dot all the i's and cross all the t's in her speeches, when she goes abroad she prepares all the menus for the banquets she has to give to return the hospitality of her hosts.

Everyone who has seen her is struck by the neatness of her appearance and her excellent taste in clothes. She obviously takes great pains over her appearance. Her hair is well-coiffured, the distinct swathe of white which runs upwards from the middle of her forehead gives her a touch of the regal. Without having to wear a crown she looks every inch the Empress of India. She is at once the most simply and most elegantly dressed woman one can see anywhere. She wears no make-up or perfume and, apart from the rudraksha necklace, wears no jewellery of any kind. Her saris as well as her salwar kameez and shawls are made of coarse, handspun cottons or silks available at the Khadi Bhandars. She chooses her own clothes and has her shirts and blouses stitched under her own supervision. Most of her saris are of light pastel shades. In any party of women gaudily attired in brocades and chiffons, dripping with gold and diamonds, Indira Gandhi stands out as the one dressed simply but in impeccable taste.

Unlike the common run of Indian politicians, Indira Gandhi rarely talks about herself or indulges in gossip about others. But she is not averse to listening to gossip as long as she is not brought into it. I recall once making an adverse remark about Jatti and asking her what made her choose such a nondescript character to be Vice President of India. Her answer was a frozen stare. I never again took the liberty of soliciting her views on anyone. Her favourite pastime is to recount anecdotes of her early days with her parents and the celebrities she has met. She has few other interests. She has no time to indulge in music or going to dance recitals. She never watches television and only once or twice in the year goes to see a movie—an English, never a Hindi, movie.

Indira Gandhi provides very poor copy to journalists but can be a most rewarding person to have as a guest. Unlike most of her countrymen who see no discourtesy in keeping their hosts and other guests waiting for hours, Indira Gandhi will turn up on the expected minute. And unlike other important Indians who are totally absorbed in their own importance, Indira Gandhi is observant, will discuss children and clothes with women, speak words of appreciation to the cook and take care to talk to everyone in the party. She honoured my home on a few occasions to meet foreign correspondents posted in Delhi.

She missed nothing about my little apartment. I had lit oil lamps around the stone Ganapati at the entrance. She sensed this had been done in her honour. She examined it, asked how old it was and pronounced it beautiful. She went round the shelves looking at the books. She examined old maps on the walls (I have a collection of sixteenth-century maps of India) and all the paintings. A large photograph of the interior of the Madurai temple taken by my friend T. S. Nagarajan attracted her attention. 'That's a very good photograph,' she remarked. 'If you like good photographs I'll show you a better one in my study,' I said. In my study was the framed cover of an issue of *The Illustrated Weekly of India* with three faces of Indira Gandhi in different moods. A faint blush of a compliment accepted spread on her face. She made no comment but it obviously put her in a happy mood. Even when Peter Niesewand of *The Guardian* and Mark Tully of the BBC (who reminded her that she had had him expelled from India during the Emergency) tried to bait her, she refused to rise to their baits and remained cool and smiling.

I had gone to some trouble in getting a bottle of sherry as I had been told by a retired ambassador with whom she had stayed in Tokyo on an official visit that it was the only alcoholic drink that she took. 'Where on earth did you get the idea that I take sherry?' she demanded. I told her. 'Absolute rubbish! I have never touched any alcohol in my life. Since everyone offers it abroad at every party and if you say "I don't drink" they want to know why, I usually take a glass of sherry and keep it beside me throughout the party. It saves me from having to argue about it.'

The evening passed very pleasantly. Some of the correspondents were pretty rough with Sanjay. 'Do you want to become prime minister of India?' I heard someone ask him. He kept his cool and replied, 'I haven't given the prospect much thought.' After Indira Gandhi and Sanjay had left, the other guests stayed on, discussing the mother and son over coffee and cognac. 'She's charming! She's gracious! You can hardly believe she can cope with these ruffianly politicians she has to deal with!' were some of the comments they made. Even Sanjay came in for many compliments: 'He's all there! Heard so much against him, I couldn't believe this polite young fellow was the same man! But he has a hard streak in him…like someone who's been hurt.' And so on.

I also had occasion to see Indira Gandhi at several embassy receptions. She was invariably the greatest draw wherever she went. No sooner had the President or Vice President been ushered in with the fanfare of national anthems, they were left to themselves and the guests swarmed around Indira Gandhi. Even if the ambassadors maintained diplomatic aloofness, their wives and children clustered round her to be photographed with her. At an Iftar party at the Kuwait Embassy, the ambassador's young son insisted on shaking her by the hand. 'I want you to be prime minister of India again,' he said gushing with enthusiasm.

'And why do you want me to be prime minister?' asked Indira Gandhi.

'Because I want to have my Coca Cola again!'

Another trait that marks Indira Gandhi as very different from other Indian politicians is that she measures every word she speaks. Experience has taught her never to commit herself in words which might be misconstrued when repeated. Even to a direct question her answer is never a straight 'Yes' or 'No'. Very often the answer is a blank stare that leaves one guessing. It is often alleged that she who is so astute in judging political situations, is a poor judge of people and is kaan ki kacchi—soft in the ear and influenced by gossip. There is little doubt that although she has the gift of passionate intuition about situations, it does not extend to an insight into human character. She is known to extend her patronage generously to people of little substance. She has often no better reason for doing so than a woman's reason: 'I think him so, because I think him so.'

It had so often mystified me how so many men and women, picked out of nowhere and put on the national stage, disowned her in times of crisis. The answer often given is that Indira Gandhi does not have the human warmth of the kind her father had; she is also said to be unusually suspicious of people's motives and therefore unable to command the sort of loyalty that held colleagues to Pandit Nehru despite his quick and explosive temper. R. K. Dhawan who has served both the father and the daughter has a different view: 'Nehru took the PM's chair when he was already a national hero. He could provide all the ambitious politicians and civil servants with jobs vacated by the British. Nehru also had no occasion to test the loyalties of these people because he never faced a real challenge to his leadership. It was different for Indira. By the time she took her father's place all the posts had been filled: the ambitions of ambitious men and women serving under her could not be fully realized. The sense of patriotism that had fired Nehru's generation had also vanished. Many of those that Indiraji raised to situations of importance either became frustrated because they could go no further or succumbed to temptations and had much to hide. Whenever Indiraji's position as a leader was questioned and they felt she might lose, they went over to what they felt was the winning side either to realize their unfulfilled ambitions or to get away with their misdeeds.' Dhawan is right. If you go over the list of ditchers and examine the circumstances in which they deserted her you will see that one of the two caps—unfulfilled ambition or corruption—fits their skulls.

They say Nehru was quick to temper and was sometimes unable to control his fits of rage. But these fits went as soon as they came and he never bore a grudge for too long. They say that Indira seldom loses her temper but once she is put off by a person she never forgives him or her. There is little truth to this. She seldom loses her cool and never raises her voice. What her father did with angry words she does with a deftly administered snub. But like her father, she also does not harbour a grievance for too long. In her political work, which includes collections of funds for her party, she has always had to trust people with the job to act on her behalf. Many have in the process lined their own pockets. She has borne with them patiently and when convinced of their corruption, quietly relieved them of the task without any fanfare.

It is no exaggeration to say that Indira's moods have often made and unmade the careers of people about her. Shibli wrote about this kind of awesome power to mould the destinies of the state in his lines to Noor Jehan, wife of Emperor Jehangir:

Us ki peyshani-i-nazuk peh jo parhti thi girah
Ja ke ban jati thi avraq-i-hakoomat peh shikan

When, in displeasure, wrinkles appeared on her forehead,
They were translated into commandments in documents of state.

37

SANJAY GANDHI
(1946–1980)

I have been criticized and attacked more often than most people I know. It does not bother me; I ignore it all or laugh it off. The one criticism I have faced that I take seriously is to do with my support for Sanjay Gandhi. In 1975, after Mrs Gandhi declared Emergency in the country, I ran a cover story in the Independence Day issue of *The Illustrated Weekly* on her second son and partner-in-politics, Sanjay. I called it 'The Man Who Gets Things Done'. I have never lived this down, but I stand by the story. I believed that Sanjay was what the country needed at the time—a man of action who would bring discipline to public offices, crack down on smugglers, clean up our cities and, most important, take serious steps to control our explosive population growth. I believed that he was doing all those things and I supported him, perhaps blindly. Outside the moment, it is easy to see the full picture.

I met Sanjay in the mid-1970s when he was already unpopular among intellectuals and many of my fellow liberals who saw him as an extra-constitutional power and a potential tyrant. When I met him, I found him to be reasonable and courteous. He was the one who had called the meeting. He wanted to talk to me about his Maruti car business and wanted me to write about it. I went with him to the factory site. I was disappointed; it looked like the workshop of a blacksmith. He took me around the site in a prototype of the Maruti car, driving fast and talking about how important the project was. I was more impressed by his passion and enthusiasm than by the physical set-up. It was being said in those days that Haryana's chief minister, Bansi Lal, had given Sanjay land for free for his factory. I found these allegations to be false. Sanjay had paid a fair price. I wrote this in my story on Maruti. That was how our association began. We became friends.

Sanjay was good-looking. He had an eye for pretty girls, but the good sense not to get carried away. He was also a teetotaller, but not self-righteous. Always polite, Sanjay sought me out for company and advice. I was flattered. Our friendship was strengthened after his marriage to Maneka, whose family I knew. They made a handsome couple. I was past sixty then and, like many people reaching old age, I enjoyed the attention of young and spirited people.

Since I also had a good equation with Mrs Gandhi in those days,

I was dubbed the Gandhis' chamcha, especially when I supported the Emergency. Even now, after all these years, I think the Emergency was necessary, because the Opposition had unleashed chaos and nothing in the country functioned. I had no idea then that it could be and would be misused and abused. Sanjay was always extremely courteous to me, so I found it hard to believe stories about his dictatorial ways. When I first got to know him, he really did seem like a committed man who was always true to his word. He had a conscience. And he was a doer, impatient to bring about changes. Maybe that was what made him dictatorial.

A year or so into the Emergency, he became very unpopular because of the forced nasbandi (sterilization) programme, censorship and arbitrary slum demolitions. It was bruited about that he had ordered bulldozers to raze the jhuggis of innocent people, and that men had been pulled out of buses and cinema halls and forcibly sterilized. Many of these were wild rumours, but it is true that Sanjay and his thuggish friends—they more than he—were beginning to run the country like their fiefdom. Mrs Gandhi had come to depend heavily on her dynamic younger son and had almost handed over the reins of power to him. Nobody could understand the hold he had on her. She both loved and feared him. There is a story that Sanjay once slapped his mother at the dinner table, with outsiders present, and she took it quietly.

What Sanjay did, or was alleged to have done, during the Emergency had given him the image of a monster. He and Maneka came to see me in Bombay shortly after the Congress had been voted out of power, with Mrs Gandhi losing badly in her constituency. When they came to my apartment on Arthur Bunder Road, there were mobs in the streets baying for Sanjay's blood. I had to drive the couple to the airport at some risk.

I stood by the Gandhi family during their days in the doghouse, when they were being persecuted by the Janata Party government, many of whose leaders the Gandhis had persecuted during the Emergency. My family and friends were very critical of me, and I had to face a great deal of flak. I watched with some satisfaction as Mrs Gandhi and Sanjay fought back and won the elections of 1980. But the happiness was brief. On the morning of 23 June 1980, Sanjay crashed his two-seater plane on the southern ridge in Delhi. Both he and his co-pilot, Captain Saxena, were killed. After his tragic death, it was left to his older brother, Rajiv—with whom he had had very little interaction—to support a shattered Indira Gandhi. There is some truth in the belief that she was never quite herself after Sanjay's death.

I liked Sanjay. But I am certain that if he had lived, this country would not have been a democracy. There would have been order and much faster development, but no democracy. I have been asked if, in that case, I would still have supported him. I don't know. He would probably have got around me. He could be a real charmer. Besides, he was a friend, and he had been good to me. It was because of him that I was nominated to the Rajya Sabha. And it was he who called up K.K. Birla and told him to give me the editor's job at the *Hindustan Times*. He did not need to do that, but he did. He was loyal, and so was I.

38

KRISHNA MENON
(1896–1974)

After Partition, I found myself back in London with a job as an information officer with the public relations department of India House. I was to stay with Arthur and Sheila Lall in Knightsbridge until my family arrived and we found a place of our own. Arthur was very taken with Krishna Menon. He assured me that Krishna Menon was the finest brain he had ever met and compared favourably with Stalin (who was not known to have a particularly fine brain). I had briefly met Krishna Menon in my college days and had not detected any signs of genius in him. He was a sour-tempered barrister without briefs and spent his energies building up his India League and paying court to Pandit Nehru whenever he was in England. His appointment as high commissioner was badly received in India and the Indian community in England; people considered it gross favouritism. But after hearing Arthur go on about him, I thought I had perhaps been wrong in my estimate of Menon, or perhaps he had matured into a better man.

I reported for work at India House and introduced myself to Sudhir Ghosh. He didn't seem very pleased to see me. Beneath the glass slab of his working table were a number of photographs and originals of letters exchanged between Gandhi and Sir Stafford Cripps, Gandhi and Prime Minister Attlee, all praising Sudhir Ghosh. It was quite evident that Sudhir was having trouble with Krishna Menon and was not on good terms with Indian journalists. He showed me to the tiny cubicle I was to occupy and introduced me to an English girl, Pamela Cullen, who was to be my assistant. He did not tell me what I was to do. 'You can ask Menon when you meet him,' he said. He studiously avoided calling Menon high commissioner, or even adding a mister to his name.

I had no idea what public relations meant, nor what I was to do to promote them. Not having been briefed or charged with a specific task, I decided that perhaps the best I could do was produce booklets on India—its people, resources, flora, fauna, etc. For the first four days after my arrival in London, I reported for work at India House every morning. I signed the visitors' book and reminded Sudhir Ghosh to introduce me to the high commissioner. He didn't think it was urgent. I asked Arthur. He said it was not for him but Sudhir to do so. However, he told Menon that I had wanted to call on him. On the fifth day, Sudhir Ghosh took me up to Menon's room.

I had a broad grin on my face when I greeted Krishna Menon and extended my right hand. He brushed it aside with his claw-like fingers. Instead of a smile of welcome, he had an angry frown on his face. I cheerfully reminded him that I had once travelled with him and Rajni Patel to Paris. He ignored my self-introduction and barked, 'Sardar, haven't they taught you any manners in India? You have been here four days and haven't had the courtesy to call on me. I am the high commissioner, you know!' My smile froze. I protested I had done my best—signed the visitors' book, and asked both Sudhir Ghosh and Arthur Lall to get me an appointment. Sudhir interrupted to say that it was his fault. 'I'll send for you later,' said Menon, dismissing me. 'I want to speak to Mr Ghosh.'

I returned to my cubicle very shaken. No one had ever spoken to me the way Menon had done and without any reason whatsoever. I was determined not to put up with it. I swore to myself that the next time Menon said anything harsh I would hit back, put in my letter of resignation and tell him to stuff it up his dirty bottom. I was out of sorts all afternoon. Instead of doing any work, I took a long stroll along the Thames embankment till my temper came down a little.

In the evening, there was a tea party in the main reception room. I went, took a cup of tea and sat down in a corner. Menon breezed in; I pretended not to have seen him. He came up to me and put his arm around my shoulders. 'Sorry for ticking you off this morning,' he said. 'I hope you had the sense to realize it was not meant for you.' I stood up, somewhat flabbergasted at the change of tone. 'I was a little taken aback,' I replied. 'If you don't have that much common sense, you'll never do as an information officer,' he said to me. He then patted me on my back and went to shake other hands. I was utterly deflated. The fellow obviously meant to be friendly towards me; it was Sudhir Ghosh he was gunning for. Menon had a convoluted mind.

It did not take me long to get the hang of India House politics. Krishna Menon had his coterie of faithfuls. At the top of the list was Arthur Lall, his trade commissioner. His other favourites were junior members of his staff; some, like his personal secretary, Captain Srinivasan of the Indian Navy, he savaged till they proved their loyalties to him. Menon had scant respect for the deputy high commissioner, R. S. Mani, also of the ICS and his number two man. Mani was a flabby man with a flabbier Belgian wife. He did his best to ingratiate himself with Menon and suffered being treated like a doormat—he remained a doormat. Menon was also allergic to men in uniform and treated his military, naval and air force attachés with unconcealed contempt. His bête noire was Sudhir

Ghosh, who was determined to run the public relations department as an independent establishment of his own.

Sudhir regarded himself as Gandhi's personal envoy to well-meaning Britons who had sided with the freedom movement. Most of them were Quakers. He entrusted them with official missions without consulting Menon. 'Let Menon do his job and let him leave me alone to do mine,' he often told me as he gloated over the photographs and letters on his table. 'I have spent many years with Gandhiji. I have no hatred in my heart against anyone,' he assured me over and over again. Then he resumed his tirade against Menon.

Menon had an eye for good-looking women. He treated the husbands of good-looking women as friends. If he sensed tension between the couple, he became especially considerate towards them—he had great understanding for misunderstood wives. Sheila Lall and my wife (after the family joined me) fell in that category. Arthur and I became his number one and number two favourites. But topping us was young Kamla Jaspal, who had joined his clerical pool.

Kamla was a Sikh—light-skinned, with curly black hair and a charming squint in one eye. She came to office dressed as if she were going to a cocktail party. She wore bright-coloured chiffon saris, with blouses that left most of her middle, including her belly button, exposed. She wore bracelets of silver, gold and glass; they covered most of her forearms and jingle-jangled whenever she brushed her untidy locks from across her face, which was often. Being scantily clad, she often caught colds and had a running nose. She dropped names of English poets, and she danced a few steps of Bharatanatyam badly; she also wrote bad prose and poetry. She was loud and aggressive in asserting herself. But she worshipped Krishna Menon as if he were an incarnation of Lord Vishnu. Like a good Hindu wife she never referred to him by his name or as high commissioner but as HE—His Excellency. To Krishna Menon, who had been away from India for several decades, Kamla Jaspal represented modern Indian womanhood. He responded to her adoration with flowers and favours, including the use of his Rolls-Royce to take her home. He was tiring of his ageing English mistress, Bridgette, who looked after the India League, and was on the lookout for a replacement. For a while Kamla courted Bridgette and soon discovered that she could oust her. In India House, everyone knew that in order to get on with Krishna Menon one had to get on with Kamla Jaspal. During that posting in London, I cultivated both Bridgette and Kamla.

Menon had reason to trust me more than Sudhir Ghosh and decided to use me as an instrument to get rid of him. He did not have to wait long for the opportunity to do so. I first discovered how bad things were when I chanced to see a confidential letter Menon had written to Pandit Nehru. He described Ghosh as a 'Patelite'. Evidently, Nehru's relations with his deputy prime minister, Sardar Patel, were strained. He also argued that foreign publicity should be under the foreign minister (Nehru) and not under the home and information minister (Patel). Before Panditji could respond to this letter, the incident of the missing chit occurred, which proved Sudhir Ghosh's undoing.

One morning, Menon sent a note to Sudhir Ghosh on a scrap of paper in his own hand, asking him to send me up to see him as soon as I reached the office. Sudhir took no notice of it till a couple of hours later, when Kamla Jaspal came down to check whether or not I had arrived. I went to Sudhir's office to find out what it was about. 'Oh, yes, Menon wants to see you without me,' he said, reading the chit. He crumpled it and threw it into his wastepaper basket. When I went to see Menon, he asked me why it had taken me two hours to come up. I told him I had known nothing about it till Kamla told me and I had then gone to Sudhir's room. Sudhir was summoned. He blankly denied having received any message from Menon. I left them going at each other, returned to Sudhir's room and pulled out the crumpled chit from his wastepaper basket. Through Kamla Jaspal, I had the chit handed over to Menon. I do not know how the Gandhian Sudhir got out of the blatant lie he had told. The next day, he left for India; Menon followed him a few days later.

While they were away, I received telegraphic orders transferring me to Canada. P. L. Bhandari, whom I had known as a junior reporter with *The Civil and Military Gazette* of Lahore and who regarded himself as an expert in public relations, was named Sudhir's successor. A few days later, Menon and Sudhir returned to London. The latter made only one appearance in India House, to take away his pictures and testimonials from his table. His parting kick was to host a large luncheon party at the Savoy Hotel for his English friends. He did not bother to invite me or any other colleagues. At that one party, he blew up the entire year's entertainment allowance of the public relations department.

Menon was a complex character—the most unpredictable and prickly I have ever met. I had first met him on the London-Paris train when he and Rajni Patel were on their way to attend some conference. At Dover, he and Rajni jumped the queue of passengers awaiting immigration clearance. When the immigration officer told them to go back to the line, Menon accused him of racial prejudice. The fellow let them through. Menon had a chip on his shoulder about being 'a black' and picked quarrels on imaginary racial insults. For a time, he had worked as a waiter at restaurants to pay for his studies at the Bar. He never picked up any practice but got to know socialist politicians and was on the panel of editors of the Pelican series of books. Till he became high commissioner, he was always very hard-up and eager to accept any hospitality extended to him.

Menon was slim, middle-sized and dark, with sharp features and bright, shining eyes. He had a broad forehead, his curly black hair greying at the temples, a large nose and high cheekbones. Women found him handsome. He was very tense; his face was never at rest and twitched with animation. He was always very well-dressed, in suits made by a well-known firm of tailors; he could not bear others being badly dressed. Once he cancelled his morning appointments, took me to his tailor, chose the material and had me measured for two suits. I thought he meant to gift them to me and thanked him profusely. They were not gifts; I had to shell out several hundred pounds. But they were the best suits I had and lasted me over twenty years. Menon was not generous with his money except when it came to his lady friends and children; even then, it was seldom more than bouquets of roses for the one, cheap plastic toys for the other.

Menon lived frugally in a room alongside his office. He ate very little but filled himself with cups of sugared tea and salted biscuits. However, he did not mind blowing up large sums of money buying a Rolls-Royce for the high commissioner (that is to say, himself) and a fleet of Austin Princesses for the use of Indian visitors and India House officials. With his limited requirements, he had no need to accumulate wealth; nevertheless, he did so. He didn't spend a penny of his salary but set up many sub-organizations of his India League and got money from rich Indians and his English friends as donations to those organizations; in return, he gave them contracts for the supply of arms to India. He had no scruples in business matters. He was also a congenital liar and regarded truth as good enough for the simple-minded and lying as the best exercise for the mind.

Menon's first reaction to any proposal put to him was to reject it. Those who got to know him better learnt to put their proposals in the negative and invariably got his approval by his rejection of them. He built up a reputation of being a workaholic. He kept long hours, which he wasted on trivialities such as checking the menus of the canteen and the consumption of petrol by the office cars. He forced me to sleep in the office on many nights. There was never enough work to justify imposing this discomfort on me. He knew that I was very keen on games and looked forward to Saturday afternoons, when I played tennis or hockey. Without fail, he would ring me up before lunch on Saturday and ask me to attend some meeting he was holding in the afternoon. He had a strong streak of sadism.

Menon's bad temper and discourtesy had to be experienced to be believed. As with many men, he was at his worst in the mornings before his gastric juices started flowing. I saw him hurling a file in the face of Jagannath Khosla and yelling: 'Have you any brains in your head? Get out!' Then he put his head between his hands to cool off and asked me, 'I shouldn't have spoken to him like that, should I have?' I conceded he had been a little rough with a senior officer. He summoned Khosla back and apologized. Khosla replied, 'Sir, it is a privilege to be ticked off by you.' One morning, when Menon failed to get a long-distance call, he screamed at the operator. The plucky English girl shouted back: 'Don't you dare talk to me like that! I am quitting. You can keep your bloody job.' Menon ran down the stairs, put his arms around the angry girl and apologized. Once I brought David Astor, the owner-proprietor of *The Observer*, and his aide William Clarke to meet Menon. He called the English a race of brigands. On the way down, in the elevator, David remarked to me: 'You must have quite a job doing public relations for Menon!' His deputy, Ashok Chanda, knowing Menon's predilection for denying anything he said if he later found it embarrassing, insisted that he put all his orders in writing. He often breezed into my office and triumphantly announced: 'Hum shala ko phaeel mein aisa mara! Bhoolega nahin' (I gave the fellow whose sister I fuck such a hiding in the file, he'll never forget it). Sir Dhiren Mitra, our legal advisor, never lost his cool; he continued placidly puffing his pipe and dismissed Menon with: 'Paagal hai' (He is mad).

Those who silently suffered Menon's tantrums were handsomely rewarded. Of them the most dramatic was the instance of Brigadier Harnarain Singh and his wife, Rani. Menon took an instant dislike to the brigadier. The latter described himself as the chief of Moron, a small zamindari near Phillaur in the Punjab. Menon always addressed him as the 'chief of the morons'. The brigadier did not know what the English word meant and would protest in his nasal whine: 'Sir, who cares for such titles these days!' His wife also liked to be treated as an aristocrat. She was the daughter of Sardar Sohan Singh, a wealthy landowner of Rawalpindi; her name, Rani, confirmed her aristocratic assumptions. Menon got to know that she had been spreading scandal about his affair with Kamla Jaspal. He summoned her to the office, roundly ticked her off and called her a bitch. A very tearful Rani craved forgiveness. Thereafter, the couple assiduously courted Kamla Jaspal and became Menon's favourites. Another two senior officers who were treated like scum but accepted their treatment without protest were Captain Srinivasan and D. N. Chatterjee. Srinivasan, a married man with children, impregnated his attractive English stenographer. It was after Menon had extracted many pounds of flesh off the hapless naval captain that he allowed him to divorce his Indian wife, marry the vastly pregnant English girl—and retain his job. Chatterjee had divorced his Bengali wife (one of Lord Sinha's progeny) and wanted to marry a Belgian heiress. By the rules of the Foreign Service, he was required to submit his resignation before his application could be considered. Chatterjee had to suffer months of humiliation before Menon forwarded his application with the recommendation that it be accepted. Chatterjee retired as an ambassador.

Merit did not matter very much to Menon; unquestioned loyalty did. He persuaded the prime minister to constitute a panel to interview applicants living in England for the Foreign Service. He got Harold Laski appointed chairman with him and someone else to constitute it. The panel selected P. N. Haksar (the only one who merited selection), Jagannath Khosla, Kamla Jaspal and Rukmini Menon (a clerk and the sister of a junior officer in the military attaché's department). Later, Menon also managed to get Keki Darashah and Prithi Singh, who had an English wife, in the subordinate Foreign Service. He held out similar promises to me; he would have me elected to Parliament and perhaps made a minister in the government. But my days as a Menon favourite were fast drawing to a close.

Menon was never rude to me. For many months, I enjoyed special favours and my colleagues who wanted things done by him used me as their via media. I travelled with him to distant towns in England where he was invited to speak. Kamla Jaspal briefed me on his personal requirements. Amongst items I had to carry were bottles of lemonade: he drank a glass for his nightcap. Though his English was heavily Malayalam-accented, Menon was a witty speaker. He was full of acid wit and sarcasm against the English and people who could not retaliate. At his first meeting with senior army, navy and air force officers training in England, he addressed them as 'Macaulay's children'. He did not enjoy other speakers scoring over him and could be quite childish in the ways in which he got the better of them. Once, speaking at the Convention of Master Cutlers at Leeds, he was at his acid best and extracted much laughter from his audience—the English enjoy laughing at themselves. Unfortunately for Menon, the chief host who rose to propose the vote of thanks turned out to be a better orator than Menon; his jokes and anecdotes got even louder applause. I saw Menon beckon a waiter and ask for another cup of tea. As the speaker was building up to a climax, Menon raised his cup with a shaking hand. Just as the speaker was about to deliver his punch line, Menon dropped the cup and spilt tea all over the table. The punch line remained undelivered and the banquet came to an abrupt end.

My most memorable venture with Menon was a visit to Dublin, where we were to open an embassy—Ireland's first full diplomatic mission. Menon decided to take his defence attachés and their wives with him. I was included in the party and asked to bring my wife along. Our party was received at Dublin airport with a guard of honour and we were put up in Dublin's swankiest hotel. The next morning, Menon was to present his credentials to the Irish president.

My phone rang early in the morning. It was a very sick-sounding Menon asking me to come to his room at once. I found him groaning in bed.

'I am very sick,' Menon moaned. 'Cancel all the day's engagements.'

I was aghast. 'Sir, they must have made a lot of preparations. Let me get the hotel doctor and see what he has to say.'

'Can't you see I am a sick man?' he growled.

I got the hotel doctor. He could not diagnose anything wrong with Menon except that he might be suffering from exhaustion. Menon was inconsolable. 'Get the chief of protocol on the line.' While I was trying to get the right number, we heard the stamp of marching feet come to a halt beneath our window. 'What is that?' asked Menon. I looked out. 'Soldiers drawing up. I expect they are to escort you to the Presidential Palace.' Menon began to feel better. He went to the bathroom to shave, and brush his teeth. When he came out, we heard the sounds of a military band down the road and coming to a halt outside the hotel. Menon had a quick look from his window. He got into a black sherwani and churidar and told me, 'Sardar, go and get dressed. We don't have much time.' Menon was now in great form. We were taken in a convoy led by a band and a troop of soldiers. Curious Dubliners lined the roads and Menon waved to them. The credentials were presented and accepted.

The president invited Menon to his home for a cup of tea in the afternoon and Menon asked me and my wife to accompany him. We were led to a book-lined study with a peat fire smouldering in the grate. The president made polite enquiries about India; Menon launched into a long harangue about India's mineral and hydro-electric resources, its industries and agricultural potential. The president listened in silence. At the end of his long monologue, Menon asked the president how Ireland was faring. 'Nothing much worth the talking,' drawled the president. 'We don't have much to export, except invisible items like poets, novelists and dramatists.'

That evening, we held a reception for the Irish president, prime minister and leaders of the Irish Opposition. Amongst those who turned up was Eamon De Valera. Following classical music, as we were being shown to our box, an announcement came over the loudspeaker that Ireland's first foreign ambassador had arrived. The audience rose to applaud him. A beam of light searched the crowded hall to pick up Menon. Instead of him, it focused on me—with my turban and beard, I looked more authentically Indian than anyone else in our party. I tried to dodge the beam by going to the back row, but the beam pursued me. Menon enjoyed my discomfiture and kept pushing me to the front. No one was able to acknowledge the applause of the audience.

Nothing specific happened to sour my relations with Menon. Of the two women he was close to, over time I became friendlier with Bridgette, who was very distressed by Menon's infatuation with Kamla Jaspal. She regarded Kamla as a designing seductress who had brought Menon a bad name. I made the mistake of saying this to Menon; he snubbed me and told me to mind my own business. Then some comment on Kashmir appeared in *The Manchester Guardian*. Menon and Haksar drafted the reply; it was sent to me for my signature as the press attaché. I could have drafted a similar reply—and perhaps have phrased it better—but I was not even consulted. The correspondence continued in the paper. In all, I signed three letters I had not written. I felt slighted and let my hurt be known to everyone in the office. Then, instead of talking to me directly, Menon began to convey his orders through Kamla Jaspal. I told her not to bring messages to me as I was always available to the high commissioner on the phone. Menon accused me of being rude to Kamla; his infatuation was at its peak at the time.

The time had come to bid a final farewell to India House. When I went to say goodbye to Jamal Kidwai, who had taken my place, he told me that Menon wanted to give a farewell reception for me. I told him flatly that I wanted no reception and did not wish to see Menon. He pleaded with me and said that he would give the reception and Menon would come only for a few moments. I knew Menon would do nothing of the sort, but agreed to go to Kidwai's party. Reluctantly, I also went to see Menon. He was courteous and said that despite our misunderstanding he regarded me as a friend. 'You don't have any friends,' I told him bluntly as I left. As I had anticipated, Menon did not turn up at the farewell reception. Kidwai apologized on his behalf to say that Menon was unwell and confined to his bed. But I saw him go briskly down the steps and get into his Rolls-Royce—lying was Menon's second nature and came as easily to him as discourtesy.

Why Menon got where he did under the patronage of Pandit Nehru remains, and probably will remain, unexplained. Panditji had him elected to Parliament and sent him to the United Nations to lead the Indian delegation. His marathon thirteen-hour speech on Kashmir won India a unanimous vote against it. He was then made defence minister against the wishes of almost all the members of the cabinet. He wrecked army discipline by promoting favourites over the heads of senior officers. He was vindictive against those who stood up to him. More than anyone else, he was responsible for the humiliating defeat of our army at the hands of the Chinese in 1962. And yet, Pandit Nehru stuck by him to the last.

The last time I spoke to Menon was on the telephone. I happened to be in London working at the India Office Library. I was sharing a flat with Sheila Lall and we had a common telephone. Every night, she would be out with one of her many lovers. The telephone would ring, but when I would pick up and say hello the line would go dead. I complained to Sheila. 'That must be Krishna,' she told me. 'He wants me to be his mistress—no strings attached.' The next time the telephone rang, instead of saying the customary 'hello' I spat out with venom: 'You bloody bastard, I know who you are! Stop ringing up at this hour or you will hear worse.' There were no calls after that.

Menon is the subject of a couple of biographies and a road is named after him. I think in my long years I got to know him better than his biographers or any of the leftists who acclaim him as a great son of India. General Shiv Varma summed him up aptly when he said, 'Menon was a bachelor, the same as his father.'

39

MOTHER TERESA
(1910–1997)

It has been more than thirty years since I was asked to do a profile of Mother Teresa for *The New York Times*. I wrote to Mother Teresa seeking her permission to call on her. Having got it, I spent three days with her, from the early hours of the morning to late at night. Nothing in my journalistic career has remained as sharply etched in my memory as those three days with her in Calcutta.

Before I met her, I read Malcolm Muggeridge's book on her, *Something Beautiful for God*. Malcolm was a recent convert to Catholicism and prone to believing in miracles. He had gone to make a film on Mother Teresa for the BBC. They first went to the Nirmal Hriday Home for dying destitutes close to the Kalighat temple. The team took some shots of the building from outside and of its sunlit courtyard. The camera crew was of the opinion that the interior was too dark and they had no lights that would help them take the shots they needed. However, since some film was left over, they decided to use it for interior shots. When the film was developed later, the shots of the dormitories inside were found to be clearer and brighter than those taken in sunlight. The first thing I asked Mother Teresa was if this was true.

'But of course,' she replied. 'Such things happen all the time.' Then she added with greater intensity: 'Every day, every hour, every single minute, God manifests Himself in some miracle.'

She narrated other miracles of the days when her organization was little known and always short of cash. 'Money has never been much of a problem,' she told me. 'God gives through His people.' She told me that when she started her first school in the slums, she had no more than five rupees with her. But as soon as people came to know what she was doing, they brought money and other things.

The first institution she took me to was Nirmal Hriday. It was in 1952 that the Calcutta Corporation had handed over the building to her. Orthodox Hindus were outraged. Four hundred Brahmin priests attached to the Kali temple gathered outside the building. 'One day, I went out and spoke to them. "If you want to kill me, kill me. But do not disturb the inmates. Let them die in peace." That silenced them. Then one of the priests staggered in. He was in an advanced stage of galloping phthisis. The nuns looked after him till he died.' That changed the priests' attitude towards Mother Teresa. Later, one day, another priest entered the home, prostrated himself at her feet and said, 'For thirty years, I have served the Goddess Kali in her temple. Now the Goddess stands before me.'

On my way back, Mother Teresa dropped me at the Dum Dum Airport. As I was about to take leave of her, she said, 'So?' She wanted to know if I had anything else to ask her.

'Tell me, how can you touch people with loathsome diseases like leprosy and gangrene? Aren't you revolted by people filthy with dysentery and cholera vomit?'

'I see Jesus in every human being,' Mother Teresa replied. 'I say to myself, this is hungry Jesus. This one has gangrene, dysentery or cholera. I must wash him and tend to him.'

I wrote a humble tribute to her for *The New York Times* and put her on the cover of *The Illustrated Weekly*. Till then, she was little known outside Calcutta; after that, more people got to know about her work. She sent me a short note of thanks, which I have in a silver frame in Kasauli. It is among my most valued possessions. It says: 'I am told you do not believe in God. I send you God's blessings.'

40

MADHAV SADASHIV GOLWALKAR
(1906–1973)

As I think on the communal beast that threatens India today, I realize that part of the Sangh Parivar's success over the years can be attributed to the charm and charisma of many of its leaders. They were men of polite manners, obvious sophistication and intelligence, who cloaked their fascist ideas in sweet reasonableness, with impeccable etiquette.

I met Madhavrao Sadashivrao Golwalkar, the then head of the RSS, around forty years ago. Guru Golwalkar had long been at the top of my hate list because I could not forget the RSS's role in communal riots and the assassination of Mahatma Gandhi, and its attempt to change India from a secular state to a Hindu rashtra. There were passages in his 1939 tract, *We, or Our Nationhood Defined*, that seemed to suggest that Golwalkar shared Hitler's ideas about racial purity and approved of his methods to purge Germany of Jews. I could thus not resist the chance of meeting him in November 1972, and interviewed him for the *Weekly*.

I expected to run into a cordon of uniformed swayamsevaks. There were none. Not even plainclothes CIDs to take down the number of my car. I arrived at what looked like a middle-class apartment. It seemed as though there was a puja going on inside—there were rows of sandals outside, the fragrance of agarbatti, the bustle of women behind the scenes, the tinkle of utensils and crockery. I stepped inside.

It was a small room. In it sat a dozen men in spotless white kurtas and dhotis—all looking newly washed as only Maharashtrian Brahmins can manage. And there was Guru Golwalkar—a frail man in his mid-sixties, black hair curling to his shoulders, a moustache framing his mouth, a wispy grey beard dangling down his chin. He wore an inerasable smile and his dark eyes twinkled through his bifocals. He looked like an Indian Ho Chi Minh. For a man who had only recently undergone surgery for breast cancer, he seemed remarkably fit and cheerful. Being a guru, I had imagined that he might expect chela-like obeisance. But he did not give me the chance. As I bent to touch his feet, he grasped my hand with his bony fingers and pulled me down on the seat beside him.

'I am very glad to meet you,' he said. 'I had been wanting to do so for some time.' His Hindi was very shuddh.

'Me too,' I replied clumsily. 'Ever since I read your *Bunch of Letters*.'

'*Bunch of Thoughts*,' he corrected me. He did not want to know my views on it. He took one of my hands in his and patted it. 'So?' He looked enquiringly at me.

'I don't know where to begin. I am told you shun publicity and your organization is secret.'

'It is true we do not seek publicity, but there is nothing secret about us. Ask me anything you want to.'

'I read about your movement in Jack Curran's *The RSS and Hindu Militarism*. He says...'

'It is a biased account,' interrupted Golwalkar. 'Unfair, inaccurate. He misquoted me and many others. There is no militarism in our movement. We value discipline—which is a different matter.'

I told him that I had read an article describing Curran as the head of CIA operations in Europe and Africa. 'I would never have suspected it,' I said naively. 'I have known him for twenty years.'

Golwalkar beamed a smile at me. 'This does not surprise me at all.' I did not know whether his remark was a comment on Curran being part of the CIA or my naivety.

'There is one thing that bothers me about the RSS,' I said to him. 'If you permit me, I will put it as bluntly as I can.'

'Go ahead.'

'It is your attitude towards the minorities, particularly the Christians and the Muslims.'

'We have nothing against the Christians except their methods of gaining converts,' said Golwalkar. 'When they give medicines to the sick or bread to the hungry, they should not exploit the situation by propagating their religion to those people. I am glad there is a move to make the Indian churches autonomous and independent of Rome.'

'What about the Muslims?' I said.

'What about them?' Golwalkar countered.

'I have no doubt in my mind that the dual loyalties that many Muslims have towards both India and Pakistan is due to historical reasons, for which Hindus are as much to blame as they. It also stems from a feeling of insecurity that they have been made to suffer since Partition. In any case, one cannot hold the entire community responsible for the wrongs of a few.' I had begun to get eloquent. 'Guruji, there are six crores of Indian Muslims here with us. We cannot eliminate them, we cannot drive them out, we cannot convert them. This is their home. We must reassure them, make them feel wanted. Let us win them over with love...'

'I would reverse the order,' Golwalkar interrupted. 'As a matter of fact, I would say the only right policy towards Muslims is to win their loyalty by love.'

I was startled. Was he playing with words? Or did he really mean what he said?

He qualified his statement: 'A delegation of Jamaat-i-Islami came to see me. I told them that Muslims must forget that they ruled India. They should not look upon foreign Muslim countries as their homelands. They must join the mainstream of Indianism.'

'How?'

'We should explain things to them. Sometimes one feels angry with Muslims for what they do, but then Hindu blood never harbours ill-will for very long. Time is a great healer. I am an optimist and feel that Hinduism and Islam will learn to live with each other.'

Tea was served. Guruji's glass mug provided a diversion. I asked him why he didn't drink the beverage out of porcelain like the rest of us.

He smiled. 'I have always taken it in this mug. I take it with me wherever I go.'

Golwalkar's closest companion, Dr Thatte, who had dedicated his life to the RSS, explained: 'Porcelain wears off and exposes the clay beneath. Clay can harbour germs.'

I returned to my theme. 'Why do you pin your faith on religion when most of the world is turning irreligious and agnostic?'

'Hinduism is on firm ground because it has no dogma. It has had agnostics before; it will survive the wave of irreligiousness better than any other religious system.'

'How can you say that?' I argued. 'The evidence is the other way. The only religions that are standing firm and even increasing their hold on the people are those based on dogma—Catholicism and, more than Catholicism, Islam.'

'It is a passing phase,' replied Golwalkar. 'Agnosticism will overtake them; it will not overtake Hinduism. Ours is not a religion in the dictionary sense of the word; it is a dharma, a way of life. Hinduism will take agnosticism in its stride.'

I had taken more than half an hour of Golwalkar's time by now. But he showed no sign of impatience. When I asked for leave, he again grasped my hands to prevent me from touching his feet.

As has become abundantly clear in the past decades, the RSS is blatantly and fiercely anti-Muslim and anti-Christian. It junks Jesus just as it rejects roza. Golwalkar even raised an objection when Abdul Hamid and the Keeler brothers were honoured by the Indian government for their bravery during the Indo-Pak War—the gallant men were non-Hindus.

I remember being impressed with Guru Golwalkar in 1972 because he did not try to persuade me to agree with his point of view. Instead, he made me feel that he was open to persuasion. I even accepted his invitation to visit him in Nagpur and see things for myself. I had thought then that I could perhaps bring him around to making Hindu-Muslim unity the main aim of his RSS. I had been a simple-minded Sardar.

41

AMRITA SHER-GIL
(1913–1941)

Women seduce. That is a fact. I have been seduced by women all my life, right from the time I was attracted to my first love, Ghayoor—it was she who had held my hand. Most women have made the first pass at me, led me on, with the exception of two women, where I took the lead. Even when I was attracted to a woman, I had little confidence to make the first move; instead, I was terribly flattered when women made a pass at me. Looking back, I wish I had had the confidence to make the first move, for I could have got closer to several women, like the now legendary painter Amrita Sher-Gil. Amrita, you see, had threatened to seduce me. It happened in Shimla in the mid-1930s.

Amrita came into my sitting room (and my life) one day and introduced herself. She told me of the flat she had rented across the road, and wanted advice about carpenters, plumbers, tailors and the like. I tried to size her up. I couldn't look her in the face too long because she had that bold, brazen kind of look that makes timid men like me turn their gaze down.

She was short and sallow-complexioned (being half Sikh and half Hungarian). Her hair was parted in the middle and tightly bound at the back. She had a bulbous nose, with blackheads showing. She had thick lips with a faint shadow of a moustache. Politeness, I discovered, was not one of her virtues; she believed in speaking her mind, however rude or unkind it be.

As a baby, my son, Rahul, was in the playpen, learning to stand on his feet. Everyone was paying him compliments: he was a very pretty little child with curly hair, large, questioning eyes and dimpled cheeks. 'What an ugly little boy!' remarked Amrita. Others protested their embarrassment. My wife froze. Amrita continued to drink her beer without concern.

Later, when she heard what my wife had to say about her manners, that she had described her as a 'bloody bitch', Amrita told her informant: 'I will teach that woman a lesson. I will seduce her husband.'

There were stories that Amrita had seduced many well-known characters of that time. People like the art critic Karl Khandalawala, Iqbal Singh and her nephew, the painter Vivan Sundaram, have written books on Amrita; Badruddin Tyabji has given a vivid account of how he was seduced by her—she simply took off her clothes and lay naked on the carpet by the fireplace. Vivan admits to her having many lovers; according to him, her real passion in life was another woman.

Unfortunately, Amrita couldn't carry out her threat of seducing me because she died a few months later. She was not yet thirty.

42

NIRAD C. CHAUDHURI

(1897-1999)

'There is nothing more dreadful to an author than neglect, compared with which reproach, hatred and opposition are names of happiness.' These words of Dr Johnson were inscribed by Nirad Chaudhuri on my copy of his book *A Passage to England.* These words hold the key to Nirad's past life and present personality. They explain the years of neglect of one who must have, at all times, been a most remarkable man; his attempt to attract attention by cocking a snook at people who had neglected him; and the 'reproach, hatred and opposition' that he succeeded in arousing as a result of his rudeness.

Nirad had been writing in Bengali for many years. But it was not until the publication of his first book in English *The Autobiography of an Unknown Indian* that he really aroused the interest of the class to which he belonged and which, because of the years of indifference to him, he had come heartily to loathe—the anglicized upper-middle class of India. He did this with calculated contempt. He knew that the wogs were more English than Indian but were fond of proclaiming their patriotism at the expense of the British. That having lost their own traditions and not having fully imbibed those of England, they were a breed with pretensions to intellectualism that seldom went beyond reading blurbs and reviews of books.

He therefore decided to dedicate the work 'To the British Empire...' The wogs took the bait and, having read only the dedication, sent up a howl of protest. Many people who would not have otherwise read the autobiography, discovered to their surprise that there was nothing anti-Indian in its pages. On the contrary, it was the most beautiful picture of eastern Bengal that anyone had ever painted. And at long last, India had produced a writer who did not cash in on naive Indianisms but could write the English language as it should be written—and as few, if any, living Englishmen could write.

Nobody could afford to ignore Nirad Chaudhuri any more. He and his wife Amiya became the most sought-after couple in Delhi's upper class circles. Anecdotes of his vast fund of knowledge were favourite topics at dinner parties.

The first story I heard of the Chaudhuri family was of a cocktail party given by the late Director General of All India Radio, Colonel

Lakshmanan. Nirad had brought his wife and sons (in shorts and full boots) to the function. After the introductions, the host asked what Nirad would like to drink: he had some excellent sherry.

'What kind of sherry?' asked the chief guest. Colonel Lakshmanan had, like most people, heard of only two kinds. 'Both kinds,' he replied. 'Do you like dry or sweet?' This wasn't good enough for Nirad, so he asked one of his sons to taste it and tell him. The thirteen-year-old lad took a sip, rolled it about his tongue and after a thoughtful pause replied, 'Must be an Oloroso 1947.'

Nirad Babu could talk about any subject under the sun. There was not a bird, tree, butterfly or insect whose name he did not know in Latin, Sanskrit, Hindi and Bengali. Long before he left for London, he not only knew where the important monuments and museums were, but also the location of many famous restaurants. I heard him contradict a lady who had lived six years in Rome about the name of a street leading off from the Coliseum—and prove his contention. I've heard him discuss stars with astronomers, recite lines from an obscure fifteenth-century French poet to a professor of French literature, advise a wine dealer on the best vintages from Burgundy. At a small function in honour of Halldór Laxness, the Icelandic winner of the Nobel Prize in Literature, I heard Nirad lecture him on Icelandic literature.

Nirad was a small, frail man, little over five feet tall. He led a double life. At home he dressed in dhoti-kurta and sat on the floor to do his reading and writing. When leaving for office, he wore European dress: coat, tie, trousers and a monstrous khaki sola topi. As soon as he stepped out street urchins would chant 'Johnnie Walker, left, right, left, right'.

Nirad Babu was not a modest man; he had much to be immodest about. He was also a very angry man. When he was dismissed from service by a singularly half-baked Minister of I & B, Dr B.V. Keskar, he exploded with wrath. Years later, it was the Government of India which wanted him to do a definitive booklet on the plight of the Hindu minority in East Pakistan and offered him a blank cheque for his services. Nirad, who was in dire financial straits, turned it down with contempt. 'The government may have lifted its ban on Nirad Chaudhuri but Nirad Chaudhuri has not lifted his ban on the Government of India,' he said to me when I conveyed Finance Minister T.T. Krishnamachari's proposal to him.

Chaudhuri's second book *A Passage to England* received the most glorious reviews in the English press. Three editions were rapidly sold out and it had the distinction of becoming the first book by an Indian author to have become a bestseller in England. The bay windows of London's famous bookshop, Foyles, were decorated with large-sized photographs of Nirad. Some Indian critics were, as in the past, extremely hostile. Nirad's reaction followed the same pattern. At first he tried not to be bothered by people 'who didn't know better', then burst out with invective against the 'yapping curs'. I asked him how he reconciled himself to these two attitudes. After a pause he replied, 'When people say nasty things about my books without really understanding what I have written, I feel like a father who sees a drunkard make an obscene pass at his daughter. I want to chastise him.' Then, with a typically Bengali gesture demonstrating the form of chastisement, 'I want to give them a shoe-beating with my chappal.'

A few years ago Nirad Babu wrote an article for a prestigious London weekly in which he mentioned how hard he was finding life in Oxford, living on his royalties from books. I published extracts from it in my column. K. K. Birla wrote to me to tell Nirad Babu that he would be happy to give him a stipend for life for any amount in any currency he wanted. I forwarded Birla's letter to Nirad. He wrote back asking me to thank Birla for his generous offer but refused to accept it. It is a pity that he accepted a CBE (Commander of the British Empire) from the British government. He deserved a peerage because he was in fact a peerless man of intellect and letters.

43

R. K. NARAYAN
(1906-2001)

It must be over forty years ago that I first met R. K. Narayan in his hometown, Mysore. I had read some of his short stories and novels. I marvelled at how a storyteller of modern times could hold a reader's interest without injecting sex or violence in his narratives. I found them too slow-moving, without any sparkling sentences or memorable descriptions of nature or of his characters. Nevertheless, the one-horse town of his invention, Malgudi, had etched itself on my mind. And all my south Indian friends raved about him as the greatest of Indians writing in English. He certainly was among the pioneers comprising Raja Rao, Govind Desani and Mulk Raj Anand. Whether or not he was the best of them is a matter of opinion.

Being with Narayan on his afternoon strolls was an experience. He did not go to a park but preferred walking up to the bazaar. He walked very slowly and after every few steps he would halt abruptly to complete what he was saying. He would stop briefly at shops to exchange namaskaras with the owners, introduce me and exchange gossip with them in Kannada or Tamil, neither of which I understood. I could sense these gentle strolls in crowded bazaars gave him material for his novels and stories. I found him very likeable and extremely modest despite his achievements.

We saw a lot more of each other during a literary seminar organized by the East-West Centre in Hawaii. Having said our pieces and sat through discussions that followed, we went out for our evening walks, looking for a place to eat. It was the same kind of stroll that we had taken in Mysore, punctuated by abrupt halts in the middle of crowded pavements till he was ready to resume walking. Finding a suitable eatery posed quite a problem. Narayan was a strict teetotaller and a vegetarian; I was neither. We would stop at a grocery store where he bought himself a carton of yoghurt. Then we would go from one eatery to another with R. K. Narayan asking, 'Have you got boiled rice?' Eventually we would find one. Narayan would empty his carton of yoghurt on the mound of boiled rice. The only compromise he made was to eat it with a spoon instead of his fingers, which he would have preferred. Such eateries had very second-rate food and no wines. Dining out was no fun for me.

One evening I decided to shake off Narayan and have a ball on my own. 'I am going to see a blue movie. I don't think you will like it,' I told him. 'I'll come along with you, if you don't mind,' he replied. So we found ourselves in a sleazy suburb of Honolulu watching an extremely obscene film depicting all kinds of sexual deviations. I thought Narayan would walk out, or throw up. He sat stiffly without showing any emotion. It was I who said, 'Let's go.' He turned to me and asked kindly: 'Have you had enough?'

We should get Narayan in the proper perspective. He would not have gone very far but for the patronage of Graham Greene who also became a kind of literary agent for him. He also got the enthusiastic patronage of *The Hindu*. N. Ram and his former English wife, Susan, wrote an excellent biography of Narayan. Greene made Narayan known to the English world of letters; *The Hindu* made him a household name in India.

Narayan was a very loveable man, but his humility was deceptive. Once when All India Radio invited a group of Indian writers to give talks and offered them fees far in excess of their usual rates, while all others accepted the offer, Narayan made it a condition that he should be paid at least one rupee more than the others. In his travelogue, *My Dateless Diary,* he writes about a dialogue at a luncheon party given in his honour. 'I blush to record this, but do it for documentary purposes. After the discussions [between two publishers declaring which of Narayan's novels is their favourite one, and ranking him with Hemingway and Faulkner as the world's three greatest living writers] have continued on these lines for a while, I feel I ought to assert my modesty—I interrupt them to say, "Thank you, but not yet…" They brush me aside and repeat, "Hemingway, Faulkner and Narayan, the three greatest living…"' Narayan goes on at some length about the argument between the publishers over whether to include Greene or Hemingway, besides Narayan himself, among the three greatest.

I was foolish enough to write about this in my column. Narayan never spoke to me again.

44

DOM MORAES
(1938–2004)

Dom Moraes's interest in poetry was born very early in his life. In his preface to a collection of his poems, he wrote, 'I was about ten years old when I started to read poetry... I had an instinctive feel, even at that age, for the shape and texture of words.' By the time he was fourteen, Dom—Domsky to his friends—had begun to write poetry himself, and he learnt French in order to be able to read Villon in the original. Poetry became a lifelong passion and he continued to write till the end of his life.

Dom was my friend from his years at Jesus College, Oxford. He was a complex character who disliked everything about India, particularly Indians—the only exceptions he made were the good-looking women he took to bed. Although he was born in Bombay and was dark as a Goan, Dom considered himself English, spoke no Indian language and wished to be buried in the churchyard of Odcombe, a tiny village in Somerset. Never a practising Christian, he selected Odcombe because one Thomas Coryate, who hailed from the village, had travelled all the way from England to India in the seventeenth century and died in Surat, where he is buried—and Dom went to Odcombe with Sarayu Srivatsa, his companion during the last decade and a half of his life, to collect material on Coryate's background for his biography. Despite his distaste for India, however, Dom's descriptions of the Indian countryside—of the heat and dust storms of summer, of the monsoons—were lyrically beautiful. His characters too came alive in his writing; notwithstanding his ignorance of Indian languages, Dom was able to comprehend what people said in their dialects and in Indian English.

Like his father, Frank Moraes, Dom was a heavy drinker. Because of his love for the bottle, Dom could not be depended on to meet deadlines or stick to the subject he was commissioned to write on. Ramnath Goenka of *The Indian Express* sacked Dom for spending his time in a Calcutta hotel, drinking and consorting with a lady, instead of going on his assignment to the Northeast. His friend, R.V. Pandit, fired him for drinking in his office in Hong Kong. *The Times of India* appointed him editor of a magazine they intended to bring out, but they fired him before the first issue came out; Dom vented his anger on poor Prem Shankar Jha, who was appointed in his stead, by grabbing his tie and demanding: 'Fatty boy! What do you know about journalism?'

I had got Dom an assignment from the Dempos, shipping magnates and mine-owners of Goa; Dom produced a very readable book on Goa without mentioning the Dempos—I had to add four pages on the family. He was commissioned by the Madhya Pradesh tourism department to do a book on the state's historical sites; he did a creditable job of describing the beauty of the landscape and the state's full-bosomed tribal women, without bothering about historical sites. Dom never allowed facts or truths to stand in the way of his writing. He did not write reference books; instead, he painted pictures in vivid colours to the songs of flutes.

Dom is said to have married thrice. When he was married to the actress Leela Naidu (his third wife), I stayed with them in Hong Kong; they, in turn, visited me several times in Delhi. At the best of times, Dom spoke in a low mumble, hard to understand—when I had asked Indira Gandhi, whom he interviewed many times to write her biography, if she understood what he said, she had beamed and replied, 'No, Leela Naidu translated for me.' Dom's second wife, Judy, bore him a son, although I don't think Dom paid for his education; neither am I sure if he had church or civil weddings and court divorces. In any event, he certainly did not pay any alimony to his former wives—he never earned enough to do so.

Dom was not choosy about his women: if any of them were willing, he was always ready to oblige. The only real love of his life, I think, was Sarayu, a Tamilian Brahmin married to a Punjabi and the mother of two children.

Sarayu was instrumental in helping Dom overcome the writers' block that plagued him for seventeen long years, from 1965 to 1982. In partnership with her, Dom wrote *Out of God's Oven*, perhaps the most fascinating example of his condemnation of all things Indian that he hated. Between them, Dom and Sarayu traversed the length and breadth of India, interviewing poets, writers, editors, film producers, Naxalites, Ranbir Sena leaders, dacoits and politicians—and Dom decried the resurgence of Hindu fundamentalism in the Bajrang Dal, the Shiv Sena, the Hindu Vishwa Parishad, the Bharatiya Janata Party and its progenitor, the Rashtriya Swayamsevak Sangh, exposing their vandalism, their penchant for violence and their pathological hatred of Muslims.

While his prose was limpid and lyrical, Dom's verse was not easy to read. His words had resonance, but one had to read every line two or three times before one could comprehend its meaning—people brought up on simple rhyming verse such as 'Twinkle, twinkle, little star' would likely find Dom's poems difficult. One could, however, detect a few themes that recurred consistently in his poems: he was obsessed with death; the hawk was the symbol of doom; his mother's insanity haunted him all his life; and he sought escape in hard liquor and making love. He summed it up in 'A Letter':

> My father hugging me so hard it hurt,
> My mother mad, and time we went away.
>
> We travelled, and I looked for love too young.
> More travel, and I looked for lust instead.
> I was not ruled by wanting: I was young,
> And poems grew like maggots in my head...

◆

When Dom was stricken with cancer, he refused to undergo chemotherapy. It was as if he almost wallowed in the prospect of an early end, with the ghost of his insane mother hovering over him.

> From a heavenly asylum, shrivelled Mummy,
> glare down like a gargoyle at your only son.
> ... That I'm terminally ill hasn't been much help.
> There is no reason left for anything to exist.
> Goodbye now. Don't try to meddle with this.

Dom Moraes died in his sleep on the evening of Wednesday, 2 June 2004, and was buried in the Sewri Christian Cemetery in Bombay. He was only sixty-eight. He was the best Indian poet of the English language, and the greatest writer of felicitous prose.

45

SIR VIDIA

(B. 1932)

When I got the news of V. S. Naipaul being awarded the Nobel Prize in Literature, I was delighted and felt that I had been vindicated. I was delighted because I have known him as a friend for over thirty-five years. I have met his first wife, who was English, and get on famously with his charming, vivacious present wife, Nadira, who is Pakistani Punjabi. I met his late brother, Shiva, and saw quite a lot of his mother when she visited Delhi. Whether it was in Delhi or Bombay, throwing a party for Vidia was a must. I took him with me wherever I went. He liked being entertained and meeting new people. He never returned hospitality. That did not matter as everyone felt privileged to have him in their house and to be able to drop his name.

I feel vindicated because every time I wrote about him, I said he deserved the Nobel Prize in Literature as he was a much better writer than many other Nobel laureates. He handled the English language with greater finesse than any contemporary writer and his range of interests was wider: humour, history, travelogues, religion, the clash of civilizations, personal profiles. Why the coveted prize eluded him for so long I could only attribute to some kind of deep-seated prejudice against writers who did not write in their mother tongue or to political considerations. Although Naipaul is a Trinidad-born Hindu, English is his mother tongue and he is essentially an objective observer of political movements, bold enough to come to his own conclusions.

When I first met Naipaul, I had only read his *A House for Mr Biswas*. I sensed then that a new star had risen in the literary firmament. That book has remained my top favourite. I can't recall exactly how we met. Perhaps he rang me up from his hotel and I invited him and his English wife over to my home. I became his escort in Delhi. He was a shy man of few words. His wife was even shyer and hardly spoke. It was evident that they were not enjoying their visit to the land of his forefathers. She was under the weather, bothered by the heat, dust and pestilence of flies. One early morning I took them to Surajkund. We stood on a ridge, looking at the rock-strewn valley ablaze with flame of the forest in flower. Vidia looked at the scene for a long time. I thought I would read a memorable description of it in his next book. Then I took him to Tughlaqabad. I had brought sandwiches and coffee. As we sat munching our sandwiches, village urchins gathered around us. They had nothing but loincloths to cover their nakedness. Their eyes and noses were running and they had flies all over their faces. In *An Area of Darkness,* Naipaul dismissed the bewitching scene of the flame of the forest trees in flower in a couple of lines but had more to say about the semi-naked urchins with flies around their eyes. It was the same with his visit to Kashmir. He visited Pamposh on a moonlit night. He had less to say about the autumn crocus (saffron) scent pervading the atmosphere and more about Kashmiri women lifting their pherans and squatting to defecate. Squalor and stench attracted his attention more than scenic beauty and fragrance.

Naipaul could be very edgy. Once when I invited him to my flat to meet a few friends over drinks, he seemed to be getting on famously with an attractive Parsi lady. But as soon as she fished out a camera from her bag and asked, 'Do you mind if I take a photograph?' Vidia snapped back sourly: 'As a matter of fact, I do mind.' The poor woman was squashed. It took some time for the others to resume conversation.

At another time the owner of a big industrial house invited me to a cocktail reception at the Taj in Bombay. I took Naipaul and my son, Rahul, who had become closer to him than I was. When we entered the ballroom on time, there were very few guests who had arrived. But seated in a row were a few attractive girls. We made a beeline for them. I introduced Vidia and my son to them. None of them spoke English, nor were they related to our hosts. It transpired that they were call girls, invited for the amusement of the guests. For Naipaul, it was an insight into the methods adopted to promote business here.

Naipaul's *Among the Believers: An Islamic Journey* caused a lot of uneasiness among Muslims. Even Salman Rushdie accused him of harbouring anti-Muslim feelings. What Naipaul wrote cannot be faulted. He observed that people who accepted Islam wrote off their pre-Islamic past. This phenomenon can be verified in Muslim countries today. In Egypt, the Pharaonic period which produced the pyramids, the Sphinx and many beautiful temples is only of historic interest, bringing in tourists and foreign exchange. It is the same in Pakistan. They have consigned their Hindu and Buddhist past to archives, museums and history books. Even the period of Sikh dominance is brushed aside as of little consequence. The destruction of the Buddhas in Bamiyan is a recent example of erasing a pre-Islamic past. This can be seen in all Muslim nations, including the most westernized like Turkey, Morocco and Tunisia. Naipaul did not invent this fact of history; he only exposed it.

I had the opportunity of interviewing Naipaul with Bhaichand Patel on 8 May 2000. He doesn't relish being interviewed. Patel and I were very exercised over the destruction of the Babri Masjid and heckled him for what was widely believed to be the Sangh Parivar's view of the act of vandalism. Naipaul stood his ground. He was an outside observer not concerned with the rights or wrongs of destroying a mosque. The phrase he used was explanatory: 'It was a balancing of history.' I interpreted this to imply that deep in the Hindu psyche was the resentment that Muslim invaders had destroyed hundreds of their temples. So what was so devilish about destroying a dilapidated old mosque?

◆

Ever since Naipaul married the highly animated and attractive Nadira, he has mellowed a great deal. He is not as gruff and edgy as he was. And for good reason is writing about sex with remarkable candour and erotic artistry. His latest work, *Half a Life,* has a few memorable episodes of lusty encounters between men and women other than their spouses.

Most writers who have won the Nobel Prize tend to rest on their laurels and write little of any significance thereafter. I hope this does not happen to Sir Vidia Naipaul.

THE FEROCITY &
FLAMBOYANCE OF
NATURE

THE MONSOON
NATURE'S FESTIVAL OF COLOURS
IN THE HEAT OF THE SUMMER

46

THE MONSOON

Monsoon is not another word for rain. As its original Arabic name indicates, it is a season. There is a summer monsoon as well as a winter monsoon, but it is only the nimbus southwest winds of summer that make a 'mausam'—the season of rains. The winter monsoon is simply rain in winter. It is like a cold shower on a frosty morning. It leaves one chilled and shivering. Although it is good for the crops, people pray for it to end. Fortunately, it does not last very long.

The summer monsoon is quite another affair. It is preceded by several months of working up a thirst so that when the waters come they are drunk deep with relish. From the end of February, the sun starts getting hotter and spring gives way to summer. Flowers wither. Flowering trees take their place. First come the orange flowers of the flame of the forest and the vermilion of the coral. They are followed by the flamboyant gulmohar and the soft golden cascades of the laburnum. Then the trees also lose their flowers. Their leaves fall. Their bare branches stretch up to the sky begging for water, but there is no water. The sun comes up earlier than before and licks up the drops of dew before the fevered earth can moisten its lips. It blazes away all day long in a cloudless grey sky, drying up wells, streams and lakes. It sears the grass and thorny scrub till they catch fire. The fires spread and dry jungles burn like matchwood.

The sun goes on, day after day, from east to west, scorching relentlessly. The earth cracks up and deep fissures open their gaping mouths asking for water; but there is no water—only the shimmering haze at noon making mirage lakes of quicksilver. Poor villagers take their thirsty cattle out to drink and are struck dead. The rich wear sunglasses and hide behind curtains of khus on which their servants pour water.

The sun makes an ally of the breeze. It heats the air till it becomes loo (India's khamsin) and sends it on its errand. Even in the intense heat, the loo's warm caresses are sensuous and pleasant. It brings up prickly heat. It produces a numbness which makes the head nod and eyes heavy with sleep. It brings on a stroke which takes its victim as gently as the breeze bears a fluff of thistledown.

Then comes a period of false hope. The temperature drops. The air becomes still. From the southern horizon a black wall begins to advance. Hundreds of kites and crows fly ahead. Can it be...? No! It is a dust storm. A fine powder begins to fall. A solid mass of locusts covers the sun.

They devour whatever is left on the trees and in the fields. Then comes the storm itself. In furious sweeps it smacks open doors and windows, banging them forward and backward, smashing their glass panes. Thatched roofs and corrugated iron sheets are borne aloft into the sky like bits of paper. Trees are torn up by the roots and fall across power lines. The tangled wires electrocute people and set fire to houses. The storm carries the flames to other houses till there is a conflagration. All this happens in a few seconds. Before you can say 'Chakravarti Rajagopalachari', the gale is gone. The dust hanging in the air settles on your books, furniture and food; it gets in your eyes and ears and throat and nose.

This happens over and over again until the people have lost all hope. They are disillusioned, dejected, thirsty and sweating. The prickly heat on the backs of their necks is like emery paper. There is another lull. A hot petrified silence prevails. Then comes the shrill, strange call of a bird. What, has it left its cool bosky shade and come out in the sun? People look up wearily at the lifeless sky. Yes, there it is with its mate! They are like large black-and-white bulbuls with perky crests and long tails. They are pied crested cuckoos who have flown all the way from Africa ahead of the monsoon. Isn't there a gentle breeze blowing? And hasn't it a damp smell? And wasn't the rumble which drowned the bird's anguished cry the sound of thunder? The people hurry to the roofs to see. The same ebony wall is coming up from the east. A flock of herons fly across. There is a flash of lightning which outshines the daylight. The wind fills the black sails of the clouds and they billow out across the sun. A profound shadow falls on the earth. There is another clap of thunder. Big drops of rain fall and dry up in the dust. A fragrant smell rises from the earth. Another flash of lightning and another crack of thunder like the roar of a hungry tiger. It has come! Sheets of water, wave after wave. The people lift their faces to the clouds and let the abundance of waters cover them. Schools and offices close. All work stops. Men, women and children run madly about the streets, waving their arms and shouting 'Ho, ho'—hosannas to the miracle of the monsoon.

The monsoon is not like the ordinary rain which comes and goes. Once it is on, it stays for three to four months. Its advent is greeted with joy. Parties set out for picnics and litter the countryside with the skins and stones of mangoes. Women and children make swings of branches of trees and spend the day in sport and song. Peacocks spread their tails and strut about with their mates; the woods echo with their shrill cries.

But after a few days, the flush of enthusiasm is gone. The earth becomes a big stretch of swamp and mud. Wells and lakes fill up and burst their bounds. In towns, gutters get clogged and streets become turbid streams. In villages, mud walls of huts melt in the water and thatched roofs sag and descend on the inmates. Rivers, which keep rising steadily from the time the summer's heat starts melting the snows, suddenly turn to floods as the monsoon spends itself on the mountains. Roads, railway tracks and bridges go under water. Houses near the river banks are swept down to the sea.

With the monsoon the tempo of life and death increases. Almost overnight grass begins to grow and leafless trees turn green. Snakes, centipedes and scorpions are born out of nothing. The ground is strewn with earthworms, ladybirds and tiny frogs. At night a myriad moths flutter around the lamps. They fall in everybody's food and water. Geckos dart about filling themselves with insects till they get heavy and fall off ceilings. Inside rooms, the hum of mosquitoes is maddening. People spray clouds of insecticide and the floor becomes a layer of wriggling bodies and wings. Next evening, there are many more fluttering around the lampshades and burning themselves in the flames.

While the monsoon lasts, the showers start and stop without warning. The clouds fly across, dropping their rain on the plains as it pleases them, till they reach the Himalayas. They climb up the mountainsides. Then the cold squeezes the last drops of water out of them. Lightning and thunder never cease. All this happens in late August or early September. Then the season of the rains gives way to autumn.

The monsoon is the most memorable experience in our lives. For others to know India and her people, they have to know the monsoon. It is not enough to read about it in books, or see it on the cinema screen, or hear someone talk about it. It has to be a personal experience because nothing short of living through it can fully convey all it means to a people for whom it is not only the source of life, but also our most exciting impact with nature. What the four seasons of the year mean to the European, the one season of the monsoon means to the Indian. It is preceded by desolation; it brings with it the hopes of spring; it has the fullness of summer and the fulfilment of autumn all in one.

It is not surprising that much of India's art, music and literature is concerned with the monsoon. Innumerable paintings depict people on rooftops looking eagerly at the dark clouds billowing out from over the horizon with flocks of heron flying in front. Of the many melodies of Indian music, Raaga Malhar is the most popular because it brings to the mind distant echoes of the sound of thunder and the pitter-patter of raindrops. It brings the odour of the earth and of green vegetation to the nostrils; the cry of the peacock and the call of the koel to the ear. There is also the Raaga Desh which invokes scenes of merry-making.

Of swings in mango groves and the singing and laughter of girls. Most Indian palaces had specially designed balconies from where noblemen could view the monsoon downpour. Here they sat listening to court musicians improvising their own versions of monsoon melodies, sipping wine and making love to the ladies of their harem. The commonest theme in Indian songs is the longing of lovers for each other when the rains are in full swing. There is no joy greater than union during monsoon time, there is no sorrow deeper than separation during the season of the rains.

Our attitude to clouds and rains remains fundamentally different from that of the westerner. To the one, clouds are symbols of hope; to the other, of despair. The Indian scans the heavens and if nimbus clouds blot out the sun his heart fills with joy. The westerner looks up and if there is no silver lining edging the clouds, his depression deepens. The Indian talks of someone he respects and looks up to as a great shadow, like the one cast by the clouds when they cover the sun. The westerner, on the other hand, looks on a shadow as something evil and refers to people of dubious character as shady types. For him, his beloved is like the sunshine and he thinks of her smile as sunny. He escapes clouds and rain whenever he can seek summer climes. An Indian, when the rain comes, runs out into the street shouting with joy and lets himself be soaked to the skin.

47

NATURE'S FESTIVAL OF COLOURS

The vagaries of the weather make Holi, the festival of colours, a chancy affair. It usually falls sometime between the latter part of February and the end of March. Some years only the young are out with their long tube syringes, buckets of coloured water and red powder to fight mock battles yelling, 'Holi hai! Holi hai!' Other years it is warm enough for the middle-aged and the old to risk being doused.

For the last ten years or so, I have celebrated Holi sitting out in my back garden, admiring the beauty of the latest love in my life, my kosam tree. I planted it some fifteen years ago. Now it is over sixty feet tall. Most of the year, it has a thick cluster of broad green leaves to screen a variety of birds that come for shelter—crows, babblers, barbets, bulbuls, doves and many others. They prefer this tree to the mango, which also has thick, dark green leaves; I haven't found out why. My love for the kosam is roused in February when it begins to shed its leaves. At first, one or two at a time. Then the tempo increases: the leaves come down by the dozen. If there is a gust of wind, it becomes a shower of leaves and the ground below a rough carpet of dried leaves.

By Holi, most of the tree is stripped to its bare branches with only a few clusters of yellow leaves clinging on for dear life. Just about the same time, new leaves begin to sprout. Much to my surprise and joy, this time they first appeared at the top. The leaves are of a fiery red colour and glow like live embers when the sun comes up. Then more appear at the end of the branches. For a few days, the tree looks like a pyramid ablaze with flames rising to the skies. I sit mesmerized for hours gazing at it because I can't recall seeing anything more beautiful. In its own mysterious way, the kosam also tells me the story of life, death and rebirth. It occurred to me that the colour of regeneration is red. At Holi time, the flame of the forest (dhak) and coral also come into flower. All of them are of deep red colour. It is nature's way of celebrating the festival of colours with its own brand of gulaal made of red leaves and flowers.

By mid-March the mulberry tree (shahtoot in Hindi; *Morus alba* in Latin for the variety whose fruit range white to purple and are usually sweet) has both flowers and foliage. For a few days its caterpillar-like fruit is free to all for picking. *Bauhinias* are still in flower, though now with leaves around them. Mango trees are covered with a powdery beige cluster of blossoms.

I have said that New Delhi is at its loveliest in February. March can be almost as enchanting. Whichever way you look, it is a splash of colour.

In March both birth and death are much in evidence. On the one hand you can see the grapevine and madhumalati—*Quisqualis* (meaning who? what?) *indica*, a name given to it by a Dutch botanist because of its eccentric manner of growth—add new leaves everyday; on the other there are neem, mahua, jamun, peepal and banyan trees shedding their foliage. For the next week or two gardeners will be busy sweeping dead leaves into mounds and making funeral pyres of them. While the pyres still smoulder, those very trees will come into new leaf. Of the dying and the reborn, the peepal and banyan have the most delicate of new leaves: pale pink, silky-soft and beautifully shaped. If you want an offering from nature as your bookmark, you cannot do better than press their leaves in your album.

The peepal (*Ficus religiosa*, so called because the Buddha attained nirvana under it) is a bit of a sponger. It will begin to sprout out of crevices in walls, even out of boles of trees where is a little mud. There is a splendid example of a peepal almost strangling its host tree in the Lodi Gardens, west of the Bara Gumbad mosque. The peepal is a splendid example of an epiphyte.

Bird courtship, begun in February, is vigorously consummated in March. Vultures and kites which started off earlier are busy making nests, usually on the same kinds of trees they used for trysting. For some years I have watched a couple of white-backed vultures choose the same cleft in the branches of the ailanthus overlooking the Golf Club swimming pool. This tree is common in Delhi. Its Latin name *Ailanthus* (tree of heaven) *excelsa* (very tall) is summed up by its Hindi name maharukh, 'the great tree'. There are quite a few giant specimens in the Golf Club and along many roads. Its flowers, which come out late in February, are hardly visible and its fruit, which drops by June, is of no use except for propagation. However, its soft wood is used for making packing cases and match splints.

Some vultures seem to have a sense of history and like to rear their young in ancient buildings. A pair of *Neophrons* (pharaoh's chickens) have for years occupied the same niche in the western wall of the Bara Gumbad in Lodi Gardens. Amongst twigs, straw and feathers I have often noticed sanitary napkins—which must have been much softer than other nest material for fragile eggs and newly hatched chicks.

Just as Englishmen have a fetish about hearing the first cuckoo in spring, so do I record the first time I hear the koel's full-throated cry, rather than the half-hearted gurgles that one hears during winter months.

In Delhi their throats open in the first week of March, and get clearer as the days get warmer and the time for courtship draws near. About the same time papeehas (brainfever birds or hawk-cuckoos) begin to announce their presence.

Birdsong can be heard round the clock: crow pheasants' deep-throated *hook, hook, hook,* treepies' grating overture followed by a tinkling of bells and golden orioles' fluty mellifluous calls can be heard every morning. On warm afternoons the *tuk, tuk* of coppersmiths (basanta or the crimson-breasted barbet) sound very much like short blasts made by diesel-operated flour mills in villages. No songbird in India can match the magpie-robin (dhaiyal). It sounds like the European blackbird or thrush except that its arias are much shorter and it usually sings only in the early hours of the morning or at dusk—matins and evensong.

It is time I introduced you to another family of birds seen everywhere in Delhi, the mynah. We have four varieties: the common, the Asian pied starling, the bank and the brahminy starling. Fifty years ago I rarely saw bank mynahs anywhere except on railway station platforms, crowded streets and the banks of the Yamuna, where they really belong. Now bank mynahs have found new abodes in water outlets on the sides of New Delhi's many overbridges. The bank mynah has brick-red naked skin around its eyes while the common has yellow. Bank mynahs chitter incessantly and are a shade smaller than their common cousins. Brahminies remain the least noticed members of the family. They are stubby, beige coloured with a streak of black on the head. The common are indeed very common and the only kind that have the audacity to enter homes and offices to carry on their guttural mutterings on windowsills and fanlights. At dusk they gather in their hundreds of thousands on jamun and gulmohar trees and, along with the equally numerous parakeets, create a racket that drowns the roar of traffic. There were not many Asian pied starlings to be seen in my childhood days; or perhaps I did not recognize them as mynahs. Now I would hazard a guess that they outnumber their three cousins. They are black and white and their fluting call is much pleasanter than the calls of other members of their tribe.

In March, the Lodi Gardens and the Buddha Jayanti Park are much frequented by picnickers. Buddha Jayanti Park specializes in planting masses of the same flower for each bed; Lodi Gardens has quite a few flowering trees and beds of pansies, phlox, salvias, violets and other delicate varieties. A good time for visiting parks is the afternoon of Holi after the coloured water sports are over and most revellers are tired or engaged in post-Holi feasting. Since drinking concoctions with bhang (a derivative of marijuana) is de rigueur at Holi, many are likely to be sleeping it off, leaving parks free of crowds and noise. In Lodi Gardens purple bougainvillea, the most luxuriant and pristine variety of the species, makes a splendid show. To be seen among the birds are owlets, sitting in holes of old walls, taking the sun with their eyes shut, and shrikes. You can generally spot the bay-backed and long-tailed shrikes on the lower branches of trees. The shrike is also known as the butcher bird because of its nasty habit of impaling live insects on thorns to keep them fresh for consumption.

48

IN THE HEAT OF THE SUMMER

May is the month of the Indian laburnum. Although gulmohars continue to blaze their fierce scarlets, oranges and yellows, you can see they are losing some of their fire and passing Nature's baton, as it were, to the laburnums.

The Indian laburnum (*Cassia fistula*) or amaltas has become as great a favourite of Delhiwalas as the gulmohar for the simple reason that both are quick growing and colourful. Of the two, the Indian laburnum makes the more spectacular entry. It first sheds its leaves; by the second fortnight of April only the long, brown-black tubular (hence *'fistula'*) fruit can be seen hanging from its bare branches. Then suddenly blossoms appear in clusters like bunches of golden grapes. The beauty of the Indian laburnum defies description. No poet or writer has ventured to put it to paper. Only painters have been able to do it justice. Alas! Its glory has a very short lease—less than a fortnight—after which its leaves take over. The seed of the laburnum, when crushed, makes a powerful purgative and its bark, which is aromatic like cinnamon, is also used for tanning.

An equally beautiful flowering tree which is in bloom this time of the year and outlives the Indian laburnum by several weeks is the pink cassia (*Cassia javanica*). It is a thorny tree with slender branches adorned with pink and white blossoms like bracelets on the arms of a beautiful woman.

May is also the month of searing heat, with the glass seldom falling below 40° centigrade, often touching 42° and even 45° in shade. As one wag remarked, 'India has only two seasons: hot and hotter.' With the heat comes the loo, the hot wind from the deserts of Rajasthan. Our loo, like the equally warm khamsin (sirocco) and the chilly mistral, takes its toll of lives. On the hottest days its torrid embrace beguiles the unwary and lulls them to eternal sleep.

Kipling has many memorable descriptions of the heat, dust and sandstorms that visit northern India during May and June. In his story 'False Dawn', he writes: 'I had felt that the air was growing hotter and hotter, but nobody seemed to notice it until the moon went out and a burning hot wind began lashing the orange trees with a sound like the noise of the sea. Before we knew where we were, the dust storm was on us, and everything was a roaring, whirling darkness.' Kipling depicts in another poem the lassitude and weariness that come with the endless days of heat and dust:

No hope, no change! The clouds have shut us in,
And through the cloud the sullen Sun strikes down
Full on the bosom of the tortured Town,
Till Night falls heavy as remembered sin
That will not suffer sleep or thought of ease,
And, hour on hour, the dry-eyed Moon in spite
Glares through the haze and mocks with watery light
The torment of the uncomplaining trees.
Far off, the Thunder bellows her despair
To echoing Earth, thrice parched. The lightnings fly
In vain. No help the heaped-up clouds afford,
But wearier weight of burdened, burning air.
What truce with Dawn? Look, from the aching sky,
Day stalks, a tyrant with a flaming sword!

The days, hard enough to bear, get longer and longer. On the first of the month the sun rises at 5.40 a.m. and sets at 6.56 p.m., giving us more than thirteen-and-a-quarter hours of hell. By the end of the month the sun rises sixteen minutes earlier (5.24 a.m.) and sets seventeen minutes later (7.13 p.m.) adding more than half an hour of unwelcome daylight. However, dry heat is easier to bear than the moist, sticky, warm stillness that pervades our coastal towns and cities. Even though perspiration is profuse, it is healthier than the body ooze that surfaces on the skin in humid climates. There is of course the nuisance of prickly heat (pitt) which erupts round the neck, but I hold to the theory my grandmother used to expound—that prickly heat is a sign of good health. For those who find it too oppressive, there are air-coolers which convert hot winds into fragrant breezes by blowing them through dampened screens of khus fibre. These smell of earth after the first drops of rain.

May is also the month of dust storms, cloudbursts and hailstorms. They come with little warning. There is of course a preliminary lull; but after days of windless calm you hardly notice it. Only black kites wheeling in the grey sky portend that something is on the way. Then suddenly it sweeps across with gale fury, blowing dust into eyes and nostrils. It is usually followed by a cloudburst. The gale and rain take their toll of trees. I have seen ancient banyans, which stood for years like gigantic sentinels on either side of Parliament Street, torn up from their roots and ignominiously flung across the tarmac road. One May afternoon a weather-beaten neem on Kasturba Gandhi Marg, under whose shade half a dozen cars sheltered from the blazing sun, came crashing down and broke a Fiat car into two. A fifty-year-old mulberry (the only leafy tree outside my apartment, to whose shade I staked my claim every summer by parking my car under it in the early hours of the morning) was mauled by one of these storms. One afternoon as I left for the swimming pool, a fierce wind came up. I had barely gone a hundred yards when three branches of the mulberry were torn from the trunk and fell down on the exact spot where my car had rested. If my frail new Maruti had been there it would have been mashed to a pulp. If I had been in it, I would not be writing this. That afternoon I drove through lashing rain along Moti Lal Nehru Marg, up Shankar Road to the Ridge past Buddha Jayanti Park. The entire route was littered with branches of jamuns, neems and mahuas. Since fragile eucalyptus trees have no branches worth speaking of, many had been brought down to earth in one piece. It was hazardous driving along these avenues and for safety I drove in the middle of the road.

Despite the intense heat during May and June, you can also have, besides dust storms and cloudbursts, an occasional hailstorm which brings the temperature down for a few hours. Usually the hailstones are very small, almost like gravel but sometimes they are of the size of pigeons' eggs. Hailstones the size of cricket balls have been known to kill cattle and humans. A hailstorm in Moradabad in 1888 is said to have killed over 246 people in a few minutes.

Deciduous trees like neems, banyans, peepals and mahuas continue to shed their leaves and don new vestments. Semuls have by now yielded all they have to give to humans. In May you will see families of poor gathering semul cotton in sacks to sell to the makers of pillows and quilts.

Petals shed by flowering trees lie about their boles. Indian laburnums spread golden carpets about their feet; maulsaris weave them in beige, papdis in pink and white looking very much like a spread of tiny hailstones.

What is true of the flora is true of the fauna. In the feathered world, May is the month of birdsong, courtship and fulfilment. Kites and vultures which began courting in the winter sit hunchbacked watching over their nests high up in the branches of the ailanthus or semul trees. The screams of koels become louder and more strident. Crows grow suspicious of the intentions of koels and can be seen chasing them away as soon as they come anywhere near their nests.

If you listen attentively to the koel's calls, you will notice a clear pattern. It is amongst the earlier callers. As soon as the eastern sky turns grey, male koels lay claim to their airspace by a series of staccato *urook, urook, urook,* repeated over half a dozen times. In human language this could be interpreted as a warning to other males: 'Keep off and that means you!' The rest of the day the call is a monotonous *kuoo-oo, kuoo-oo.* While courting, it is the female pursued by her suitor who emits sharp cries of *kik, kik!* as she courses through the foliage.

One rarely sees koels in the act of mating. Once the female is ready to lay her eggs, her paramour takes the lead in luring crows away from their nests. The female koel then quickly deposits her eggs amongst the clutch of crows' eggs and signals to her partner that her mission has been successful by triumphant cries of *kuil, kuil, kuil!*

This cuckolding of crows requires a lot of cunning and a fine sense of timing. Koels have first to locate a crow's nest which has some eggs already laid, otherwise the crows would become suspicious. The eggs must resemble those of crows and must hatch earlier. While the crow's eggs take over a fortnight to incubate, koel chicks are ready to emerge a couple of days earlier. They also have the capacity to edge crow chicks out of the nest and hog all the food their foster parents bring. By late August and early September you can often see koel chicks being fed by crows and hear them cawing like their foster parents.

Asian pied starlings rebuild their homes every year. For many years I have seen a pair remake theirs in the same cleft of the siris which stands at one end of the tennis court. And while playing I catch the honeyed notes of golden orioles from sheesham trees, the trumpet calls of peacocks from a neighbouring park and papeehas calling in the distance.

I generally see more of nature at dawn on my way to the club, in the hour I play tennis and on my way back home, than I do during the rest of the day which I spend closeted in my study. I did not realize for years, being too absorbed in the game, that the source of the fragrance that pervaded the courts was the siris. By the middle of May its pale yellow powder-puff blossoms fall and mingle with the dust to look like bedraggled fluffs of wool. It was the same with the gulmohar under which chairs are laid out for people awaiting their turn to play. I had taken its presence for granted and rarely did my gaze rest on it till, one summer, the elements compelled me to open my eyes and take notice of its flamboyant beauty.

Khushwant Singh with
the Sujan Singh Park cats

With his parents, brothers and sister. KS is at the top extreme right

In this Haveli' was born
KHUSHVANT SINGH
Eminent novelist' historian and
promoter of Indo-Pakistan friendship
خشونت سنگھ
اس حویلی میں پیدا ہوئے

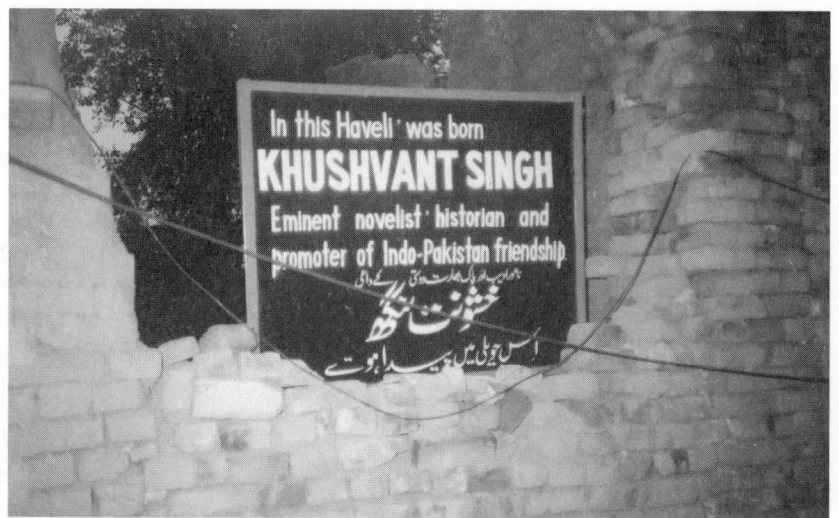

Hadali

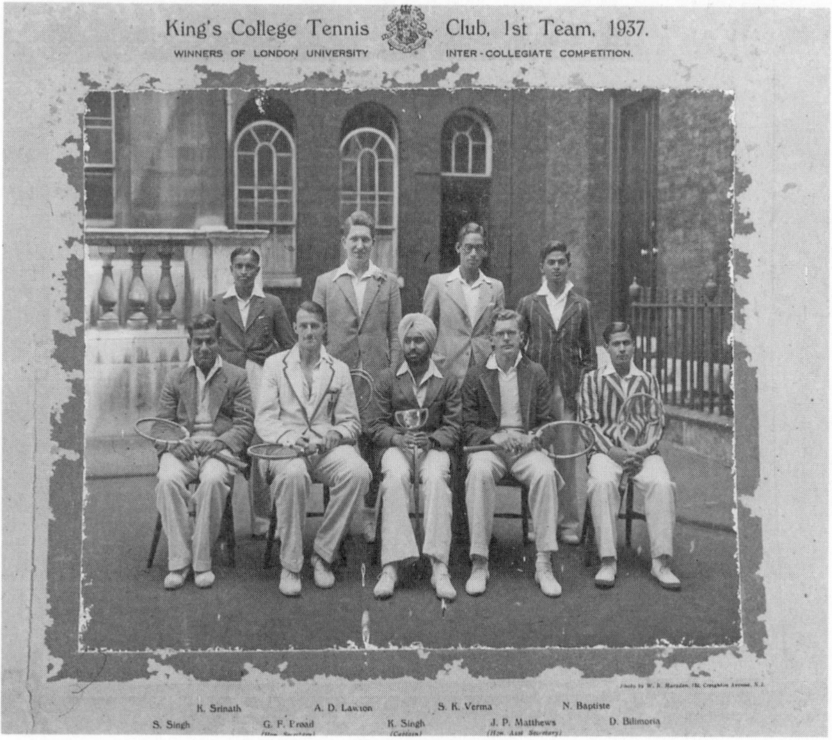
King's College Tennis Club, 1st Team, 1937.
WINNERS OF LONDON UNIVERSITY INTER-COLLEGIATE COMPETITION.
K. Srinath
A. D. Lawton
S. K. Verma
N. Baptiste
S. Singh
G. F. Froad
(Hon. Secretary)
K. Singh
(Captain)
J. P. Matthews
(Hon. Asst Secretary)
D. Bilimoria

Captain of the King's College Tennis Club

With Kaval, soon after the wedding

With the legendary Barney Rosset, the first publisher of Train to Pakistan

With his wife, Kaval, his parents and children, Mala and Rahul

Rahul and Mala

Simba and his family

In the room where he did much of his writing

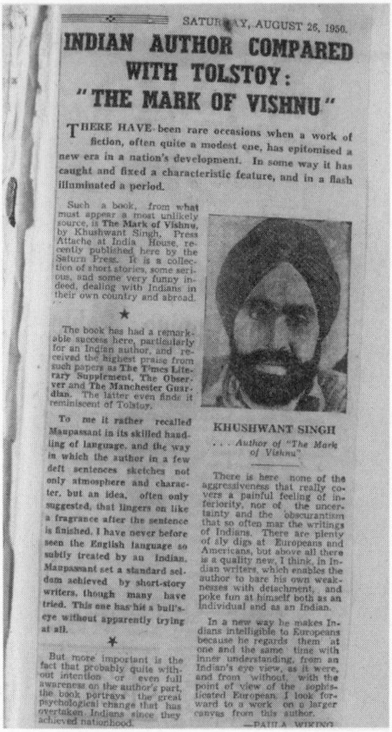

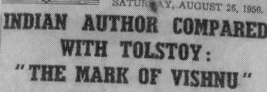

INDIAN AUTHOR COMPARED WITH TOLSTOY: "THE MARK OF VISHNU"

THERE HAVE been rare occasions when a work of fiction, often quite a modest one, has epitomised a new era in a nation's development. In some way it has caught and fixed a characteristic feature, and in a flash illuminated a period.

Such a book, from what must appear a most unlikely source, is The Mark of Vishnu, by Khushwant Singh, Press Attache at India House, recently published here by the Saturn Press. It is a collection of short stories, some serious, and some very funny indeed, dealing with Indians in their own country and abroad.

KHUSHWANT SINGH
... Author of "The Mark
of Vishnu"

＊

The book has had a remarkable success here, particularly for an Indian author, and received the highest praise from such papers as The Times Literary Supplement, The Observer and The Manchester Guardian. The latter even finds it reminiscent of Tolstoy.

To me it rather recalled Maupassant in its skilled handling of language, and the way in which the author in a few deft sentences sketches not only atmosphere and character, but an idea, often only suggested, that lingers on like a fragrance after the sentence is finished. I have never before seen the English language so subtly treated by an Indian. Maupassant set a standard seldom achieved by short-story writers, though many have tried. This one has hit a bull's-eye without apparently trying at all.

＊

But more important is the fact that probably quite without intention or even full awareness on the author's part, the book portrays the great psychological change that has overtaken Indians since they achieved nationhood.

There is here none of the aggressiveness that really covers a painful feeling of inferiority, nor of the uncertainty and the obscurantism that so often mar the writings of Indians. There are plenty of sly digs at Europeans and Americans, but above all there is a quality new, I think, in Indian writers which enables the author to bare his own weaknesses with detachment, and poke fun at himself both as an individual and as an Indian.

In a new way he makes Indians intelligible to Europeans because he regards them at one and the same time with inner understanding, from an Indian's eye view, as it were, and from without, with the point of view of the sophisticated European. I look forward to a work on a larger canvas from this author.

—PAULA WIKDON

Receiving the Grove Press Award in 1955 for
Mano Majra, *later published as* Train to Pakistan

With Kaval, and Ravi Dayal, his son-in-law

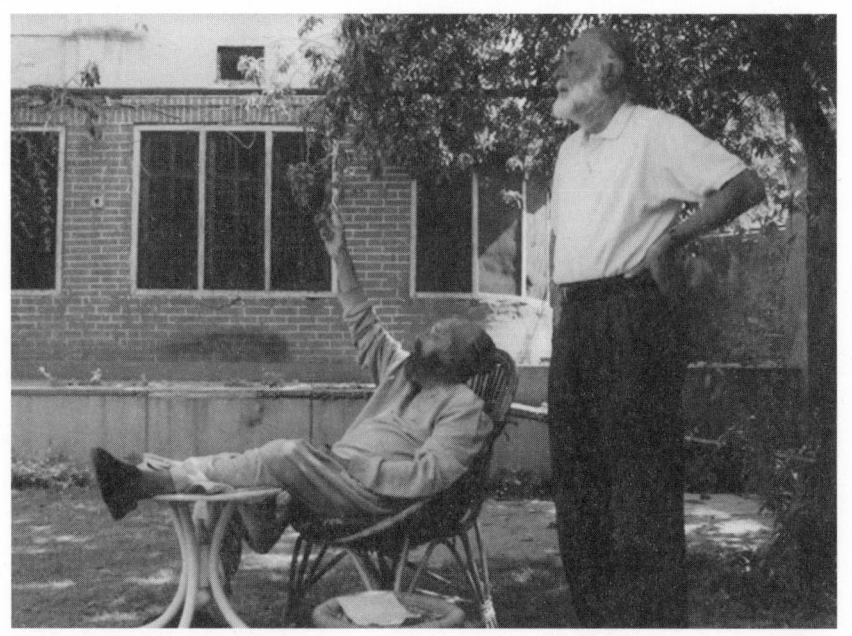

With Rahul in his Sujan Singh Park garden

With his granddaughter, Naina, and her cat

With Pandit Nehru at the first Commonwealth Prime Ministers' Conference in London

With Eamon de Valera, President of the Irish Republic, and Krishna Menon

With Sanjay Gandhi

With Zia-ul-Haq, President of Pakistan, just after the execution of Bhutto

Receiving the Padma Bhushan

With Giani Zail Singh

Receiving the Padma Vibhushan

With Manmohan Singh

An artist works on a bust of Khushwant Singh as Amrita Pritam looks on

Editing a manuscript

Sitting on the steps in Sujan Singh Park

In Memoriam

The plaque in Hadali

SEX
ON MY
MIND

IN THE LAND OF THE *KAMASUTRA*

SEX ON MY MIND

ON KISSING

THE RAJNEESH APPROACH TO SEX

TO THE VICTOR GO THE SPOILS

49

IN THE LAND OF THE *KAMASUTRA*

If you write about sex, you will be censured. Much worse, you will be condemned as a person with a dirty mind who wallows in filth. So few, very few, people dare to talk or write about sex because they know they are bound to be misunderstood. One man who had the courage to speak his mind on matters of sex without caring what people said about him was Acharya Rajneesh, known to his disciples as Osho. He was right in holding that our so-called civilized society refused to accept nudity and sex as normal and natural. We have become a 'peeping tom' society. I have my own 'peeping tom' story to tell.

Many winters ago I happened to be travelling by a night train from Delhi to Bhopal. It was a fast express that made only a few halts at major stations. I found myself in a compartment of five berths: three below and two on the sides above. I had a lower berth, as did the other two passengers who were there before me. The upper berths were reserved in the names of a Professor and Mrs Saxena. Fifteen minutes before the train was due to leave, a party of men and women escorting a bride decked in an ornate sari drawn discreetly across her face, her arms loaded with ivory bangles stopped by our compartment, read the names on the panel and came in. They were dismayed to see the two berths reserved for them were separated by a fifteen-foot chasm of space. One of the party approached me and asked if I could take one of the upper berths to accommodate the newly married couple. I readily agreed and moved my bedding roll. Another passenger who had the middle berth also moved up to the other upper berth so that the bridal couple could be alongside each other. I heard one of the party stop the conductor guard and tell him to wake up the pair at a particular junction where the train was to make a brief three-minute halt at 3 a.m.

As the conductor guard blew his whistle and waved his green flag, the party took leave of the bridal pair with much embracing and sobbing. No sooner had the train cleared the lighted platform, the bride blew her nose and uncovered her face. She was a woman in her mid-twenties: pale-skinned, round-faced and wearing thick-lensed glasses. I couldn't see much of her figure but could guess that she would be forever fighting a losing battle against fat. Her groom looked a couple of years older than her ('professor' being an honorific for a junior lecturer) and, like his bride, was sallow-faced, corpulent and bespectacled. From the snatches of conversation that I could hear (I was only four feet above them) I gathered that they were total strangers and their marriage had been arranged by relatives and through the matrimonial columns of the *Hindustan Times*. They talked of their papajis and mummyjis. Then of their time in college (the halcyon days for most educated Indians) and of their friends: 'like a brother to me' or 'better than my own real sister'. After a while the conversation began to flag; I saw the man's hand resting on his woman's on the window.

The lights were switched off, leaving only a nightlight which bathed the compartment in blue. I could not see very much except when the train ran past brightly lit platforms of wayside railway stations.

The couple did not bother to use the middle berth vacated for them and decided to make themselves as comfortable as they could on a four-foot-wide wooden plank. They ignored the presence of other passengers in the small compartment and were totally absorbed in getting to know each other. Such was their impatience that they did not find time to change into more comfortable clothes. They drew a quilt over themselves and were lost to the world.

The sari is both a very ornamental as well as a functional dress. Properly draped, it can accentuate the contours of the female form giving a special roundness to the buttocks. A well-cut blouse worn with the sari elevates the bosom, and exposes the belly to below the navel. There is no other form of female attire which can both conceal the physical shortcomings of the wearer as well as expose what deserves exposure. A fat woman looks less fat in a sari than she would in a dress and a thin woman looks more filled out. At the same time a sari is very functional. All a woman has to do when she wants to urinate or defecate is to lift it to her waist. When required to engage in quick sexual intercourse, she needs to do no more than draw it up a little and open her thighs. Apparently this was what Mrs Saxena was called upon to do. I heard a muffled 'Hai Ram' escape her lips and realized that the marriage had been consummated.

The Saxenas did not get up to go to the bathroom to wash themselves but began a repeat performance. This time they were less impatient and seemed to be getting more out of their efforts. More than once the quilt slipped off them and I caught a glimpse of the professor's heaving buttocks and his bride's bosom which he had extricated out of her choli. Above the rattle and whish of the speeding train, I heard the girl's whimper and the man's exultant grunts. They had a third go at each other before peace descended on our compartment. It was then well past the hour of midnight. Thereafter it was only the wail of the engine tearing through the dark night and the snores of my elderly companions that occasionally disturbed our slumbers.

We were rudely disturbed by someone thumping on the door, slapping the window-panes and yelling 'Get up, get up. It is Sehore. The train will leave in another minute.' It was the conductor guard.

I pressed the switch and the compartment was flooded with light. A memorable sight it was! Professor Saxena fast asleep with his buttocks exposed; Mrs Saxena also fast asleep, her mouth wide open, breasts bare, lying supine like a butterfly pinned down on a board. Her hair was scattered on her pillow. Their glasses lay on the floor.

Whatever embarrassment they felt was drowned in the hustle and bustle of getting off the train. We heaved out their beds and suitcases. The professor stumbled out on the cold platform adjusting his fly. She followed him covering her bare bosom with a fold of her sari. As the train began to move, she screamed: one of her earrings was missing. The friendly guard brought the train to a halt. All of us went down on our knees scouring the floor. The errant earring was found wedged in a crevice of the seat. We resumed our journey.

'It is love,' remarked one of my travelling companions with great understanding. 'They are newly married and this was their first night together. All should be forgiven to people in love.'

'What kind of love?' I asked in a sarcastic tone. 'A few hours ago they were complete strangers. They haven't the patience to wait till they get home and start having sex without as much as exchanging a word of affection. You call that love?'

'Well,' he replied pondering over the episode. 'They may not get another chance for some days. There will be his relatives: his mother, sisters, brothers. And lots of religious ceremonies. Youth is impatient and the body has its own demands. Let us say it is the beginning of love.'

'It may be the beginning of another family but I don't see where love comes in,' I remarked. 'I can understand illiterate peasants coupling like the cattle they rear but I cannot understand two educated people—a lecturer in a college and a schoolteacher—so totally lacking in sophistication or a sense of privacy as to begin copulating in the presence of three strangers.'

'You have foreign ideas,' said the third man dismissing me. 'Anyway, it is 3.30 in the morning. Let's get some sleep.' He switched off the light and the argument.

The episode stayed in my mind because it vividly illustrated the pattern of the man-woman relationship that exists among the vast majority of Indians. Love, as the word is understood in the West, is known only to a tiny minority of the very westernized living in the half a dozen big cities of India who prefer to speak English rather than Indian languages, read only English books, see only Western movies and even dream in English. For the rest, it is something they read about in poems or see on the screen but it is very rarely a personal experience. Arranged marriages are the accepted norm; 'love' marriages a rarity. In arranged marriages the parties first make each other's acquaintance physically through the naked exploration of each other's body and it is only after some of the lust has been drained out of their system that they get the chance to discover each other's mind and personality. It is only after lust begins to lose its potency and there is no clash of temperaments that the alliance may in later years develop bonds of companionship. But the chances of this happening are bleak. In most cases, they suffer each other till the end of their days.

I have no idea what became of the Saxenas whose nuptial consummation I witnessed. It is likely that by now they have produced a small brood of Saxenas. He is probably a full professor teaching romantic poetry and occasionally penning a verse or two to some younger lady professor ('like a sister to me') or to some pig-tailed student ('like my own daughter'). Mrs Saxena probably tries to retain her husband's interest by dog-like devotion, prayer and charms brought from 'holy' men. On the rare occasions when the professor mounts her, she has to fantasize about one of his younger colleagues ('exactly like a real brother to me') before she shudders in the throes of an orgasm with the name of God on her lips: 'Hai Ram'.

The Saxenas are luckier than most Indian couples because they live away from their families and are assured a certain amount of privacy. To most newly married Indian couples, the concept of privacy is as alien as that of love. They rarely get a room to themselves; the bride-wife sleeps with other women members of her husband's family, the husband's charpai is lined alongside his father's and brothers'. Occasionally, the mother-in-law, anxious to acquire a grandson, will contrive a meeting between her son and his wife. The most common technique is to get her to take a tumbler of milk to the lad when other male members are elsewhere. The lad grabs the chance for the 'quickie'. Hardly ever do the couple get enough time for a prolonged and satisfying bout of intercourse. Most Indian men are not even aware that women also have orgasms; most Indian women share this ignorance because although they go from one pregnancy to the next, they have no idea that sex can be pleasurable. This is a sad commentary on the people of a country which produced the most widely read treatise on the art of sex, *Kamasutra*, and elevated the act of sex to spiritual sublimity by explicit depictions in its temples.

50

SEX ON MY MIND

Indians have sex more often in their brains than anywhere else. Sex is an elemental passion. It's an integrated part of our life. All human relationships are based on the desire to have sex. When it is not fulfilled, it comes out in perverted forms. That is why celibacy does not work. The desire to have multiple partners is also normal. Married people commit adultery in their mind—the idea of a happy married life is a façade.

◆

Our forefathers understood sex as the most potent emotion in life and gave it the importance it deserved in their writings, paintings and sculptures. You can find examples in John Brough's translation of *Poems from the Sanskrit*, as well as in illustrated editions of the *Kamasutra*. It was a time when sculptors were decorating walls of temples in Khajuraho and Konark, depicting lusty men and beautifully rounded women copulating with gay abandon. Censoring by state or society did not exist.

Things changed with the invasion of Muslims in northern India. Islamic puritanism took over. Though they gave India many of its beautiful buildings, depictions of sex in writing, painting or sculpture became taboo. After them came the British who introduced their own brand of morality based on Victorian prudery of what could be printed and what deserved to be censored. After independence we had puritanical leaders who continued to censor and be hypocritical about sex.

I have always been extremely forthright in my views on sex. I think, for example, that sex is much more important than romance. I've never really had the time nor the inclination for romance. Romantic interludes take up a lot of time and are a sheer waste of energy, for the end result isn't very much. Sex is definitely more important, though sex with the same person can get boring after a while...you know, routine. Phir wo baat nahin rahti hai... A partner once bedded becomes a bore. Even the best-looking man or woman becomes boring. When it comes to sex, I don't think looks matter much.

I have many women friends. And I also keep in touch with those I've made love to in the past. I can't stand women who are not animated. She could be the most beautiful woman, but if she's not lively, then, as far as I'm concerned, there's no point. I've been with many women over the years. I've never worried about infections or sexually transmitted diseases.

You don't think of all this while making love. You just go for it. Once it's up it has to go in there—there's no other way!

I've had affairs that I've used as material for my writing. They contributed to the love-making scenes and passages in my stories and novels. The affairs were very good while they lasted but then you move on, without any unpleasantness. You just drift apart. And in the instances where the women have persisted, I've withdrawn after a point—I've always wanted my space and have never wanted anyone to get too close to me emotionally. I value my space and have guarded it because of my writing. Writing is a solitary task and I'm more comfortable being alone. I get impatient with people and places, so I move on. I've been like this all my life.

I have been with women of almost every nationality and they are the same in bed. Foreigners *don't* make love differently; their attitude towards love-making might be different. And all those notions about the French being great lovers or that Englishwomen are frigid—they are all myths. Years ago, before I'd travelled to England, I had heard that Englishwomen were frigid, cold and reserved. Nothing could be more wrong. That sort of stereotyping—it's absolute rubbish. Nationalities, even religious backgrounds, make no difference at all. It's the desire, the intensity, that's important; there has to be that attraction. Of course, there could be problems if one of the partners has an insatiable appetite and the other has little interest in sex! As far as I'm concerned, I've never been in a situation like this, so I've never really had any awkward moments.

And like nationality or religious background, size does not matter either—whether it's the size of the penis or that of the breasts, whether the lips are full... None of it matters. There just has to be desire on both sides, and reciprocation of feelings. And there should be no suppression or holding back. For if you withhold your urges it will come out in some other form; there's bound to be some aberration. There's far too much sexual frustration in our country and this probably explains the rapes and molestations we hear about every other day. They happen in other countries too, but in India it seems to be a problem now more than ever before. And it's linked to sexual repression and our hypocrisy—we Indians are very interested in sex, we have the curiosity and the drive but we pretend to be prudish and conservative.

◆

I had my first sexual encounter when I was around nineteen. It was 1934. After having spent the summer vacations in Delhi I had to get back to England, where I was studying. From Delhi I took the Frontier

Mail to Bombay and had to spend the night there, before the ship set sail the next morning. I spent that night in Bombay's Victoria Terminus Station. I went out to explore the neighbourhood. While I was walking around, I strolled much beyond, towards Kamathipura, Bombay's red-light area—narrow lanes and by-lanes with women looking out of their homes, beckoning, gesturing, smiling... One of those women kept calling out to me and somehow I found myself responding. 'Which way?' I asked her. She pointed to a staircase leading up to her room. I went up the dark flight of steps. The room was dingy, lit by a single oil lamp. There was a boy sitting there. The woman came forward to receive me. She was fat, dark, middle-aged and dressed in a salwar kameez. Without a word of welcome, she said in Punjabi, 'It will be Rs 10.' I pulled out a ten-rupee note and handed it to her. She gave the boy a five-rupee note and ordered him to give it to her landlord. Then she bolted the door from inside. The room had no furniture save a charpai covered with a greasy durrie and a dirty pillow. There was a pitcher of water and a lota covering its mouth. She turned around to address me. 'You Sardars are such fine-looking men; why do you grow this fungus around your chins?' she asked running her hand over my beard. I did not reply. She sensed I was a novice and asked me whether it was my first time. Hearing me say yes, she slipped off her salwar, tucked her shirt above her waist, baring her fat bottom. She went to the pitcher, filled the lota and splashed water between her thighs and dried her middle with a dirty rag. Then, laying herself on the charpai she raised her legs, bent at the knees, to her chest. 'Come!' she said, stretching out both her arms. Till then I had never had a good look at a woman between her thighs. I was not sure where to enter her. As I undid my trousers and bent over her, she took my penis in one hand and directed it to its target. As I entered her, I spent myself.

◆

The first time I saw female genitals it was a sight! It wasn't attractive or appealing at all—on the contrary, it was appalling! Appalling! I was in my teens and there was a lunch being hosted on the lawns of the teachers' quarters in my school. When this lady teacher tried sitting on the grass, her sari rode up and exposed her thighs and much more. That fleeting glimpse of the teacher's private parts revolted me but it was also then that my curiosity about a woman's body was whetted and I would try and peep when women labourers were bathing semi-clad... It was with that glimpse that I first became aware of desire.

Another time, when I was recovering from yet another bout of typhoid, a nurse hired to look after me went beyond her call of duty—she did more than sponge my body. I was still young, in my teens, but that didn't deter her from holding my penis and even kissing it. I was too young to know what was happening, and also too weak and too ill to respond, react or enjoy it.

And long before that, when I was a young child, a cousin tried exploring my body. She must have been around the same age as I was. We tried touching each other and somehow it aroused something—a strange curiosity about the female form. That's how it all began.

◆

Since then, I have always been a bit of a lecher. From the tender age of four onwards, lechery has been uppermost in my mind. I have never been able to conform to the Indian ideal of regarding women as my mother, sister or daughter. Whatever their age, to me they were, and are, objects of lust.

51

ON KISSING

Some three years ago, I took the liberty of greeting the daughter of the then Pakistan high commissioner, Ashraf Jehangir Qazi, with a kiss. She was around sixteen; I was nearing ninety. Her grandfather and grand-uncle were in college with me in England. A photograph of me embracing the teenager appeared in *The Indian Express* and was picked up by some Pakistani papers. It created a furore in Pakistan. Qazi was summoned to Islamabad to explain his daughter's conduct. He did so to their satisfaction. They felt pretty foolish about it. A few days later, a Pakistani family, including their young daughters, came to call on me. As I opened the door to welcome them, the father said to me, 'First, give my daughters a kiss, then we will come in'. And before the Qazis left India for the US, they came to say goodbye to me. This time it was their daughter who took the initiative and kissed me on both sides of my bearded cheeks.

I often wonder what would have happened if, instead of Qazi's little girl, I had taken the same liberty with her grand-aunt, Pyari Begam, who was a great beauty and in my age group. Perhaps it would have led to a war between the Baluchis and Sikhs. It was truly said by Don Marquis on kissing: 'Mayhem, death and arson have followed many a thoughtless kiss not sanctioned by a person.'

There are infinite ways of kissing: an avuncular on the forehead, the fraternal on both cheeks, the more intricate on the lips, or side of the neck. The choice largely depends on the female recipient because males are overeager to convert the gesture into an intimate relationship. It is said high-heeled shoes were invented for short women who were tired of being kissed on their foreheads.

An honest kiss demands the meeting of the lips. Even with this, there are countless ways of expressing emotions. Vatsyayan made a list of over sixty in his silly sex classic, *Kamasutra*. In the matter of kissing no one needs a textbook to guide him or her. All of us know all there is to know from the day we are born. Nor do we have to wait for astral signs to tell us of auspicious days to go ahead. There is an old English saying; 'Kissing is not in season when the gorse is not in bloom.' Gorse is in full blossom right through the year. It grows in profusion in the Shivaliks.

One does not have to define a kiss. Henry Gibbons made a silly attempt which robbed it of all the joy it yields: 'The anatomized juxtaposition of two orbicularis oris muscles in a state of contraction.' Nonsense! Poet

231

Robert Herrick was closer to the mark when he wrote: 'What is a Kiss? Why this, as some approve: The sure, sweet cement, glue and lime of love.'

Kisses can be lethal as well as life-giving. There was the kiss of Judas which betrayed Jesus Christ and led to his crucifixion—it was the kiss of death. There is also the prolonged kiss of resuscitation to save the life of a drowned person. There is the kiss that reveals a past relationship. There is a kiss which means nothing but a meeting of lips. As an old Italian proverb says: 'A kiss on the lip does not always touch the heart.' It is the kind of kiss that film actors plant on each other in front of cameras with dozens of people watching them. Meanwhile, I find solace in an old Spanish saying: 'A kiss without a moustache is like an egg without salt.' I have plenty of moustache.

52

THE RAJNEESH APPROACH TO SEX

There are many ways of attaining godhood, say teachers of religion. Acharya Rajneesh disagrees and says there is only one way, and sexual intercourse is the first step towards it. He maintains that religion as it is practised is false, and its propagators are agents of Satan. They have degraded love and taught us the negation of life. The philosophy of religion has always been death-oriented instead of being life-oriented. He goes on to add: 'I call religion the art of living. Religion is not a way to undermine life; it is a medium for delving deeply into the mysteries of existence. Religion is not turning one's back on life; it is facing life squarely. Religion is not escaping from life; religion is embracing life fully. Religion is the total realization of life.'

Since love is the essence of all religions and sex the essence of love, you cannot sidestep it to proceed on your voyage of discovery. Rajneesh writes, 'Sex is the beginning of the journey to love. The origin, the Gangotri of the Ganges of Love, is sex, passion—and everybody behaves like it's the enemy. Every culture, every religion, every guru, every seer has attacked this Gangotri, this source, and the river has remained bottled up. The hue and cry has always been, "Sex is sin. Sex is irreligious. Sex is poison". But we never seem to realize that ultimately, it is the sex energy itself that travels to and reaches the inner ocean of love. Love is the transformation of sex energy.'

Because sex has been condemned and suppressed 'it has become an obsession, a disease, a perversion', says the Acharya, and advises us to 'accept sex with joy. Acknowledge its sacredness… When a man approaches his wife he should have a sacred feeling, as if he were going to a temple. And when a wife goes to her husband she should be full of the reverence one has nearing God. In the moments of sex, lovers pass through coitus, and that stage is very near to the temple of God, to where he is manifest in creative formlessness.' He conjectures that man has his first glimpse of Samadhi during sexual intercourse culminating in a climax when the mind becomes empty of thoughts. Thus vishyanand (bliss of coitus) and Brahmanand (bliss of union with God) are much the same; one is ephemeral, the other eternal.

Not all sexual intercourse is an experience of divinity. For that you have to first get rid of your ego. 'Unless I dissolve myself, how can the other unite with me?' he asks. Love always gives; the ego is ever

233

the grabber; love is motiveless, the ego always motivated; the ego only understands the language of taking; the language of giving is love. The second condition to be fulfilled is the feeling of timelessness. 'In orgasm, the sense of time is non-existent. There is no past, no future, there is only the present moment.'

The Acharya has some practical suggestions to overcome an unhealthy obsession with sexuality. Children should be allowed to remain nude as much as possible in the home so that they do not develop prurient curiosity in private organs. They should also be taught to meditate (on what, he does not say) in silence for at least one hour every day. They should be taught what sex is all about before they are old enough to engage in it. He writes, 'Sex is the most mysterious, most profound, most precious and, at the same time, the most accursed subject; and we are in total darkness about it. We never pay attention to this important phenomenon. A man goes through the routine of coitus throughout his life, but he does not know what it is.'

The Acharya, who claims to have had sexual fulfilment in his previous life which cleared his mind of sexuality for his present incarnation and those to come, tells us how to get the best out of coitus. Most of us are used to quickies that end in frustration and incite us to have more of the same thing. Coitus, he tells us, must be prolonged as much as possible. In the way of technique, he suggests slowing down one's breathing and focusing awareness to a point between the eyes, the seat of the agnichakra. If you can prolong intercourse to one hour, you need not think of sex for the rest of your life; if you can prolong it to three hours, you will be liberated from sexuality for your lives to come. A third essential condition is that you should approach sex with reverence. 'Give sex a sacred status in your life,' he says. 'At the time of coitus, we are close to God.'

The Acharya tells us the sculptors of erotica on the temples of Konark, Khajuraho and Puri had the right approach to sex. We should have such temples all over India. Tantriks were also on the right path; preachers of religious dogma suppressed them. He concludes: 'The journey to kama is also the journey to Rama. The journey to lust is also the journey to light. The tremendous attraction for sex is also the search for the sublime.'

I am not sure how seriously one should take Rajneesh.

53

TO THE VICTOR GO THE SPOILS

There are two themes I wish to illustrate through this almost entirely true short story. The first is that God compensates women. He does not endow with good looks in His own mysterious ways. A plain-looking, homely type of girl need not envy her better-looking sisters because men are more likely to make passes at her than at girls who resemble Marilyn Monroe or Prema Narayan. He makes good-looking lasses haughty and arrogant and only gigolo types have the confidence to approach them. That is why the plainer-looking have a better time with men and end up making better marriages than pretty ones who seldom have a satisfying sex life and usually make disastrous marriages.

The second theme is somewhat hackneyed: only the brave deserve the fair, equally well expressed in the maxim, 'Nothing ventured, nothing gained.'

Now to the illustrative story.

Some thirty years ago I was living in a two-bedroom basement flat in Highgate, London. I had recently resigned from the diplomatic service but still had my large American limousine with a 'CD' numberplate and a sizeable stock of duty-free champagne, Scotch, wines and liqueurs. My family had returned to India and I had three months of freedom to finish a book I was working on and whatever else I wanted to do in the way of keeping myself amused. The apartment above mine was occupied by a stenotyping agency which closed in the evening. The one above the agency was occupied by a young lady who, I was told, was a stage actress. She went to work late in the evening and returned home after the second show, sometime after midnight. All three flats had one entrance. Since the only garage attached to the premises was too small to house my limousine, it was parked outside the entrance. The only source of natural light for my basement flat was a large window, half of which was above ground level alongside a bus stop. Sitting in my armchair I could see the legs of people queueing up outside or alighting from buses.

I spent most of my days working on my book. In the evenings, a girl who had been my secretary at India House came to collect whatever I had scribbled during the day and have tea with me before she departed. After she left I would take a walk round Hampstead Heath and return home to light a fire, drink, listen to music, eat a sandwich supper and read till I felt sleepy. This was rarely before midnight. And soon I began to time my retirement with the sound of the opening of the entrance door and the footsteps of the actress going up the stairs to her apartment.

And it was not much after that that I discovered her identity. The lady who came to clean my flat also did the other two apartments. One morning I casually asked her about the occupant of the top flat. 'That will be Miss Dawson,' she replied, 'Jennifer Dawson, pretty as a picture she is. And very very nice too. She gave me two free tickets for her show. She's got a very small role. But mark my words, she'll go far. One day I'll be proud of having worked for her.'

Thereafter I kept a lookout for the last bus that stopped by my apartment. And soon got to recognize the pair of shapely legs that alighted and then took their owner up the steps.

One Sunday morning I contrived to make her acquaintance. I had noted that she went to the midmorning service and since there was no show on Sundays, spent the afternoons at home, presumably washing her clothes. As soon as I heard her footsteps coming down, I came out of my apartment. She extended her hand and said, 'We are neighbours but we have never met. I am Jennifer Dawson. Mrs Markham has told me you are Mr Singh. Nice to meet you.'

I took her proffered hand and replied, 'Mrs Markham told me you were pretty but not how pretty you were. I am honoured living beneath a famous actress.'

'Famous, my foot!' she said with a laugh. 'I'm only a miserable extra. If you want to see how extra I am, I will be happy to give you a ticket for the show. That's the only thing I can afford; I get it free.'

I opened the front door for her and asked, 'Can I drop you anywhere? I have nothing much to do except take my car for an airing.'

She looked at my chariot-sized limousine. 'Cor blimey! Must drink up gas by the gallon! I am going to the church round the corner, I don't mind being driven in your American Rolls-Royce.'

I dropped her at the church. 'I can pick you up on my way back; how long will the service last?' I asked. 'You are most kind!' she replied. 'I should be through in an hour. Sure you don't mind?'

'On this fine Sabbath morning I have nothing whatsoever to do save eat the English air. Allah is in His heaven and all's right with the world.'

I went back to my apartment to freshen up and was back outside the church. I switched on the radio. I was lucky. It was Beethoven's Ninth Symphony, the only piece of Western classical music I was familiar with. It was coming across in all its mellifluous beauty.

She was among the first to step out of the church. She shook hands with the vicar and ran towards the car. She certainly was a beauty: hazel-brown hair tumbling down on her shoulders, broad forehead, large brown eyes, lovely neck and as shapely a figure as you would see in a Miss Universe beauty contest. Beethoven's magic worked. 'Let's not go home till the symphony is over,' she pleaded.

I drove slowly round the heath, along Spaniard's Inn Road and the Vale of Heath. She kept humming softly to herself and tossing her head to the music, completely oblivious of my presence. We were passing Keats' Grove when the symphony reached its climactic end. 'That was wonderful,' she sighed. 'Thank you ever so much for indulging me. I have wasted all your precious morning.'

'It was a pleasure,' I replied. 'I wish you would waste more of them. I get awfully lonely having no one to talk to except Mrs Markham and my secretary for a few minutes every day. The rest of the time, it is books. And silence.'

She did not rise to the bait. Nor accept my invitation to have a bite with me before she went up. 'Who will do all my laundry and ironing, write my weekly letter to Ma and cook my supper? Thanks for a wonderful time.' She patted me on the shoulder and ran upstairs.

Next Sunday I slipped a note under her door inviting her for a drink in the evening after she had done her Sunday chores. She did not send a reply but as it turned dark and the street lights came on, I heard her footsteps come down the stairs and a gentle tap on my door. I leapt up from my chair to welcome her. 'It is very thoughtful of you to have invited me,' she said. She looked round the dimly lit room with only one tablelamp above my armchair. I switched on the room light and went to help her take off her overcoat. 'It's freezing cold. Don't mind if I keep it on?' she asked.

Mrs Markham always laid coal in the grate. I took a bottle of gin and splashed it over the heap and threw a lighted match on it. The grate exploded into a blue flame and soon we had a blazing fire going. 'How extravagant can one be!' she exclaimed. 'Never heard of anyone lighting fire with gin.'

'Duty-free diplomatic privilege,' I replied. 'Costs me very little and is quicker than newspapers or woodchips to get a fire going. What would you like, Scotch, sherry, gin, vodka, champagne?'

She slipped her overcoat off her shoulders and warmed her hands before the grate. 'If you are flush with liquor I would not mind some champagne,' she replied.

I got a bottle of Mouton Rothschild from the freezer, uncorked it with professional skill and poured the frothing, bubbling liquor into the best cut-glasses I had. I raised mine and proposed the toast, 'To the most beautiful girl in the world!' Her face flushed with pleasure as she raised her glass and replied, 'To the world's nicest old man and the greatest liar.'

She curled up in an armchair and sipped champagne; I replenished her glass several times. The fire in the grate glowed on her face and lit the curls on her hair. 'Jennifer, you must have lots of admirers and boyfriends,' I said.

'Why do you say that?' she asked.

'Now you are fishing. Your mirror must tell you why every time you look into it.'

'You are nice!' she replied. 'Believe it or not I have never had any boyfriends. Admirers, yes. A few. They pay me compliments. And that's that.'

I paid her more compliments. Quoted lines I knew of English poets in praise of beautiful women. She listened with a distant look in her eyes, gazing into the embers of coal glowing in the grate. I put on music. She shut her eyes.

I made sandwiches and coffee and brought them in a tray for her. I gently tapped her on the shoulder. 'Asleep?'

She woke with a start. 'Not really. Day-dreaming to the music. I should have been doing all that, not you,' she said, looking at the tray. 'You are spoiling me.'

We ate our sandwiches and drank our coffee in silence. I felt her large eyes fixed, questioning, on me. Did I dare make an advance? No, she was too beautiful for the likes of me and I did not want to lose her friendship by taking a false step. After a while she stood up. 'I don't want to go but I must drag myself away. Beauty sleep and all that—can't afford to look dowdy on the stage.' She gave me a peck on my nose. 'Thank you for a wonderful, wonderful evening.' She left and shut the door behind her.

I had established rapport, proved that I was a gentleman who would not take unwelcome liberties with her. The rest, I would leave to time. And her.

I changed my working hours to suit hers. Every night she came back from the theatre, I had the fire lit, a bottle of champagne in the freezer, sandwiches on a tray and a steaming pot of hot coffee. She had her nightcap with me. We spent our Sundays together. She told me that she went to church because she had nothing better to do and much preferred to drive out to the country, walk in the woods and end the Sabbath by my fireside. We did Kenwood and Kew; Burnham Beeches and the Cotswolds and Stratford-on-Avon. I got no closer to her than I had on the first evening.

Then an old friend of my college days in Lahore arrived in London.

He had very little money and gratefully accepted my invitation to stay with me. He was a small, effeminate Sardarji whose chief qualification was being a good listener. No one would suspect him of a being a ladies' man or regard him as a rival. I told him about Jennifer, her goddess-like aloofness, and cautioned him to treat her with respect.

The first time they met he was on his best behaviour. She gave him a ticket for her show. They came back together. I was happy they had hit it off. The following Sunday I asked a few Indian friends we had known in Lahore and their wives for drinks. Needless to say, Jennifer was the main attraction. And a great success.

She acted the hostess and talked to all the women. From the way my guests looked at me I could sense that they felt Jennifer was my woman and I had something very nice going for me while my family was away. I did not want to disabuse them.

The party went on late into the night with vast quantities of Scotch and champagne going down their gullets. Everyone was in high spirits, particularly my house guest who took more than his share of liquor. Around midnight, the guests departed, leaving Jennifer and the Sardarji with me. They relaxed in their armchairs while I removed empty glasses and ashtrays. My Sardarji friend planted himself on the carpet beside Jennifer's feet, looking soulfully at her with his large cocker spaniel eyes. He rested his head against her thighs and began stroking her shapely legs.

'Please tell your friend to behave himself,' said Jennifer to me.

I spoke to him in Punjabi. He was too far gone to listen to me in any language. Jennifer got up from her chair and sat down in another. After a while the Sardarji hauled himself up, planted himself on the arm of the same chair and began stroking Jennifer's hair. I spoke more sharply this time. It was no use. 'Jennifer, I think you should go to your apartment,' I suggested.

Jennifer only changed her chair. The Sardarji followed her and resumed his ministrations. I lost my temper. 'For God's sake, stop pestering Jennifer! You are drunk. You better go to bed.'

He took no notice of me. It became like a game of hide-and-seek between the two with me playing the role of a referee. Neither took my advice to retire to their respective beds. Then in the game of chase, the Sardarji slipped and fell. His turban came off and he was sick all over my carpet. I was very angry. Jennifer apologized and left. I went off to my bedroom and left my house guest wallowing in his vomit.

The next morning I told my Sardarji friend to find lodgings elsewhere. He left without protest or apology. I wrote a note to Jennifer, apologizing for his behaviour and hoping that she would not drop me because of what had happened. I thought it best not to leave my door open to welcome her when she returned from the theatre and let her, if she wanted, knock at my door. I found a note from her saying not to worry. But she did not knock at my door. Night after night I saw her legs as she alighted from the bus, heard the click of the lock opening the front door and her footsteps going up the stairs. I felt let down and punished for no fault of mine.

And lonely. I could not concentrate on my work. My peace of mind was gone. I felt that if I met my Sardarji friend again I would punch him on the nose for what he had done by ruining a beautiful friendship.

Came next Sunday. Bright and sunny with peals of church bells from distant spires, the loudest being from 'Jennifer's round the corner'. I could not contain myself any more. I decided to go up to her bed-sitting room apartment—she had never invited me—and take her out for a drive into the country as we had done in the past. I was sure she would relent and make up.

I went up the dark stairway to the top floor. Beside the doorbell was a strip of paper with the name 'Jennifer Dawson'. I rang the bell. I heard Jennifer's voice shouting, 'See who it is. Maybe a telegram or something.' The door opened. Facing me stood my Sardarji friend in his pyjamas.

A

MERRY

HEART

54

INDIAN HUMOUR

Until I read Lee Siegel's *Laughing Matters* I was not aware of the fact that we do have a tradition of humour coming down to us from ancient times. Our ancients poked fun at their kings, statesmen and army commanders. They were lampooned as important men controlled by their wives and mistresses who offloaded their bastard children on their unsuspecting husbands. Then we had court jesters like Birbal, Tenali Raman and Gopal Bhore. They specialized in solving riddles put to them by their patrons or scoring points against other royal advisors. Their sense of humour was not sophisticated but they continue to enjoy esteem among common people to this day. According to Siegel every generation of Indians has produced its own humourists. I may be the one for the present generation.

◆

We may have had a great tradition of humour but today lack a sense of humour. Let me analyse why. The first condition, the sine qua non—without which nothing humorous can be created—is our inability to laugh at ourselves. We take ourselves too seriously and are easily offended by those who do not share our self-esteem. Sometime or the other, every one of us makes an ass of himself. But how rare it is to hear an Indian tell a joke about himself in which he is shown in a poor light!

Let me give you a couple of instances of how seriously we take ourselves. This is a true story about a minister of government. You know what most of our ministers are like! No sooner do they become powerful than they lose all sense of proportion and get inflated with self-esteem. Well, this minister I am going to tell you about was sitting all by himself in a corner of a restaurant. I went up to him and invited him to join my friends. He graciously agreed to do so. I introduced him and added, 'My friends were saying that of all the important people in this country, you are the only one who has not lost his head and retains his sense of modesty.'

The minister blushed to the roots of his grey beard and replied: 'Hanji, everyone says I am very modest. In school and college I never stood second in my class [in case you don't know, that is an Indianism for saying you were always tops] but I never gave up my modesty. I had the biggest legal practice in my district, but I never gave up my modesty. And now I am the youngest ever man to be made a full minister but I remain as modest as ever.'

With great difficulty I kept myself from breaking out into guffaws of laughter. But I couldn't retain this gem, illustrative of our national character, in my belly for too long. I narrated the dialogue at many parties and also wrote about it saying that as a nation we were unable to stomach success and even a modest Indian was not happy unless he could prove himself to be the most modest man in the world. Needless to say, all this got back to the minister. He never forgave me for making him out to be a bit of an ass. And once when I went to see him to ask for a favour, he dismissed me very curtly: 'Aap mera mazaak uratey rahtey hain (You keep making fun of me).'

The other anecdote, also true, is about a young and very bright student who had topped in every exam he took and ended up with a scholarship at Oxford University where also he got a first class first. He became a kind of guru and gave sermons on Vedanta. The main theme of the message he preached was that the source of all evil was hum hain—I am, the ego which inflated into ahamkara—arrogance. And that unless you conquered this ego, you could not hope to better yourself. One day one of his disciples asked him: 'Sir, I agree with all you say, but how exactly does one conquer one's ego?'

'A very good question,' replied our philosopher. 'I know something about it, because the problem of conquering the ego because of my many achievements is much tougher for me than for any of you. I recommend that each one of you devise your own formula. What I do is to sit padmasan and repeat to myself every morning and evening, "I am not so-and-so who stood first in every exam I took. I am not so-and-so who broke all examination records of my university. I am not so-and-so who became president of the university union. I am not so-and-so, the most brilliant philosopher of the Orient. I am merely a spark of the divine."'

Needless to say that those of us who spread this story about the formula to conquer the ego came in for some very uncharitable lambasting from this human spark of the divine.

The second reason for our lacking in humour is that we are very touchy about a large number of topics. We must not make jokes about God or religion; we must not make jokes about our elders; we must not make jokes about revered figures of our history except those which have been sanctioned by tradition—like for example those of Akbar and Birbal or about Maharaja Ranjit Singh and Akali Phula Singh. Try and crack a joke about Chhatrapati Shivaji within earshot of a Maharashtrian and you'll understand what I mean. We are equally sensitive about community jokes, which form a rich storehouse of humour of other countries. Although we have lots of proverbs of different castes and subcommunities like Julahas,

Naees, Jats, Banias, Marwaris and others, we do not think it is right to relate these or jokes based on stereotypes in the presence of members of those subgroups. This phenomenon is in acute contrast to the Jews who not only tell jokes about themselves but heartily participate in jokes other people tell about them.

With so many taboos, what are we left with? Precious little. Turn the pages of any of our magazines. Most of them devote a page or so to what they think is humorous. The most popular form is an item entitled 'Answers to Your Questions' where readers' queries are answered by a hired wit or by the editor himself. When I read them I do not know whether to laugh or cry. The other item usually bears some silly title like 'Smile Awhile', 'Laugh', 'Laffs' or 'Laughing Matter'. Without exception, all the jokes printed under this heading are taken from some international syndicates or lifted from foreign magazines and occasionally rephrased to make them sound Indian. Almost all the strip-cartoons and comics are likewise taken from foreign sources. I have a sizeable collection of books on humour; I have yet to come across one on Indian humour which is not almost entirely plagiarized.

State legislatures and parliaments are a rich source of humour in all countries. This particular brand of humour requires a ready wit so that the retort can be fired back as soon as a remark is made, not thought of much later: what the French call the staircase wit—something you think you should have said going down the stairs after the party is over.

We have had some parliamentarians who were quick-witted in their repartees but their best efforts were not especially memorable.

Some of the finest sallies of wit and humour were fired by A. P. Herbert, Aneurin Bevan and above all Winston Churchill in the British House of Commons. I will not narrate them as most of you are likely to have heard them before. But let me tell you an absolute gem of a retort that I picked up from, of all places, the Parliament of Uruguay. An Opposition member was attacking a minister. The minister got up to intervene. The member shouted back, 'But I haven't finished yet.' This was repeated many times but every time the minister rose to defend himself the Opposition man yelled, 'Sit down! I haven't finished yet.' When at long last the man finished his speech, the minister asked: 'Have you finished now?'

'Yes,' replied the man taking his seat.

'Then pull the chain,' snapped the minister amidst thunderous applause.

55

THE JOKER

Laughter is evidently the elixir of life—the best tonic in the world to ensure a long and happy life. Laughter is not only the best tonic but humorous writing and relating other people's jokes is very lucrative, as both my publishers and I have found. Every one of my joke books has gone into more than a dozen reprints. They are to be seen on pavements, railway station and airport bookstalls.

But not everyone enjoys jokes, especially when they are the target. This is especially true of politicians who have notoriously thin skins. We have had quite a few very good cartoonists—Shankar Pillai, R. K. Laxman, O. V. Vijayan, Rajinder Puri, Mario Miranda. Their cartoons have enlivened our newspapers and magazines and brought a smile to our faces. But many politicians and political parties take themselves very seriously and consider far too many topics as sacred cows not to be laughed about. They take umbrage at being the butt of jokes.

Laughter for them is no laughing matter. They serve those who poke fun at them with legal notices—or worse.

I cannot take credit for the jokes appearing in my joke books. A large number were sent to me by readers who have been acknowledged by their names. Some I made up or moulded from jokes I picked up from friends, books and magazines.

At the end of the day, more than my other work as a novelist, short story writer, historian of the Sikhs or translator, I am known for my joke books. At every gathering, I am implored, 'Koi joke-shoke ho jai'—let there be a joke or two. I am known as a joker.

56

A MAN'S LIFE

God created a mule, and told him, 'You will be a mule, work constantly from dawn to dusk, and carry heavy loads on your back. You will eat grass and lack intelligence. You will live for fifty years.'

The mule answered, 'To live like that for fifty years will be too much. Please, Lord, give me no more than twenty years.' And it was so. Then God created a dog, and told him, 'You will hold vigilance over the dwellings of man to whom you will be the greatest companion. You will eat his table scraps and live for twenty-five years.'

The dog responded, 'Lord, to live twenty-five years as a dog like that will be too much. Please, Lord, give me no more than ten years.' And it was so.

God then created a monkey and told him, 'You will be a monkey. You will swing from tree to tree and act like an idiot. You will be funny, and you will live for twenty years.'

The monkey responded, 'Lord, to live twenty years as the clown of the world will be too much. Please, Lord, give me no more than ten years.' And it was so.

Finally, God created man and told him, 'You will be the only rational being that walks on the earth. You will use your intelligence to have mastery over other creatures of the world. You will dominate the earth and live for twenty years.'

The man responded, 'Lord, to be a man for only twenty years will be too little. Please, Lord, give me the thirty years the mule refused, the fifteen years the dog refused, and the ten years the monkey refused.' And it was so.

Ever since the grant of that wish man's life goes somewhat like this: He lives the first twenty years as a man enjoying himself without a worry in the world, then he marries and has children; to support them he has to work like a mule and carry the heavy responsibility (load) of his family on his shoulders. This goes on till he is forty. The next fifteen years he lives a dog's life guarding his house and eating leftovers after the children have emptied the pantry. Finally, in his old age, he lives the last ten years as a monkey, entertaining his grandchildren by acting like an idiot. And so it has been ever since.

57

BLISSFUL IGNORANCE

Once Albert Einstein went to a New York restaurant. Having forgotten his reading glasses at home, he asked the waiter to read out the menu for him. 'Sorry, sir,' he replied, 'I am like you. I cannot read or write either!'

(Contributed by Manjitinder Singh Johal, Ludhiana)

58

FILE IT, FORGET IT

This is a true story of an ingenious politician who was head of a government company that was to buy forty buses for its transport fleet. After getting his palm duly greased, he asked his procurement-in-charge to put up a note recommending that the buses be bought from a particular firm. The note was duly put up. The politician wrote 'Approved' below the note and signed. Meanwhile, another firm had got wind of the deal, so they approached the politician with a better kickback offer.

The politician recalled the file and added 'Not' in front of 'Approved'. The original supplier then landed up and offered the politician a further cut. The politician calmly recalled the file a second time and added an 'e' after 'Not', so that now it read 'Note Approved'.

(Contributed by Rajeshwari Singh, New Delhi)

59

POWER OF NATURAL GAS

Indian defence ministers are notorious for their lack of familiarity with military weapons and skills.

There was a time when the army was under attack by the enemy, which was using chemical weapons in the form of gas. The Indian Army was short of gas masks.

The general telephoned the Indian defence minister and said: 'I am running drastically short of means to fight the gas attack.'

And the defence minister promptly said: 'Try taking two tablets of soda bicarb dissolved in a glass of water. That should take care of the gas.'

(Contributed by Priya Nath Mehta, Gurgaon)

60

DYING FOR LOVE

Banto, who was at her maika (mother's house) for a couple of days, phones her husband: 'Darling, in the last fifteen days that I have been away from you, I have reduced by half. When are you coming to fetch me?'

He replied: 'In a month or so.'

(Contributed by Shashank Shekhar, Mumbai)

61

DEALING WITH SANTA

Santa was flying to Chandigarh from Pune. He was allotted a middle seat but he decided to take the window seat which had been allotted to an old lady. The old lady requested Santa to exchange seats with her. He refused, saying, 'I want to see the view from the window.' The lady then complained to the air hostess. The air hostess made the same request. Santa was adamant and bluntly refused.

The air hostess told the assistant captain. He came and requested Santa, but in vain. Finally the captain came. He whispered something in Santa's ears. Santa immediately vacated the window seat and took the middle seat.

Astonished, the air hostess and the assistant captain asked the captain what he had said to Santa. The captain replied: 'I just told him that only the middle seats will go to Chandigarh. All others will go to Jalandhar.'

(Contributed by Jyotica Sikand, New Delhi)

ENTHUSIASMS,
RANTS &
SOLILOQUIES

WHY I SUPPORTED THE EMERGENCY

ANGREZI HATAO

SEEING ONESELF

THE JOYS OF FARTING

62

WHY I SUPPORTED THE EMERGENCY

The Emergency has become a synonym for obscenity. Even men and women who were pillars of Emergency rule and misused their positions to harass innocent people against whom they had personal grudges try to distance themselves from their past in the hope that it will fade out of public memory forever. We must not allow them to get away with it. Because of them many mistakes were made which must be avoided the next time conditions require the suspension of democratic norms for the preservation of law and order.

With some reservations I supported the Emergency proclaimed by Mrs Indira Gandhi on 25 June 1975. Let me explain why. I concede that the right to protest is integral to democracy. You can have public meetings to criticize or condemn government actions. You can take out processions, call for strikes and closure of businesses. But there must not be any coercion or violence. If there is any, it is the duty of the government to suppress it by force, if necessary. By May 1975, public protests against Mrs Gandhi's government had assumed nationwide dimensions and often turned violent. With my own eyes I saw slogan-chanting processions go down Bombay's thoroughfares, smashing cars parked on the roadsides and breaking shop windows as they went along. The local police was unable to contend with them because they were too few, the protesters too many. The leaders of Opposition parties watched the country sliding into chaos as bemused spectators, hoping that the mounting chaos would force Mrs Gandhi to resign.

The unquestioned leader of the anti-Mrs Gandhi movement was Jayaprakash Narayan, a man for whom I had enormous respect and admiration. He had become the conscience keeper of the nation. But Lok Nayak, as he came to be known, crossed the Lakshman rekha of democratic protest. His call for 'total revolution' included preventing elected members of state legislatures from entering Vidhan Sabha buildings. He announced his intention to gherao Parliament House and even asked the police and the army to revolt against the government. I wrote to Jayaprakash protesting that what he was advocating was wrong and undemocratic. He wrote back justifying his stand. I published both my letter and his much-longer reply in *The Illustrated Weekly of India* which I then happened to be editing. I believe, and still believe, freedom to speak one's mind is the basic principle of democracy.

In early June I was attending a conference in Mexico City. I arrived back in Bombay the day the Emergency was declared. The night before, all the Opposition leaders had been picked up from their homes and put in jails across the country. *The Times of India* offices were in pandemonium. We were told that censorship had been imposed on the press: we had to toe the line or get out. I was determined to resist and thought if editors of other papers published by Bennett, Coleman & Co. would form a united front against censorship we would succeed in making the government change its mind against the press. I expected Sham Lal, editor of *The Times of India*, to become our leader. He bluntly refused to do so. Sham Lal's number two, Girilal Jain, resident editor in Delhi, went one better by lauding the emergence of Sanjay Gandhi as the new leader. Not one other editor was willing to risk his job. Editors of the *Navbharat Times*, *Maharashtra Times*, *Dharmyug*, *Filmfare*, *Femina*, *Sarika* decided to stay away from the protest meeting we organized. Inder Malhotra's behaviour was enigmatic. He kept going up and down the floors greeting everyone with 'jai ho' and moving on. He never looked anyone in the eye. To this day I don't know whether he was for or against the Emergency. For three weeks I refused to publish the *Weekly*. My friend from my college years in England, Rajni Patel, who became the dominant voice on the board of directors, told me bluntly: 'My friend, if you are looking for martyrdom, we'll give it to you.' The board chairman, Justice (retd) K. T. Desai, was gentler. 'You don't realize how serious the government is about censorship on the press. If you refuse to publish the journal we will have no option but to find another editor. Why not give it a try to see how it goes?' I agreed to give it a try. After all, I had criticized Jayaprakash Narayan's call for a 'total revolution' as undemocratic. The Allahabad High Court judgement declaring Mrs Gandhi's membership of Parliament invalid weakened her position and she was persuaded by her closest advisers to strike out.

The Emergency, when first imposed, was generally welcomed by the people. There were no strikes or hartals, schools and colleges re-opened, business picked up, buses and trains began to run on time. People are under the impression that the Emergency administrators were very efficient. They were not. A few days after it was promulgated I got a call from H. Y. Sharada Prasad asking me to come over to see the prime minister. I was not to tell anyone about the appointment. The next day I met her in her South Block office. I pleaded with her to withdraw censorship on the press. 'Editors like me who support you have lost credibility. Nobody will believe that we are doing so of our free will and not being dictated to,' I argued. She remained adamant. 'There cannot be any Emergency without censorship on the press,' she maintained. I returned to Bombay disappointed. Back in the office, I found in my mail a letter reading, 'How did your meeting with Madame Dictator go?' Signed George. George Fernandes had gone underground but someone (obviously in the PMO) had informed him about my meeting. The same afternoon four leading members of the RSS, against whom warrants of arrest had been issued, boldly walked into my office and for half an hour questioned me about what had passed between the PM and me. And then, as boldly, walked out.

The censorship was also selective and eccentric. Some papers like *The Indian Express* were made targets of Mrs Gandhi's ire. Others like *The Times of India* and the *Hindustan Times* were left alone. As was the weekly, *Blitz*, owned by the most unprincipled editor of our times, Russi Karanjia, who enthusiastically supported Mrs Gandhi. Kuldip Nayar was arrested. For no reason whatsoever, so was his eighty-two-year-old father-in-law, Bhim Sen Sachar, once chief minister of Punjab. Romesh Thapar, once very close to Mrs Gandhi, closed down his *Seminar*. His sister, Dr Romila Thapar, who kept her distance from politics, was harassed by income tax sleuths for many days. Mrs Gandhi could be very vindictive against people she had once been close to.

In Bombay, censorship had its lighter side. Vinod Mehta, who edited the sleazy girlie magazine *Debonair*, was asked to have his articles and pictures cleared before they were sent to the printer. The censor looked over the pages. 'Porn? Theek hai! Politics, no.' Most of it was soft porn. It was quickly cleared. I was not subjected to the indignity of pre-censorship except for a few hours. I happened to be at a luncheon reception given by Governor Ali Yavar Jung in honour of President Fakhruddin Ali Ahmed. Out of the blue the president turned to me and said loudly, 'What is all this you keep publishing in your journal? Don't you know there is an Emergency?' I didn't know what he was referring to. Nor did S. B. Chavan, chief minister of Maharashtra, who overheard the president's remark. When I returned to my office I found a pre-censorship order slapped under the CM's authorization on the *Weekly*. The offending article had in fact appeared in *Femina* and not in my journal. I rang up Sharada Prasad. Mrs Gandhi was due to go abroad the next day. Chavan was told to withdraw the censorship order immediately. He did so as tamely as the braggadocio with which he had imposed it.

During the Emergency I was frequently in Delhi to help out Maneka Gandhi and her mother, Amtesh, with their magazine *Surya*. I saw something of the caucus which was running the government. Siddhartha Shankar Ray had drafted the regulations; Sanjay was the kingpin. Besides his kitchen cabinet comprising his wife and mother-in-law, there was the old family retainer, Mohammad Yunus (Chacha); civil servant Navin

Chawla; Kishan Chand, Lieutenant Governor of Delhi, who later ended his life by jumping into a well; and Jagmohan, who was put in charge of clearing slums, which he did with ruthless zeal. There was the Rasputin figure of Dhirendra Brahmachari, swamiji to the royal household; and two pretty women, Ambika Soni and Rukhsana Sultana—Sanjay had an eye for pretty women. He also had an enthusiastic supporter in Bansi Lal who had allotted him land in Haryana where he was CM, basing his decision on the rustic truism 'bachda pakad lo toh ma toh peechey chali ayegee'—catch the calf and its mother is bound to follow you. He had I.K. Gujral packed off to Moscow and replaced by the more amenable Vidya Charan Shukla as information and broadcasting minister.

Because of my frequent visits to Delhi to monitor the progress of *Surya*, I saw quite a bit of the Gandhi family, particularly Sanjay and his in-laws. He was more relaxed with Maneka's family than with his own. He was a man of few words but with enormous zest for work. He was a strict teetotaller and even avoided drinking tea, coffee, aerated drinks and iced water. In some ways he epitomized the slogan he had coined: kaam ziyaada, baatein kum—work more, talk less. He was a young man in a hurry to get things done. He had no patience with tedious democratic processes and red tape, no time for long-winded politicians or bureaucrats. The fact that he had no legitimacy for imposing his fiats on the country, besides being the son of the prime minister, was of little importance to him. Unlike Maneka, he never used strong language and was extremely courteous towards older people like me. In his younger days he was known to have stolen cars—he had a passion for cars. He had been in many brawls: despite his modest size he rippled with muscles. I took to him as a lovable goonda.

For many months this coterie ruled the country. Anyone who crossed their paths was promptly put behind bars. There was not a squeak of protest. Virtually the only party which kept up a passive resistance movement throughout the period were the Akalis. Long before the Emergency was lifted, it had lost public support. Arbitrary arrests, the ruthless way Jagmohan bulldozed slums in Delhi, made people believe the wildest canards, of the way men were picked up from bus and cinema queues to be forcibly sterilized, as true. Nobody ever verified the facts but most people lent willing ears to stories of Sanjay's excesses. The Emergency, which was even justified by a sage like Acharya Vinoba Bhave, initially, was distorted into an abominated monster which had to be destroyed for ever. There may be other occasions to impose an Emergency in the country. If we do not make the mistakes of 1975–1977, we will be able to keep the country on the right track when it begins to wobble.

63

When anyone asks me, 'What is your mother tongue?' I reply without hesitation: 'English.'

They regard my swarthy complexion, the turban on my head and my greying beard. The contemptuous look in their eyes leaves me in no doubt that they see me as a leftover of the breed of toadying spittlelickers of the British. When I add, 'My mother tongue is English though my mother cannot speak one word of it,' they roar with laughter. They think it is a big joke. How can a black man born in India deriving sustenance from the dung heap of a Punjabi village describe English as his native tongue except in jest?

I do not jest. I call English my mother tongue because I am more familiar with it than with any other language. Since most people I mix with are also more at ease with English than with what they call their mother tongues, I hear more English spoken than any other language. Most of what I read is in English. All my work is done in English. I write it better than my three Indian languages, Punjabi, Hindi and Urdu. I know that in writing English I make errors in grammar and my vocabulary is limited. I try to better my diction, improve my syntax and endeavour to turn out a polished sentence which is at once pregnant with meaning and pleasing to the ear. With me English is a passion. No other language gives me quite the same pleasure. I find it more musical and much richer in its literature than any other language of the world.

When I make these assertions, my friends shake their heads; cluck their tongues and remark: 'Even if all you say about English is true, it still does not make it your mother tongue.'

I bark back: 'So much the worse for definitions! If a person cannot speak the language spoken by his mother (not an inconceivable situation, for example, children of Indian parents in England or even children in westernized Bombay and Delhi) it is a travesty of fact to describe that language as a mother tongue. Let us redefine it as the language one is most at home with and which one loves. So defined, Jawaharlal Nehru's mother tongue was English. His daughter Indira Gandhi's mother tongue is also English. And it is also mine.'

'English, though it has been recognized by our Constitution as a language to be used in India, is not an Indian language,' asserted the poet Dinkar at a meeting to felicitate him on the receipt of the Jnanpith

Award. He was loudly cheered. I was made to appear as Rai Bahadur Maska Lal trying to unfurl the Union Jack: he, a khadi-clad Bhagat Singh yelling 'Jai Hind'. Neither the poet's patriotic outburst nor the applause he received squashed me. 'Why,' I asked my black friends, 'do you deny English the status of an Indian language? Is it because it was brought to India by foreign conquerors? So also were Arabic and Persian. So indeed was Sanskrit by our Aryan forefathers.

'Both Hindi and Urdu were born out of these once-foreign languages. English only happens to be the last of these importations. It has been with us for over two hundred years. It has insinuated itself in the speech of the illiterate peasant as well as the most sophisticated urbanite. Not one of us can carry on a conversation on any topic without a liberal profusion of English words. Famous and patriotic Indians like Raghunath Hari Navalkar of Maharashtra and Raja Rammohun Roy of Bengal wanted English to be made compulsory and developed as our national language. Very rightly we got rid of our English rulers; but must we foolishly also give up the good with the bad? Must we throw out the lovely babbling baby with the dirty English bathwater?'

The Angrezi hataowalas change their line of attack. 'English is spoken by barely 2 per cent of the population of the country; how can it ever be given the status of a national language?' they demand. I reply: 'Many languages, e.g., Kashmiri, Sindhi, Assamese, Punjabi are spoken by fewer or as many Indians as is English. And the 2 per cent who speak English matter more in national affairs than speakers of other languages. All your cabinet ministers, chief ministers, judges, ambassadors, civil servants, defence personnel, scientists, economists, managers of factories are English speaking. Name anyone who matters and in nine cases out of ten the language he or she speaks best is English. If you weigh languages in terms of the power they wield, you will see that English outweighs all the other Indian languages recognized in the Constitution put together. Most of our work is still done in English because no other language is capable of handling the technicalities of administration, justice, technology, science.

'Let us not forget how English served us in the past and does so today. It was the language of our protest against our rulers—a powerful weapon wielded by Tilak, Gokhale, Sri Aurobindo, Gandhi and Nehru. More than any other language it gave us the sense of Indianness. It is not surprising that more people read English newspapers and magazines than publications in any other language.'

'What about the masses?'

What about them? A survey carried out amongst illiterate peasants and workers around Delhi revealed that, when asked what language they would like to learn, the majority opted for English. It is not only the link language which will keep India together but also the language of opportunity. It opens the window of a village hovel to the city; it opens the window of India to the world.

Of course, we Angreziwalas derive solace from the conviction that no matter how much the Desi Bhashawalas scream in protest, English has come to stay in India and will remain the chief link language between the different states of our union and the only means of communication with the world outside... So, dear Bhashawalas, make peace with Angrezi. Drape her in a Benaras brocade sari as you would if your son brought home a foreign daughter-in-law. But don't waste your energies fighting against her because she has come to stay 'till death do us part'.

64

SEEING ONESELF

The gods in their wisdom did not grant me the gift of seeing myself as others see me. They must have thought that knowing what others thought of me might engender suicidal tendencies in me and decided to let me stew in my own self-esteem. Now I am up against the formidable task of having to write about myself.

It is a daunting assignment. Have you ever tried to look yourself squarely in the eyes in your own mirror? Try it and you will understand what I mean. Within a second or two you will turn your gaze from your eyes to other features—as women do when they are putting on make-up or men do when they are shaving. Looking into the depths of one's own eyes reveals the naked truth. The naked truth about oneself can be very ugly.

I know I am an ugly man. Physical ugliness has never bothered me nor inhibited me from making overtures to the fairest of women. I am convinced that only empty-headed nymphomaniacs look out for handsome gigolos. They have no use for the likes of me; I have no use for the likes of them. My concern is not with my outward appearance, my untidy turban, unkempt beard or my glazed look (I have been told that my eyes are those of a lustful badmaash) but with what lies behind the physical—the real me compounded of conflicting emotions like love and hate, general irritability and occasional equipoise, angry denunciation and tolerance of another's point of view, rigid adherence to a self-prescribed regimen and accommodation of others' convenience. And so on. It is on these qualities that I will dwell in making an estimate of myself.

First, I must dispose of the question which people often ask me: 'What do you think of yourself as a writer?' Without appearing to wear the false cloak of humility, let me say quite honestly that I do not rate myself very highly. I can tell good writing from the not so good, the first rate from the passable. I know that of the Indians or the Indian-born, Nirad Chaudhuri, V.S. Naipaul, Salman Rushdie, Amitav Ghosh and Vikram Seth handle the English language better than I. I also know I can, and have, written as well as any of the others— R.K. Narayan, Mulk Raj Anand, Manohar Malgonkar, Ruth Jhabvala, Nayantara Sahgal or Anita Desai. What is more, unlike most in the first or the second category, I have never laid claim to being a great writer. I regard self-praise to be the utmost form of vulgarity. Almost every Indian writer I have met is prone to laud his or her achievements. This is something I have never done. Nor ever solicited awards or recognition. Nor ever spread false stories of being considered for the Nobel Prize in Literature. The list of prominent Indians who spread such canards about themselves is formidable: Vatsyayan (Agyeya), G. V. Desani, Dr Gopal Singh Dardi (former Governor of Goa), Kamala Das and many others.

Am I a likeable man? I am not sure. I do not have many friends because I do not set much store by friendship. I have found that friends, however nice and friendly they may be, demand more time than I am willing to spare. I get easily bored with people and would rather read a book or listen to music than converse with anyone for too long. I have had a few very close friends in my time. I am ashamed to admit that when some of them dropped me, instead of being upset, I felt relieved. And when some died, I cherished their memory more than I did their company when they were alive.

I have the same attitude towards women whom I have liked or loved. It does not take much for me to get deeply emotional about women. Often at the very first meeting I feel I have found the Helen I was seeking, and like Majnoon sifting the sands of desert wastes, my quest for Laila is over. None of these infatuations lasted very long. At times betrayal of trust hurt me deeply but nothing left lasting scars on my psyche. The only lesson I learnt was that as soon as you sense the others cooling off, be the one to drop them. Dropping people gives you a sense of triumph; being dropped one of defeat, which leaves the ego wounded. I do not have the gift of friendship. Nor the gift of loving or being loved.

Hate is my stronger passion. Mercifully, it has never been directed against a community but only against certain individuals. I hate with a passion unworthy of anyone who would like to describe himself as civilized. I try my best to ignore them but they are like an aching tooth which I am periodically compelled to feel with my tongue to assure myself that it still hurts. My hate goes beyond people I hate. I drop people who befriend them. My enemy's friends become my enemies.

Hate does not always kill the man who hates, as is maintained by the sanctimonious. Unrepressed hate can often be cathartic. Shakespeare could gnash his teeth with righteous hatred:

You common cry of curs! whose breath I hate
As reek o' the rotten fens, whose loves I prize
As the dead carcasses of unburied men
That do corrupt the air...

Fortunately there are not many people I hate. I could count them on the tips of the fingers of one hand—no more than four or five. And if

I told you why I hate them, you may agree that they deserve contempt and hatred.

I hate name-droppers. I hate self-praisers. I hate arrogant men. I hate liars. Is there anything wrong in hating them? People ask me, why can't you leave them alone? Why can't you ignore their existence? Now, that is something I cannot do. I cannot resist making fun of name-droppers, calling liars liars to their faces. And I love abusing the arrogant. I have been in trouble many times because of my inability to resist mocking these types. And since most name-droppers, self-praisers and arrogant men go from success to success, become ministers, governors and win awards they don't deserve, my anger often explodes into denouncing them in print. I have been dragged into courts and before the Press Council. This can be a terrible waste of time and money. I think I will have wax images of my pet hates and vent my spleen on them by sticking pins in their effigies. May the fleas of a thousand camels infest their armpits! I am not a nice man to know.

65

THE JOYS OF FARTING

Farting is one of the three great joys of life. First, sex; second, oil rubbed on a scalp full of dandruff; third, a long, satisfying fart. With the onset of middle age I have reversed the order of merit: farting now tops my list of life's pleasures.

The king of farts is the Trumpet—known to our ancestors as Uttam Paadam—its noise rendered as *phadakaam*. It is an act of will, it is proclamatory, it is masculine. It has much sound, little smell. The louder, the less odorous. My friend, the bald, beady-eyed photographer who has done considerable research on the subject is an exponent of the Trumpet. He is of the considered opinion that the Trumpet can only be produced by people who restrict their diet to fresh fruits and non-fibrous vegetables grown above the ground. Such food is sattvik (pure). (Poultry, fish and meat, though nourishing, are of the secondary rajas category. Spices, stale food like pickles, preserves and chutneys; vegetables which grow underground like potatoes, radishes, carrots and garlic, or are attached to the earth like onions, cabbages, turnips and cauliflowers are definitely tamas). My photographer friend demonstrated the Trumpet by consuming a succulent watermelon on an empty stomach. An hour later he was airborne like a jet plane.

Second in the order of the farts is the Shehnai—our ancestors also give it a secondary status—Madhyamaa—and its sound it rendered as *thain, thain*. I prefer to compare it to the shehnai, a wind instrument made famous by the maestro Ustaad Bismillah Khan of Varanasi. Like the Trumpet, the Shehnai is also an act of will and may be produced by a simple shift in position or gentle pressure on the paunch. It differs from the Trumpet in its softer tone and longer duration. The opening notes of a Scottish bagpipe sound very much like it—*pheenh*.

The third variety is the Scraper which makes a sound like a squelch of uncured leather or the rustling of old parchment. It is in fact not one but a succession of little farts—*pirt, pirt, pirt, pirt*. The Scraper is a by-product of eating too much of tamasik food. It is also a phenomenon of rectal muscles softened by age.

The fourth is the Tabla. It proclaims itself with a single *phut* like a tap on a bongo drum. The Tabla is its own master as it escapes without the host's consent causing him or her deep embarrassment if they happen to be in company.

The fifth is the noiseless stink bomb, the Phuskin. Since it is unspoken it is best suited to be planted on a neighbour as a secret gift—gupta daan. The donor can assume a 'not-I' look on his face or hold his nostrils and turn towards someone else with an accusing look. But he must heed the Japanese saying: 'He who talks is the one who farted'. If you have let off a stinking gupta daan, let others guess the identity of the benefactor.

Nations have different attitudes towards farting. The Europeans and Americans are quite shameless about it. It is a part of their Greek inheritance. Niarchos (first century AD) extolled the virtues of farting any time wind built up in the belly:

> If blocked, a fart can kill a man;
> If let escape, a fart can sing
> Health-giving songs; farts kill and save.
> A fart is a powerful king.

Niarchos knew the difference between a noiseless stink bomb and the audible varieties of wind-breaking. To wit:

> Does Henry sigh, or does he fart?
> His breath is strong from either part.

Exhortations to the fart are also found in contemporary English literature:

> Men of letters ere we part
> Tell me why you never fart?
> Never fart? Dear Miss Bright,
> I do not need to fart, I write.

Although white races eat black rajas food which does not produce much wind, when they have it, they release it in company with total unconcern for propriety. This is particularly revolting in the case of the wine-drinkers making a gupta daan: wind produced by wine is singularly stenchful. The ultimate in white people's vulgarity was a Frenchman who displayed his fart-power on stage. He had a slit made in the back of his trousers and for a small wager would blow out a candle placed three feet from his posterior.

If the whites are disgusting, the Indians are not much better. Indians have a very poor sense of humour and treat farting as a topic of jest. Since they eat highly spiced tamasik foods, they are the world's champion farters and have much occasion to laugh at each other. Once a minister of cabinet recording a talk for the External Services of All India Radio let out a Trumpet. The talk had to be re-recorded. However, when the time came, by mistake the original recording was put on the air. It gave an

Indian the unique distinction of having his fart heard around the world. The *Guinness Book of Records*, please note.

For an unrelenting attitude towards farting, the palm must be given to the Persians and the Arabs. There is a tale told of a young Iranian who broke wind in a mehfil. He was so overcome with remorse that he left the town. After many years in self-imposed exile he returned home hoping that his small misdemeanour would have been forgotten. Naming himself, he asked some boys to direct him to his old home. 'You mean the home of so-and-so the farter?' demanded the urchins. The poor man went back into exile.

The first prize for courtesy extended to farters goes to Sufi Abdul Rahman Hatam Ibn Unwan al-assam of Balkh, known for reasons of his noble attitude to farting as Hatam the Deaf. It is said that while he was explaining a matter of some theological import to an old woman, the lady farted. The saintly Sufi raised his voice and said, 'Speak louder, I am hard of hearing.' And for the fifteen long years that the woman continued to live, Hatam pretended to be hard of hearing and suffered people shouting in his ears. Hatam the Deaf is the patron saint of embarrassed farters.

HOW TO LIVE,
HOW TO DIE

66

HOW TO LIVE LONG AND BE HAPPY

Having lived a reasonably contented life, I was musing over what a person should strive for to achieve happiness. Here is my list of the essentials:

+ First and foremost is good health. If you do not enjoy good health you can never be happy. Any ailment, however trivial, will deduct from your happiness.

+ Second, a healthy bank balance. It need not run into crores but should be enough to provide for creature comforts and something to spare for recreation, like eating out, going to the pictures, travelling or going on holidays to the hills or by the sea. Shortage of money can be only demoralizing. Living on credit or borrowing is demeaning and lowers one in one's own eyes.

+ Third, a home of your own. Rented premises can never give you the snug feeling of a nest which is yours for keeps that a home provides. If it has a garden space, all the better. Plant your own trees and flowers, see them grow and blossom, cultivate a sense of kinship with them.

+ Fourth, an understanding companion, be it your spouse or a friend. If there are too many misunderstandings, they will rob you of your peace of mind. It is better to be divorced than to bicker all the time.

+ Fifth, lack of envy towards those who have done better than you in life—risen higher, made more money, or earned more fame. Envy can be very corroding; avoid comparing yourself with others.

+ Sixth, do not allow other people to descend on you for gup-shup. By the time you get rid of them, you will feel exhausted and poisoned by their gossip-mongering.

+ Seventh, cultivate some hobbies which can bring you a sense of fulfilment, such as gardening, reading, writing, painting, playing or listening to music. Going to clubs or parties to get free drinks or to meet celebrities is a criminal waste of time.

+ Eighth, every morning and evening, devote fifteen minutes to introspection. In the morning, ten minutes should be spent on stilling the mind and then five in listing things you have to do that day. In the evening, five minutes to still the mind again, and ten to go over what you had undertaken to do.

Nathaniel Cotton summed up my views on the subject in one verse:

If solid happiness we prize,
Within our breast this jewel lies,
And they are fools who roam.
The world has nothing to bestow;
From our own selves our joys must flow,
And that dear hut—our home.

67

DEALING WITH ADVERSITY

I had had two extensions of my contract with Bennett, Coleman & Co. and expected to get a third one. However, conditions in the company and the country had changed radically. After many years under government control, Bennett, Coleman & Co. was returned to its proprietors, the Jains. Mrs Gandhi was voted out of power and replaced by Morarji Desai. I was not able to come to terms with either Ashok Jain, who became chairman of the company, or Morarji Desai, who became prime minister. I continued to support Mrs Gandhi and defend her son, Sanjay. In one issue we had carried a readers' opinion poll on the most popular man in the country. The vote was overwhelmingly in favour of Sanjay Gandhi, a man more hated by the new government than even his mother. Morarji Desai was upset with the *Weekly* which remained the most widely-read journal in the country. On writing to him asking for an interview when he came to Bombay, I got a three-line reply telling me to see him at Santa Cruz airport to find out if he would have time to receive me. I went to the airport, muscled my way through his crowd of admirers and greeted him. He looked angrily at me and mumbled, 'So you think Sanjay is the hero of the country!' I protested that it wasn't my opinion but that of the readers. 'What readers?' he snapped. 'It was all rigged.' As he was about to get into his car, I said to him, 'Morarjibhai, I take it you don't want to see me.' He paused a while before replying. 'No, I will see you. You come to my son's apartment at 5 p.m.'

When I arrived at Kanti Desai's residence there was another crowd of people in the verandahs and in his father's bedroom. Morarji was sitting on his bed talking to them. He saw me and told his callers to leave. 'I have given him an appointment, I would like to talk to him alone,' he ordered. The crowd left. Morarji asked me to sit by him on his bed. He was a different man from the one I had met that morning at the airport. He accepted my version that a majority of the readers had voted for Sanjay but maintained that the whole thing must have been rigged. (He was right as later I discovered—a single person had sent a hundreds of 'readers' votes in favour of Sanjay.) I switched on the tape-recorder and asked him a whole range of questions about the Emergency, his detention in jail and his plans for India. I asked him specifically whether he intended to re-impose prohibition after it had flopped everywhere it had been tried. He was adamant: prohibition was a directive clause of the Constitution,

271

it had succeeded in many parts of the country, particularly in his native Gujarat and he intended to enforce it all over the country. When I had run out of my questions he asked me to switch off the tape-recorder: he wanted to talk to me man to man, or as friends. 'You make fun of my insistence on prohibition and advocating urine therapy. If I persuade you that drinking is bad for you, will you give it up?'

'Morarjibhai, I have been drinking for fifty years and have never been drunk even once in my life. If I persuade you that drinking is not bad for you, will you have a drink?' I asked in reply.

He thought over my suggestion for a while and replied, 'That is a fair offer; if you persuade me that drinking alcohol is not bad for my health, I promise to try it.'

He went on to extol the benefits of urine therapy. He told me innumerable cases of sickness, which had been declared incurable by doctors, responding to fresh urine. 'I have a prescription for curing cancer as well. Give up every kind of food. Just live on grapes and warm water and it will get cancer out of your system.'

He was friendly enough for me to question him on another of his fads. 'Morarjibhai, I have also written about your vow of abstinence from sex.' Before I could proceed further, he cut me short, 'I do not wish to discuss the subject with you.' The interview, which had lasted well over an hour, was over.

Morarji Desai, despite his fads, was a straight and honest man who rarely told a lie. That did not go for his son, Kanti, on whom he doted. As far as he was concerned, Kanti could do no wrong. A few days later, when Ashok Jain invited me for breakfast at his house in Delhi, I broached the subject of my contract. Quite gently but firmly, he told me that Kanti Desai had strong reservations about my continuing as editor and that my contract would not be renewed. Weeks later, when it became known that my tenure as editor was to end within a few months because of pressure brought by the Desais on the proprietors, Morarji rang me up from Delhi. 'Do you believe me that I did not say a word against you to Ashok Jain?' I replied, 'Morarjibhai, if you say so, I will believe it because I know that you do not tell a lie.' That did not apply to Ashok Jain or Kanti Desai. Ashok Jain denied ever having told me that the Desais had said anything to him about me. When questioned by the Avinashlingam Commission set up by Morarji's government to look into the charges of vindictiveness made against it, Kanti Desai went on record to say that he did not know who I was.

I returned to Bombay to settle my affairs. I had three months to hand over charge to my successor and took three months leave to look for another job or work on my novel *Delhi*. On my own I recommended the name of R. G. K. as my successor. It was summarily rejected. The date of my departure was fixed. I wrote a last sentimental piece of farewell on my editorial page saying that my bulb logo would not be appearing in the *Weekly* any more. Some mischief-maker conveyed to the management that I had written a nasty piece against Bennett, Coleman & Co. A week before I was to relinquish my post, I came to the office as usual an hour before anyone else. At ten o'clock, a senior clerk came in with a letter from the general manager, Ram Tarneja: 'Sir, I tried to deliver it to you yesterday, but you had gone home. I am sorry to be the courier. I hope you will forgive me,' he said. It was a one-paragraph letter informing me that my services were terminated forthwith and I was to hand over charge to M. V. Kamath with immediate effect. In short, I was fired one week before I was due to retire.

I sent for Fatma Zakaria, gave her the letter and asked her to inform the staff after I had left. I picked up my umbrella and walked out of *The Times of India* building.

Gratuitous discourtesy towards editors had become the hallmark of the Jain family. They had treated their most distinguished editor, Frank Moraes, with the same lack of courtesy. Inder Malhotra and Prem Shankar Jha, both distinguished in their respective fields, were humiliated and forced to quit. Girilal Jain who spent his life serving them and edited *The Times of India* with distinction for over nine years was shown the door with less regard than I.

I got to work on the next chapter of my manuscript of *Delhi*. There were Allama Iqbal's lines to inspire me:

Jahaan mein ahle-eemaan soorat-e-khursheed jeetay hain,
Idhar doobey, udhar nikley; udhar doobey, idhar niklay.

In this world men of faith and self-confidence are like the sun,
They go down on one side to come up on the other.

68

ADVICE TO WOULD-BE WRITERS

I have often wondered why some people develop the itch to write while others do not. It has very little to do with their academic background. Many toppers in their school and college days are unable to write anything worth reading, while others who are barely able to scrape through their exams turn into good storytellers.

Some professions make it easier to get access to the world of literature. Journalism is the best because meeting deadlines imposes discipline and switching from reporting to commenting on events is not very difficult. Only, one has to guard against using journalistic jargon. The same applies to teaching. A teacher can take to creative writing but must guard himself against becoming pedantic. Doctors often make good writers because they are enriched by close contact with sickness, the process of dying and death. Lawyers seldom make good writers. They tend to itemize their writing as they do affidavits. Soldiers are best advised to stick to writing about soldiering and battles they fought.

◆

Today, the world of writers and publishers has changed beyond recognition. The pioneers of Indian writing in English—Mulk Raj Anand, R. K. Narayan and Raja Rao either had patrons who helped them find publishers or organizations which sponsored their works. They made some noise in literary circles but not much money. Literary agents were little known. The only one I'd heard of then was Curtis Brown. It was said that if a literary agent took your work on, they would find you a good publisher and take their cut on royalties due to you. Today a literary agent has become a powerful factor in publishing: the best writers use them because it is the agents who get publishing houses to cough up huge sums as advance royalties. The whole business resembles a whorehouse. Publishers can be compared to brothel keepers, literary agents to bharooahs (pimps) who find eligible girls and fix rates of payment; writers can be likened to prostitutes. Newcomers are naya maal (virgins) who draw the biggest fees so they can be deflowered. I, for one, never went through a literary agent—nor did I have problems finding a good publisher. I was happy with the 8 to 10 per cent they gave me on the sales of my books.

◆

I have often been asked how one becomes a good writer. I'd say that one has to slog and be totally honest and fearless. Always speak out. One might face problems but one mustn't give in. Along with hard work, read whatever you can—whether it's classics or fairy tales or even nonsense verse. Reading—reading as much as you can—will make you capable of distinguishing between bad and good writing.

Also, one should never be pretentious; don't show off by using difficult words. That comes in the way of communicating with the reader. Always do your homework. A writer's responsibility—whether you're an essayist or a novelist—is to inform your reader while you provoke or entertain him. The challenge is to tell your reader something he doesn't know. Don't talk down to the reader; level with him. Above all, don't be afraid to be yourself.

69

THE PREOCCUPATIONS OF MIDDLE AGE

What preoccupies the minds of men past their middle age after they have done their day's work and have nothing else to do? Based on introspection, I have come to the conclusion that they think of three things whose proportions vary with age but which are concerned with the basic needs of survival, then with procreation, and after that reflections on their past years and uncertainty about the future.

If they are still working, they first think of how their work is progressing and what remains to be accomplished. They are concerned with their bread and butter, the instinct of survival. Then they think of sexual affairs they have had or wanted to have—that is, basically, the instinct to procreate. And finally, they go over their past—friends they've had, misunderstandings or deaths that ended relationships; and what the future holds for them.

Mohammed Rafi Sauda (1713-1781), poet laureate of the Mughal court, thought along the same lines:

Firk-e-maash, ishq-e-butaan, yaad-e-raftgaan
Is zindagi mein ab koi kya kya karey?

(Concern for livelihood, love for women, memories of the past
What else is there left to man in his life?)

Mirza Asadullah Khan Ghalib had much the same thing to say, except that he was obsessed with impending death. He craved for fursat—a break from the all-consuming business of making a living, in order to focus his mind on other things:

Jee dhoondta hain phir vahi fursat ke raat din
Baithey rahen tassavure-e-jaanam kiye huay

(The heart yearns for those days and nights of leisure
When one could just sit imagining one's beloved)

In later life, a man spends less time thinking of his livelihood. Recollections of affairs with women recede into the background, as do memories of departed friends. He begins to worry more about his unknown future.

Most people are in reasonably good shape until their seventies. Instead of worrying, older people should either find ways of making a living or if they can afford to retire completely, find hobbies to keep themselves busy. Gardening, painting, music, learning a new language or volunteering time to those who need help are all ways to keep busy.

But to do nothing is to be nothing—a sure way of hastening the end.

70

OLD AGE

Whenever my son, living in Mumbai, was asked why he was going to Delhi, his reply was 'to see my A Pees'. A Pees stood for Aged Parents. Now that he is himself what in modern parlance is described as a senior citizen, and his mother has passed away, he answers the same question with 'to see old Pop'.

With the passing of generations, the attitude of younger people towards the old has changed. When I was a young man, we used to describe aged people as oldies, or worse sattreah bahattreah (in his seventies and feeble-minded). Now persons in their seventies are not considered old; new attitudes and a sizeable vocabulary have been evolved to describe them.

One way to show respect to the aged seems to be to keep a respectful distance from them.

So we have old people's homes a good distance from homes their inhabitants once lived in and ruled over. There is much to be said in favour of old people's homes. The few I have visited in England and the USA are as luxurious as any five-star hotel; separate cottages with modern amenities like world radio and TV, spacious dining and sitting rooms where you can meet and chat with others in your own age groups, light tasty food and wines, billiards rooms, card tables for bridge, rummy or patience. There are spacious lawns and flower beds. Above all, there are nurses and doctors in attendance round the clock. They cost a packet. Inmates are happy blowing up their life's savings to live out their last days in comfort because they are aware they can't take anything with them when they go. Their offspring don't grudge them this because they are relieved of the responsibility of looking after their parents and can get on with their own lives. The notion of a family gathered round the bed of a dying patriarch or matriarch is as dead as a dodo.

However much I approve of old people's homes, I resent being described as a gerry (for geriatric), old boomer, fuddy-duddy, gaffer or old fogey, codger, coot, geezer, etc. Some new coinages like dinosaur, fossil, cotton top, cranky, crumbly are downright offensive. Eighty years ago Chesterton wrote in his essay 'On the Prudery of Slang': 'There was a time when it was customary to call a father a father... Now...it appears to be considered a mark of advanced intelligence to call our father a bean or a scream. It is obvious to me that calling the old gentleman "father" is facing the facts of nature. It is also obvious that calling him a "bean" is merely weaving a graceful fairy tale to cover the facts of nature.'

Call us oldies or what you will, but bear in mind that just as saas bhi kabhi bahu thhi (the mother-in-law was once a bride) you too will one day become an old person, and slang terms like codger, geyser or fuddy-duddy can be hurtful even to an oldie who is hard of hearing.

71

THE DEATH OF LOVED ONES

There are two schools of thought on the subject—Eastern and Western. Orientals believe that the best way of coping with the death of a loved one like a parent, spouse or child is to cry your heart out till you are drained of tears. The custom of vain (chants of lament) and breast-beating were regarded as cathartic. All this is followed by chautha, chaleesveen, boh, antim ardas or a prayer meeting in memory of the departed soul. Friends are expected to call in the belief that grief shared is grief halved. Westerners believe that grief is a private matter and should not be exhibited in public. Shedding tears is unmanly. One should put up a stoic front and get over the shock of loss by oneself.

I had to cope with the problem myself very recently. Being an agnostic, I could not find solace in religious rituals. Being essentially a loner, I discouraged friends and relations coming to condole with me on the death of my wife. Most of them ignored my request and came to see me. I found this commiseration even more traumatic. I spent the first night alone sitting in my chair in the dark. At times I broke down, but soon recovered my composure. A couple of days later, I resumed my usual routine of work from dawn to dusk. That took my mind off the stark reality of having to live alone in an empty home for the rest of my days. But friends persisted in calling and upsetting my equilibrium. So I packed myself off to Goa to be alone by myself. I was not sure if it would work out.

Everyone has to evolve his or her own formula of coping with grief. People who believe in God turn to Him. The words of Psalm 34 are pertinent: 'The Lord is close to the broken-hearted and saves those who are crushed in spirit.' Jesus Christ, who was an Oriental, was not ashamed of weeping before everyone when he lost a friend. So it is recorded in the Bible (John 11:33-38): 'When Jesus saw many weeping and the Jews who had come along with him also weeping, he was deeply marred in spirit and troubled: "Where have you laid him?" he asked. "Come and see Lord," they replied. Jesus wept. Then the Jews said, "See how he loved him!"'

As one would expect, Osho Rajneesh made light of the darkest of subjects, including ways of coping with grief. In his collection of sermons *Walking in Zen, Sitting in Zen*, he cites the case of an Italian, Perelli, and his method of getting over the shock of losing his wife:

At the funeral of his wife, Perelli made a terrible scene, so terrible and heart-rending, in fact, that friends had to forcibly restrain him from jumping into the grave and being buried with his beloved Maria. Then, still overcome with grief, he was taken home in the rented limousine and immediately went into complete seclusion.

A week passed and nothing was heard of him. Finally, worried about the poor guy, his late wife's brother went to the house. After ringing the doorbell for ten minutes—and still worried—the brother-in-law jimmied the front door, went upstairs and found his dead sister's husband with the maid.

The bedroom was a mess—empty champagne bottles everywhere. 'This is terrible, Perelli!' the brother-in-law declared in shocked tones. 'Your dead wife, my sister, has been dead only a week and you're doing this!' So busy was Perelli that he managed only to turn his head. 'How do I know what I'm doing?' he said. 'I got such grief! I got such grief!'

At one time Jains, Hindus and Sikhs celebrated the passing of elders who had led a full life. They decorated their biers with balloons and bunting, and funeral processions were led by brass bands playing tunes right from their homes to the cremation grounds. It is a pity that not many today follow this custom. The death of aged people, particularly those who have died after prolonged illnesses, should be looked upon as a reprieve from suffering, and celebrated.

72

DEATH AND DYING

'Have you ever thought about death?'

This was the second time he was asking me this. S. Prasher, retired commissioner of income tax, the moving spirit behind the Save Kasauli Society, has this disturbing habit of tossing questions at me to which I have no answers.

'Indeed I have,' I replied. 'I think about it all the time. I've read as much about it as I could. I found no answers.'

I quoted my favourite lines on the subject:

There was a Door to which I found no Key
There was a Veil beyond which I could not see;
Some talk awhile of Thee and Me
Then no more of Thee or Me.

'Omar Khayyam!' he said triumphantly. 'But surely there is more to it than just admitting that you do not know?'

'The body goes, perhaps with it the mind as well. Your memory remains in some people's minds while they are alive. After them even that is gone. You may leave charitable trusts in your name; you may write books that may be read after you are gone.'

'That is not what I mean,' Prasher said. 'What about consciousness?'

'Consciousness of what?' I asked. 'Where does it survive? It has to be something more tangible than the notion of consciousness.'

He proceeded to explain at great length. Most of it was beyond my comprehension. I tried to bring him down to earth. 'Most thinkers play with words, some talk of death as an integral part of life. I agree. Some compare life to a journey on a train; some get off at one station, others continue a little further. Bhola Nathji in his *The Secret of Death* writes, "One can deny the existence of God, but one cannot deny the existence of death... Life is that which must go, and death, that which must come." I entirely agree, but does that tell us where we go when we die? Does anything of us remain when we are gone?'

Most people who have written on the subject have dwelt more on the inherent fear of dying rather than death. They give false assurances that death is nothing to be scared of. For example, John Donne (1572-1631) describes it as 'merely a form of rest and sleep':

Death, be not proud, though some have called thee
Mighty and dreadfull, for thou art not so;
For those whom thou think'st, thou dost overthrow
Die not, poore Death, nor yet canst thou kill me.

For Donne, death was:

One short sleepe past, wee wake eternally,
And death shall be no more; death, thou shalt die.

John Keats (1795-1821), who died at the young age of twenty-five, had no such illusions of something surviving after he 'ceased to be'. He knew that he had a lot more to give but felt he was a 'fair creature of an hour' after which love and fame would sink to nothingness.

The key word, I told Prasher, is 'nothingness'. Death erases our bodies, our minds and everything our bodies or minds may have achieved in our lives. Prasher was not satisfied with my answer. But he had no answers to offer besides conjecturing that consciousness remained. He exhorted me to think more deeply on the subject. I promised to do so, fully aware it would get me nowhere.

As far as I am concerned, I would like to go the way my ninety-year-old father went. He was enjoying his evening drink. He felt a little uneasy and lay down on his bed to let the uneasiness pass. It was one for the long road to the unknown. He rose no more.

One way to overcome the fear of death is to make fun of it. On his seventy-fifth birthday, Winston Churchill was asked what he thought about it. 'I am ready to meet my Maker. Whether my Maker is prepared for the ordeal of meeting me is another matter,' he replied. Lord Palmerston on his deathbed told his physician, 'Die, my dear doctor? That is the last thing I shall do.'

◆

One day in Kolkata, I was waiting for a taxi when a man who was about ninety years old looked at my suitcase and asked, 'Where are you going?'

'On a short trip,' I replied.

The old man said, 'I'll be going on a long trip soon.'

Touched, I said, 'Well, we all have to take that long trip one day. If I'm fortunate and live to be your age, I'll be very happy about it.'

His look changed from that of attentive listening to one of impatience. 'Young man!' he retorted, 'I'm going to my grandson in London!'

73

SOME CODES TO LIVE BY

+ Ahimsa is more than non-violence, it is also the absence of the intention to hurt anyone. It is the first rule of civilization and the central principle of a good life. But it must also be accompanied with a determination to fight bigotry and hate with all one's might.
+ Religion has very little to do with goodness. Belief in a god does not make a person a better human being, nor does questioning his existence make him an evil one.
+ Work is worship; worship is not work.
+ Try not to lie. If you think someone has done you wrong, use truth to bring him around. Nothing is stronger than the truth.
+ Anger is a waste of time and energy. If you cannot forgive, withdraw.
+ Learn to share what you have. Be generous, and have the intelligence to know when you are being taken for a ride.
+ To be happy, rid yourself of greed, envy and hypocrisy.
+ Connect with nature. Respect it. Find a shady tree and sit under it for some time every day, watching the life in and around it. It is better than prayer.
+ Life is not always fair. Sometimes the good suffer for their deeds and the wicked prosper. So there is no use telling anyone that there are rewards for the good in life.
+ Goodness of the heart should be a habit, and its own reward.

74

HOW I WOULD LIKE TO BE REMEMBERED

I
would
like
to
be
remembered
as
someone
who
made
people
smile.

FICTION & POETRY

THE
NOVELS

TRAIN TO PAKISTAN: **DACOITY/KALYUG**

I SHALL NOT HEAR THE NIGHTINGALE:
SHOOTING THE CRANE

DELHI: A NOVEL: **DELHI**

THE COMPANY OF WOMEN: **DHANNO**

BURIAL AT SEA: **VICTOR JAI BHAGWAN**

THE SUNSET CLUB: **LODI GARDENS**

75

TRAIN TO PAKISTAN
DACOITY/KALYUG

The summer of 1947 was not like other Indian summers. Even the weather had a different feel in India that year. It was hotter than usual, and drier and dustier. And the summer was longer. No one could remember when the monsoon had been so late. For weeks, the sparse clouds cast only shadows. There was no rain. People began to say that God was punishing them for their sins.

Some of them had good reason to feel that they had sinned. The summer before, communal riots, precipitated by reports of the proposed division of the country into a Hindu India and a Muslim Pakistan, had broken out in Calcutta, and within a few months the death toll had mounted to several thousand. Muslims said the Hindus had planned and started the killing. According to the Hindus, the Muslims were to blame. The fact is, both sides killed. Both shot and stabbed and speared and clubbed. Both tortured. Both raped. From Calcutta, the riots spread north and east and west: To Noakhali in East Bengal, where Muslims massacred Hindus; to Bihar, where Hindus massacred Muslims. Mullahs roamed the Punjab and the Frontier Province with boxes of human skulls said to be those of Muslims killed in Bihar. Hundreds of thousands of Hindus and Sikhs who had lived for centuries on the Northwest Frontier abandoned their homes and fled towards the protection of the predominantly Sikh and Hindu communities in the east. They travelled on foot, in bullock carts, crammed into lorries, clinging to the sides and roofs of trains. Along the way—at fords, at crossroads, at railroad stations—they collided with panicky swarms of Muslims fleeing to safety in the west. The riots had become a rout. By the summer of 1947, when the creation of the new state of Pakistan was formally announced, ten million people—Muslims and Hindus and Sikhs—were in flight. By the time the monsoon broke, almost a million of them were dead, and all of northern India was in arms, in terror, or in hiding. The only remaining oases of peace were a scatter of little villages lost in the remote reaches of the frontier. One of these villages was Mano Majra.

Mano Majra is a tiny place. It has only three brick buildings, one of which is the home of the moneylender Lala Ram Lal. The other two are the Sikh temple and the mosque. The three brick buildings enclose a triangular common with a large peepal tree in the middle. The rest of the village is a cluster of flat-roofed mud huts and low-walled courtyards, which front on narrow lanes that radiate from the centre. Soon the lanes dwindle into footpaths and get lost in the surrounding fields. At the western end of the village there is a pond ringed round by keekar trees. There are only about seventy families in Mano Majra, and Lala Ram Lal's is the only Hindu family. The others are Sikhs or Muslims, about equal in number. The Sikhs own all the land around the village; the Muslims are tenants and share the tilling with the owners. There are a few families of sweepers whose religion is uncertain. The Muslims claim them as their own, yet when American missionaries visit Mano Majra the sweepers wear khaki sola topis and join their womenfolk in singing hymns to the accompaniment of a harmonium. Sometimes they visit the Sikh temple, too. But there is one object that all Mano Majrans—even Lala Ram Lal— venerate. This is a three-foot slab of sandstone that stands upright under a keekar tree beside the pond. It is the local deity, the deo to which all the villagers—Hindu, Sikh, Muslim or pseudo-Christian—repair secretly whenever they are in a special need of blessing.

Although Mano Majra is said to be on the banks of the Sutlej River, it is actually half a mile away from it. In India villages cannot afford to be too close to the banks of rivers. Rivers change their moods with the seasons and alter their courses without warning. The Sutlej is the largest river in the Punjab. After the monsoon its waters rise and spread across its vast sandy bed, lapping high up the mud embankments on either side. It becomes an expanse of muddy turbulence more than a mile in breadth. When the flood subsides, the river breaks up into a thousand shallow streams that wind sluggishly between little marshy islands. About a mile north of Mano Majra the Sutlej is spanned by a railroad bridge. It is a magnificent bridge—its eighteen enormous spans sweep like waves from one pier to another, and at each end of it there is a stone embankment to buttress the railway line. On the eastern end the embankment extends all the way to the village railroad station.

Mano Majra has always been known for its railway station. Since the bridge has only one track, the station has several sidings where less important trains can wait, to make way for the more important.

A small colony of shopkeepers and hawkers has grown up around the station to supply travellers with food, betel leaves, cigarettes, tea, biscuits and sweetmeats. This gives the station an appearance of constant activity and its staff a somewhat exaggerated sense of importance. Actually the stationmaster himself sells tickets through the pigeonhole in his office, collects them at the exit beside the door, and sends and receives messages over the telegraph ticker on the table. When there are people to notice him, he comes out on the platform and waves a green flag for trains which do not stop. His only assistant manipulates the levers in the glass cabin on the platform which control the signals on either side, and helps shunting engines by changing hand points on the tracks to get them on to the sidings. In the evenings, he lights the long line of lamps on the platform. He takes heavy aluminium lamps to the signals and sticks them in the clamps behind the red and green glass. In the mornings, he brings them back and puts out the lights on the platform.

Not many trains stop at Mano Majra. Express trains do not stop at all. Of the many slow passenger trains, only two, one from Delhi to Lahore in the mornings and the other from Lahore to Delhi in the evenings, are scheduled to stop for a few minutes. The others stop only when they are held up. The only regular customers are the goods trains. Although Mano Majra seldom has any goods to send or receive, its station sidings are usually occupied by long rows of wagons. Each passing goods train spends hours shedding wagons and collecting others. After dark, when the countryside is steeped in silence, the whistling and puffing of engines, the banging of buffers, and the clanking of iron couplings can be heard all through the night.

All this has made Mano Majra very conscious of trains. Before daybreak, the mail train rushes through on its way to Lahore, and as it approaches the bridge, the driver invariably blows two long blasts of the whistle. In an instant, all Mano Majra comes awake. Crows begin to caw in the keekar trees. Bats fly back in long silent relays and begin to quarrel for their perches in the peepal. The mullah at the mosque knows that it is time for the morning prayer. He has a quick wash, stands facing west towards Mecca and with his fingers in his ears cries in long sonorous notes, 'Allah-o-Akbar'. The priest at the Sikh temple lies in bed till the mullah has called. Then he too gets up, draws a bucket of water from the well in the temple courtyard, pours it over himself, and intones his prayer in monotonous singsong to the sound of splashing water.

By the time the 10:30 morning passenger train from Delhi comes in, life in Mano Majra has settled down to its dull daily routine. Men are in the fields. Women are busy with their daily chores. Children are out grazing cattle by the river. Persian wheels squeak and groan as bullocks go round and round, prodded on by curses and the jabs of goads in their hindquarters. Sparrows fly about the roofs, trailing straw in their beaks. Pye-dogs seek the shade of the long mud walls. Bats settle their arguments, fold their wings, and suspend themselves in sleep.

As the midday express goes by, Mano Majra stops to rest. Men and children come home for dinner and the siesta hour. When they have eaten, the men gather in the shade of the peepal tree and sit on the wooden platforms and talk and doze. Boys ride their buffaloes into the pond, jump off their backs, and splash about in the muddy water. Girls play under the trees. Women rub clarified butter into each other's hair, pick lice from their children's heads, and discuss births, marriages and deaths.

When the evening passenger from Lahore comes in, everyone gets to work again. The cattle are rounded up and driven back home to be milked and locked in for the night. The women cook the evening meal. Then the families foregather on their rooftops where most of them sleep during the summer. Sitting on their charpais, they eat their supper of vegetables and chapatis and sip hot creamy milk out of large copper tumblers and idle away the time until the signal for sleep. When the goods train steams in, they say to each other, 'There is the goods train.' It is like saying goodnight. The mullah again calls the faithful to prayer by shouting at the top of his voice, 'God is great.' The faithful nod their amens from their rooftops. The Sikh priest murmurs the evening prayer to a semicircle of drowsy old men and women. Crows caw softly from the keekar trees. Little bats go flitting about in the dusk and large ones soar with slow graceful sweeps. The goods train takes a long time at the station, with the engine running up and down the sidings exchanging wagons. By the time it leaves, the children are asleep. The older people wait for its rumble over the bridge to lull them to slumber. Then life in Mano Majra is stilled, save for the dogs barking at the trains that pass in the night.

It had always been so, until the summer of 1947...

◆

Early in September the time schedule in Mano Majra started going wrong. Trains became less punctual than ever before and many more started to run through at night. Some days it seemed as though the alarm clock had been set for the wrong hour. On others, it was as if no one had remembered to wind it. Imam Baksh waited for Meet Singh to make the first start. Meet Singh waited for the mullah's call to prayer before getting up. People stayed in bed late without realizing that times had changed and the mail train might not run through at all. Children did not know when to be hungry, and clamoured for food all the time. In the evenings, everyone was indoors before sunset and in bed before the express came by—if it did come by. Goods trains had stopped running altogether, so there was no lullaby to lull them to sleep. Instead, ghost trains went past at odd hours between midnight and dawn, disturbing the dreams of Mano Majra.

This was not all that changed the life of the village. A unit of Sikh soldiers arrived and put up tents near the railway station. They built a six-foot-high square of sandbags about the base of the signal near the bridge, and mounted a machine gun in each face. Armed sentries began to patrol the platform and no villagers were allowed near the railings. All trains coming from Delhi stopped and changed their drivers and guards before moving on to Pakistan. Those coming from Pakistan ran through with their engines screaming with release and relief.

One morning, a train from Pakistan halted at Mano Majra railway station. At first glance, it had the look of the trains in the days of peace. No one sat on the roof. No one clung between the bogies. No one was balanced on the footboards. But somehow it was different. There was something uneasy about it. It had a ghostly quality. As soon as it pulled up to the platform, the guard emerged from the tail end of the train and went into the stationmaster's office. Then the two went to the soldiers' tents and spoke to the officer in charge. The soldiers were called out and the villagers loitering about were ordered back to Mano Majra. One man was sent off on a motorcycle to Chundunnugger. An hour later, the sub-inspector with about fifty armed policemen turned up at the station. Immediately after them, Mr Hukum Chand drove up in his American car.

The arrival of the ghost train in broad daylight created a commotion in Mano Majra. People stood on their roofs to see what was happening at the station. All they could see was the black top of the train stretching from one end of the platform to the other. The station building and the railings blocked the rest of the train from view. Occasionally a soldier or a policeman came out of the station and then went back again.

In the afternoon, men gathered in little groups, discussing the train. The groups merged with each other under the peepal tree, and then everyone went into the gurdwara. Women, who had gone from door to door collecting and dropping bits of gossip, assembled in the headman's house and waited for their menfolk to come home and tell them what they had learned about the train.

This was the pattern of things at Mano Majra when anything of consequence happened. The women went to the headman's house, the men to the temple. There was no recognized leader of the village. Banta Singh, the headman, was really only a collector of revenue—a lambardar. The post had been in his family for several generations. He did not own any more land than the others. Nor was he a head in any other way. He had no airs about him: he was a modest, hard-working peasant like the rest of his fellow villagers. But since government officials and the police dealt with him, he had an official status. Nobody called him by his name. He was 'O Lambardara', as his father, his father's father, and his father's father's father had been before him.

The only men who voiced their opinions at village meetings were Imam Baksh, the mullah of the mosque, and Bhai Meet Singh. Imam Baksh was a weaver, and weavers are traditionally the butts of jokes in the Punjab. They are considered effeminate and cowardly—a race of cuckolds whose women are always having liaisons with others. A series of tragedies in his family had made him an object of pity, and then of affection. The Punjabis love people they can pity. His wife and only son had died within a few days of each other. His eyes, which had never been very good, suddenly became worse and he could not work his looms any more. He was reduced to beggary, with a baby girl, Nooran, to look after. He began living in the mosque and teaching Muslim children the Quran. He wrote out verses from the Quran for the village folk to wear as charms or for the sick to swallow as medicine. Small offerings of flour, vegetables, food, and castoff clothes kept him and his daughter alive. He had an amazing fund of anecdotes and proverbs which the peasants loved to hear. His appearance commanded respect. He was a tall, lean man, bald save for a line of white hair which ran round the back of his head from ear to ear, and he had a neatly trimmed silky white beard that he occasionally dyed with henna to a deep orange-red. The cataracts in his eyes gave them a misty philosophical look. Despite his sixty years, he held himself erect. All this gave his bearing dignity and an aura of righteousness. He was known to the villagers not as Imam Baksh or the mullah but as Chacha, or 'Uncle'.

Meet Singh inspired no such affection and respect. He was only a peasant who had taken to religion as an escape from work. He had a little land of his own which he had leased out, and this, with the offerings at the temple, gave him a comfortable living. He had no wife or children. He was not learned in the scriptures, nor had he any faculty for conversation. Even his appearance was against him. He was short, fat, and hairy. He was the same age as Imam Baksh, but his beard had none of the serenity of the other's. It was black, with streaks of grey. And he was untidy. He wore his turban only when reading the scripture. Otherwise, he went about with his long hair tied in a loose knot held by a little wooden comb. Almost half of the hair was scattered on the nape of his neck. He seldom wore a shirt and his only garment—a pair of shorts—was always greasy with dirt. But Meet Singh was a man of peace. Envy had never poisoned his affection for Imam Baksh. He only felt that he owed it to his own community to say something when Imam Baksh made any suggestions. Their conversation always had an undercurrent of friendly rivalry.

The meeting in the gurdwara had a melancholic atmosphere. People had little to say, and those who did spoke slowly, like prophets.

Imam Baksh opened the discussion. 'May Allah be merciful. We are living in bad times.'

A few people sighed solemnly, 'Yes, bad days.'

Meet Singh added, 'Yes, Chacha—this is Kalyug, the dark age.'

There was a long silence and people shuffled uneasily on their haunches. Some yawned, closing their mouths with loud invocations to God: 'Ya Allah. Wah Guru, wah Guru.'

'Lambardara,' started Imam Baksh again, 'you should know what is happening. Why has not the Deputy sahib sent for you?'

'How am I to know, Chacha? When he sends for me I will go. He is also at the station and no one is allowed near it.'

A young villager interjected in a loud cheery voice: 'We are not going to die just yet. We will soon know what is going on. It is a train after all. It may be carrying government treasures or arms. So they guard it. Haven't you heard—many have been looted?'

'Shut up,' rebuked his bearded father angrily. 'Where there are elders, what need have you to talk?'

'I only...'

'That is all,' said the father sternly. No one spoke for some time.

'I have heard,' said Imam Baksh, slowly combing his beard with his fingers, 'that there have been many incidents with trains.'

The word 'incident' aroused an uneasy feeling in the audience. 'Yes, lots of incidents have been heard of,' Meet Singh agreed after a while.

'We only ask for Allah's mercy,' said Imam Baksh, closing the subject he had himself opened.

Meet Singh, not meaning to be outdone in the invocation to God, added, 'Wah Guru, wah Guru.'

They sat on in silence punctuated by yawns and murmurs of 'Ya Allah' and 'Hey wah Guru'. Several people, on the outer fringe of the assembly, stretched themselves on the floor and went to sleep.

Suddenly a policeman appeared in the doorway of the gurdwara. The lambardar and three or four villagers stood up. People who were asleep were prodded into getting up. Those who had been dozing sat up in a daze, exclaiming, 'What is it? What's up?', then hurriedly wrapped their turbans round their heads.

'Who is the lambardar of the village?'

Banta Singh walked up to the door. The policeman took him aside and whispered something. Then as Banta Singh turned back, he said loudly: 'Quickly, within half an hour. There are two military trucks waiting on the station side. I will be there.'

The policeman walked away briskly.

The villagers crowded round Banta Singh. The possession of a secret had lent him an air of importance. His voice had a tone of authority.

'Everyone, get all the wood there is in his house and all the kerosene oil he can spare and bring these to the motor trucks on the station side. You will be paid.'

The villagers waited for him to tell them why. He ordered them off brusquely. 'Are you deaf? Haven't you heard? Or do you want the police to whip your buttocks before you move? Come along quickly.'

People dispersed into the village lanes whispering to each other. The lambardar went to his own house.

A few minutes later, villagers with bundles of wood and bottles of oil started assembling outside the village on the station side. Two large mud-green army trucks were parked alongside each other. A row of empty petrol cans stood against a mud wall. A Sikh soldier with a sten gun stood on guard. Another Sikh, an officer with his beard neatly rolled in a hair net, sat on the back of one of the trucks with his feet dangling. He watched the wood being stacked in the other truck and nodded his head in reply to the villagers' greetings. The lambardar stood beside him, taking down the names of the villagers and the quantities they brought. After dumping their bundles of wood on the truck and emptying bottles of kerosene into the petrol cans, the villagers collected in a little group at a respectful distance from the officer.

Imam Baksh put down on the truck the wood he had carried on his head and handed his bottle of oil to the lambardar. He retied his turban, then greeted the officer loudly, 'Salaam, Sardar sahib.'

The officer looked away.

Imam Baksh started again, 'Everything is all right, isn't it, Sardar sahib?'

The officer turned around abruptly and snapped, 'Get along. Don't you see I am busy?'

Imam Baksh, still adjusting his turban, meekly joined the villagers.

When both the trucks were loaded, the officer told Banta Singh to come to the camp next morning for the money. The trucks rumbled off towards the station.

Banta Singh was surrounded by eager villagers. He felt that he was somehow responsible for the insult to Imam Baksh. The villagers were impatient with him.

'O Lambardara, why don't you tell us something? What is all this big secret you are carrying about? You seem to think you have become someone very important and don't need to talk to us any more,' said Meet Singh angrily.

'No, Bhai, no. If I knew, why would I not tell you? You talk like children. How can I argue with soldiers and policemen? They told me nothing. And didn't you see how that pig's penis spoke to Chacha? One's self-respect is in one's own hands. Why should I have myself insulted by having my turban taken off?'

Imam Baksh acknowledged the gesture gracefully. 'Lambardar is right. If somebody barks when you speak to him, it is best to keep quiet. Let us all go to our homes. You can see what they are doing from the tops of your roofs.'

The villagers dispersed to their rooftops. From there the trucks could be seen at the camp near the station. They started off again and went east along the railway tracks till they were beyond the signal. Then they turned sharp left and bumped across the rails. They turned left again, came back along the line towards the station, and disappeared behind the train.

All afternoon, the villagers stood on their roofs shouting to each other, asking whether anyone had seen anything. In their excitement they had forgotten to prepare the midday meal. Mothers fed their children on stale leftovers from the day before. They did not have time to light their hearths. The men did not give fodder to their cattle nor remember to milk them as evening drew near. When the sun was already under the arches of the bridge everyone became conscious of having overlooked the daily chores. It would be dark soon and the children would clamour for food, but still the women watched, their eyes glued to the station. The cows and buffaloes lowed in the barns, but still the men stayed on the roofs looking towards the station. Everyone expected something to happen.

The sun sank behind the bridge, lighting the white clouds which had appeared in the sky with hues of russet, copper, and orange. Then shades of grey blended with the glow as evening gave way to twilight and twilight sank into darkness. The station became a black wall. Wearily, the men and women went down to their courtyards, beckoning the others to do the same. They did not want to be alone in missing anything.

The northern horizon, which had turned a bluish grey, showed orange again. The orange turned into copper and then into a luminous russet. Red tongues of flame leaped into the black sky. A soft breeze began to blow towards the village. It brought the smell of burning kerosene, then of wood. And then—a faint acrid smell of searing flesh.

The village was stilled in a deathly silence. No one asked anyone else what the odour was. They all knew. They had known it all the time. The answer was implicit in the fact that the train had come from Pakistan.

That evening, for the first time in the memory of Mano Majra, Imam Baksh's sonorous cry did not rise to the heavens to proclaim the glory of God.

76

'There should be a baptism in blood. We have had enough of target practice.'

The trunk of a tree thirty yards away bore imprints of their marksmanship. Its bark was torn; in its centre was a deep, yellow gash oozing a mixture of gum and sap. From one branch dangled a row of metal heads of electric bulbs; their glass was strewn on the ground and shone like a bed of mica. Littered about the tree were tin cans and tattered pieces of cardboard sieved with holes.

'What about it, leader?' asked the smallest boy in the party, slapping the butt of his rifle. 'We should sprinkle blood on our guns and say a short prayer to baptize them. Then they will never miss their mark and we can kill as many Englishmen as we like.'

Sher Singh smiled. He tossed his revolver in the air and caught it by the handle. He took careful aim at an empty sardine can and fired another six shots. The bullets went through into the earth kicking up whiffs of dust. His Alsatian dog, Dyer, began to whine with excitement. He leapt up with a growl and ran down the canal embankment. He sniffed at the tin and pawed it gingerly to make sure that it was dead, then picked it up in his mouth and shook it from side to side. He ran back with it and laid it at his master's feet.

'Why waste good bullets on tin cans and trees? What have they done to us?' asked another member of the party.

'That is why I say we should have a baptism in blood,' repeated the little boy.

'We will have our blood baptism when the time comes,' replied Sher Singh pompously. 'Let us be prepared for action. When duty calls, we will not be found wanting.'

'Brother, it is an old Hindu custom to baptize weapons before using them. Our ancient warriors used to dip their swords in a tray of goat's blood and lay them before Durga, Kali or Bhavani or whatever name the goddess of destruction was known by. We should keep up the tradition.'

Sher Singh could not make up his mind. He had never killed anything before. Even the sight of a headless chicken spouting blood as it fluttered about had made him turn cold with horror. He had been full of loathing for the cook who had wrenched off the fowl's head, and had given up eating meat of any kind for some months. But this was different. They were training to become terrorists. They had to learn how to take life—to become tough. He, more than the others, because he was their leader.

'My gun is thirsty,' went on the little boy. 'If it can't get the blood of an Englishman or a toady it must drink that of some animal or bird.'

There was a general murmur of assent. Only Sher Singh was reluctant. 'You don't want to smear the blood of a jackal or a crow on your guns, do you? What else can you find this time of the year? The shooting season closed two months ago.'

'We will find something or other round about the swamp,' assured Madan. 'There may be deer coming to drink. Perhaps a duck or two which could not migrate.'

That decided him finally. Madan was the strong man of the university. He had won his colours in many games and had played cricket for his province. His performance against a visiting English side—he had carried his bat after scoring a century—had made him a local hero. He had brought the other boys with him and would have been the leader of the band except that he knew little of politics. And it was Sher Singh, and not he, who had arranged the smuggling of rifles and hand grenades from across the frontier. Although Sher Singh had assumed the leadership of the group, Madan was its backbone. He was both Sher Singh's chief supporter and rival: one whose presence was an encouragement and a challenge at the same time.

'OK, brother, OK,' said Sher Singh in English and stood up. 'We must be quick. It will be dark in an hour.' He collected the empty cases lying on the ground and put them in his pocket. The boys also stood up and brushed the dust off their clothes. They put their guns in the jeep. One of them volunteered to stay back.

Sher Singh loaded his rifle and led the party down the canal bank towards the marsh. Dyer ran ahead barking excitedly.

They crossed the stretch of chalky saltpetre and got to the edge of the swamp. There were no birds on the water. On the other side was a peepal tree on which there was a flock of white egrets. Right on the top was a king vulture with its bald red head hunched between its black shoulders. Beneath the tree were bitterns wading in the mud. The birds were over a hundred yards away; well beyond Sher Singh's range of marksmanship.

The party surveyed the scene and considered the pros and cons of taking a shot from that distance. The vulture stuck out its head and the egrets began to show signs of nervousness. Suddenly there came the loud, raucous cry of a sarus crane followed by another from its mate. They were in a cluster of bulrushes not fifty yards away. The boys sat down on their haunches and stopped talking. The cranes continued calling alternately for a few minutes and then resumed their search for frogs. The vulture and the egrets on the opposite bank went back to sleep.

'Kill one of these. They are as big as any black buck,' whispered the small boy.

'Who kills cranes?' asked Sher Singh. 'They are no use to anyone. And I am told if one of a pair is killed, the other dies of grief.'

'If you are going to funk shooting birds, you will not do much when it comes to shooting Englishmen,' taunted Madan. 'You will say, "Why kill this poor chap, his widow and children will weep", or "His mother will be sad". Sher Singhji, this is what is meant by baptism in blood; get used to the idea of shedding it. Steel your heart against sentiments of kindness and pity. They have been the undoing of our nation. We are too soft.'

That was enough to provoke Sher Singh—particularly as it came from Madan. 'Oh no! Nothing soft about me,' he answered defiantly. 'If it is a sarus crane you want, a sarus crane you will have. Come along, Dyer—and if you bark, I'll shoot you too.'

Sher Singh got down on his knees and crawled up behind the cover of the pampas grass, his dog following warily behind. He stopped after a few yards and parted the stalks with the muzzle of his rifle. One of the birds was busy digging in the mud with his long beak; the other was on guard, turning its head in all directions, looking out for signs of danger. Sher Singh decided to be patient. He wanted to get a little closer and also get enough time to take aim. Missing a bird of that size would be bad for his reputation.

After a few minutes, he looked through the stalks again. Both the cranes were now busy rummaging in the reeds. He crept up another ten yards, Dyer behind him. He paused for breath and once again parted the pampas stalks with the muzzle of his rifle. One of the birds was again on the lookout. Sher Singh drew the bead on the other—at the easiest spot to hit: the heavy, feathered middle of its body. The sentry crane spotted Sher Singh. It let out a warning cry and rose heavily into the air. Its mate looked up. Before it could move, Sher Singh fired. The bullet hit its mark. A cloud of feathers flew up and the bird fell in the mud. Dyer ran across to seize it. The boys came up from behind, clapping and shouting.

Sher Singh clicked open the catch; the metal case of the bullet flew out and fell on the ground. He picked it up and put it in his pocket. He blew into the barrel and saw the smoke shoot out of the other end. He was a jumble of conflicting emotions of guilt and pride. He had mortally wounded a harmless, inedible bird. But this was his first attempt to take life and it had succeeded. Then his friends came up, slapped him on the back and shook his hand by turn. The feeling of remorse was temporarily smothered.

The shot had not killed the crane. It flapped its wings and dragged itself out of the pool of blood and pecked away fiercely with its long, powerful beak. The snarling and snapping Alsatian kept a discreet distance. Then the other crane flew back and began to circle overhead, crying loudly. It dived down low over the dog to frighten it away.

'Leader, give the other one its salvation too. Let them be together in heaven or hell.'

'Yes, let's see you take a flying shot,' added Madan.

The argument appealed to Sher Singh. The anguished cry of the flying crane was almost human. If he did not silence it, it would continue to haunt him for a long time. If both of the pair were dead, perhaps they would be together wherever cranes went after death. Sher Singh took out the magazine of his rifle and pressed six bullets in it. He followed the crane's flight with his barrel and fired when the bird was almost above him. The bullet went through one of the wings. The bird wavered badly in its flight and some feathers came floating down. Sher Singh fired the second shot. Then the third and the fourth and emptied the magazine. The crane flew away across the swamp, ducking nervously as the bullets whistled by in quick succession.

Sher Singh blew the smoke out of the barrel once more.

In his excitement he forgot to pick up the empty cases.

'Its time is not up yet,' said Madan to console him. 'Put this one out of its agony.'

Once having embarked on the bloody business, Sher Singh could not stop halfway. He walked up to the injured bird and put his right foot on its neck. The crane began to kick violently and gasp for breath. Its beak opened wide showing its thin, long tongue. Sher Singh took out his revolver and fired two shots into its body. The bird's dying gurgle was stifled in its throat. Its legs clawed the air and then slowly came to a stop in an attitude of prayer. Blood started trickling from its beak and a film covered its small black eyes.

'This one is finished. Let us take it to the jeep and baptize our weapons in its blood.'

Two of the boys caught the crane by the wings from either end and dragged it out of the swamp. Dyer sniffed at the dead bird's head dangling between its trailing legs and began to run round in circles, yapping deliriously. Sher Singh saw his handiwork and a lump came up in his throat. He did not respond to the backslapping and hilarity of his companions.

Before they got clear of the swamp, the other crane flew back and started circling over them. They saw it high above in the deep blue sky; then heard its cries piercing the stillness of the dusk. Sher Singh ignored requests to have another go at the flying bird; in any case it was too high and the light was failing fast. When they got to the canal bank, it became dark. The crane flew lower and lower till they could see its grey form with its long legs almost above their heads. They shooed it off. The bird disappeared in the dark only to come back again and again. Its crying told them it was there all the time, trying to reclaim its dead mate. Sher Singh wanted to get away from the place as fast as his jeep could take him. That was not to be.

When they got to the jeep, they saw a Sikh peasant talking to the boy they had left behind. He was obviously waiting for them. When the man saw what the boys had brought, he spat on the ground: 'Sardarji, why did you have to take the life of this poor creature? Is anyone going to eat it?' He spoke to Sher Singh as Sher Singh was the only one carrying a gun.

'Oi Sardara, what do you know about these things? Be on your way,' answered the boy holding one end of the crane's wings.

The peasant spat again, the spittle fell near the foot of the boy who had spoken rudely. 'The shooting season closed two months ago and you are still going about killing birds. Have you a licence?' he asked.

'Oi, who do you think you are?'

The peasant stood up. He was a big man standing well over six feet. He was also broad and hairy. Long strands of hair trickled out from all sides of his clumsily-tied turban. A thick, black beard covered most of his chest. He carried a bamboo staff shod with iron at either end.

'Keep quiet,' said Sher Singh angrily, silencing his companion; then turned calmly to the peasant. 'There is no open or closed season for birds like these; that is only for game.'

'Nevertheless, you have to have a gun licence,' continued the other truculently. 'I am the headman of the village beyond the swamp. I heard the firing. It sounded like machine-gun practice. You have to show me all your arms licences.'

'There is only one gun,' said Sher Singh with presence of mind. 'I will show you mine.'

He fished out his father's shot-gun licence from his pocket and wrapped a five rupee note in its folds. He put his arm around the peasant's shoulder and took him aside: 'Come along, Lambardar sahib, you have become angry for no reason. You can see the licence and anything else you like.'

Madan felt that he was entitled to join them. Before Sher Singh could hand over the licence, Madan spoke to the headman: 'Lambardarji, you know who you are talking to? This is Sher Singh, son of Sardar Buta Singh, Magistrate. You have heard the name of Sardar Buta Singh, I hope.'

The headman turned to Sher Singh. He looked at him for a brief moment and then took Sher Singh's hands in his. The scowl on his face turned to a broad, friendly grin. 'Who doesn't know of Sardar Buta Singh?' he asked. 'But how should I have known! Do forgive me, Sardar sahib.'

'Not at all,' answered Sher Singh. 'It is you who must forgive us for speaking rudely! You are a lambardar and we should respect you!'

'I am your slave,' said the peasant, touching Sher Singh's knee. 'The slave of your slaves. You must come to my humble home for some water or something.'

'That is very kind of you; we will, another day. Do see my licence. And this is for your children.'

'No, no, Sardar sahib,' protested the headman. 'Do not shame me. I am not short of money. By the Guru's blessing I have plenty to eat and drink. I only need your kindness. If you step into the hut of Jhimma Singh I will ask nothing more. Your slave is named Jhimma Singh.'

They re-joined the party. The headman's mood had changed completely. 'Babuji,' he said, addressing them all, 'if you are fond of shikar, you only have to say the word and I will arrange one for you. I could get the villagers to beat through the fields and you could shoot to your hearts' content. Partridge, hare, deer, wild pig—anything.'

'We will ask you when the shooting season opens,' answered Madan.

'Now you are making fun of me; I was only doing my duty as a headman. Sardar Buta Singh is the king of this district, who dare tell his son when he can or cannot shoot? Isn't that so Babuji... Babuji... what is your name?'

Before Madan could reply, Sher Singh answered, 'He is Mr Nasir Ali; he is a captain in the army.'

The boys took up the game eagerly and introduced each other to him with false names. The peasant shook hands with all of them. 'What have I to do with names? You are all friends of Sardar Sher Singh, that is enough for me,' he said with a knowing smile.

'If we have your permission,' said Madan, taking the peasant's hand again. 'It is getting very late and I have to report at the cantonment by nine.'

'Of course, of course, Captain sahib. Please forgive me for detaining you. You promise to let me know when you come next time?'

They all promised and parted the best of friends.

The boys threw the dead crane into the canal without the ceremonial baptism and turned back homewards.

It was evident that Sher Singh was still upset. One of the boys tried to draw him out. 'That was a narrow escape,' he said cheerfully. 'You know what these village headmen are! All informers. They would inform against their own parents to please the police. Leader, you were very clever in not letting him know Madan's name. Wasn't he?'

'Very clever. Great presence of mind,' they agreed.

'He knows mine,' said Sher Singh grimly.

Madan felt he had to explain. 'If I had not mentioned your father's name, he would not have let us go. He will never dare to say a word about you to anyone, you take my word for it. I know his type. He will probably come to you with presents of tins of clarified butter or farm produce. Really, you have no need to worry.'

Sher Singh did not answer. They all fell silent.

When they got to the end of the canal road, they found the way barred by the gate meant to keep off general traffic. The gateman heard the car and came out of his hut with his log book. Sher Singh took it from him and entered a name and a car number and handed it back. The gateman took the log book and examined the entry in front of the headlight. He looked at the number plate on the jeep and came back. He spoke politely but firmly: 'Sardar sahib, I do not know English but I am not illiterate. You have put in a wrong number for the car. I will have to report it to the canal officer.'

'It is not his car, it is mine,' replied Madan promptly. 'He does not know the number. You enter the correct number and report it to anyone you like. Tell them it was the car of Mr Wazir Chand, Magistrate, driven by his son, Madan Lal. Now open the gate.'

The tone of authority did not fail to impress the gateman. He walked quietly to the gate and unlocked it. He salaamed as the jeep went past.

Everyone was convinced that Madan had atoned for his earlier indiscretion—if any. Even Sher Singh felt he had been a little mean in his resentment. 'If we let ourselves be bothered by informers and canal road gatemen, we won't get far with our plans. To hell with them. Revolutions cannot be stopped by vermin,' he proclaimed loudly.

'Indeed not,' added Madan. 'And what has anyone learnt anyhow? That you have a gun. Of course you have a gun—and a licence for it too. And that your father's jeep used the canal road! What more?'

Sher Singh felt very relieved. His fears were purely imaginary. He pulled up the jeep. 'I've had too much tea,' he announced. 'I will dedicate its remains to the lambardar and the gateman.'

They roared with laughter and leapt out of the jeep. They lined up along the deserted road. 'On the headman,' said one.

'On the headman and all informers.'

'On the headman, all informers, and all Englishmen.'

'No,' said the smallest boy, 'mine is for the Englishmen's memsahibs.' They laughed louder and continued laughing for a long time.

'Quiet!' ordered Sher Singh. 'Listen.'

The laughter died down and they listened. Above the purring of the motor engine they heard the cry of the sarus crane. They looked up into the black sky studded with stars. A large grey form flew up from the side of the road they had come. It circled over the jeep a couple of times and landed right in front of the glaring head lights. The crane called to its mate.

'It's been following us all the way; thinks we've got the other one in the car,' said the little boy. Even he could not bring himself to repeat the suggestion that Sher Singh should kill the bird. 'Brother Sarus,' he said addressing the crane, 'your dear mate is in heaven. Don't cry. Go and find yourself another wife.'

The crane turned to him without any sign of fear. It spread out its enormous wings and charged. The boy ran round the jeep. Dyer began to growl and bark but even he did not have the courage to attack the angry bird. The other boys came up yelling loudly and the crane retreated. It kept calling all the time.

The boys got back into the jeep and Sher Singh stepped on the accelerator as hard as he could. They heard the crane calling above them for a little distance till they mixed with the traffic going into the city.

77

DELHI: A NOVEL
DELHI

I return to Delhi as I return to my mistress Bhagmati when I have had my fill of whoring in foreign lands. Delhi and Bhagmati have a lot in common. Having been long misused by rough people they have learnt to conceal their seductive charms under a mask of repulsive ugliness. It is only to their lovers, among whom I count myself, that they reveal their true selves.

To the stranger, Delhi may appear like a gangrenous accretion of noisy bazaars and mean-looking hovels growing round a few tumbledown forts and mosques along a dead river. If he ventures into its narrow, winding lanes, the stench of raw sewage may bring vomit to his throat. The citizens of Delhi do little to endear themselves to anyone. They spit phlegm and bloody betel juice everywhere; they urinate and defecate whenever and wherever the urge overtakes them; they are loud-mouthed, express familiarity with incestuous abuse and scratch their privates while they talk.

It is the same with Bhagmati. Those who do not know her find her unattractive. She is dark and has pockmarks on her face. She is short and squat; her teeth are uneven and yellowed as a result of chewing tobacco and smoking beedis. Her clothes are loud, her voice louder, her speech bawdy and her manners worse.

This is, as I say, only on the surface—like the evil-smelling oil people smear on their skins to repel mosquitoes, midges and other blood-sucking vermin. What you have to do for things to appear different is to cultivate a sense of belonging to Delhi and an attachment to someone like Bhagmati. Then the skies over Delhi's marbled palaces turn an aquamarine blue; its domed mosques and pencil-like minarets are spanned by rainbows, the earth exudes the earthly aroma of khus, of jasmine and of maulsari. Then the dusky Bhagmati glides towards you swaying her ample hips like a temple dancer; her mouth smells of fresh cloves and she speaks like her imperial Majesty the Empress of Hindustan. Only when making love does she behave, as every woman should, like a lusty harlot. It is a simple formula: use your heart not your head, your emotion not your reason.

I make Delhi and Bhagmati sound very mysterious. The truth is that I am somewhat confused in my thoughts. What I am trying to say is that although I detest living in Delhi and am ashamed of my liaison with Bhagmati, I cannot keep away from either for too long. In these pages I will explain the strange paradox of my lifelong, love-hate affair with the city and the woman. It may read like a *Fucking Man's Guide to Delhi: Past and Present* but that is not what I mean it to be.

◆

The plane touches down at Palam at 2100 hours, one hour behind schedule. 'Air India planes used to arrive on the dot till the government took it over,' says someone. A voice over the speaker system orders us to remain seated. 'Why?' I demand of an air hostess gliding past me. She confides in my ear: 'Health!' India, mother of most diseases known to mankind, does not want to add any more to her list. We sit encapsuled in light, talking in whispers and preventing our newspapers from rustling.

Someone slaps the plane with a heavy hand: thump, thump. The steward yanks open the door. Two men in medical white waft in with a gust of hot air. They go down the aisle distributing printed forms. We busy ourselves filling in the answers: Where did you spend the last ten days? Nine days? Yesterday? One man takes a canister out of his pocket and strides up the aisle spraying us with hospital smell. We can disembark.

We file out. Near the base of the ramp, attached to the first class exit, stands an enormous grey Rolls-Royce bearing the president's three-faced lion insignia on its number plate. Beside the car, stand the president's ADC and an orderly with an armful of flowers. Behind them are half a dozen photographers with cameras raised to their noses. A white woman carrying a fur coat over one arm and a hat-box in her other hand comes down the steps. Flash bulbs explode. The ADC clicks his heels and salutes. He takes the white woman's fur coat and hat-box and hands them to the orderly. He garlands the woman, presents her with the bouquets and salutes her again. She flashes her teeth at him. They get into the Rolls-Royce. The Rolls-Royce purrs away into the dark.

Who is she?

We are herded together and directed to follow an Air India official. We shade our eyes against the glare of the airport lights and showers of moths. We skirt long-snouted bandicoots skating on their bellies and enter a door marked 'International'. A large poster with a picture of Pandit Nehru bids us *Welcome to India.*

A police sergeant scrutinizes our health forms and stacks them in the 'out' basket on his table. A sub-inspector inspects our passports, stamps them and hands them back to us. A customs officer gives us sheaves of forms to fill in triplicate. Three each for what we have bought abroad; three each for what we have in foreign currency. We spend half an hour filling them. Customs men eye us to see if our expressions betray undeclared items. We look bored; our expressions betray nothing.

Forty minutes later trollies rattle into the customs shed. Coolies offload cases on the floor. I locate my valise and grab a customs inspector. I have bought nothing and have no foreign currency. He does not believe me. He examines my declaration forms and my passport. He opens my valise and fires a stream of questions at me as he digs through my clothes.

'Any whisky-shisky?'

'No.'

'No tape recorder?'

'No.'

'Transistor-shransistor?'

'No.'

'Camera-shamera?'

'No.'

'Watch-shotch?'

'No.'

He grabs my hand and examines the shiny new Vulcan alarm watch on my wrist. I bought it at Beirut's duty-free shop in the airport store for thirty-five pounds.

'How much?'

I produce a receipt for the watch I bought for my cook which is tucked into my hip pocket. 'Seven pounds.'

He is a bad loser. He chalks my valise as if he were writing 'Fuck off'. One takes a lot from these customs bastards.

A porter grabs my valise. We pierce through a wall of clamorous taxi drivers and find a cab. The porter dumps my valise on the rear seat and exclaims: 'Okay, sir, salaam!' Airport rules say don't tip porters. He takes five rupees off me.

The Sikh cab driver has a Sikh friend in the front seat. Twenty minutes later we arrive at my destination. The cab driver lights a match and reads the meter, 'Eighteen fifty plus two for the luggage. Twenty fifty.'

'Eighteen fifty?' I pack as much disbelief as I can into my voice. 'It is more than double what I paid on my way out to Palam airport a few weeks ago.'

'Eighteen fifty,' repeats the cabbie. His friends lights another match and reads: 'Eighteen fifty. See meter.'

One Sikh may argue with one Sikh. One Sikh must never argue with two Sikhs—certainly not after dark. I pay twenty rupees fifty paise plus another two rupees as tip.

The nightwatchman of our block of apartments is also a Sikh. When I go out of Delhi, I leave the key of my flat with him. He is an honest fellow but a little soft under his turban. He was discharged from the army for his eccentricities. Although he was only a truck driver he never forgets he once wore a soldier's uniform. He jumps up from his charpai and orders himself: 'Salute!' And salutes me as if I were the colonel of his regiment. 'How was His Majesty the King of England?' he asks me in English.

'England now has a Queen.'

He thinks that a matter of small detail. 'Very well, sir. Did you ask His—beg pardon—Her Majesty, why he/she did not answer my letters?'

'Budh Singh, how long have you been like this?' I enquire very gently. Budh (knowledge) Singh gets this way three times in the year; then he becomes a Budhoo (simpleton) Singh. One has to be very gentle with Budhoo Singh.

His eyes burn. 'You think I mad?' he screams. 'You want dismiss me?' I do not answer. He unlocks the door, switches on the light and lets me in. He carries my valise to the unlit bedroom mumbling to himself. He comes back and presents me the key of the apartment with both his hands like a vanquished general surrendering his sword. 'Sir, here is your key and here is your job!'

'Budh Singh, I only asked you how long you have been like this,' I say taking the key.

'Yes, but I know truth,' says he peering into my eyes. 'Public say Budh is Budhoo again. Sahib sack him when he back from foreign. I say Hunooz Dilli door ast: you know what that mean? It is a long way to Delhi.'

'But I am back in Delhi,' I remind him. He looks at me more intensely. 'Okay! Forgive and forget.'

He assures me the apartment has been swept, furniture dusted. 'All okay. Cold machine okay, air condition okay. Come and look,' he commands. I follow him to the bedroom and press the switch. *Click.* No result. *Click, clock, click, clock.* No result. 'Excuse me, bulb fooze,' explains Budh Singh. He presses another switch. The burst of light gives him a shock. He leaps in the air and pirouettes like a dancing dervish.

He puts a finger to his turban and explains. 'Springtime something happen here. Don't mind, salute!'

'It will pass,' I reassure him. He comes close to me till his beard almost touches mine. He says in a conspiratorial whisper, 'Excuse me! Your hijda come many time to enquire if you back.'

Budh Singh does not like my mistress Bhagmati because she called him Pagal (mad) Singh. Budh Singh has never forgiven her. He calls her a him or a hijda (hermaphrodite). Bhagmati has a small bosom and a

The Novels   311

heavy voice. 'Excuse me,' he confides to my beard, 'everyone is talking about it. They say, take woman, take boy—okay! But a hijda! That's not nice. Don't mind my saying so!'

I say nothing. Budh Singh takes it as a reprimand. He stands stiffly to attention, salutes for the umpteenth time and orders himself: 'Right turn!' He turns right. 'By the left, quick march.' And marches out with measured steps.

Hah!

I peel off my clothes and go into the bathroom. I turn on the tap. A muddy ooze trickles down into the bucket. It is followed by a little muddy water. Then a fart. No water. I give up.

I go to my study, pick up the phone and dial the number of the caretaker on night duty. Two girls are on the line yakking away about their daddyji and uncleji. I put down the receiver, slap a mosquito against my paunch and try again. They are still at it; this time about their mummyji and auntyji. I put down the receiver, extract fluff out of my navel, inhale its shitty smell and try a third time. They are exulting over the piquancy of the chaat in Bengali Market: 'Yum! Yum!' I lose my temper and tell them that it is almost midnight and they should be doing what their mummyjis are doing to their daddyjis. 'Some dirty fellow on our line,' says one. 'Will buzz you later. Ta-ta.'

I dial my number. Engaged. Three minutes later I dial again. Engaged. I dial Complaints. The man at the other end tells me to dial Assistance. I dial Assistance. This operator tells me: 'Number out of order, please dial Complaints.' I give up.

I go to my bedroom to let the air conditioner cool my naked flesh and raw temper. It welcomes me with a distinct lowering of tone, but soon its drone lulls me to slumber. In a short while, however, it resents my indifference and goes off in a sulk. The bedroom becomes like the Black Hole of Calcutta.

Power cut. No light, no fan. I come out into my patch of garden and flop into a cane chair. It's hot, humid, dark and still. There are a few stars, but they are very very far away. And there are too many mosquitoes. I think angry thoughts. I will write letters to the papers about delays at the airport, the manners of customs inspectors, cheating by cab drivers, the inefficiency of the electricity company, Delhi telephones, Delhi water supply... Then I think of Bhagmati. I wonder how much whoring she has done while I have been away. She likes to tell me of her exploits because she knows it rouses my desire for her. I sit in the dark many hours. I am angry, I am wanton. Then less angry, more wanton. A pale, old moon wanders into the sky. A light goes up in the temple behind my apartment. The electricity is back when it is not needed. I get up and drag my feet into the sitting room.

I switch on the table lamp. 5.15 a.m. I throw open the window. The curtains flutter. A cool breeze fragrant with the madhumalati which covers the outside wall drives away the dank fuzz of yesterday's dead air. I sink into my armchair and gaze out of the window. Streetlights go off with a silent bang. Through the foliage of the mulberry tree appears the grey dawn.

Flying foxes wing their soundless way back to perch on massive arjun trees. The old lady who lives in the apartment above mine slish-sloshes along the road. She stops by my hibiscus hedge, looks around to see if anyone is looking, quickly plucks some flowers, thrusts them in her dupatta and slish-sloshes on towards the temple. Her old man follows her. He also stops by my hedge, looks around to see if anyone is listening, presses his paunch, and lets out a long, painful fart. He walks on with a lighter step and a 'who did that?' look on his face. A light goes on in the opposite block. A woman draws the curtains, ties her untidy hair into a bun and stretches her arms towards me. More lights are switched on and off. The morning star is barely visible in the pink sky. Crows begin cawing to each other. Sparrows start quarrelling in the mulberry tree. The muezzin's voice rises to the heavens. Temple bells peal to awaken the gods from their slumbers. The milkman cycles round the block with a noisy clanging of milk cans. Another cyclist follows tinkling his bell and shouting 'Paperwala! Ishtaitman, Taim of India, Hindustan Taim, Express, Herald, paperwala!' I hear the slush of papers being pushed under my door. I stay in my armchair. The morning breeze wafts the light of dawn into the room. It is cool, fragrant, pregnant with sadness and longing; it is the bad-i-saba—the morning breeze—sacred to lovers. And I am back in my beloved city.

◆

I settle down to the *Hindustan Times*. The front page has a picture of the white woman who came off the plane last night. 'Lady Hoity-Toity says it's great to be back home in Delhi.' So that's who she is! She has come to collect material for a book on archaeology. She is staying with the president at Rashtrapati Bhavan.

I glance over the headlines and look at the pictures.

My cook-bearer enters with a welcome grin. I give him the Japanese watch I bought for him. His grin changes into a smile. He gives me a mug of black coffee and asks me if I will be in for lunch. No. Dinner? Yes, but I may be late, so leave it on the table. What would I like? I know he's thinking of Bhagmati because she eats only Indian food and I eat Anglo-Indian ishtoo or sawset with kashtar for a putteen. I do not know how, when or where I will find Bhagmati. But I am not going to tell him, so I reply 'Anything.' He goes away constipated with curiosity.

It is time to catch up with Delhi. A quick shower and I am off in my Hindustan Ambassador. More roads and roundabouts have had their names changed. The Windsors, Yorks, Cannings and Hardinges have been replaced by the Tilaks, Patels, Azads and Nehrus. There are red flags outside a petrol station with three men chanting 'Death to petrol-stationwala.' Red flags outside Dr Sen's nursing home. Six men yelling 'Death to Doctors.' Red flags outside the Food and Agriculture Ministry building. Four men in garlands sit cross-legged on the lawn. A placard in front of them says *Third Day of Relay Hunger Strike*. A procession with saffron flags goes along Parliament Street chanting 'Our religion and our country are one. The cow is our mother. Death to cow-eaters.' On the lawns of Connaught Circus there is a political meeting. The speaker yells into the mike: 'All together cry—Jai Hind.' The crowd obeys: 'Jai Hind.' The man at the mike is not happy. 'That's not good enough. We cannot fight those Chinese pigs with such feeble voices, can we? Let your voices be heard as far as Peking. All together—Jai Hind.'

'JAI HIND.'

Pekinese pigs, piss in your pants. With enemies like Indians you've nothing to lose except your piddle.

I park my car beside the stalls of Tibetan 'antique' dealers on Janpath (once Queensway). The same brand of American tourists bargain for the same kind of brass and stone bric-à-brac. The same set of Sikh fortune-tellers mumble the same kind of talk of romances and travel to foreigners. One fellow spots my Mark and Sparks T-shirt. 'You come from phoren, you go phoren again,' he assures me. 'One minute you give me and I tell you love affairs. Rich white lady passioning for you. I tell you name. I tell you how to make her and her much fortune your own.' I speak to him in Punjabi. 'Tell these things to the Amreekans, I have no money.' He knows his victim. 'Money?' he sneers indignantly, 'Money is dirt on back of hand. You great future. Much riches. Much love affairs with phoren ladies. One evil star stopping you. Close palm.' Without thinking I clench my fist. 'Now open.' I unclench my hand. There is a black spot in the middle of my palm. 'See!' he says triumphantly, 'Black star! You give rupee one only. From Amreekans I take rupees ten. I tell you how conquer black star.' I give him a rupee and am instructed in the art of seducing foreign women. 'Sardarji, your lady love name begin with J. H. T. Yes?' I know no woman with the initials J. H. T. He goes on: 'When you get white lady with J. H. T. in name you remember Natha Singh, world-famous palmist-astrologer.'

I arrive at the All India Cooperative Coffee House. More red flags. One banner says *Give us our demands.* A man hands me a leaflet listing the demands. I roll it up and return it to him with an obscene gesture. He returns the compliment. Nasty man!

I cast my eyes over the noisy throng. Can't see anyone I'd care to be with. I buy a copy of *Delhi Underworld* from the newsstand, grab a table just as it is vacated and tilt three chairs against it. I plunge into my weekly ration of Delhi scandals. A minister of cabinet (name to be disclosed next week) has impregnated his daughter-in-law. There's nepotism for you! Free service to the son! 'Confessions of a Connaught Circus Girl.' Poor thing complains of misuse by the Indian staff of an African embassy. She says Africans are better endowed than Indians. They also pay more money. A college lad writes a letter complaining that his stepmother raped him while his father was out on tour. The editor appends an angry footnote in italics: '*How can you put your instrument in the same place as your father's which gave you birth?... Your stepmother is a disgrace to Indian womanhood.*' He promises to give advice on how to deal with such women in the next issue. I drool over drawings of 'sex cats' with bosoms like the protrusions on the fenders of American cars. The next issue also promises a full disclosure of goings-on in Tihar Jail (women's section). Bhagmati has told me quite a lot about that. She's been to Tihar many times.

I see two of our gang come in. One is a photographer, the other a journalist. Both claim to be Delhi's champion womanizers. They see me and advance with their arms wide open. 'Hullo, hullo. How's the little one?' asks the photographer, tapping my middle. 'Did it do its duty to the memsahibs?' I tap his fly: 'And how's Delhi's champion stud bull?' He shrugs his shoulders. 'Fifteen days no action. I stick to my motto: when you find a woman, fornicate, when you do not, be celibate. No self-abuse, no boys, no hijdas.' That's hitting me below the belt.

'And you great pen-pusher, what's your Qutub Minar been up to?' I ask the journalist. He's a big fellow with pubic-sized growth on his face. He also replies in verse. 'When I get a woman I copulate. When I don't, I masturbate. No complaints. The great Guru is in His heaven and the mashooka in my bed!' He plucks a hair out of his beard and examines it with philosophical detachment. A third friend joins us. He is an Upper Division Clerk in the Ministry of Defence. He is utilizing his unutilized sick leave. He disapproves of this kind of talk! 'Five million Indians are dying of hunger in Bihar and all you fellows can think of is women.' He

shakes his foot, then jerks his legs like the arms of a nutcracker. He puts
his feet on the chair and continues to amuse himself. A fart escapes his
fat arse: *poonh*. He is embarrassed. He puts his feet down and apologizes:
'Sorry, it was slip of the tongue.'

Another of our cronies comes along. He is a politician of sorts and
our political expert. He made a name during the last famine by organizing
a 'miss-a-chapati-a-week' movement. Now he is contemplating a similar
campaign for family planning based on the slogan 'If you want good
luck: In one week only one...' The slogan hasn't got off the bed yet. We
return to sex and corruption and inefficiency and five million starving in
Bihar. We drink many cups of coffee and nibble many plates of cashew
nuts. So passes the morning.

A heavy depression overtakes me. I take leave of my coffee house
friends and drive along the Ring Road which skirts the old city. I pass
along the Mughal city wall and Zeenat Mahal's mosque. I slow down at
the electric crematorium. No customers, no smoke. I move on through
the arches of three bridges to Nigambodh Ghat cremation ground on the
Jumna. I park my car and go in.

What's happened to the Delhiwalas? They are not even dying as they
used to! Only one pyre burning and three heaps of smouldering ashes.
No mourners. I walk up to the edge of the bank to see if there is any
life there. Quite a scene!

Down the steps running into the river is a corpse draped in a red
shroud. A dozen men and women are screaming and beating their breasts.
A Brahmin priest pushes them aside, chants Sanskrit mumbo-jumbo and
sprinkles water on the body. A middle-aged man uncovers its face. It's
a young girl—very waxen and in deep slumber. The man stares at her
face, moans and shakes his head in disbelief. A woman on the other side
of the corpse smacks her forehead many times and clasps the dead girl
in her arms. Other people gently remove the wailing couple and cover
up the face of the corpse. The priest puts out his palm. Somebody gives
him a rupee. He looks at the silver coin with disdain, then clip-clops up
the stairs in his wooden sandals. The middle-aged couple resume their
mourning. The woman throws dust in her hair and smacks her head with
both her hands screaming. 'Hai! Hai! Hai!' The man again uncovers the
dead girl's face, gazes intently for a minute and then groans, 'Hai Rabba!'
He cannot take his eyes off the dead child. He presses her arms and legs,
massages the soles of her feet. The pyre is ready. The corpse is lifted and
placed on it. More wood and pampas stalks are placed over the body and
a brass lota full of clarified butter emptied on it. A man lights a stick
with a bundle of rags soaked in kerosene and takes the torch round the

pyre. It bursts into flames. Another man takes a sharp-pointed bamboo pole, prods the flaring, crackling pyre to locate the dead girl's head and then lunges into her skull.

The parents bury their faces in the dust, slap the ground and wail. The Toofan Mail from Calcutta rumbles over Jumna's iron bridge towards Delhi railway station.

I leave Nigambodh Ghat with the heat of the flames on my face and the helpless cry of the stricken parents ringing in my ears. There is real grief! It stabs through the heart like a needle. There, but for the grace of God, it could have been I pouring dust on to my head to mourn the death of my child! Here, by the grace of God, I am driving my Ambassador back to my apartment! What are my irritations, envies and frustrations compared to the sorrow of the people I have left behind! They will go home and miss their daughter. I'll get home and drink my Scotch.

Budh Singh awaits me. He presents arms with his stave. I refuse to be embarrassed. He comes closer and confides. 'Excuse me, sir, your hijda came to see you. I told her you have not come back from phoren. I hope you not angry with me. Take a woman, take a boy, but a hijda...'

I could slap Budhoo Singh across his bearded face. Instead I gently shut the door behind me and fix myself a drink.

That's Delhi. When life gets too much for you all you need to do is to spend an hour at Nigambodh Ghat, watch the dead being put to flames and hear their kin wail for them. Then come home and down a couple of pegs of whisky. In Delhi, death and drink make life worth living.

78

THE COMPANY OF WOMEN
DHANNO

The sweeper woman came in carrying her broom, a bucket of phenyl water and a mop and asked him if she could do the floors. She had taken orders from Sonu about which room to do first: their bedroom, the children's room and the bathrooms were given priority; the sitting-dining room came last. Without looking up at her Mohan nodded his head.

As she sat on her haunches mopping the floor with a piece of rag soaked in phenyl, Mohan noticed her rounded buttocks separated by a sharp cleavage. He could not take his eyes off her ample behind. He had never bothered to look at her before nor did he know her name. She was just the jamadarni—the sweeper's wife. She often brought her three children with her. He had sometimes seen them playing in the garden while their mother was busy in the house. The sweeperess stood up, turned her face towards him and brushed aside a strand of hair from her forehead. He noticed she was also full-bosomed and had a narrow waist. She was dark but not unattractive. The woman got down on her haunches again to do another part of the room. Mohan turned to his paper.

He recalled his college days in India. One of the boys had told him that sweeper women made the best lovers; they were uninhibited, wild and hot. Apparently there was no better antidote for sore eyes than sex with a sweeperess. Mohan did not suffer from any eye ailment but he had noticed that as a class the so-called untouchable women were in fact the most touchable. What about this one in his own house? It would not be difficult to persuade her to come to his bedroom when the other servants were in their quarters or out buying provisions. He could double her salary, give her children toys and sweets. Such master-servant liaisons were not uncommon. Poorly paid menials welcomed a second income and their spouses were not very particular about infidelity provided it brought in some money. No messy hassles with women demanding attention and presents and wanting to be taken to parties. There was also the advantage of convenience: sex on the tap, as it were. Mohan decided to keep the sweeper woman in mind in the event of failure on other fronts. She would provide no companionship but would at least solve his most important problem.

The next morning, when the jamadarni came to do the floors, he spoke to her for the first time. 'What is your name?' he asked as she hitched

318

up her salwar and squatted a few feet ahead of him to mop the floor.

'Dhanno,' she replied, without looking up at him, but clearly expecting to be asked more questions.

'What does your husband do?'

'He is a sweeper with the municipality, sahib.'

'What does he earn?'

'One thousand rupees per month. We have three children. Even with what I earn we barely manage to feed and clothe ourselves. My husband is a sharabi, sahib, wastes a lot of money on liquor.'

Mohan was not sure what he paid her: her salary was paid by his office along with the salaries of the other servants and was clubbed together as essential household expenses. He merely signed the cheques every month. If he wanted to give her more, it would have to be in cash. He fished out a hundred-rupee note from his wallet and held it out for her. 'Take this. It is for your children.' The woman took the note, touched it to her forehead and tucked it in her bra. 'Will memsahib not be coming home any more?' she asked directly. 'She has taken her luggage and the children with her.'

Mohan was taken aback by her audacity; working class people did not believe in dropping hints or being tactful: they were direct and blunt. He snubbed her. 'Get on with your work,' he said gruffly...

◆

One day, instead of driving back home, he decided to take a drive round the city. He had not done this for a long time. He gave his chauffeur the evening off and drove to India Gate. He got out to take in the scene. In the east rose the dark grey walls of Purana Qila, built by Humayun, the second Mughal Emperor. Blocking the lower half of the view was the sports stadium built on the orders of a half-crazy vicereine, Lady Willingdon, to perpetuate the name of her dynasty. This was after Lutyens had built his city. The architect could do nothing about the stadium except gnash his teeth. It ruined his vision of a broad, tree-lined boulevard running down from the Viceregal Palace through the War Memorial arch and past the stone canopy under which stood the statue of King George V, right up to the imposing western entrance of Purana Qila. The rulers of Free India had removed the statue of the British king, but at least the canopy looked more beautiful with nothing under it. Mohan recalled that some politicians had wanted to demolish the whole structure because it was a remnant of the Raj. Bloody vandals! Fortunately they had been unable to do anything to the majestic War Memorial arch except change its name to India Gate. They kept a flame burning under it to honour those who fell fighting for India.

The rest was much the same as Lutyens had designed it: a boulevard flanked by a succession of water tanks and flowering lagerstroemia leading to the secretariats and a slight gradient to the black-domed Viceregal Palace, now Rashtrapati Bhavan. There were clouds on the western horizon. The setting sun broke through them and lit up the entire panorama of massive buildings, lawns, water tanks and flowering trees in soft amber hues. A sight for the gods, said Mohan to himself. Delhi was the only city in the world which gave him a sense of belonging. On days like this the city could even make him forget the absence of a woman in his life.

He brought four large coloured balloons and two bricks of vanilla ice cream from vendors, their carts bright with green and white neon lights, who clustered around India Gate every evening. He had done this before when his children were with him. What was the point of buying balloons and ice cream when they were no longer around?

When Mohan got home, Dhanno was going over the floors once again: in Delhi you had to dust everything at least twice a day. Her children were, as usual, playing in the garden, waiting for their mother to finish. They eyed the balloons but knew they were not for them. Sahib had never brought anything for them. Mohan handed over the balloons and ice cream to Dhanno: 'These are for your children,' he said as he switched on the TV.

A minute later Dhanno brought in her children, each holding a balloon. 'Touch the sahib's feet,' she ordered them. 'He has also brought you ice cream.'

The children touched his feet and ran out as fast as they could. Had Dhanno got the message?

He got his answer the next morning. She was later than usual—after the cook had left for the bazaar to buy the day's groceries and the bearer had gone to his quarter to have his bath. She wore a freshly washed and ironed salwar kameez and had kajal in her eyes. She said nothing and got down on her haunches to mop the floor. She seemed to sense the sahib's eyes on her. Twice she turned round and caught him staring at her behind. She blushed coyly, turned her face away to get on with her job. Mohan concluded the answer was yes.

He decided not to hurry matters. He must first weigh the pros and cons of taking on his cleaning woman as a mistress. There were fewer hassles than in having an affair with a woman of his own class. There would be less talk. No doubt his two male servants would soon suspect that something was going on between their sahib and the sweeperess. To them she was an untouchable: they never let her enter the kitchen. They avoided physical contact with her, and when she came to take the leftovers, they dropped dal-roti or whatever had been eaten by their master into utensils she brought with her. If they smelt something, they would tell the neighbours' servants who, in turn, would tell their employers. Dhanno was not likely to confide in her husband, but if he had any sense he would begin to suspect his wife's behaviour. Perhaps the extra money she brought in would keep him quiet. Perhaps it would not. But all these anxieties weighed little against the great advantage of being able to have sex whenever he wanted—she would not expect more than a little extra, nor any claims to his emotions or his time.

His mind became obsessed with the possibility of taking Dhanno. She hovered before his eyes in the office, at home. He wanted to make sure he did not slip up on any detail. The next morning he asked her when her husband left for work. 'He leaves very early in the morning, sahib. I pack a paratha and some sabzi for his afternoon meal. He returns quite late in the evening. The first few days of the month, after he has got his pay, he drinks with his cronies and doesn't return till midnight.'

'And what about the children? Do you always take them with you wherever you work?'

'No, sahib. Many mornings I ask other servants' wives to keep an eye on them. When I am at home, I look after their children.'

Dhanno sensed what was on the sahib's mind. She let him choose the day and time for their tryst. She did not have to wait long. Two days later she heard him tell the cook to get fresh fish from INA market. 'Everything in INA market is fresher and cheaper than elsewhere,' he was explaining, 'fish, crabs, prawns, vegetables, fruit, everything. All the people I know shop there for their daily needs.' The INA market was almost an hour by bicycle from Maharani Bagh. Going, coming and shopping would keep the cook away for at least three hours. Then the sahib wrote something on a piece of paper and gave it to the bearer. He had run out of his cigars, he said. The kind he smoked were only available at MR Stores in Connaught Circus. He had put the name on the paper. The bearer was to take the bus to Connaught Circus and get a box for the sahib. He handed the bearer several hundred-rupee notes. 'Be sure to get a receipt,' he added. The bearer would also be away for a couple of hours.

Dhanno took good care to leave the house while the other two servants were still there. Back in her quarter she took a second bath, soaping herself vigorously and scrubbing her body. She saw the servants leave on their errands and quietly slipped back into the house.

Mohan was waiting for her. When she came upstairs, he got up from his chair and gently guided her by her shoulders into his bedroom and bolted the door from inside. He kissed her on the lips and fondled her breasts. She responded vigorously. He slipped his hand inside her kameez to feel her breasts. They were firmer than his wife's and the nipples much harder. Dhanno slipped her shirt off over her shoulders and coyly looked down at her feet. Mohan undid the cord of her salwar and let it fall to the floor. Dhanno was stark naked. 'Not like this, sahib,' she murmured. 'You must be like me.' She unbuckled his belt and pulled his trousers down. She gasped. 'Sahib, I have never seen anything so big!'

'How many have you seen?' asked Mohan with a leer as he took her hand and put it on his penis. Dhanno blushed as she tried to correct herself. 'Only my husband's. He is less than half your size. I haven't seen any man's—Saunh Rabb dee (I swear by God).' Mohan knew she was lying. Dhanno knew that the sahib knew she was lying. But why waste time on trivial details?

Mohan took off his shirt, then pushed her on to his bed. He started making love. When he tried to slip on a condom, she held his hand. 'After my third child I had nasbandi; you will enjoy me more without this thing on you.'

Each time Mohan made love to a new body, it was like exploring a new landscape. Women were much the same in their essentials but enchantingly different in detail. Dhanno's body had a musky odour unlike his wife's which always smelt of French cologne. Mohan could not hold out very long. He lay back defeated. Dhanno was patient with him. She massaged his body gently from head to foot till he was roused once more. This time she came a lot quicker than he.

In the frenzy of orgasm she dug her nails into his scalp, bit his lips before she collapsed with a long gurgle like an animal being slaughtered. Mohan felt triumphant and proud of his manliness.

They washed together in the bathroom. And dressed together in the bedroom. Mohan took two one-hundred rupee notes from his wallet and pressed them into Dhanno's hands. 'There is no need for this,' she said, tucking the notes into her kameez between her breasts. 'I am your baandee. Whenever you want her, your slave will be at your service.'

79

BURIAL AT SEA
VICTOR JAI BHAGWAN

Jai Bhagwan's father, Krishan Lal Mattoo, wanted to bring up his only son as an English aristocrat. He often told his wife (semi-literate to him since she could only read and write Hindi) and children that in order to deal with the British, one had to speak English like them, mix with them socially as an equal, learn to eat their kind of food on expensive china using silver forks and knives, and serve them premium Scotch and vintage French wines of better quality than they could afford. Then one should tell them to their faces that it was time for them to buzz off from India and let Indians manage their own affairs.

Mattoo could afford to hold such views. He had made a tidy fortune as a practicing lawyer in the Delhi and other high courts of India. Many a time he had confronted English barristers and got the better of them because of his grasp of the law and oratory. Indian princes, zamindars and industrialists engaged him as their counsel and paid him whatever he asked for as fees. So formidable was his reputation that people said that if you got Mattoo to appear for you, you won half the battle even before he had opened his mouth. Early in his career, Mattoo had built himself a double-storeyed mansion in Delhi's Civil Lines with an annexe for his office, a two-bedroom villa for his guests, and a spacious garden growing exotic flowers, including varieties of roses no one had seen in India before. He named it Shanti Bhavan. It was his grandest possession and he enjoyed showing it off to the rich and powerful, both Indian and English, whom he entertained as often as he could. He was a generous host. Princes of royal blood and English governors of provinces were eager to be invited by him, for he served the best of food and wine and sometimes, as a bonus and with admirable discretion, arranged for the most cultured whores from the city's old quarter to perform mujra songs and dances for them.

Among the many people who stayed with Mattoo whenever he was in Delhi was Mahatma Gandhi. The two men shared a special bond. Mattoo had at first been amused and faintly irritated by news of a half-naked nationalist leader come from South Africa who went about preaching non-violence, celibacy and the boycott of everything foreign. He was even said to have a fetish for fasting and enemas and personally cleaned latrines! When they first met at the house of an Indian National Congress leader in Delhi, Mattoo was prepared for self-righteous lecturing. To his immense surprise, Gandhi praised him for bringing honour and self-respect to India by worsting the British in their own law. 'Mattoo sahib, this too is fighting for freedom,' he said. Mattoo had suffered for years from a vague guilt because people who resented his success accused him of being anti-Indian and a slave to English custom. Gandhi's words came as a balm. He became an open admirer of Gandhi, though he never gave up his expensive tastes or English ways.

On one of Gandhi's visits to Delhi, Mattoo put to him his views on anglicizing his children. He expected him to have strong reservations against it. The Mahatma listened to him in silence, then said, 'I agree. We have to have some Indians who can tell the English when to get out in a language they can understand. But don't take it so far that they are ashamed of being Indian. Their roots must remain firmly embedded in Indian soil.' Mattoo was delighted. He brought his family to be blessed by Gandhi. The Mahatma took the five-year-old Jai Bhagwan in his lap and asked, 'Beta, what do you want to be when you grow up?' The boy replied without hesitation, 'Bapu, I want to become a Mahatma like you.'

The Mahatma hugged the boy close to his chest. 'You will become a bigger man than your Bapu. May Ishwara give you a long life!'

80

THE SUNSET CLUB
LODI GARDENS

Lodi Gardens is within easy walking distance from Rajpath, and has a vast variety of trees, birds and medieval monuments. It is perhaps the most scenic historic park in India. At one time it was a scatter of tombs and mosques in a village called Khairpur. In the 1930s the villagers were moved out and the monuments taken under government protection.

Then the vicereine, Lady Willingdon, who was somewhat batty and wanted her name to go down in posterity, had the scattered monuments enclosed within walls and an entrance gate erected on the north side, bearing the inscription 'Lady Willingdon Park'. She also had a cinder track laid out for sahibs and their mems to ride on. All that is history. No one now calls it Lady Willingdon Park, the cinder track has become a cobbled stone footpath, and the park is known as Lodi Gardens because most of its monuments were built during the rule of the Lodi dynasty. Today it has three more entrances. A second one is also in the north, with a small car park. People have to walk across an old stone bridge called aathpula (eight-spanned), over a moat which once guarded the walled enclosure of the tomb of Sikandar Lodi, built in 1518, through an avenue of maulsari trees to the centre of the park. There is another entrance on the eastern side, along the India International Centre, and one more in the south, close to a palm-lined avenue leading to the oldest tomb in the complex, that of Muhammad Shah Sayyid, built in 1450.

For good reason, the most popular place in the park is the extensive lawn on the southern side of what must have been the main mosque, the Jami Masjid, built in 1494. The reason for its popularity is its dome, which is an exact replica of a young woman's bosom including the areola and the nipple. Most mosques and mausolea have domes but they have metal spires put on top of them which rob them of their feminine charm. Not the Bara Gumbad, the Big Dome. You can gape at it for hours on end and marvel at its likeness to a virgin's breast. You will notice that men sprawled on the lawns have their face towards it; their womenfolk sit facing the other way. It also has a bench facing it. Regular visitors to the park call it Boorha Binch, old men's bench, because, for years, three old men have been sitting on it after they have hobbled round the park. While they talk, their gaze is fixed on the Bara Gumbad. English-speaking Indians call them the 'Sunset Club' because the three men who occupy

325

the bench are seen on it every day at sunset. All three are in their late eighties, the sunset years of their life.

◆

Let me introduce you to the members of the Sunset Club. First, Pandit Preetam Sharma, because he is the oldest of the three. He is a Punjabi Brahmin, an Oxford graduate who served as cultural counsellor in London and Paris and rose to the highest position in the Ministry of Education before he retired. He is well preserved, bald in front but with white locks flowing down his skull and curling up around his shoulders. They give him a scholarly look. He is in good health but needs glasses to read, a hearing aid to hear and dentures to eat. He believes in Ayurveda and homeopathy. Although there were a succession of women, foreign and Indian, in his life, he narrowly escaped marrying one. He lives with his spinster sister, Sunita, who is almost twenty years younger than him and works with an NGO. They live in a ground-floor flat close to Khan Market. It has two bedrooms and two bathrooms, a large drawing-dining room, a study and two verandahs.

One wall of the drawing room has a bookshelf packed with books which he has not read, nor intends to read. They create the impression that he is a man of culture. Other walls have paintings he made after he retired from service. No one except he understands what they are about but they do create the impression that he is a man of culture. He writes long poems in blank verse. He has them printed in Khan Market and gives copies freely to his visitors. Having risen to the top in the Ministry of Education, he is chairman of many cultural and social organizations and school boards. He makes a very good chairman as he makes profound statements like 'Culture knows no frontiers; all religions teach truth and love'; etc., etc. He has no enemies. All the men and women who know him love him. For company, he has had a succession of apsos named Dabboo One, Two and Three. He has a car and a chauffeur provided by a school whose chairman he is. It takes him, his servant Pavan and Dabboo Three to the northern entrance of Lodi Gardens. He does a round of the park followed by Pavan and the dog before he takes a seat on the Boorha Binch. His servant and dog sit behind him on the lawn.

Second is Nawab Barkatullah Baig Dehlavi. He is a Sunni Mussalman whose Pathan ancestors settled in Delhi before the British took over the country. They combined soldiering with the practice of Unani (Greek) medicine. They were granted land close to what is today Nizamuddin. Barkatullah's father set up a chain of Unani dawakhanas (pharmacies) in the old city but preferred living in his large house in Nizamuddin. It is a spacious mansion named Baig Manzil. It has many rooms, verandahs, a large garden in front and staff quarters at the back. Baig does not believe in amassing books; he finished with them after school and college. He has a few diwans of Urdu poets and an impressive collection of artefacts from Mughal times which are on display in his sitting room. He is a powerfully built six-footer with grey-white hair, a handlebar moustache and a short clipped beard.

Like all good Muslims from well-to-do families, Baig went to Aligarh Muslim University before he took over his father's business and, on his demise, his mansion. He is married to his cousin Sakina. They have a brood of children. But for occasional visits to Chawri Bazaar, the courtesans' street, and bedding his wife's maidservants in his younger days, he has been a faithful husband. After the partition of the country in 1947, he stayed on in India, joined the Congress Party and is a supporter of the Nehru-Gandhi dynasty. For over forty years he has been a regular stroller in Lodi Gardens. The chauffeur of his Mercedes-Benz drops him at the southern entrance of the park. He does his rounds of the monuments followed by a servant pushing a wheelchair, before he takes his seat on the bench facing Bara Gumbad. Even in his eighties, Baig is in good shape: no glasses, no hearing aid, no false teeth, though he is occasionally short of breath.

Third is Sardar Boota Singh. He is a stocky Sikh with a paunch. The unshorn hair on his head is snow-white. Instead of tying a six-yard-long turban he has taken to wearing a cotton or woollen cap. He dyes his beard and looks younger than his eighty-six years. He suffers from many ailments: chronic constipation, incipient diabetes, fluctuating blood pressure, enlarged prostate and periodic bouts of gout. He has been wearing glasses since his schooldays, half a denture as all his lower teeth are gone, and for some years, a hearing aid as well. He professes to be an agnostic sybarite, but every morning when he gets up around 4 a.m., he prays for his health and repeats Aum Arogyam many times, followed by the Gayatri Mantra and a Sikh hymn designed to keep sorrows at a distance:

> May ill-winds not touch me, the Lord is my Protector.
> Around me Rama has drawn a wall to protect me;
> No harm will come to me, brother.
> The True Guru, who put the Universe together
> Gave me Rama's name as panacea against all ills;
> Meditate on Him and Him alone.
> He saves those who deserve saving; He removes all doubts
> Says Nanak, the Lord is merciful. He is my helper.

He explains the contradictions in his agnosticism and hedonism by saying: 'Who knows! They say prayers can work miracles. No harm in trying them out.'

Prayers seldom help him, so he supplements them with a variety of pills from dawn to after dinner.

Boota had his higher education in England and served with Indian missions in London and Paris before he returned to Delhi and took to writing for newspapers. He lives in a flat close to Sharma's. The walls of his sitting room are lined with books banned as pornographic. His favourites are books of quotations and anthologies of poetry, both Urdu and English. He has memorized quite a few and comes out with them at every opportunity. People think he is a man of learning but he knows he is a bit of a fraud.

Boota is a widower with two children. His son has migrated to Canada. His daughter, who is widowed, lives close by with her daughter. Though he lives alone, he is never lonely; he has a constant stream of ladies visiting him in the evening when he opens his bar. He is a great talker and a windbag. He makes up salacious stories of his conquests, which keep his audience spellbound. He uses bad language as if it was his birthright. When he is tired of company, he simply says, 'Now bugger off.' If he disapproves of a person, he calls him 'phuddoo', which is Punjabi for fucker. And every other person including himself is a 'chootia'—cunt-born. Every evening he drives down to the India International Centre. He spends an hour there sipping coffee, then enters Lodi Gardens through its eastern entrance past the Kos Minar. He too takes a couple of rounds of the park before he joins the other two on the bench facing the Bara Gumbad.

THE PORTRAIT OF
A LADY &
OTHER STORIES

KARMA

THE PORTRAIT OF A LADY

POSTHUMOUS

81

KARMA

Sir Mohan Lal looked at himself in the mirror of a first-class waiting room at the railway station. The mirror was obviously made in India. The red oxide at its back had come off at several places and long lines of translucent glass cut across its surface. Sir Mohan smiled at the mirror with an air of pity and patronage.

'You are so very much like everything else in this country, inefficient, dirty, indifferent,' he murmured.

The mirror smiled back at Sir Mohan.

'You are a bit of all right, old chap,' it said. 'Distinguished, efficient—even handsome. That neatly trimmed moustache—the suit from Savile Row with the carnation in the buttonhole—the aroma of eau de cologne, talcum powder and scented soap all about you! Yes, old fellow, you are a bit of all right.'

Sir Mohan threw out his chest, smoothed his Balliol tie for the umpteenth time and waved a goodbye to the mirror.

He glanced at his watch. There was still time for a quick one.

'Koi hai!'

A bearer in white livery appeared through a wire gauze door.

'Ek chota,' ordered Sir Mohan, and sank into a large cane chair to drink and ruminate.

Outside the waiting room, Sir Mohan Lal's luggage lay piled along the wall. On a small grey steel trunk Lachmi—Lady Mohan Lal—sat chewing a betel leaf and fanning herself with a newspaper. She was short and fat and in her mid-forties. She wore a dirty white sari with a red border. On one side of her nose glistened a diamond nose ring, and she had several gold bangles on her arms. She had been talking to the bearer until Sir Mohan had summoned him inside. As soon as he had gone, she hailed a passing railway coolie.

'Where does the zenana stop?'

'Right at the end of the platform.'

The coolie flattened his turban to make a cushion, hoisted the steel trunk on his head, and moved down the platform. Lady Lal picked up her brass tiffin carrier and ambled along behind him. On the way she stopped by a hawker's stall to replenish her silver betel leaf case, and then joined the coolie. She sat down on her steel trunk (which the coolie had put down) and started talking to him.

'Are the trains very crowded on these lines?'

'These days all trains are crowded, but you'll find room in the zenana.'

'Then I might as well get over the bother of eating.'

Lady Lal opened the brass carrier and took out a bundle of chapatis and some mango pickle. While she ate, the coolie sat opposite her on his haunches, drawing lines in the gravel with his finger.

'Are you travelling alone, sister?'

'No, I am with my master, brother. He is in the waiting room. He travels first class. He is a vizier and a barrister, and meets so many officers and Englishmen in the trains—and I am only a native woman. I can't understand English and don't know their ways, so I keep to my zenana inter-class.'

Lachmi chatted away merrily. She was fond of a little gossip and had no one to talk to at home. Her husband never had any time to spare for her. She lived in the upper storey of the house and he on the ground floor. He did not like her poor, illiterate relatives hanging about his bungalow, so they never came. He came up to her once in a while at night and stayed for a few minutes. He just ordered her about in anglicized Hindustani, and she obeyed passively. These nocturnal visits had, however, borne no fruit.

The signal came down and the clanging of the bell announced the approaching train. Lady Lal hurriedly finished off her meal. She got up, still licking the stone of the pickled mango. She emitted a long, loud belch as she went to the public tap to rinse her mouth and wash her hands. After washing she dried her mouth and hands with the loose end of her sari, and walked back to her steel trunk, belching and thanking the gods for the favour of a filling meal.

The train steamed in. Lachmi found herself facing an almost empty inter-class zenana compartment next to the guard's van, at the tail end of the train. The rest of the train was packed. She heaved her squat, bulky frame through the door and found a seat by the window. She produced a two-anna bit from a knot in her sari and dismissed the coolie. She then opened her betel case and made herself two betel leaves charged with red and white paste, minced betel nuts and cardamoms. These she thrust into her mouth till her cheeks bulged on both sides. Then she rested her chin on her hands and sat gazing idly at the jostling crowd on the platform.

The arrival of the train did not disturb Sir Mohan Lal's sangfroid. He continued to sip his Scotch and ordered the bearer to tell him when he had moved the luggage to a first-class compartment. Excitement, bustle and hurry were exhibitions of bad breeding, and Sir Mohan Lal was eminently well-bred. He wanted everything 'tickety-boo' and orderly.

In his five years abroad, Sir Mohan Lal had acquired the manners and attitudes of the upper classes. He rarely spoke Hindustani. When he did, it was like an Englishman's—only the very necessary words and properly anglicized. But he fancied his English, finished and refined at no less a place than the University of Oxford. He was fond of conversation and, like a cultured Englishman, he could talk on almost any subject—books, politics, people. How frequently had he heard English people say that he spoke like an Englishman!

Sir Mohan wondered if he would be travelling alone. It was a cantonment and some English officers might be on the train. His heart warmed at the prospect of an impressive conversation. He never showed any sign of eagerness to talk to the English as most Indians did. Nor was he loud, aggressive and opinionated like them. He went about his business with an expressionless matter-of-factness. He would retire to his corner by the window and get out a copy of *The Times*. He would fold it in a way in which the name of the paper was visible to others while he did the crossword puzzle. *The Times* always attracted attention. Someone would like to borrow it when he put it aside with a gesture signifying 'I've finished with it'. Perhaps someone would recognize his Balliol tie which he always wore while travelling. That would open a vista leading to a fairyland of Oxford colleges, masters, dons, tutors, boat races and rugger matches. If both *The Times* and the tie failed, Sir Mohan would 'Koi hai' his bearer to get the Scotch out. Whisky never failed with Englishmen. Then followed Sir Mohan's handsome gold cigarette case filled with English cigarettes. English cigarettes in India? How on earth did he get them? Sure he didn't mind? And Sir Mohan's understanding smile—of course he didn't mind. But could he use the Englishman as a medium to commune with his dear old England? Those five years of grey bags and gowns, of sports blazers and mixed doubles, of dinners at the Inns of Court and nights with Piccadilly prostitutes. Five years of a crowded glorious life. Worth far more than the forty-five in India with his dirty, vulgar countrymen, with sordid details of the road to success, of nocturnal visits to the upper storey and all-too-brief sexual acts with obese old Lachmi, smelling of sweat and raw onions.

Sir Mohan's thoughts were disturbed by the bearer announcing the installation of the sahib's luggage in a first-class coupé next to the engine. Sir Mohan walked to his coupé with a studied gait. He was dismayed. The compartment was empty. With a sigh he sat down in a corner and opened the copy of *The Times* he had read several times before.

Sir Mohan looked out of the window down the crowded platform. His face lit up as he saw two English soldiers trudging along, looking in all the compartments for room. They had their haversacks slung behind their backs and walked unsteadily. Sir Mohan decided to welcome them, even though they were entitled to travel only second class. He would speak to the guard.

One of the soldiers came up to the last compartment and stuck his face through the window. He surveyed the compartment and noticed the unoccupied berth.

"Ere, Bill,' he shouted, 'one 'ere.'

His companion came up, also looked in, and looked at Sir Mohan.

'Get the nigger out,' he muttered to his companion.

They opened the door, and turned to the half-smiling, half-protesting Sir Mohan.

'Reserved!' yelled Bill.

'Janta—Reserved. Army—Fauj,' exclaimed Jim, pointing to his khaki shirt.

'Ek dum jao—get out!'

'I say, I say, surely,' protested Sir Mohan in his Oxford accent.

The soldiers paused. It almost sounded like English, but they knew better than to trust their inebriated ears. The engine whistled and the guard waved his green flag.

They picked up Sir Mohan's suitcase and flung it on the platform. Then followed his thermos flask, briefcase, bedding and *The Times*. Sir Mohan was livid with rage.

'Preposterous, preposterous,' he shouted, hoarse with anger. 'I'll have you arrested—guard, guard!'

Bill and Jim paused again. It did sound like English, but it was too much of the King's for them.

'Keep yer ruddy mouth shut!' And Jim struck Sir Mohan flat on the face.

The engine gave another short whistle and the train began to move. The soldiers caught Sir Mohan by the arms and flung him out of the train. He reeled backwards, tripped on his bedding, and landed on the suitcase.

'Toodle-oo!'

Sir Mohan's feet were glued to the earth and he lost his speech. He stared at the lighted windows of the train going past him in quickening tempo. The tail end of the train appeared with a red light and the guard standing in the open doorway with the flags in his hands.

In the inter-class zenana compartment was Lachmi, fair and fat, on whose nose the diamond nose ring glistened against the station lights. Her mouth was bloated with betel saliva which she had been storing up to spit as soon as the train had cleared the station. As the train sped past the lighted part of the platform, Lady Lal spat and sent a jet of red dribble flying across like a dart.

82

THE PORTRAIT OF A LADY

My grandmother, like everybody's grandmother, was an old woman. She had been old and wrinkled for the twenty years that I had known her. People said that she had once been young and pretty and had even had a husband, but that was hard to believe. My grandfather's portrait hung above the mantelpiece in the drawing room. He wore a big turban and loose-fitting clothes. His long white beard covered the best part of his chest and he looked at least a hundred years old. He did not look the sort of person who would have a wife or children. He looked as if he could only have lots and lots of grandchildren. As for my grandmother being young and pretty, the thought was almost revolting. She often told us of the games she used to play as a child. That seemed quite absurd and undignified on her part and we treated them like the fables of the prophets she used to tell us.

She had always been short and fat and slightly bent. Her face was a criss-cross of wrinkles running from everywhere to everywhere. No, we were certain she had always been as we had known her. Old, so terribly old that she could not have grown older, and had stayed at the same age for twenty years. She could never have been pretty; but she was always beautiful. She hobbled about the house in spotless white, with one hand resting on her waist to balance her stoop and the other telling the beads of her rosary. Her silver locks were scattered untidily over her pale, puckered face, and her lips constantly moved in inaudible prayer. Yes, she was beautiful. She was like the winter landscape in the mountains, an expanse of pure white serenity breathing peace and contentment.

My grandmother and I were good friends. My parents left me with her when they went to live in the city and we were constantly together. She used to wake me up in the morning and get me ready for school. She said her morning prayer in a monotonous sing-song while she bathed and dressed me in the hope that I would listen and get to know it by heart. I listened because I loved her voice but never bothered to learn it. Then she would fetch my wooden slate which she had already washed and plastered with yellow chalk, a tiny earthen ink pot and a reed pen, tie them all in a bundle and hand it to me. After a breakfast of a thick, stale chapati with a little butter and sugar spread on it, we went to school. She carried several stale chapatis with her for the village dogs.

My grandmother always went to school with me because the school was attached to the temple. The priest taught us the alphabet and the morning prayer. While the children sat in rows on either side of the verandah singing the alphabet or the prayer in a chorus, my grandmother sat inside reading the scriptures. When we had both finished, we would walk back together. This time the village dogs would meet us at the temple door. They followed us to our home growling and fighting each other for the chapatis we threw to them.

When my parents were comfortably settled in the city, they sent for us. That was a turning point in our friendship. Although we shared the same room, my grandmother no longer came to school with me. I used to go to an English school in a motor bus. There were no dogs in the streets and she took to feeding sparrows in the courtyard of our city house.

As the years rolled by we saw less of each other. For some time she continued to wake me up and get me ready for school. When I came back she would ask me what the teacher had taught me. I would tell her English words and little things of Western science and learning, the law of gravity, Archimedes' principle, the world being round, etc. This made her unhappy. She could not help me with my lessons. She did not believe in the things they taught at the English school and was distressed that there was no teaching about God and the scriptures. One day I announced that we were being given music lessons. She was very disturbed. To her music had lewd associations. It was the monopoly of harlots and beggars and not meant for gentlefolk. She rarely talked to me after that.

When I went up to university, I was given a room of my own. The common link of friendship was snapped. My grandmother accepted her seclusion with resignation. She rarely left her spinning wheel to talk to anyone. From sunrise to sunset she sat by her wheel, spinning and reciting prayers. Only in the afternoon she relaxed for a while to feed the sparrows. While she sat in the verandah breaking the bread into little bits, hundreds of little birds collected round her, creating a veritable bedlam of chirrupings. Some came and perched on her legs, others on her shoulders. Some even sat on her head. She smiled but never shooed them away. It used to be the happiest half-hour of the day for her.

When I decided to go abroad for further studies, I was sure my grandmother would be upset. I would be away for five years, and at her age one could never tell. But my grandmother could. She was not even sentimental. She came to leave me at the railway station but did not talk or show any emotion. Her lips moved in prayer, her mind was lost in prayer. Her fingers were busy telling the beads of her rosary. Silently she kissed my forehead, and when I left I cherished the moist imprint as perhaps the last sign of physical contact between us.

But that was not so. After five years I came back home and was met by her at the station. She did not look a day older. She still had no time for words, and while she clasped me in her arms I could hear her reciting her prayer. Even on the first day of my arrival, her happiest moments were with her sparrows, whom she fed longer and with frivolous rebukes.

In the evening a change came over her. She did not pray. She collected the women of the neighbourhood, got an old drum and started to sing. For several hours she thumped the sagging skins of the dilapidated drum and sang of the homecoming of warriors. We had to persuade her to stop to avoid overstraining. That was the first time since I had known her that she did not pray.

The next morning she was taken ill. It was a mild fever and the doctor told us that it would go. But my grandmother thought differently. She told us that her end was near. She said that, since only a few hours before the close of the last chapter of her life she had omitted to pray, she was not going to waste any more time talking to us.

We protested. But she ignored our protests. She lay peacefully in bed, praying and telling her beads. Even before we could suspect, her lips stopped moving and the rosary fell from her lifeless fingers. A peaceful pallor spread on her face and we knew that she was dead.

We lifted her off the bed and, as is customary, laid her on the ground and covered her with a red shroud. After a few hours of mourning we left her alone to make arrangements for her funeral.

In the evening we went to her room with a crude stretcher to take her to be cremated. The sun was setting and had lit her room and verandah with a blaze of golden light. We stopped halfway in the courtyard. All over the verandah and in her room right up to where she lay dead and stiff, wrapped in the red shroud, thousands of sparrows sat scattered on the floor. There was no chirping. We felt sorry for the birds and my mother fetched some bread for them. She broke it into little crumbs, the way my grandmother used to, and threw it to them. The sparrows took no notice of the bread. When we carried my grandmother's corpse off, they flew away quietly. Next morning the sweeper swept the bread crumbs into the dustbin.

83

POSTHUMOUS

I am in bed with fever. It is not serious. In fact, it is not serious at all, as I have been left alone to look after myself. I wonder what would happen if the temperature suddenly shot up. Perhaps I would die. That would be really hard on my friends. I have so many and am so popular. I wonder what the papers would have to say about it. They couldn't just ignore me. Perhaps the *Tribune* would mention it on its front page with a small photograph. The headline would read 'Sardar Khushwant Singh Dead'—and then in somewhat smaller print:

> We regret to announce the sudden death of Sardar Khushwant Singh at 6 p.m. last evening. He leaves behind a young widow, two infant children and a large number of friends and admirers to mourn his loss. It will be recalled that the Sardar came to settle in Lahore some five years ago from his hometown, Delhi. Within these years he rose to a position of eminence in the Bar and in politics. His loss will be mourned generally throughout the province.
>
> Amongst those who called at the late Sardar's residence were the PA to the prime minister, the PA to the chief justice, several ministers and judges of the high court.
>
> In a statement to the press, the hon'ble the chief justice said: 'I feel that the Punjab is poorer by the passing away of this man. The cruel hand of death has cut short the promise of a brilliant career.'

At the bottom of the page would be an announcement:

The funeral will take place at 10 a.m. today.

I feel very sorry for myself and for all my friends. With difficulty I check the tears which want to express sorrow at my own death. But I also feel elated and want people to mourn me. So I decide to die—just for the fun of it as it were. In the evening, giving enough time for the press to hear of my death, I give up the ghost. Having emerged from my corpse, I come down and sit on the cool marble steps at the entrance to wallow in posthumous glory.

In the morning I get the paper before my wife. There is no chance of a squabble over the newspaper as I am downstairs already, and in any case my wife is busy pottering around my corpse. The *Tribune* lets me down. At the bottom of Page 3, Column 1, I find myself inserted in little brackets of obituary notices of retired civil servants—and that is all. I feel annoyed. It must be that blighter Shafi, special representative. He never liked me. But I couldn't imagine he would be so mean as to deny me a little importance when I was dead. However, he couldn't keep the wave of sorrow which would run over the province from trickling into his paper. My friends would see to that.

Near the high court the paper is delivered fairly early. In the house of my lawyer friend Qadir it is deposited well before dawn. It isn't that the Qadirs are early risers. As a matter of fact, hardly anyone stirs in the house before 9 a.m. But Qadir is a great one for principles and he insists that the paper must be available early in the morning even if it is not looked at.

As usual, the Qadirs were in bed at 9 a.m. He had worked very late at night. She believed in sleep anyhow. The paper was brought in on a tray along with a tumbler of hot water with a dash of lime juice. Qadir sipped the hot water between intervals of cigarette smoking. He had to do this to make his bowels work. He only glanced at the headlines in bed. The real reading was done when the cigarette and lime had had their effect. The knowledge of how fate had treated me had to await the lavatory.

In due course Qadir ambled into the bathroom with the paper in one hand and a cigarette perched on his lower lip. Comfortably seated, he began to scan it thoroughly and his eye fell on news of lesser import. When he got to Page 3, Column 1, he stopped smoking for a moment, a very brief moment. Should he get up and shout to his wife? No, he decided, that would be an unnecessary demonstration. Qadir was a rationalist. He had become more of one since he married a woman who was a bundle of emotions and explosions. The poor fellow was dead and nothing could be done about it. He knew that his wife would burst out crying when he told her. That was all the more reason that he should be matter-of-fact about it—just as if he was going to tell her of a case he had lost.

Qadir knew his wife well. He told her with an air of casualness, and she burst out crying. Her ten-year-old daughter came running into the room. She eyed her mother for a little while and then joined her in the wailing. Qadir decided to be severe.

'What are you making all this noise for?' he said sternly. 'Do you think it will bring him back to life?'

His wife knew that it was no use arguing with him. He always won the arguments.

'I think we should go to their house at once. His wife must be feeling wretched,' she said.

Qadir shrugged his shoulders.

'I am afraid I can't manage it. Much as I would like to condole with his wife—rather widow—my duty to my clients comes first. I have to be at the tribunal in half an hour.'

Qadir was at the tribunal all day and his family stopped at home.

◆

Not far from the city's big park lives another friend, Khosla. He and his family, consisting of a wife, three sons and a daughter, reside in this upper-class residential area. He is a judge and very high up in the bureaucracy.

Khosla is an early riser. He has to rise early because that is the only time he has to himself. During the day he has to work in the courts. In the evenings he plays tennis—and then he has to spend some time with the children and fussing with his wife. He has a large number of visitors, as he is very popular and enjoys popularity. But Khosla is ambitious. As a lad he had fancied himself as a clever boy. In his early youth his hair had begun to fall off and had uncovered a large bald forehead. Khosla had looked upon it as nature's confirmation of his opinion about himself. Perhaps he was a genius. The more he gazed upon his large head in the mirror, the more he became convinced that fate had marked for him an extraordinary career. So he worked harder. He won scholarships and rounded off his academic career by topping the list in the civil service examination. He had justified the confidence he had in himself by winning laurels in the stiffest competitive examination in the country. For some years he lived the life of a contented bureaucrat. In fact, he assured himself that he was what people called 'a success in life'.

After some years this contentment had vanished. Every time he brushed the little tuft at the back of his head and ran his hands across his vast forehead he became conscious of unrealized expectations. There were hundreds of senior civil servants like him. All were considered successes in life. The civil service was obviously not enough. He would work—he would write—he knew he could write. There it was written in the size of his head. So Khosla took to writing. In order to write well he took to reading. He amassed a large library and regularly spent some hours in it before going to work.

This morning Khosla happened to be in a mood to write. He made himself a cup of tea and settled in a comfortable armchair by the electric radiator. He stuck the pencil in his mouth and meditated. He couldn't think of what to write. He decided to write his diary. He had spent the previous day listening to an important case. It was likely to go on for some days. The courtroom had been packed and everyone had been looking at him—that seemed a good enough subject. So he started to write.

Khosla was disturbed by the knock of the bearer bringing in the paper. He opened the news-sheet to read the truths of mundane existence.

Khosla was more interested in social affairs, births, marriages and deaths, than events of national or international import. He turned to Page 3, Column 1. His eye caught the announcement and he straightened up.

He just tapped his notebook with his pencil, and after a wake-up cough informed his wife of the news. She just yawned and opened her large dreamy eyes wide.

'I suppose you will close the high court today?' she said.

'I am afraid the high court doesn't close at just any excuse. I'll have to go. If I have any time I'll drop in on the way—or we can call on Sunday.'

The Khoslas did not come. Nor did many others for whose sorrow at my demise I had already felt sorrowful.

At 10 o'clock a little crowd had collected in front of the open space beneath my flat. It consisted mainly of people I did not expect to see. There were some lawyers in their court dress, and a number of sightseers who wanted to find out what was happening. Two friends of mine also turned up, but they stood apart from the crowd. One was a tall, slim man who looked like an artist. With one hand he kept his cigarette in place, the other he constantly employed in pushing his long hair off his forehead. He was a writer. He did not believe in attending funerals. But one had to hang around for a little while as a sort of social obligation. It was distasteful to him. There was something infectious about a corpse—so he smoked incessantly and made a cigarette smokescreen between himself and the rest of the world.

The other friend was a communist, a short, slight man with wavy hair and a hawkish expression. His frame and expression belied the volcano that they camouflaged. His approach to everything was coldly Marxist and sentiment found no place in it. Deaths were unimportant events. It was the cause that mattered. He consulted the writer in a polite whisper.

'How far are you going?'

'I plan dropping off at the coffee house,' answered the other. 'Are you going the whole way?'

'No ruddy fear,' said the communist emphatically. 'Actually I had to be at a meeting at ten, and I was planning to be free of this by 9.30—but you know our people haven't the foggiest idea about time. I'll get along to the party office now and then meet you at the coffee house at 11.30. Incidentally, if you get the opportunity, just ask the hearse driver if he is a member of the Tongawala Union. Cheers.'

A little later a hearse, drawn by bony brown horse, arrived and pulled up in front of my doorstep. The horse and his master were completely oblivious to the solemnity of the occasion. The driver sat placidly chewing his betel nut and eyeing the assembly. He was wondering whether this was the type likely to produce a tip. The beast straightaway started to piddle and the crowd scattered to avoid the spray which rebounded off the brick floor.

The crowd did not have to wait very long. My corpse was brought down, all tied up in white linen, and placed inside the hearse. A few flowers were ceremoniously placed on me. The procession was ready to start.

Before we moved, another friend turned up on his bicycle. He was somewhat dark and flabby. He carried several books on the carrier and had the appearance of a scholarly, serious-minded professor. As soon as he saw the loaded hearse, he dismounted. He had great respect for the dead and was particular to express it. He put his bicycle in the hall, chained it, and joined the crowd. When my wife came down to bid her last farewell he was visibly moved. From his pocket he produced a little book and thoughtfully turned over its pages. Then he slipped through the people towards my wife. With tears in his eyes he handed the book to her.

'I've brought you a copy of the Gita. It will give you great comfort.' Overcome with emotion, he hurriedly slipped back to wipe the tears which had crept into his eyes.

'This,' he said to himself with a sigh, 'is the end of human existence. This is the truth.'

He was fond of thinking in platitudes—but to him all platitudes were profound and had the freshness and vigour of original thought.

'Like bubbles,' he said to himself, 'human life is as momentary as a bubble.'

But one didn't just die and disappear. Matter could not immaterialize— it could only change its form. The Gita put it so beautifully:

'Like a man casts off old garments to put on new ones...so does the soul, etc., etc.'

The professor was lost in contemplation. He wondered what new garments his dead friend had donned.

His thoughts were disturbed by a movement between his legs. A little pup came round the professor's legs, licking his trousers and looking up at him. The professor was a kind man. He involuntarily bent down and patted the little dog, allowing him to lick his hands.

The professor's mind wandered—he felt uneasy. He looked at the corpse and then at the fluffy little dog at his feet, who after all was part of God's creation.

'Like a man casts off old garments to put on new ones...so does the soul...'

No, no, he said to himself. He shouldn't allow such uncharitable thoughts to cross his mind. But he couldn't check his mind. It wasn't impossible. The Gita said so, too. And he bent down again and patted the pup with more tenderness and fellow feeling.

The procession was on the move. I was in front, uncomfortably laid within the glass hearse, with half a dozen people walking behind. It went down towards the river.

By the time it had passed the main street, I found myself in solitude. Some of the lawyers had left at the high court. My author friend had branched off to the coffee house, still smoking. At the local college, the professor gave me a last, longing, lingering look and sped up the slope to his classroom. The remaining six or seven disappeared into the district courts.

I began to feel a little small. Lesser men than myself had had larger crowds. Even a dead pauper carried on a municipal wheelbarrow got two sweepers to cart him off. I had only one human being, the driver, and even he seemed to be oblivious of the enormity of the soul whose decayed mansion he was transporting on its last voyage. As for the horse, he was positively rude.

The route to the cremation ground is marked with an infinite variety of offensive smells. The climax is reached when one has to branch off the main road towards the crematorium along a narrow path which runs beside the city's one and only sewer. It is a stream of dull, black fluid with bubbles bursting on its surface all the time.

Fortunately for me, I was given some time to ruminate over my miscalculated posthumous importance. The driver pulled up under a large peepal tree near where the road turns off to the cremation ground. Under this peepal tree is a tonga stand and a water trough for horses to drink out of. The horse made for the water and the driver clambered off his perch to ask the tonga drivers for a light for his cigarette.

The tonga drivers gathered round the hearse and peered in from all sides.

'Must be someone rich,' said one. 'But there is no one with him,' queried another. 'I suppose this is another English custom—no one goes to funerals.'

By now I was thoroughly fed up. There were three ways open to me. One was to take the route to the cremation ground and, like the others that went there, give myself up to scorching flames, perhaps to be born again into a better world, but probably to be extinguished into nothingness. There was another road which forked off to the right towards the city. There lived harlots and other people of ill-repute. They drank and gambled and fornicated. Theirs was a world of sensation and they crammed their lives with all the varieties which the senses were capable of registering. The third one was to take the way back. It was difficult to make up one's mind. In situations like these the toss of a coin frequently helps. So I decided to toss the coin; heads and I hazard the world beyond; tails and I go to join the throng of sensation seekers in the city; if it is neither heads nor tails and the coin stands on its edge, I retrace my steps to a humdrum existence bereft of the spirit of adventure and denuded of the lust for living.

TOBA TEK SINGH:
FICTION IN TRANSLATION

84

UMRAO JAN ADA

MIRZA MOHAMMAD HADI RUSWA

Umrao Jan Ada's *author, Mirza Mohammad Hadi Ruswa (1857-1931),
writes that the Lucknow courtesan called Umrao Jan narrated the 'novel'
to him in a series of interviews. Kidnapped from her parental home in
Faizabad, when she was little more than a child, by the thug Dilawar
Khan and his accomplice Peer Baksh, Umrao Jan is sold to a well-known
madam in Lucknow by her captors.*

Asked the bird of the fowler: 'It is my first night in the cage.
Let me beat my wings against the bars.'

You have already heard of my first night in captivity. I still wonder how I
ever lived through it. I will not forget the utter helplessness to my dying
day. It must have been hard for my soul not to have given up.

As for Dilawar Khan, he got the punishment he deserved. But it
did not quench the fires of hate in my heart. I would not have had any
compunction in seeing him cut up into small pieces and his flesh fed
to the crows and kites. I am certain that even in hell he is flogged with
burning faggots night and day and if God is just, a worse fate awaits
him on the day of judgement.

It would have been better if Dilawar Khan had killed me. A handful
of dust would have covered my virtue, and my evil deeds would not have
tarnished the fair name of my parents. I would also have been spared the
blackening of my face in front of man and God.

I met my mother once again. But that was a long time ago. God
alone knows whether she is still alive. I have heard that my younger
brother has a son who, by the grace of Allah, is now fourteen or fifteen
years old. He has also two daughters. I have a strong desire to see them
all. They live in Faizabad which is not very far. One wretched rupee could
get me there. But my hands are tied.

Those days there were no railway trains and it used to take four days
to travel from Faizabad to Lucknow. But Dilawar Khan, fearing lest my
father pursue him, took a roundabout route through the wilderness and
it took us eight days to reach Lucknow. How would a useless creature
like me know where Lucknow was? It was from the talk between Dilawar
Khan and Peer Bakhsh that I gathered it was there that they were taking

me. I had heard people at home talk of Lucknow because my mother's father worked there as a gatekeeper in some nawab's mansion. Once he came to visit us at Faizabad and brought lots of sweets and toys for me. I never forgot him.

Dilawar Khan and Peer Bakhsh took me across the Gomti to the home of Karim's father-in-law which was a dingy mud hovel. Karim's mother-in-law was an old hag who looked like a bather of corpses. She took me inside and locked me up in a cell and kept me locked up all morning and afternoon. Then a youngish woman (who I later learnt was Karim's wife) came in and brought me three chapatis, a spoonful of lentil soup in a saucer of clay and some water in an earthen jug. Even this simple fare was like a feast for me, because for one whole week, fate had deprived me of home-cooked food; on the journey I was given nothing but roasted gram or powdered corn. I ate all I was given and drank up half the jug of water. I stretched myself on the floor and fell fast asleep. Heaven alone knows how long I slept because in the cell one could not tell night from day. I woke up several times in the dark and since there was no one around, I covered my face with my dupatta and went back to sleep. Then the old hag, Karim's mother-in-law, came in muttering and jabbering.

'Her ladyship does like to sleep, doesn't she? Shout yourself hoarse and she will not turn a hair; shake her for all you are worth and she will slumber on. I think a snake must have sniffed at her. Ah, her ladyship is awake at last.'

I kept quiet and she went on jabbering till she had exhausted herself. 'Where is the cup?' she demanded. I gave it to her and she went out. The door was locked again. A little later Karim's mother came in. She unlatched a window and took me through it to a tumbledown courtyard. It did my heart good to see the open sky even though it was for a short time. I was taken back and locked up in the same dark dungeon and, as on the previous day, I was given lentil soup and a bowl of maize porridge to eat.

So passed another two days. On the third day, a girl, perhaps a year or two older than me, was brought and locked up in the same cell. God alone knows where Karim had enticed her! The poor thing was crying her heart out. Her arrival was a blessing for me. When she stopped crying, we started talking to each other in whispers.

She told me her name was Ram Dei, the daughter of a Hindu trader of a village near Sitapur. I could not see her face in the dark, but next day when the window was opened, we had a good look at each other. She was fair and petite and her features were lovely.

Ram Dei was taken away on the fourth day and I had to spend

another two days in the dark hole in utter loneliness. On the third night Dilawar Khan and Peer Bakhsh came and took me out with them. It was a moonlit night. We went across some open ground and then through a street till we came to a bridge. The river was in flood and a sharp breeze was blowing. I began to shiver with cold. A little later we found ourselves in another street and then we went through a very long and narrow lane. I had to walk its entire length and my feet ached. We came to another bazaar which was so crowded that we found it difficult to get through. At long last we came to the entrance of a house.

Mirza Ruswa, can you guess what this place was? It was here that I was to trade my honour for money, for this was the Chowk, the prostitutes' quarter. And I was where I was to get whatever was due to me from the world—honour and disgrace, fame and notoriety, failure and success. It was the establishment of Madam Khanum Jan, and its doors were open. We went in and up a staircase, through a courtyard to a verandah where she was sitting. Khanum was nearly fifty, but what a grand old lady she was! I have never seen another woman with a more dignified bearing nor one as well dressed as her. The hair about her temples had gone snow-white and neatly framed her dark face. She wore a pair of loose pyjamas made of gold thread and had a dupatta of finely wrinkled white muslin over her head. She had big bracelets of solid gold on her arms; her plain earrings became her beautiful face. Her daughter Bismillah Jan had exactly the same complexion and features but lacked that something, a certain je ne sais quoi, which made her mother so much more fascinating. I have never forgotten the impression she created on me that day. She was sitting on a low settee covered with a carpet. The room was lit by a lamp with a glass globe shaped like a lotus flower. A large and richly engraved paan leaf casket lay open in front of her. She was smoking a hookah through a long winding stem. Her daughter, the dusky Bismillah Jan, was dancing. As soon as we entered, the dancing stopped and those present left the room. The deal had apparently been settled earlier. Madam Khanum looked up and asked: 'Is this the girl?'

'Yes, madam,' replied Dilawar Khan.

She beckoned me to her side, put her arm around my shoulder and made me sit down beside her. She tilted up my face and looked closely. 'Very well,' she said at last, 'I stand by my offer for this one. What about the other girl?'

'She has already been disposed of,' replied Peer Bakhsh.

'How much did you get for her?'

'Two hundred rupees.'

'Well, then, that's settled,' she commented, and then asked: 'Who did you sell her to?'

'A begum bought her for her son.'

'She wasn't too bad to look at; I would have paid as much. You were hasty.'

'What was I to do? I did my best but my wife's brother would not listen to me.'

'This girl also has a nice face,' interrupted Dilawar Khan, 'you are the best judge.'

'She will do,' conceded Khanum, 'at least she is human.'

'Well, she is yours for the taking,' replied Dilawar Khan.

'You are a stubborn lot,' said Khanum. She called for one Husaini. A dark, buxom woman of middle age came in. 'Bring the cash box,' ordered Khanum. Husaini went and fetched the cash box. Khanum opened it and put a lot of money in front of Dilawar Khan.

I came to know later that she paid a hundred and twenty-five rupees for me. Of these, Peer Bakhsh counted out some and tied them up in his kerchief. (I was told he got fifty.) The accursed Dilawar Khan put the rest in his pouch. Both of them salaamed and took their leave. I was left with Khanum and the maidservant Husaini. Khanum spoke to her maidservant: 'Husaini, this girl does not seem too dear for the price we have paid.'

'Dear? I would say you got her very cheap.'

'Oh no, not so very cheap either,' exclaimed Khanum. 'However, she has an innocent face. I wonder whose child she is. And what a state her parents must be in! Don't these rascals have any fear of God when they abduct these girls, Husaini? Don't you agree we are absolutely blameless? It is they who will have to answer before God for deeds such as this. If I had not bought her, she would have been sold to someone else.'

'She will be much better off here,' Husaini assured her. 'Hasn't madam heard how these slave girls are treated by mistresses of respectable homes?'

'Of course I have heard! Only the other day, I was told that Sultan Jahan Begum chanced upon her slave girl talking to her husband and had the girl branded with a red hot iron till she died.'

'These women get away with murder here,' sighed Husaini, 'but on the day of judgement, those who treat their servants cruelly will have their faces blackened.'

'Only have their faces blackened!' exclaimed Khanum warming up, 'They will be thrashed by hell's burning faggots.'

'It will serve them right,' agreed the maidservant. 'That is what they really deserve.' After a while Husaini asked Khanum: 'Mistress, give this child to me; I will bring her up for you. She is your property, but let me look after her.'

'All right, you take her,' replied Khanum waving to me.

Husaini, who had remained standing all this while, sat down beside me. 'Where do you come from, child?' she asked me.

'From Bangla,' I replied sobbing.

'Where's Bangla?' Husaini asked Khanum.

'How dense you are! Bangla is another name for Faizabad.'

'What is your father's name?' Husaini asked me.

'Jemadar.'

'You are the limit,' interrupted Khanum. 'How can she know her father's name? She is only a child.'

'What is your name?' asked Husaini, proceeding with her questions.

'Ameeran.'

'I don't like the name,' interrupted Khanum again. 'We will call you Umrao.'

'Do you hear child?' said Husaini. 'Henceforth you answer to the name of "Umrao". When the mistress calls "Umrao", you reply "Yes, madam."'

From that day onwards my name became Umrao. When I grew up and took my place amongst the courtesans of Lucknow, people began to call me Umrao Jan. And when I began to write poetry, I added the pseudonym 'Ada' and came to be known as Umrao Jan Ada.

85

TOBA TEK SINGH

SAADAT HASAN MANTO

This story, by Saadat Hasan Manto (1912-1955), who by his own estimation (and that of practically every other reader of Urdu literature) was the greatest short story writer who walked the earth, has been translated by multiple translators. This translation is one of the best.

A couple of years or so after the partition of the subcontinent, the governments of Pakistan and India felt that just as they had exchanged their hardened criminals, they should exchange their lunatics. In other words, Muslims in the lunatic asylums of India should be sent across to Pakistan; and mad Hindus and Sikhs in Pakistan asylums be handed over to India.

Whether or not this was a sane decision, we will never know. But people in knowledgeable circles say that there were many conferences at the highest levels between bureaucrats of the two countries before the final agreement was signed and a date fixed for the exchange.

The news of the impending exchange created a novel situation in the Lahore lunatic asylum. A Muslim patient who was a regular reader of the *Zamindar* was asked by a friend, 'Maulvi sahib, what is this thing they call Pakistan?' After much thought he replied, 'It's a place in India where they manufacture razor blades.' A Sikh lunatic asked another, 'Sardarji, why are we being sent to India? We cannot speak their language.' The Sardarji smiled and replied, 'I know the lingo of the Hindustanis.' He illustrated his linguistic prowess by reciting a doggerel.

Hindustanis are full of shaitani
They strut about like bantam cocks.

One morning a mad Mussalman yelled the slogan 'Pakistan Zindabad' with such vigour that he slipped on the floor and knocked himself senseless.

Some inmates of the asylum were not really insane. They were murderers whose relatives had been able to have them certified and thus saved from the hangman's noose. These people had vague notions of why India had been divided and what Pakistan was. But even they knew very little of the complete truth. The papers were not very informative and the guards were so stupid that it was difficult to make any sense of what they said. All one could gather from their talk was that there was a man of the name of Muhammad Ali Jinnah who was also known as the Qaid-i-Azam. And that this Muhammad Ali Jinnah alias Qaid-i-Azam had made a separate country for the Mussalmans which he called Pakistan.

No one knew where this Pakistan was or how far it extended. This was the chief reason why inmates who were not totally insane were in a worse dilemma than those who were utterly mad: they did not know whether they were in India or Pakistan. If they were in India, where exactly was Pakistan? And if they were in Pakistan how was it that the very same place had, till recently, been known as India?

A poor Muslim inmate got so baffled with the talk about India and Pakistan, Pakistan and India, that he got madder than before. One day while he was sweeping the floor he was suddenly overcome by an insane impulse. He threw away his broom and clambered up a tree. And for two hours he orated from the branch of this tree on Indo-Pakistan problems. When the guards tried to get him down, he climbed up still higher. When they threatened him he replied, 'I do not wish to live either in India or Pakistan; I want to stay where I am, on top of this tree.'

After a while the fit of lunacy abated and the man was persuaded to come down. As soon as he was on the ground he began to embrace his Hindu and Sikh friends and shed bitter tears. He was overcome by the thought that they would leave him and go away to India.

Another Muslim inmate had a Master of Science degree in radio engineering and considered himself a cut above the others. He used to spend his days strolling in a secluded corner of the garden. Suddenly a change came over him. He took off all his clothes and handed them over to the head constable. He resumed his peregrinations without a stitch of clothing on his person.

And there was yet another lunatic, a fat Mussalman who had been a leader of the Muslim League in Chiniot. He was given to bathing fifteen to sixteen times during the day. He suddenly gave it up altogether.

The name of this fat Mussalman was Muhammad Ali. But one day he proclaimed from his cell that he was Muhammad Ali Jinnah. Not to be outdone, his cellmate who was Sikh proclaimed himself to be Master Tara Singh. The two began to abuse each other. They were declared 'dangerous' and put in separate cells.

There was a young Hindu lawyer from Lahore. He was said to have become unhinged when his lady-love jilted him. When he heard that Amritsar had gone to India, he was very depressed: his sweetheart lived in Amritsar. Although the girl had spurned his affections, he did not forget her even in his lunacy. He spent his time cursing all leaders, Hindu as well as Muslim, because they had split India into two and made his beloved an Indian and him a Pakistani.

When the talk of exchanging lunatics was in the air, other inmates consoled the Hindu lawyer with the hope that he would soon be sent to India—the country where his sweetheart lived. But the lawyer refused to be reassured. He did not want to leave Lahore because he was convinced that he would not be able to set up a legal practice in Amritsar.

There were a couple of Anglo-Indians in the European ward. They were very saddened to learn that the English had liberated India and returned home. They met secretly to deliberate on problems of their future status in the asylum: would the asylum continue to have a separate ward for Europeans? Would they be served breakfast as before? Would they be deprived of toast and be forced to eat chapatis?

Then there was a Sikh who had been in the asylum for fifteen years. And in the fifteen years he said little besides the following sentence: 'Opardi, good good di, anekas di, bedhyana di, moong di dal of di lantern.'

The Sikh never slept either at night or in the day. The warders said that they had not known him to blink his eyes in fifteen years. He did not as much as lie down. Only on rare occasions he leant against the wall to rest. His legs were swollen down to the ankles.

Whenever there was talk of India and Pakistan, or the exchange of lunatics, this Sikh would become very attentive. If anyone invited him to express his views, he would answer with great solemnity, 'Opardi, good good di, anekas di, bedhyana di, moong di dal of the Pakistan government.'

Sometime later he changed the end of his litany from 'of the Pakistan Government' to 'of the Toba Tek Singh government'.

He began to question his fellow inmates whether the village of Toba Tek Singh was in India or Pakistan. No one knew the answer. Those who tried got tied up in knots when explaining how Sialkot was at first in India and was now in Pakistan. How could one guarantee that a similar fate would not befall Lahore and from being Pakistani today it would not become Indian tomorrow? For that matter, how could one be sure that the whole of India would not become a part of Pakistan? All said and done who could put his hand on his heart and say with conviction that there was no danger of both India and Pakistan vanishing from the face of the globe one day!

The Sikh had lost most of his long hair. Since he seldom took a bath, the hair of his head had matted and joined with his beard. This gave the Sikh a very fierce look. But he was a harmless fellow. In the fifteen years he had been in the asylum, he had never been known to argue or quarrel with anyone. All that the older inmates knew about him was that he owned land in village Toba Tek Singh and was a prosperous farmer. When he lost his mind, his relatives had brought him to the asylum in iron fetters. Once a month, some relatives came to Lahore to find out how he was faring. With the eruption of Indo-Pakistan troubles their visits had ceased.

The Sikh's name was Bishen Singh but everyone called him Toba Tek Singh. Bishen Singh had no concept of time—neither of days, nor weeks, nor of months. He had no idea how long he had been in the lunatic asylum. But when his relatives and friends came to see him, he knew that a month must have gone by. He would inform the head warder that 'Miss Interview' was due to visit him. He would wash himself with great care; he would soap his body and oil his long hair and beard before combing them. He would dress up before he went to meet his visitors. If they asked him any questions, he either remained silent or answered, 'Opardi, anekas di, bedhyana di, moong di dal of di lantern.'

Bishen Singh had a daughter who had grown into a full-bosomed lass of fifteen. But he showed no comprehension about his child. The girl wept bitterly whenever she met her father.

When talk of India and Pakistan came up, Bishen Singh began to question other lunatics about the location of Toba Tek Singh. No one could give him a satisfactory answer. His irritation mounted day by day. And now even 'Miss Interview' did not come to see him. There was a time when something had told him that his relatives were due. Now that inner voice had been silenced. And he was more anxious than ever to meet his relatives and find out whether Toba Tek Singh was in India or Pakistan. But no relatives came. Bishen Singh turned to other sources of information.

There was a lunatic in the asylum who believed he was God. Bishen Singh asked him whether Toba Tek Singh was in India or Pakistan. As was his wont God adopted a grave mien and replied, 'We have not yet issued our orders on the subject.'

Bishen Singh got the same answer many times. He pleaded with 'God' to issue instructions so that the matter could be settled once and for all. His pleadings were in vain; 'God' had many pressing matters awaiting 'His' orders. Bishen Singh's patience ran out and one day he let 'God' have a bit of his mind. 'Opardi, good good di, anekas di, bedhyana di, moong di dal of wahi-i-guru ji ka khalsa and wahi-i-guruji di fateh! Jo boley so nihal, Sat Sri Akal!'

This was meant to put 'God' in his place as the God only of the Mussalmans. Surely if He had been God of the Sikhs, He would have heard the pleadings of a Sikh!

A few days before the day fixed for the exchange of lunatics, a Muslim from Toba Tek Singh came to visit Bishen Singh. This man had never been to the asylum before. When Bishen Singh saw him he turned away. The warders stopped him: 'He's come to see you; he's your friend, Fazal Din,' they said.

Bishen Singh gazed at Fazal Din and began to mumble. Fazal Din put his hand on Bishen Singh's shoulder. 'I have been intending to see you for the last many days but could never find the time. All your family have safely crossed over to India. I did the best I could for them. Your daughter, Roop Kaur...'

Fazal Din continued somewhat haltingly, 'Yes... she too is well. She went along with the rest.'

Bishen Singh stood where he was without saying a word. Fazal Din started again. 'They asked me to keep in touch with you. I am told that you are to leave for India. Convey my salaams to brother Balbir Singh and to brother Wadhawa Singh...and also to sister Amrit Kaur... Tell brother Balbir Singh that Fazal Din is well and happy. Both the grey buffaloes that they left behind have calved—one is a male, the other a female...the female died six days later. And if there is anything I can do for them, I am always willing. I have brought you a little sweet corn.'

Bishen Singh took the bag of sweet corn and handed it over to a warder. He asked Fazal Din, 'Where is Toba Tek Singh?'

Fazal Din looked somewhat puzzled and replied, 'Where could it be? It's in the same place it always was.'

Bishen Singh asked again: 'In Pakistan or India?'

'No, not in India; it's in Pakistan,' replied Fazal Din.

Bishen Singh turned away mumbling 'Opardi, good good di, anekas di, bedhyana di, moong di dal of the Pakistan and Hindustan of dur phittey moonh.'

◆

Arrangements for the exchange of lunatics were completed. Lists with names of lunatics of either side had been exchanged and information sent to the people concerned. The date was fixed.

It was a bitterly cold morning. Busloads of Sikh and Hindu lunatics left the Lahore asylum under heavy police escort. At the border at Wagah, the superintendents of the two countries met and settled the details of the operation.

Getting the lunatics out of the buses and handing over custody to officers of the other side proved to be a very difficult task. Some refused to come off the bus; those that came out were difficult to control; a few broke loose and had to be recaptured. Those that were naked had to be clothed. No sooner were the clothes put on them than they tore them off their bodies. Some came out with vile abuse, others began to sing at the tops of their voices. Some squabbled; others cried or roared with laughter. They created such a racket that one could not hear a word. The female lunatics added to the noise. And all this in the bitterest of cold when people's teeth chattered like the scales of rattlesnakes.

Most of the lunatics resisted the exchange because they could not understand why they were being uprooted from one place and flung into another. Those of a gloomier disposition were yelling slogans: 'Long Live Pakistan' or 'Death to Pakistan'. Some lost their tempers and were prevented from coming to blows in the very nick of time.

At last came the turn of Bishen Singh. The Indian officer began to enter his name in the register. Bishen Singh asked him, 'Where is Toba Tek Singh? In India or Pakistan?'

'In Pakistan.'

That was all that Bishen Singh wanted to know. He turned and ran back to Pakistan. Pakistani soldiers apprehended him and tried to push him back towards India. Bishen Singh refused to budge. 'Toba Tek Singh is on this side,' he cried, and began to yell at the top of his voice, 'Opardi, good good di, anekas di, bedhyana di, moong di of Toba Tek Singh and Pakistan.' They did their best to soothe him, to explain to him that Toba Tek Singh must have left for India; and that if anyone of that name was found in Pakistan he would be dispatched to India at once. Bishen Singh refused to be persuaded. They tried to use force. Bishen Singh planted himself on the dividing line and dug his swollen feet into the ground with such firmness that no one could move him.

They let him be. He was soft in the head. There was no point using force; he would come round on his own—yes. They left him standing where he was and resumed the exchange of other lunatics.

Shortly before sunrise, a weird cry rose from Bishen Singh's throat. The man who had spent all the nights and days of the last fifteen years standing on his feet, now sprawled on the ground, face down. The barbed-wire fence on one side marked the territory of India; another fence marked the territory of Pakistan. In the No Man's Land between the two barbed-wire fences lay the body of Bishen Singh of village Toba Tek Singh.

86

STENCH OF KEROSENE

AMRITA PRITAM

Amrita Pritam (1910-2005), the award-winning Punjabi writer,
published over seventy books and won both the Jnanpith and the Sahitya
Akademi awards.

Outside, a mare neighed. Guleri recognized the neighing and ran out
of the house. The mare was from her parents' village. She put her head
against its neck as if it were the door of her father's house.

◆

Guleri's parents lived in Chamba. A few miles from her husband's village,
which was on high ground, the road curved and descended steeply
downhill. From this point one could see Chamba lying a long way away
at one's feet. Whenever Guleri was homesick, she would take her husband
Manak and go up to this point. She would see the homes of Chamba
twinkling in the sunlight and would come back with her heart aglow
with pride.

Once every year, after the harvest had been gathered in, Guleri
was allowed to spend a few days with her parents. They sent a man to
Lakarmandi to bring her back to Chamba. Two of her friends, who were
also married to boys outside Chamba, came home at the same time of
the year. The girls looked forward to this annual meeting when they
spent many hours every day talking about their experiences, their joys
and sorrows. They went about the streets together. Then there was the
harvest festival. The girls would have new dresses made for the occasion.
They would have their dupattas dyed, starched and sprinkled with mica.
They would buy glass bangles and silver earrings.

Guleri always counted the days to the harvest. When autumn breezes
cleared the skies of the monsoon clouds she thought of little besides her
home in Chamba. She went about her daily chores—fed the cattle, cooked
food for her husband's parents and then sat back to work out how long
it would be before someone would come for her from her parents' village.

And now, once again, it was time for her annual visit. She caressed
the mare joyfully, greeted her father's servant, Natu, and made ready to
leave the next day.

Guleri did not have to put her excitement into words: the expression on her face was enough. Her husband, Manak, pulled at his chillum and closed his eyes. It seemed either as if he did not like the tobacco, or that he could not bear to face his wife.

'You will come to the fair at Chamba, won't you? Come even if it is only for the day,' she pleaded.

Manak put aside his chillum but did not reply.

'Why don't you answer me?' asked Guleri in a temper. 'Shall I tell you something?'

'I know what you are going to say: "I only go to my parents once in the year!" Well, you have never been stopped before.'

'Then why do you want to stop me this time?' she demanded.

'Just this time,' pleaded Manak.

'Your mother has not said anything. Why do you stand in my way?' Guleri was childishly stubborn.

'My mother...' Manak did not finish his sentence.

On the long awaited morning, Guleri was ready long before dawn. She had no children and therefore no problem of either having to leave them with her husband's parents or taking them with her. Natu saddled the mare as she took leave of Manak's parents. They patted her head and blessed her.

'I will come with you for a part of the way,' said Manak.

Guleri was happy as they set out. Under her dupatta she hid Manak's flute.

After the village of Khajiar, the road descended steeply to Chamba. There Guleri took out the flute from beneath her dupatta and gave it to Manak. She took Manak's hand in hers and said, 'Come now, play your flute!' But Manak, lost in his thoughts, paid no heed. 'Why don't you play your flute?' asked Guleri coaxingly. Manak looked at her sadly. Then, putting the flute to his lips, he blew a strange anguished wail of sound.

'Guleri, do not go away,' he begged her. 'I ask you again, do not go this time.' He handed her back the flute, unable to continue.

'But why?' she asked. 'You come over on the day of the fair and we will return together. I promise you, I will not stay behind.'

Manak did not ask again.

They stopped by the roadside. Natu took the mare a few paces ahead to leave the couple alone. It crossed Manak's mind that it was this time of year, seven years ago, that he and his friends had come on this very road to go to the harvest festival in Chamba. And it was at this fair that Manak had first seen Guleri and they had bartered their hearts to each other. Later, managing to meet alone, Manak remembered taking her hand and telling her, 'You are like unripe corn—full of milk.'

'Cattle go for unripe corn,' Guleri had replied, freeing her hand with a jerk. 'Human beings like it better roasted. If you want me, go and ask for my hand from my father.'

Amongst Manak's kinsmen it was customary to settle the bride price before the wedding. Manak was nervous because he did not know the price Guleri's father would demand from him. But Guleri's father was prosperous and had lived in cities. He had sworn that he would not take money for his daughter, but would give her to a worthy young man of a good family. Manak, he had decided, answered these requirements and very soon after, Guleri and Manak were married. Deep in memories, Manak was roused by Guleri's hand on his shoulder.

'What are you dreaming of?' she teased him.

Manak did not answer. The mare neighed impatiently and Guleri, thinking of the journey ahead of her, rose to leave. 'Do you know the bluebell wood a couple of miles from here?' she asked. 'It is said that anyone who goes through it becomes deaf.'

'Yes.'

'It seems to me that you have passed through the bluebell wood; you do not hear anything that I say.'

'You are right, Guleri. I cannot hear anything that you are saying to me,' replied Manak with a deep sigh.

Both of them looked at each other. Neither understood the other's thoughts.

'I will go now. You had better return home. You have come a long way,' said Guleri gently.

'You have walked all this distance. Better get on the mare,' replied Manak.

'Here, take your flute.'

'You take it with you.'

'Will you come and play it on the day of the fair?' asked Guleri with a smile. The sun shone in her eyes. Manak turned his face away. Guleri, perplexed, shrugged her shoulders and took the road to Chamba. Manak returned to his home.

Entering the house, he slumped listless on his charpai. 'You have been away a long time,' exclaimed his mother. 'Did you go all the way to Chamba?'

'Not all the way; only to the top of the hill,' Manak's voice was heavy.

'Why do you croak like an old woman?' asked his mother severely. 'Be a man.'

Manak wanted to retort, 'You are a woman; why don't you cry like one for a change!' But he remained silent.

Manak and Guleri had been married seven years, but she had never borne a child and Manak's mother had made a secret resolve: 'I will not let it go beyond the eighth year.'

This year, true to her decision, she had paid Rs 500 to get him a second wife and now, she had waited, as Manak knew, for the time when Guleri went to her parents' to bring in the new bride.

Obedient to his mother and to custom, Manak's body responded to the new woman. But his heart was dead within him.

◆

In the early hours of one morning he was smoking his chillum when an old friend happened to pass by. 'Ho Bhavani, where are you going so early in the morning?'

Bhavani stopped. He had a small bundle on his shoulder: 'Nowhere in particular,' he replied evasively.

'You must be on your way to some place or the other,' exclaimed Manak. 'What about a smoke?'

Bhavani sat down on his haunches and took the chillum from Manak's hands. 'I am going to Chamba for the fair,' he replied at last.

Bhavani's words pierced through Manak's heart like a needle.

'Is the fair today?'

'It is the same day every year,' replied Bhavani drily.

'Don't you remember, we were in the same party seven years ago?' Bhavani did not say any more but Manak was conscious of the other man's rebuke and he felt uneasy. Bhavani put down the chillum and picked up his bundle. His flute was sticking out of the bundle. Bidding Manak farewell, he walked away. Manak's eyes remained on the flute till Bhavani disappeared from view.

Next afternoon when Manak was in his fields he saw Bhavani coming back but deliberately he looked the other way. He did not want to talk to Bhavani or hear anything about the fair. But Bhavani came round the other side and sat down in front of Manak. His face was sad, lightless as a cinder.

'Guleri is dead,' said Bhavani in a flat voice.

'What?'

'When she heard of your second marriage, she soaked her clothes in kerosene and set fire to them.'

Manak, mute with pain, could only stare and feel his own life burning out.

The days went by, Manak resumed his work in the fields and ate his meals when they were given to him. But he was like a man dead, his face quite blank, his eyes empty.

'I am not his spouse,' complained his second wife. 'I am just someone he happened to marry.'

But quite soon she was pregnant and Manak's mother was well pleased with her new daughter-in-law. She told Manak about his wife's condition, but he looked as if he did not understand, and his eyes were still empty.

His mother encouraged her daughter-in-law to bear with her husband's moods for a few days. As soon as the child was born and placed in his father's lap, she said, Manak would change.

A son was duly born to Manak's wife; and his mother, rejoicing, bathed the boy, dressed him in fine clothes and put him in Manak's lap. Manak stared at the newborn baby in his lap. He stared a long time, uncomprehending, his face as usual, expressionless. Then suddenly the blank eyes filled with horror, and Manak began to scream. 'Take him away!' he shrieked hysterically. 'Take him away! He stinks of kerosene.'

87

THE DEATH OF SHAIKH BURHANUDDIN
KHWAJA AHMAD ABBAS

This story, along with 'Toba Tek Singh', is one of Khushwant Singh's 'all-time favourites'. It is also one of the finest stories of Partition to have been published. Khwaja Ahmad Abbas (1914-1987), a journalist, novelist and filmmaker, published over forty books in Urdu and a few in English.

My name is Shaikh Burhanuddin.

When violence and murder became the order of the day in Delhi and the blood of Muslims flowed in the streets, I cursed my fate for having a Sikh for a neighbour. Far from expecting him to come to my rescue in times of trouble, as a good neighbour should, I could not tell when he would thrust his kirpan into my belly. The truth is that till then I used to find the Sikhs somewhat laughable. But I also disliked them and was somewhat scared of them.

My hatred for the Sikhs began on the day when I first set my eyes on one. I could not have been more than six years old when I saw a Sikh sitting out in the sun combing his long hair. 'Look!' I yelled with revulsion, 'a woman with a long beard!' As I got older, this dislike developed into hatred for the entire race.

It was a custom amongst old women of our household to heap all afflictions on our enemies. Thus, for example, if a child got pneumonia or broke its leg, they would say 'a long time ago a Sikh (or an Englishman) got pneumonia, or a long time ago a Sikh (or an Englishman) broke his leg'. When I was older I discovered that this referred to the year 1857 when the Sikh princes helped the ferringee (foreigner) to defeat the Hindus and Muslims in the War of Independence. I do not wish to propound a historical thesis but to explain the obsession, the suspicion and hatred which I bore towards the English and the Sikhs. I was more frightened of the English than of the Sikhs.

When I was ten years old, I happened to be travelling from Delhi to Aligarh. I used to travel third class, or at the most in the intermediate class. That day I said to myself, 'Let me for once travel second class and see what it feels like.' I bought my ticket and I found an empty second-class compartment. I jumped on the well-sprung seats; I went into the bathroom and leapt up to see my face in the mirror; I switched on all the fans. I played with the light switches. There were only a couple of minutes for the train to leave when four red-faced Tommies burst into the compartment, mouthing obscenities: everything was either 'bloody' or 'damn'. I had one look at them and my desire to travel second class vanished.

I picked up my suitcase and ran out. I only stopped for breath when I got into a third-class compartment crammed with natives. But as luck would have it, it was full of Sikhs—their beards hanging down to their navels and dressed in nothing more than their underpants. I could not escape from them; but I kept my distance.

Although I feared the white man more than the Sikhs, I felt that he was more civilized: he wore the same kind of clothes as I. I also wanted to be able to say 'damn', 'bloody fool'—the way he did. And like him I wanted to belong to the ruling class. The Englishman ate his food with forks and knives, I also wanted to learn to eat with forks and knives so that natives would look upon me as advanced and as civilized as the white man.

My Sikh-phobia was of a different kind. I had contempt for the Sikh. I was amazed at the stupidity of men who imitated women and grew their hair long. I must confess I did not like my hair cut too short; despite my father's instructions to the contrary, I did not allow the barber to clip off more than a little when I went to him on Fridays. I grew a mop of hair so that when I played hockey or football it would blow about in the breeze like those of English sportsmen. My father often asked me, 'Why do you let your hair grow like a woman's?' My father had primitive ideas and I took no notice of his views. If he had had his way he would have had all heads razored bald and stuck artificial beards on people's chins... That reminds me that the second reason for hating the Sikhs was their beards, which made them look like savages.

There are beards and beards. There was my father's beard, neatly trimmed in the French style; or my uncle's, which went into a sharp point under his chin. But what could you do with a beard to which no scissor was ever applied and which was allowed to grow like a wild bush—fed with a compost of oil, curd and goodness knows what! And, after it had grown a few feet, combed like hair on a head. My grandfather also had a very long beard which he combed...but then my grandfather was my grandfather and a Sikh is just a Sikh.

After I had passed my matriculation examination I was sent to the Muslim University at Aligarh. We boys who came from Delhi, or the United Provinces, looked down upon boys from Punjab; they were crude rustics who did not know how to converse, how to behave at table, or to deport themselves in polite company. All they could do was drink large tumblers of buttermilk. Delicacies such as vermicelli with essence of kewra sprinkled on it or the aroma of Lipton's tea were alien to them. Their language was unsophisticated to the extreme, whenever they spoke to each other it seemed as if they were quarrelling. It was full of 'ussi, tussi, saadey, twhaadey'—Heaven forbid. I kept my distance from Punjabis.

But the warden of our hostel (God forgive him) gave me a Punjabi as a roommate. When I realized that there was no escape, I decided to make the best of a bad bargain and be civil to the chap. After a few days we became quite friendly. This man was called Ghulam Rasul and he was from Rawalpindi. He was full of amusing anecdotes and was a good companion.

You might well ask how Mr Ghulam Rasul gatecrashed into a story about the Sikhs. The fact of the matter is that Ghulam Rasul's anecdotes were usually about the Sikhs. It is through these anecdotes that I got to know the racial characteristics, the habits and customs of this strange community. According to Ghulam Rasul the chief characteristics of the Sikhs were the following:

All Sikhs were stupid and idiotic. At noontime they lost their senses altogether. There were many instances to prove this. For example, one day at 12 noon, a Sikh was cycling along Hall Bazaar in Amritsar when a constable, also a Sikh, stopped him and demanded, 'Where is your light?' The cyclist replied nervously, 'Jemadar sahib, I lit it when I left my home; it must have gone out just now.' The constable threatened to run him in. A passer-by, yet another Sikh with a long white beard, intervened, 'Brothers, there is no point in quarrelling over little things. If the light has gone out it can be lit again.'

Ghulam Rasul knew hundreds of anecdotes of this kind. When he told them in his Punjabi accent his audience was left helpless with laughter. One really enjoyed them best in Punjabi because the strange and incomprehensible behaviour of the uncouth Sikh was best told in his rustic lingo.

The Sikhs were not only stupid but incredibly filthy as well. Ghulam Rasul, who had known hundreds of them, told us how they never shaved their heads. And whereas we Muslims washed our hair thoroughly at least every Friday, the Sikhs who made a public exhibition of bathing in their underpants, poured all kinds of filth, like curd, into their hair. I rub lime juice and glycerine in my scalp. Although the glycerine is white and thick like curd, it is an altogether different thing—made by a well-known firm of perfumers of Europe. My glycerine came in a lovely bottle whereas the Sikh's curd came from the shop of a dirty sweetmeat seller.

I would not have concerned myself with the manner of living of these people except that they were so haughty and ill-bred as to consider themselves as good warriors as the Muslims. It is known over the world that one Muslim can get the better of ten Hindus or Sikhs. But these Sikhs would not accept the superiority of the Muslim and would strut about like bantam cocks, twirling their moustaches and stroking their beards. Ghulam Rasul used to say that one day we Muslims would teach the Sikhs a lesson that they would never forget.

Years went by.

I left college. I ceased to be a student and became a clerk; then a head clerk. I left Aligarh and came to live in New Delhi. I was allotted government quarters. I got married. I had children.

The quarters next to mine were occupied by a Sikh who had been displaced from Rawalpindi. Despite the passage of years, I remembered what Ghulam Rasul had told me. As Ghulam Rasul had prophesied, the Sikhs had been taught a bitter lesson, in humility at least, in the district of Rawalpindi. The Muslims had virtually wiped them out. The Sikhs boasted that they were great heroes; they flaunted their long kirpans. But they could not withstand the brave Muslims. The Sikhs' beards were forcibly shaved. They were circumcised. They were converted to Islam. The Hindu press, as was its custom, vilified the Muslims. It reported that the Muslims had murdered Sikh women and children. This was wholly contrary to Islamic tradition. No Muslim warrior was ever known to raise his hand against a woman or a child. The pictures of the corpses of women and children published in Hindu newspapers were obviously faked. I wouldn't have put it beyond the Sikhs to murder their own women and children in order to vilify the Muslims.

The Muslims were also accused of abducting Hindu and Sikh women. The truth of the matter is that such was the impact of the heroism of Muslims on the minds of Hindu and Sikh girls that they fell in love with young Muslims and insisted on going with them. These noble-minded young men had no option but to give them shelter and thus bring them to the true path of Islam. The bubble of Sikh bravery was burst. It did not matter how their leaders threatened the Muslims with their kirpans, the sight of the Sikhs who had fled from Rawalpindi filled my heart with pride in the greatness of Islam.

The Sikh who was my neighbour was about sixty years old. His beard had gone completely grey. Although he had barely escaped from the jaws of death, he was always laughing, displaying his teeth in the most vulgar fashion. It was evident that he was quite stupid. In the beginning he tried to draw me into his net by professions of friendship. Whenever I passed him he insisted on talking to me. I do not remember what kind of Sikh festival it was, when he sent me some sweet butter. My wife promptly gave it away to the sweeperess. I did my best to have as little to do with him as I could. I snubbed him whenever I could. I knew that if I spoke a few words to him, he would be hard to shake off. Civil talk would encourage him to become familiar. It was known to me that Sikhs drew their sustenance from foul language. Why should I soil my lips by associating with such people!

One Sunday afternoon I was telling my wife of some anecdotes about the stupidity of the Sikhs. To prove my point, exactly at 12 o'clock, I sent my servant across to my Sikh neighbour to ask him the time. He sent back the reply, 'Two minutes after 12.' I remarked to my wife 'You see, they are scared of even mentioning 12 o'clock!' We both had a hearty laugh. After this, many a time when I wanted to make an ass of my Sikh neighbour, I would ask him, 'Well, Sardarji, has it struck twelve?' The shameless creature would grin, baring all his teeth and answer, 'Sir, for us it is always striking twelve.' He would roar with laughter as if it were a great joke.

I was concerned about the safety of my children. One could never trust a Sikh. And this man had fled from Rawalpindi. He was sure to have a grudge against Muslims and to be on the lookout for an opportunity to avenge himself. I had told my wife never to allow the children to go near the Sikh's quarters. But children are children. After a few days I saw my children playing with the Sikh's little girl, Mohini, and his other grandchildren. This child, who was barely ten years old, was really as beautiful as her name indicated; she was fair and beautifully formed. These wretches have beautiful women. I recall Ghulam Rasul telling me that if all the Sikh men were to leave their women behind and clear out of Punjab, there would be no need for Muslims to go to paradise in search of houris.

The truth about the Sikhs was soon evident. After the thrashing in Rawalpindi, they fled like cowards to East Punjab. Here they found the Muslims weak and unprepared. So they began to kill them. Hundreds of thousands of Muslims were martyred; the blood of the faithful ran in streams. Thousands of women were stripped naked and made to parade through the streets. When Sikhs, fleeing from West Punjab, came in large numbers to Delhi, it was evident that there would be trouble in the capital. I could not leave for Pakistan immediately. Consequently I sent away my wife and children by air with my elder brother, and entrusted my own fate to God. I could not send much luggage by air. I booked an entire railway wagon to take my furniture and belongings. But on the day I was to load the wagon I got information that trains bound for Pakistan were being attacked by Sikh bands. Consequently my luggage stayed in my quarters in Delhi.

On 15 August, India celebrated its independence. What interest could I have in the independence of India! I spent the day lying in bed reading *Dawn* and the *Pakistan Times*. Both the papers had strong words to say about the manner in which India had gained its freedom and proved conclusively how the Hindus and the British had conspired to destroy the Muslims. It was only our leader, the great Muhammad Ali Jinnah, who was able to thwart their evil designs and win Pakistan for the Muslims. The English had knuckled under because of Hindu and Sikh pressure and handed over Amritsar to India. Amritsar, as the world knows, is a purely Muslim city. Its famous Golden Mosque—or am I mixing it up with the Golden Temple!—yes, of course, the Golden Mosque! There is the Jama Masjid, the Red Fort, the mausolea of Nizamuddin and Emperor Humayun, the tomb and school of Safdarjung—just everything worthwhile bears imprints of Islamic rule. Even so, this Delhi (which should really be called Shahjahanabad after its Muslim builder Shahjahan) was to suffer the indignity of having the flag of Hindu imperialism unfurled on its ramparts.

My heart seemed rent asunder. I could have shed tears of blood. My cup of sorrow was full to the brim when I realized that Delhi, which was once the footstool of the Muslim Empire, the centre of Islamic culture and civilization, had been snatched out of our hands. Instead we were to have the desert wastes of West Punjab, Sindh and Baluchistan inhabited by an uncouth and uncultured people. We were to go to a land where people do not know how to talk in civilized Urdu; where men wear baggy salwars like their womenfolk, where they eat thick bread four pounds in weight instead of the delicate wafers we eat at home!

I steeled myself. I would have to make this sacrifice for my great leader, Jinnah, and for my new country, Pakistan. Nevertheless, the thought of having to leave Delhi was most depressing.

When I emerged from my room in the evening, my Sikh neighbour bared his fangs and asked, 'Brother, did you not go out to see the celebrations?' I felt like setting fire to his beard.

One morning the news spread of a general massacre in old Delhi. Muslim homes were burnt in Karol Bagh. Muslim shops in Chandni Chowk were looted. This then was a sample of Hindu rule! I said to myself, 'New Delhi is really an English city; Lord Mountbatten lives here as well as the commander-in-chief. At least in New Delhi no hand will be raised against Muslims.' With this self-assurance I started towards my office. I had to settle the business of my provident fund; I had delayed going to Pakistan in order to do so. I had only got as far as Gole Market when I ran into a Hindu colleague. He said, 'What on earth are you up to? Go back at once and do not come out of your house. The rioters are killing Muslims in Connaught Circus.' I hurried back home.

I had barely got to my quarters when I ran into my Sikh neighbour. He began to reassure me. 'Shaikhji, do not worry! As long as I am alive no one will raise a hand against you.' I said to myself: 'How much fraud is hidden behind this man's beard! He is obviously pleased that the Muslims are being massacred, but expresses sympathy to win my confidence; or is he trying to taunt me?' I was the only Muslim living in the block, perhaps I was the only one on the road.

I did not want these people's kindness or sympathy. I went inside my quarters and said to myself, 'If I have to die, I will kill at least ten or twenty men before they get me.' I went to my room where, beneath my bed, I kept my double-barrelled gun. I had also collected quite a hoard of cartridges.

I searched the house, but could not find the gun.

'What is huzoor looking for?' asked my faithful servant, Mohammed.

'What happened to my gun?'

He did not answer. But I could tell from the way he looked that he had either hidden it or stolen it.

'Why don't you answer?' I asked him angrily.

Then he came out with the truth. He had stolen my gun and given it to some of his friends who were collecting arms to defend the Muslims in Daryaganj.

'We have hundreds of guns, several machine guns, ten revolvers and a cannon. We will slaughter these infidels; we will roast them alive.'

'No doubt, with my gun, you will roast the infidels in Daryaganj, but who will defend me here? I am the only Mussalman amongst these savages. If I am murdered, who will answer for it?'

I persuaded him to steal his way to Daryaganj to bring back my gun and a couple of hundred cartridges. When he left I was convinced that I would never see him again. I was all alone. On the mantelpiece was a family photograph. My wife and children stared silently at me. My eyes filled with tears at the thought that I would never see them again. I was comforted with the thought that they were safe in Pakistan. Why had I been tempted by my paltry provident fund and not gone with them? I heard the crowd yelling.

'Sat Sri Akal...'

'Har Har Mahadev.'

The yelling came closer and closer. They were rioters—the bearers of my death warrant. I was like a wounded deer, running hither and thither, with the hunters' hounds in full pursuit. There was no escape. The door was made of very thin wood and glass panes. The rioters would smash their way in.

'Sat Sri Akal…'

'Har Har Mahadev.'

They were coming closer and closer; death was coming closer and closer. Suddenly there was a knock at the door. My Sikh neighbour walked in—'Shaikhji, come into my quarters at once.' Without a second thought I ran into the Sikh's verandah and hid behind the columns. A shot hit the wall above my head. A truck drew up and about a dozen young men climbed down. Their leader had a list in his hand—'Quarter No. 8—Shaikh Burhanuddin'. He read my name and ordered his gang to go ahead. They invaded my quarters and under my very eyes proceeded to destroy my home. My furniture, boxes, pictures, books, druggets and carpets, even the dirty linen was carried into the truck. Robbers! Thugs! Cut-throats!

As for the Sikh who had pretended to sympathize with me, he was no less a robber than they! He was pleading with the rioters: 'Gentlemen, stop! We have prior claim over our neighbour's property. We must get our share of the loot.' He beckoned to his sons and daughters. All of them gathered to pick up whatever they could lay their hands on. One took my trousers; another a suitcase.

They even grabbed the family photograph. They took the loot to their quarters.

You bloody Sikh! If God grants me life I will settle my score with you. At this moment I cannot even protest. The rioters are armed and only a few yards away from me. If they get to know of my presence…

'Please come in.'

My eyes fell on the unsheathed kirpan in the hands of the Sikh. He was inviting me to come in. The bearded monster looked more frightful after he had soiled his hands with my property. There was the glittering blade of his kirpan inviting me to my doom. There was no time to argue. The only choice was between the guns of the rioters and the sabre of the Sikh. I decided rather the kirpan of the old man than ten armed gangsters. I went into the room hesitantly, silently.

'Not here, come in further,' I went into the inner room like a goat following a butcher. The glint of the blade of the kirpan was almost blinding.

'Here you are, take your things,' said the Sikh.

He and his children put all the stuff they had pretended to loot in front of me. His old woman said, 'Son, I am sorry we were not able to save more.'

I was dumbfounded.

The gangsters had dragged out my steel almirah and were trying to smash it open. 'It would be simpler if we could find the keys,' said someone. 'The keys can only be found in Pakistan. That cowardly son of a filthy Muslim has decamped,' replied another.

Little Mohini answered back: 'Shaikhji is not a coward. He has not run off to Pakistan.'

'Where is he blackening his face?'

'Why should he be blackening his face? He is in...' Mohini realized her mistake and stopped mid-sentence. Blood mounted in her father's face. He locked me in the inside room, gave his kirpan to his son and went out to face the mob.

I do not know what exactly took place outside. I heard the sound of blows; then Mohini crying; then the Sikh yelling full-blooded abuse in Punjabi. And then a shot and the Sikh's cry of pain: 'hai'.

I heard a truck engine starting up and then there was a petrified silence.

When I was taken out of my prison my Sikh neighbour was lying on a charpai. Beside him lay a torn and bloodstained shirt. His new shirt also was oozing with blood. His son had gone to telephone for the doctor.

'Sardarji, what have you done?' I do not know how these words came out of my lips. The world of hate in which I had lived all these years lay in ruins about me.

'Sardarji, why did you do this?' I asked him again.

'Son, I had a debt to pay.'

'What kind of a debt?'

'In Rawalpindi there was a Muslim like you who sacrificed his life to save mine and the honour of my family.'

'What was his name, Sardarji?'

'Ghulam Rasul.'

Fate had played a cruel trick on me. The clock on the wall started to strike... 1... 2... 3... 4... 5... The Sikh turned towards the clock and smiled. He reminded me of my grandfather with his twelve-inch beard. How closely the two resembled each other!

...6...7...8...9...We counted in silence.

He smiled again. His white beard and long white hair were like a halo, effulgent with a divine light... 10... 11... 12... The clock stopped striking.

I could almost hear him say: 'For us Sikhs, it is always 12 o'clock!'

But the bearded lips, still smiling, were silent. And I knew he was already in some distant world, where the striking of clocks counted for nothing, where violence and mockery were powerless to hurt him.

88

THE NIGHT OF THE FULL MOON
KARTAR SINGH DUGGAL

Kartar Singh Duggal (1917-2012) wrote in both Urdu and Punjabi and published over fifty books in his lifetime. He won several major awards including the Sahitya Akademi Award and the Padma Bhushan.

No one believed that Malan and Minnie were mother and daughter; they looked like sisters—Minnie was quite a bit taller than her mother. People said, 'Malan, your daughter has grown into a lovely woman!' They never stopped gaping at the girl. She was like a pearl and as charming as she was comely.

When Malan looked at her daughter she felt as if she was looking at herself. She too had been as young and as beautiful. She hadn't aged much either. And there was somebody who was willing to go to the ends of the earth for her even now.

Why had her mind wandered to this man? He must be a dealer in pearls because every time she thought of him pearls dropped from her eyes! Her daughter was now a woman; it was unbecoming of her to think of a man. She had restrained herself all these years; why did her mind begin to waver? She must hold herself in check. Her daughter was due to wed in another week; she must not entertain such evil thoughts—never! Never!

'My very own, my dearest,' he had written only yesterday, 'do not forget me.' But every time he came to the village she sent him away without any encouragement. She shut her eyes as fast as she shut her door against him. He had refused to give her up. She was his life; without her he found no peace. He had spent many years waiting for her, pleading with her, suffering the pangs of love and passion. An age had passed and now the afternoon shadows had lengthened across life's courtyard.

Malan knew in her heart that he would come that night. Every full moonlit night he knocked on her door. And tonight the moon would be full. The night would be cold, frosty and still. She had never unlatched her door for him. Would she tonight? She recalled a cold, moonlit night of many years ago. She was dancing in the mango grove when her dupatta had got caught in his hand. She had come to him bare-headed with the moonlight flecking her face with jasmine petals. He had put the dupatta across her shoulders—exactly the way it lay across her shoulders now. A shiver ran down Malan's spine.

Minnie came down the lane, tall and as slender as a cypress. Fair and fragile, she looked as if the touch of a human hand would leave a stain on her. Modestly, she had her dupatta wrapped round her face, and her eyes lowered.

Minnie was returning from the temple. She had prayed to the gods, she said softly to her mother, to grant her wish. She had prayed to the gods to grant everybody all their wishes.

Malan smiled. Something stirred her fancy. If her wish could be granted, she thought to herself, what would she ask for?

'Father has not returned!' complained Minnie.

'He is not expected back today; it will be a thousand blessings if he gets back by tomorrow. He has a lot of things to buy. At weddings and feasts it's better to have a little more than to run short,' explained Malan.

Minnie took off her sequined dupatta and spread it on her mother's shoulders. She took her mother's plain dupatta instead, and went into the kitchen.

The light of the full moon came through the branches and sprinkled itself on Malan's face. The full moon always did something to her. It made her feel like one drunk. In another four days women would come to her courtyard to sing wedding songs. They would put henna on the palms and the soles of her daughter's feet. They would help her with her bridal clothes; load her with ornaments. How would her daughter look in bright red silk? And then the groom would come on horseback and take her to his own home and make love to her. He would kiss the henna away from the girl's palms and the soles of her feet.

It wasn't so very long ago that all this had happened to her, Malan. But Minnie's father had not once kissed the soles of her feet, nor ever pressed her palms against his eyes. He always came home tired; he ate his meal and fell fast asleep. Only the desire to have a son would occasionally arouse him at midnight. And then it was over so quickly that Malan had to spend hours counting the stars to cool down and get back to sleep. These midnight efforts had produced a daughter every year. The girls came to the world uninvited and departed without leave. Only one, Minnie, remained. She was a replica of her mother; like the fruit of a tree that bears only one. Minnie had large gazelle eyes—the eyes of Malan. Her long black hair fell down to her waist. And she had a full-bosomed wantonness that often made Malan think that all her frustrated passions had been rekindled in her daughter's body.

Minnie scrubbed the kitchen utensils, bolted the door of the courtyard and went to bed in her own room. Malan was left alone.

It was late. The moon was so dazzlingly bright that it seemed to be focussing all its light in that one courtyard. Was it cold? Not really. Just pleasantly cool. Malan asked herself why she sat alone in the courtyard under the night of the full moon. Was she expecting someone? Minnie had gone to bed and her father had gone away to the city. Why was he away on a night like this? On full moon nights she used to keep herself indoors, away from temptation. But tonight she had her daughter's sequined dupatta wrapped about her face. The sequins glistened in the silvery moonlight; it seemed as if the stars were entangled in her hair; they twinkled on her eyelashes, on her face and on her shoulders. A nightjar called from the mango grove: *uk, uk, uk.* It would call like that all through the night: *uk, uk, uk.*

Her thoughts carried her with them. Her daughter would be married in a week's time. Then she would be left alone—all alone in the huge courtyard. A shiver ran through her body. The empty courtyard would terrify her. She would have to learn to live by herself. Her husband was too occupied with the pursuit of money; his moneylending and debt-collecting. He came back late in the evening only to collapse on his charpai. She had often asked him why he involved himself in so many affairs, but it had not made any difference.

Malan went indoors and saw her daughter fast asleep—dead to the world as only the young can be. Her red bangles lay beside her pillow. Silly girl! She had only to turn in her sleep and they would be crushed. Malan picked them up to put them on the mantlepiece. Before she knew it, she had slipped them on to her own arms; six on one, six on the other. They glistened even in the dark. They were new; her daughter had only bought them the day before from the bangle seller.

Malan came out into the moonlit courtyard—the sequined dupatta on her head and her arms a-jingle-jangle with bright red glass bangles. She felt like a bride—warm, lusty. Blood surged in her veins.

There was a gentle knock on the door. It was he. It was the same knock—a nervous, hesitant knock. He was there as he had written in his letter he would be: 'On the full moonlit night of December, I will knock at your door. If you are willing, open the door; if you are not willing, let it be. I will continue to knock at your door as I have always done.'

Knock, knock, knock—very soft, very sweet, a very inviting knock. Who could it be but he! The prowler on moonlit nights. Suddenly the moon went behind a cloud and it was absolutely dark.

In a moment, Malan's feet took her across the dark courtyard. With trembling hands she undid the latch. Another moment and she was in his arms. Their lips met; their teeth ground against each other. Passion that had been held in check for over twenty years burst its banks and carried them on the flood.

Malan did not know how they went to the bo tree outside the village. She did not remember how they went into the field beside the bo tree—nor how long they stayed there. She was woken by the train that passed by the village in the early hours of the dawn. She extricated herself from her lover's embrace, covered her face with her dupatta and hurried back to her home.

She slipped off the bangles from her arms and put them back beside her daughter's pillow. She folded her daughter's sequined dupatta, took her own back and went to her charpai. She fell asleep at once and slept as she had never slept before—almost as if she were making up for a lifetime of sleeplessness.

When she woke, the sun was streaming into the courtyard.

'How you slept, like a little babe!' teased Minnie. Minnie had swept the rooms and the courtyard and cooked the morning meal. She had bathed and was ready to go to the temple. She had tied jasmine flowers in her dupatta to offer to the gods.

As soon as Minnie left, Malan stretched herself lazily on a charpai in the courtyard. She was filled with sleep and her head was filled with dreams.

A soft breeze began to blow. Warm sunshine spread in the courtyard. Malan felt like a bowl of milk, full to the brim—with a few petals of jasmine floating on it. It was a strange, heady intoxication. Her eyes would close, open, and then close again.

'O Malan! Where's that slut?' cried a voice suddenly. Malan felt as if someone had slapped her face.

'Never heard of such goings on!' said another voice, 'and only four days to her wedding!'

'What has my daughter done?' shrieked Malan, rising up in anger. 'She is as innocent as a calf.'

There were derisive exclamations. Then someone sneered, 'Your little calf has been on the dung heap all night.'

Malan's body went cold, her lifeblood draining from her veins; a deathly pallor spread over her face.

Lajo, her neighbour, was speaking. 'It was barely dark when the bitch walked off with a stranger. I had got up to relieve myself when I saw them go away into the fields, with their arms entwined around each other's waists. I didn't get a wink of sleep. We have to watch the interests of our daughters. I've never heard of anyone blacken the faces of her parents in this way.'

99: Khushwant Singh

Malan sat still as if turned to stone. She did not seem to hear what was being said.

The village watchman took up Lajo's story.

'Sister-in-law Malan,' he said trying to attract her attention.

'What is it, Jumma?' Her voice seemed to come out of the depths of a deep well.

'Bhabhi, this is not the sort of thing one can talk about easily. An awful thing happened in the village last night. My hair has gone grey with the years I've been watchman of the village, but never have I known such a scandal. Your daughter blackened her face with someone under the bo tree. Twice I passed within ten paces of them. There they were locked together, limb joined to limb; oblivious of all but each other. I kept guard over your house. I said to myself "The wedding is to take place in another four days; the house must be full of new dresses and ornaments and the door wide open!" I left at dawn. I don't know what time your daughter came back after whoring. If she were my child I would break every bone in her body.'

Malan gazed at the watchman, stunned.

Jumma was followed by Ratna, the zamindar. He was in a rage.

'Where is that slut?' he roared. 'Couldn't she find another field for whoring?' Ratna leapt about as he spoke. The neighbours came out of their homes to watch and listen. Ratna continued. 'I was on my way to the well when I saw her come out of the field with her face wrapped in the sequined dupatta. I thought that the girl had come out to ease herself; but then her lover emerged from the other end of the same field. I saw them with my own eyes.'

At that moment, Minnie tore her way through the crowd. She had heard all that had been said about her. 'You are lying, Uncle!' she shrieked.

'You dare call me a liar, you little trollop! You ill-starred wretch! And how did a broken red bangle happen to be in my field?' He untied the knot in his shawl, took out a piece of red bangle and slapped it on Minnie's palm. Minnie ran her eyes over her arms and counted the bangles; there were only eleven. The world swam before her eyes and then darkened.

The women exchanged glances. They had seen Minnie buy the bangles. Yes, there were ten and then two more. And she had specially asked for red ones.

The courtyard was full of babbling men and women. Minnie's fiancé's father edged his way through; his wife was behind him. They flung all the presents they had received in front of Malan: clothes, money and rings. The crowd gaped. Women touched their ears; young girls bit their fingernails. This was drama indeed. A broken engagement was a broken life. What would Minnie do, now that she would never find a husband? It served her right, shameless harlot!

Over the sound of their angry droning, there was a loud splash. For a moment the crowd was petrified. Then someone shouted, 'The well!' and understanding dawned.

Minnie was nowhere to be seen. Gentle Minnie who never raised her voice against anyone, who was as pure as the jasmine she wove into garlands. Minnie, who never tired of praying to her gods for the happiness of everyone she knew.

Suddenly sobered, people ran to the well. Only Malan sat where she was, numb with horror, unable to move. Her courtyard was empty— emptier than it ever had been, as empty as it always would be now.

89

IDGAH

PREMCHAND

Premchand (Dhanpat Rai Srivastav, 1880-1936) was one of India's
greatest writers. He wrote in Hindi and published over a dozen novels
and nearly 300 short stories.

A full thirty days after Ramadan comes Eid. How wonderful and beautiful
is the morning of Eid! The trees look greener, the fields more festive,
the sky has a lovely pink glow. Look at the sun! It comes up brighter
and more dazzling than before to wish the world a very happy Eid. The
village is agog with excitement. Everyone is up early to go to the Idgah
mosque. One finds a button missing from his shirt and is hurrying to his
neighbour's house for thread and needle. Another finds that the leather
of his shoes has become hard and is running to the oil-press for oil to
grease it. They are dumping fodder before their oxen because by the time
they get back from the Idgah it may be late afternoon. It is a good three
miles from the village. There will also be hundreds of people to greet and
chat with; they would certainly not be finished before midday.

The boys are more excited than the others. Some of them kept only
one fast—and that only till noon. Some didn't even do that. But no one
can deny them the joy of going to the Idgah. Fasting is for the grown-
ups and the aged. For the boys it is only the day of Eid. They have been
talking about it all the time. At long last the day has come. And now
they are impatient with people for not hurrying up. They have no concern
with things that have to be done. They are not bothered whether or not
there is enough milk and sugar for the vermicelli pudding. All they want
is to eat the pudding. They have no idea why Abbajan is out of breath,
running to the house of Chaudhry Karim Ali. They don't know that if
the chaudhry were to change his mind he could turn the festive day of
Eid into a day of mourning. Their pockets bulge with coins like the
stomach of the pot-bellied Kubera, the Hindu God of Wealth. They are
forever taking the treasure out of their pockets, counting and recounting
it before putting it back. Mahmood counts 'One, two, ten, twelve'—he
has twelve paise. Mohsin has 'One, two, three, eight, nine, fifteen' paise.
Out of this countless hoard they will buy countless things: toys, sweets,
paper-pipes, rubber balls—and much else.

The happiest of the boys is Hamid. He is only four, poorly dressed, thin and famished-looking. His father died last year of cholera. Then his mother wasted away and, without anyone finding out what had ailed her, she also died. Now Hamid sleeps in Granny Ameena's lap and is as happy as a lark. She tells him that his father has gone to earn money and will return with sack loads of silver. And that his mother has gone to Allah to get lovely gifts for him. This makes Hamid very happy. It is great to live on hope; for a child there is nothing like hope. A child's imagination can turn a mustard seed into a mountain. Hamid has no shoes on his feet; the cap on his head is soiled and tattered; its gold thread has turned black. Nevertheless Hamid is happy. He knows that when his father comes back with sacks full of silver and his mother with gifts from Allah he will be able to fulfil all his heart's desires. Then he will have more than Mahmood, Mohsin, Noorey and Sammi.

In her hovel the unfortunate Ameena sheds bitter tears. It is Eid and she does not have even a handful of grain. If only her Abid were there, it would have been a different kind of Eid!

Hamid goes to his grandmother and says, 'Granny, don't you fret over me! I will be the first to get back. Don't worry!'

Ameena is sad. Other boys are going out with their fathers. She is the only 'father' Hamid has. How can she let him go to the fair all by himself? What if he gets lost in the crowd? No, she must not lose her precious little soul! How can he walk three miles? He doesn't even have a pair of shoes. He will get blisters on his feet. If she went along with him she could pick him up now and then. But then who would be there to cook the vermicelli? If only she had the money she could have bought the ingredients on the way back and quickly made the pudding. In the village it would take her many hours to get everything. The only way out was to ask someone for them.

The villagers leave in one party. With the boys is Hamid. They run on ahead of the elders and wait for them under a tree. Why do the oldies drag their feet? And Hamid is like one with wings on his feet. How could anyone think he would get tired?

They reach the suburbs of the town. On both sides of the road are mansions of the rich, enclosed all around by thick, high walls. In the gardens mango and lichi trees are laden with fruit. A boy hurls a stone at a mango tree. The gardener rushes out screaming abuses at them. By then the boys are a furlong out of his reach and roaring with laughter. What a silly ass they make of the gardener!

Then come big buildings: the law courts, the college and the club. How many boys would there be in this big college? No, sir, they are not all boys! Some are grown-up men. They sport enormous moustaches.

What are such grown-up men going on studying for? How long will they go on doing so? What will they do with all their knowledge? There are only two or three grown-up boys in Hamid's school. Absolute duds they are too! They get a thrashing every day because they do not work at all. These college fellows must be the same type—why else should they be there! And the Masonic Lodge. They perform magic there. It is rumoured that they make human skulls move about and do other kinds of weird things. No wonder they don't let in outsiders! And the white folk play games in the evenings. Grown-up men, men with moustaches and beards playing games! And not only they, but even their memsahibs! That's the honest truth! You give my granny that something they call a racket; she wouldn't know how to hold it. And if she tried to wave it about she would collapse.

Mahmood says, 'My mother's hands would shake; I swear by Allah they would!'

Mohsin says, 'Mine can grind maunds of grain. Her hand would never shake holding a miserable racket. She draws hundreds of pitchers full of water from the well every day. My buffalo drinks up five pitchers. If a memsahib had to draw one pitcher, she would go blue in the face.'

Mahmood interrupts, 'But your mother couldn't run and leap about, could she?'

'That's right,' replies Mohsin, 'she couldn't leap or jump. But one day our cow got loose and began grazing in the chaudhry's fields. My mother ran so fast after it that I couldn't catch up with her. Honest to God, I could not!'

So they proceed to the stores of the sweetmeat vendors. All so gaily decorated! Who can eat all these delicacies? Just look! Every store has them piled up in mountainous heaps. They say that after nightfall jinns come and buy up everything. 'My abba says that at midnight there is a jinn at every stall. He has all that remains weighed and pays in real rupees, just the sort of rupees we have,' says Mohsin.

Hamid is not convinced. 'Where would the jinns come by rupees?'

'Jinns are never short of money,' replies Mohsin. 'They can get into any treasury they want. Mister, don't you know, no iron bars can stop them? They have all the diamonds and rubies they want. If they are pleased with someone they will give him baskets full of diamonds. They are here one moment and five minutes later they can be in Calcutta.'

Hamid asks again, 'Are these jinns very big?'

'Each one is as big as the sky,' asserts Mohsin. 'He has his feet on the ground, his head touches the sky. But if he so wanted, he could get into a tiny brass pot.'

'How do people make jinns happy?' asks Hamid. 'If anyone taught me the secret, I would make at least one jinn happy with me.'

'I do not know,' replies Mohsin, 'but the chaudhry sahib has a lot of jinns under his control. If anything is stolen, he can trace it and even tell you the name of the thief. Jinns tell him everything that is going on in the world.'

Hamid understands how chaudhry sahib has come by his wealth and why people hold him in so much respect.

It begins to get crowded. Parties heading for the Idgah are coming into town from different sides—each one dressed better than the other. Some in tongas and ekkas; some in motor cars. All wearing perfume; all bursting with excitement.

The small party of village rustics is not bothered about the poor show they make. They are a calm, contented lot.

For village children everything in the town is strange. Whatever catches their eye, they stand and gape at it with wonder. Cars hoot frantically to get them out of the way, but they couldn't care less. Hamid is nearly run over by a car.

At long last the Idgah comes in view. Above it are massive tamarind trees casting their shade on the cemented floor on which carpets have been spread. And there are row upon row of worshippers as far as the eye can see, spilling well beyond the mosque courtyard. Newcomers line themselves behind the others. Here neither wealth nor status matters because in the eyes of Islam all men are equal. Our villagers wash their hands and feet and make their own line behind the others. What a beautiful, heart-moving sight it is! What perfect coordination of movements! A hundred thousand heads bow together in prayer! And then all together they stand erect; bow down and sit on their knees! Many times they repeat these movements— exactly as if a hundred thousand electric bulbs were switched on and off at the same time again and again. What a wonderful spectacle it is!

The prayer is over. Men embrace each other. They descend on the sweet and toy vendors' stores like an army moving to an assault. In this matter the grown-up rustic is no less eager than the boys. Look, here is a swing! Pay a paisa and enjoy riding up to the heavens and then plummeting down to the earth. And here is the roundabout strung with wooden elephants, horses and camels! Pay one paisa and have twenty-five rounds of fun. Mahmood and Mohsin and Noorey and other boys mount the horses and camels.

Hamid watches them from a distance. All he has are three paise. He couldn't afford to part with a third of his treasure for a few miserable rounds.

They've finished with the roundabouts; now it is time for the toys. There is a row of stalls on one side with all kinds of toys: soldiers and milkmaids, kings and ministers, water-carriers and washerwomen and holy men. Splendid display! How lifelike! All they need are tongues to speak. Mahmood buys a policeman in khaki with a red turban on his head and a gun on his shoulder. Looks as if he is marching in a parade. Mohsin likes the water-carrier with his back bent under the weight of the water bag. He holds the handle of the bag in one hand and looks pleased with himself. Perhaps he is singing. It seems as if the water is about to pour out of the bag. Noorey has fallen for the lawyer. What an expression of learning he has on his face! A black gown over a long, white coat with a gold watch chain going into a pocket, a fat volume of some law book in his hand. He looks like he has just finished arguing a case in a court of law.

These toys cost two paise each. All Hamid has are three paise; how can he afford to buy such expensive toys? If they dropped out of his hand, they would be smashed to bits. If a drop of water fell on them, the paint would run. What would he do with toys like these? They'd be of no use to him.

Mohsin says, 'My water-carrier will sprinkle water every day, morning and evening.'

Mahmood says, 'My policeman will guard my house. If a thief comes near, he will shoot him with his gun.'

Noorey says, 'My lawyer will fight my cases.'

Sammi says, 'My washerwoman will wash my clothes every day.'

Hamid pooh-poohs their toys—they're made of clay—one fall and they'll break into pieces. But his eyes look at them hungrily and he wishes he could hold them in his hands for just a moment or two. His hands stretch without his wanting to stretch them. But young boys are not givers, particularly when it is something new. Poor Hamid doesn't get to touch the toys.

After the toys it is sweets. Someone buys sesame seed candy, others gulab jamuns or halwa. They smack their lips with relish. Only Hamid is left out. The luckless boy has at least three paise; why doesn't he also buy something to eat? He looks with hungry eyes at the others.

Mohsin says, 'Hamid, take this sesame candy, it smells good.'

Hamid suspects it is a cruel joke; he knows Mohsin doesn't have so big a heart. But despite knowing this Hamid goes to Mohsin. Mohsin takes a piece out of his leaf-wrap and holds it towards Hamid. Hamid stretches out his hand. Mohsin puts the candy in his own mouth. Mahmood, Noorey and Sammi clap their hands with glee and have a jolly good laugh. Hamid is crestfallen.

Mohsin says, 'This time I will let you have it. I swear by Allah! I will give it to you. Come and take it.'

Hamid replies, 'You keep your sweets. Don't I have money?'

'All you have are three paise,' says Sammi. 'What can you buy for three paise?'

Mahmood says, 'Mohsin is a rascal. Hamid, you come to me and I will give you gulab jamun.'

Hamid replies, 'What is there to rave about sweets? Books are full of bad things about eating sweets.'

'In your heart you must be saying, "If I could get it I would eat it,"' says Mohsin. 'Why don't you take the money out of your pocket?'

'I know what this clever fellow is up to,' says Mahmood. 'When we've spent all our money, he will buy sweets and tease us.'

After the sweet vendors there are a few hardware stores and shops of real and artificial jewellery. There is nothing there to attract the boys' attention. So they go ahead, all of them except Hamid who stops to see a pile of tongs. It occurs to him that his granny does not have a pair of tongs. Each time she bakes chapatis, the iron plate burns her hands. If he were to buy her a pair of tongs she would be very pleased. She would never burn her fingers; it would be a useful thing to have in the house. What use are toys? They are a waste of money. You can have some fun with them but only for a very short time. Then you forget all about them.

Hamid's friends have gone ahead. They are at a stall drinking sherbet. How selfish they are! They bought so many sweets but did not give him one. And then they want him to play with them; they want him to do odd jobs for them. Now if any of them asked him to do something, he would tell them, 'Go suck your lollipop, it will burn your mouth; it will give you a rash of pimples and boils; your tongue will always crave for sweets; you will have to steal money to buy them and get a thrashing in the bargain. It's all written in books. Nothing will happen to my tongs. No sooner my granny sees my pair of tongs she will run up to take it from me and say, "My child has brought me a pair of tongs," and shower me with a thousand blessings. She will show it off to the neighbour womenfolk. Soon the whole village will be saying, "Hamid has brought his granny a pair of tongs, how nice he is!" No one will bless the other boys for the toys they have got for themselves. Blessings of elders are heard in the court of Allah and are immediately acted on. Because I have no money, Mohsin and Mahmood adopt such airs towards me. I will teach them a lesson. Let them play with their toys and eat all the sweets they can. I will not play with toys. I will not stand any nonsense from anyone. And one day my father will return. And also my mother. Then I will ask these chaps, "Do you want any toys? How many?" I will give each one a basket full of toys and teach them how to treat friends. I am not the sort who buys a paisa worth of lollipops to tease others by sucking them myself. I know they will laugh and say Hamid has brought a pair of tongs. They can go to the Devil!'

Hamid asks the shopkeeper, 'How much for this pair of tongs?'

The shopkeeper looks at him and seeing no older person with him replies, 'It's not for you.'

'Is it for sale or not?'

'Why should it not be for sale? Why else should I have bothered to bring it here?'

'Then why don't you tell me how much it is!'

'It will cost you six paise.'

Hamid's heart sinks. 'Let me have the correct price.'

'All right, it will be five paise, bottom price. Take it or leave it.' Hamid steels his heart and says, 'Will you give it to me for three?' And proceeds to walk away lest the shopkeeper scream at him. But the shopkeeper does not scream. On the contrary, he calls Hamid back and gives him the pair of tongs. Hamid carries it on his shoulder as if it were a gun and struts up proudly to show it to his friends. Let us hear what they have to say.

Mohsin laughs and says, 'Are you crazy? What will you do with the tongs?' Hamid flings the tongs on the ground and replies, 'Try and throw your water-carrier on the ground. Every bone in his body will break.'

Mahmood says, 'Are these tongs some kind of toy?'

'Why not?' retorts Hamid. 'Place them across your shoulders and it is a gun; wield them in your hands and it is like the tongs carried by singing mendicants—they can make the same clanging as a pair of cymbals. One smack and they will reduce all your toys to dust. And much as your toys may try they could not bend a hair on the head of my tongs. My tongs are like a brave tiger.'

Sammi who had bought a small tambourine asks, 'Will you exchange them for my tambourine? It is worth eight paise.'

Hamid pretends not to look at the tambourine. 'My tongs, if they wanted to, could tear out the bowels of your tambourine. All it has is a leather skin and all it can say is *dhub, dhub*. A drop of water could silence it forever. My brave pair of tongs can weather water and storms without budging an inch.'

The pair of tongs wins everyone over to its side. But now no one has any money left and the fairground has been left far behind. It is well past 9 a.m. and the sun is getting hotter every minute. Everyone is in a hurry to get home. Even if they talked their fathers into it, they could not get the tongs. This Hamid is a bit of a rascal. He saved up his money for the tongs.

The boys divide into two factions. Mohsin, Mahmood, Sammi and Noorey on the one side, and Hamid by himself on the other. They are engaged in hot argument. Sammi has defected to the other side. But Mohsin, Mahmood and Noorey, though they are a year or two older than Hamid, are reluctant to take him on in debate. Right is on Hamid's side. Also it's moral force on the one side, clay on the other. Hamid has iron, now calling itself steel, unconquerable and lethal. If a tiger were to spring on them, the water-carrier would be out of his wits; Mister Constable would drop his clay gun and take to his heels; the lawyer would hide his face in his gown, lie down on the ground and wail as if his mother's mother had died. But the tongs, the pair of tongs, Champion of India, would leap and grab the tiger by its neck and gouge out its eyes.

Mohsin puts all he has in his plea, 'But they cannot go and fetch water, can they?'

Hamid raises the tongs and replies, 'One angry word of command from my tongs and your water-carrier will hasten to fetch the water and sprinkle it at any doorstep he is ordered to.'

Mohsin has no answer. Mahmood comes to his rescue. 'If we are caught, we are caught. We will have to do the rounds of the law courts in chains. Then we will be at the lawyer's feet asking for help.'

Hamid has no answer to this powerful argument. He asks, 'Who will come to arrest us?'

Noorey puffs out his chest and replies, 'This policeman with the gun.'

Hamid makes a face and says with scorn, 'This wretch come to arrest the Champion of India! Okay, let's have it out over a bout of wrestling, Far from catching them, he will be scared to look my tongs in the face.'

Mohsin thinks of another ploy. 'Your tongs' face will burn in the fire every day.' He is sure that this will leave Hamid speechless. That is not so. Pat comes Hamid with the retort, 'Mister, it is only the brave who can jump into a fire. Your miserable lawyers, policemen, and water-carriers will run like frightened women into their homes. Only this Champion of India can perform this feat of leaping into the fire.'

Mahmood has one more try, 'The lawyer will have chairs to sit on and tables for his things. Your tongs will only have the kitchen floor to lie on.'

Hamid cannot think of an appropriate retort so he says whatever comes into his mind, 'The tongs won't stay in the kitchen. When your lawyer sits on his chair my tongs will knock him down on the ground.'

It does not make sense but our three heroes are utterly squashed—

almost as if a champion kite had been brought down from the heavens to the earth by a cheap, miserable paper imitation. Thus Hamid wins the field. His tongs are the Champion of India. Neither Mohsin nor Mahmood, neither Noorey nor Sammi—nor anyone else can dispute the fact.

The respect that a victor commands from the vanquished is paid to Hamid. The others have spent between twelve to sixteen paise each and bought nothing worthwhile. Hamid's three-paise worth has carried the day. And no one can deny that toys are unreliable things: they break, while Hamid's tongs will remain as they are for years.

The boys begin to make terms of peace. Mohsin says, 'Give me your tongs for a while, you can have my water-carrier for the same time.'

Both Mahmood and Noorey similarly offer their toys. Hamid has no hesitation in agreeing to these terms. The tongs pass from one hand to another; and the toys are in turn handed to Hamid. How lovely they are!

Hamid tries to wipe the tears of his defeated adversaries. 'I was simply pulling your leg, honestly I was. How can these tongs made of iron compare with your toys?' It seems that one or the other will call Hamid's bluff. But Mohsin's party are not solaced. The tongs have won the day and no amount of water can wash away their stamp of authority. Mohsin says, 'No one will bless us for these toys.'

Mahmood adds, 'You talk of blessings! We may get a thrashing instead. My amma is bound to say, "Are these earthen toys all that you could find at the fair?"'

Hamid has to concede that no mother will be as pleased with the toys as his granny will be when she sees the tongs. All he had was three paise and he has no reason to regret the way he has spent them. And now his tongs are the Champion of India and King of Toys.

By eleven the village was again agog with excitement. All those who had gone to the fair were back at home. Mohsin's little sister ran up, wrenched the water-carrier out of his hands and began to dance with joy. Mister Water-carrier slipped out of her hand, fell on the ground and went to paradise. The brother and sister began to fight; and both had lots to cry about. Their mother lost her temper because of the racket they were making and gave each two resounding slaps.

Noorey's lawyer met an end befitting his grand status. A lawyer could not sit on the ground. He had to keep his dignity in mind. Two nails were driven into the wall, a plank put on them and a carpet of paper spread on the plank. The honourable counsel was seated like a king on his throne. Noorey began to wave a fan over him. He knew that in the law courts there were khus curtains and electric fans. So the least he could do was to provide a hand fan, otherwise the hot legal arguments might affect his lawyer's brains. Noorey was waving his fan made of bamboo leaf. We do not know whether it was the breeze or the fan or something else that brought the honourable counsel down from his high pedestal to the depths of hell and reduced his gown to mingle with the dust of which it was made. There was much beating of breasts and the lawyer's bier was dumped on a dung heap.

Mahmood's policeman remained. He was immediately put on duty to guard the village. But this police constable was no ordinary mortal who could walk on his own two feet. He had to be provided a palanquin. This was a basket lined with tatters of discarded clothes of red colour for the policeman to recline on in comfort. Mahmood picked up the basket and started on his rounds. His two younger brothers followed him lisping, 'Shleepers, keep awake!' But night has to be dark; Mahmood stumbled, the basket slipped out of his hand. Mr Constable, with his gun, crashed to the ground. He was short of one leg.

Mahmood, being a bit of a doctor, knew of an ointment which could quickly re-join broken limbs. All it needed was the milk of a banyan sapling. The milk was brought and the broken leg reassembled.

But no sooner was the constable put on his feet than the leg gave way. One leg was of no use because now he could neither walk nor sit. Mahmood became a surgeon and cut the other leg to the size of the broken one so the chap could at least sit in comfort.

The constable was made into a holy man; he could sit in one place and guard the village. And sometimes he was like the image of the deity. The plume on his turban was scraped off and you could make as many changes in his appearance as you liked. And sometimes he was used for nothing better than weighing things down.

Now let's hear what happened to our friend Hamid. As soon as she heard his voice, Granny Ameena ran out of the house, picked him up and kissed him. Suddenly she noticed the tongs in his hand. 'Where did you find these tongs?'

'I bought them.'

'How much did you pay for them?'

'Three paise.'

Granny Ameena beat her breast. 'You are a stupid child! It is almost noon and you haven't had anything to eat or drink. And what do you buy—tongs! Couldn't you find anything better in the fair than this pair of iron tongs?'

Hamid replied in injured tones, 'You burn your fingers on the iron plate. That is why I bought them.'

The old woman's temper suddenly changed to love—not the kind of calculated love, which wastes away in spoken words. This love was mute, solid and steeped with tenderness. What a selfless child! What concern for others! What a big heart! How he must have suffered seeing other boys buying toys and gobbling sweets! How was he able to suppress his own feelings! Even at the fair he thought of his old grandmother. Granny Ameena's heart was too full for words.

And the strangest thing happened—stranger than the part played by the tongs was the role of Hamid the child playing Hamid the old man. And old Granny Ameena became Ameena the little girl. She broke down. She spread her apron and beseeched Allah's blessings for her grandchild. Big tears fell from her eyes. How was Hamid to understand what was going on inside her!

90

I TAKE THIS WOMAN

RAJINDER SINGH BEDI

Rajinder Singh Bedi (1915-1984) won the Sahitya Akademi Award for this novel in 1965. It was later made into a film.

The sun was a deeper red; the heavens were a darker crimson as if spattered with the blood of innocents: the stream of blood ran from the sky down into Tiloka's courtyard, tinting the green of the bakain with hues of purple. Beside the tumbledown mud wall where garbage was thrown sat Dabboo. He raised his head to the heavens and set up a piteous howl.

That afternoon the sweepers of the Rural District Council had come and strewn pellets of poisoned meat in the lanes. At the time Dabboo was asleep in the cool fragrance of the sand beneath the pitcher rack. The clay-scented shade had saved Dabboo from the fate which befell many of his kin—particularly his favourite, Bori. After many hours of peaceful slumber, he had risen, stretched his limbs and yawned. By that time Bori's eyes had turned to marbles. Dabboo scampered out of the courtyard and found her carcass, as stiff as a log. He sniffed at her posterior and quietly turned back homewards.

Tiloka's wife, Rano, and her neighbour, Channo, watched Dabboo come and go. Channo put a finger on the gold pin in her nose and sighed. 'Disgusting, isn't it!' she exclaimed. 'The males of the species are the same; they deserve to be strung up by the same rope.'

Rano's eyelids quivered like washing fluttering on a line. She brushed away her tears with the back of her hand and smiled, 'Channo, I hope your Dabboo is not like this one.' She was overcome with her audacity. Channo replied with a masculine oath, ran back into her house and busied herself with her household chores. By the time she had finished her work she had all but forgotten the tragic scene of the afternoon. But when she came out to throw the refuse on the garbage heap, Dabboo was there to remind her of his fate. Channo picked up her broom and shooed away the wailing Dabboo. 'Begone, you miserable dog! Why do you howl in my courtyard? If you have to wail, go and wail in the chaudhry's courtyard across the lane. The mob is there—and the money as well.'

Rano hated Chaudhry Meharban Das. She hated him because it was Meharban Das who had initiated her husband into his evil ways. Village women are like that: they will overlook every fault of their husbands by pinning them on other men. When Rano heard about Tiloka's doings from anyone, although she would be all burnt up inside, she would keep a straight face and say nothing. But when Tiloka returned home she would give him a proper tongue-lashing. She would claw his face. She would bite him. She would keep going at him till he beat her. Then she would become quiet and say with philosophical resignation: 'Just as well he spills his passion elsewhere; otherwise I would have to cope with all of it.'

It was only from gossip in the village that Rano came to know of the 'manly' qualities of her husband. It created a perverse desire in her to claim his affections exclusively for herself. She went to the holy man who had set himself up beneath the leafless peepal tree. He was said to have undergone arduous penance and thus gathered great merit. It was said that he wore a steel bracket about his loins and never deigned to look at women. This was all the more creditable as he was surrounded by hordes of women at all hours of the day and night. Some came to ask for sons; others for medicine for protection against miscarriage. Most came for charms to keep their husbands in their power.

Everyone talked of the case of Puran Dei, the Brahmin's wife. The charm that the holy one gave her not only filled her womb but also made her husband, Gian Chand, dote on her like one possessed. Rano had got some powder from the holy one. She was only awaiting the chance to administer it to Tiloka when he asked for milk. She looked forward to the night when he had taken the milk with the magic powder and his passions were roused. Then she would not let him touch her—or only after he begged her for the favour by touching her feet and rubbing his nose in the dust. But many weeks had passed without Tiloka asking for milk. Instead, he quenched his thirst with the bottle of orange liquor he got from Chaudhry Meharban Das.

Rano could forgive most things, but not drink. To her the bottle of liquor was like a second wife in the house. The stench of alcohol! Holy Mother, it made her sick to think of it! And once drunk, the devil took possession of you, body and soul. It was absolute damnation.

During the day Tiloka plied his tonga. So did many others like Nawab, Ismail and Gurdas. But in the evening it would only be Tiloka at the Naseebanwala tonga stand looking for a female passenger for Chaudhry Meharban Das's 'rest house', with its promise of dainty dishes consumed in a cosy bed. To be sure, Tiloka took all this trouble for Chaudhry Meharban Das. But everyone blamed him. And all he got for his pains was half a chop of meat and a bottle of distilled orange liquor.

Kotla was a place of pilgrimage. On one side of the chaudhry's courtyard was the shrine of the Goddess. It was said that she had rested there for a breather while fleeing from her lusty Bhairon; she had then gone on to find shelter in the hills of Sialkot and Jammu. If one looked up to the northwest one could still see a camel-hump formation peak named after the Goddess—Vaishno Devi.

The passenger that Tiloka brought to the chaudhry that evening was barely thirteen years old. When Bhairon had lusted after Vaishno Devi she had decapitated him with her trident. The poor thirteen-year-old innocent had only a pair of hands as soft as rose petals to defend herself against the chaudhry's amours. She put them together to pray to be left alone, but that was of little avail. Her skin was as soft as that of a watermelon—and as easy to pierce with the knife of lust that Meharban Das used. No wonder then the sun had turned a fiery red! And no wonder that the God Surya had, in his rage, whipped his horses to a mad gallop, driven his chariot across the village well and disappeared behind the cotton fields! He had left his angry glow in the heavens. The pale moon barely two days old shimmered in a paler sky.

Next door to the temple was the contractor's house. He was having repairs done to his roof. The red of the bricks could not be seen, but the lime plaster showed like grinning teeth. The breeze whistled through the casuarina, jamun and neem trees that lined the watercourse. Beside the pond, the stunted peepal which had sheltered Baba Hari Das clapped its few leaves as if beating time to music. Tiloka was driving through the bazaar of the village, past its only flour and grain shop, when he chanced to see a lone woman. It was the Arain woman, Jehlum, buying wheat. Tiloka shouted to her: 'What about it, Jehlum, old girl?'

It is a well-known saying that a poor man's wife is everyone's sister-in-law. Jehlum was used to villagers making passes at her. She did not bother to look round. She continued filling her sack as she replied, 'If your mother's willing, why not go to her?'

Tiloka laughed and continued on his way.

Tiloka's twin sons were playing ludo on a charcoal-drawn pattern under the neem tree. One boy scored a kill; the other objected. They began to fight. The boys cursed in the language used by their elders, and pulled each other's hair. As soon as they heard their father's footsteps, they separated, grabbed their primers, and quickly sat down beside the old lamp. Tiloka called to them. The elder of the two replied by reciting loudly from his book: 'Look, the owl hoots in yonder tree.' Tiloka knew his sons. 'You bastards! Don't try these tricks on me!' he yelled. The younger one took up the recitation: 'We should never use bad language.' Tiloka realized the import of the words of wisdom and held his tongue.

Besides the twins, Bantey and Santey, there were two more. Their older child, the first-born, the parents had, for the sake of simplicity and posterity, named Waddi, the elder. She lent her mother a helping hand in the home; and when the chores were done, she looked after the youngest, the one-year-old, Chummoo.

My brother's come back from play, he's hungry
I'll roll and bake him a maund to eat.

Even when she played pat-ball with other girls of the neighbourhood, Waddi's songs were about her little brother:

We've come on to our rooftop
I've a brother tall as a bamboo
My brother's wife is slender as the cypress
My brother's wife wears gold in her nose.

In this way Waddi brought people and objects familiar to her into her verses: sugar cane, her little brother, her sister-in-law and her nose ring, the leafless peepal tree, her husband's elder brother (her horizon had expanded to her future husband's elder brother—but she had only a vague and hazy notion of who or what he or it might be).

There was another member of the household who was rapidly catching on to the facts of life. This was Tiloka's younger brother, Mangal. Mangal was an incorrigible idler, a good-for-nothing drone, quarrelling and getting into brawls, forever adjusting his tehmad round his waist. And Rano, who really liked him, always feigned ill-temper when she chided him: 'Patience, you big oaf! Who do you think I've cooked all this stuff for but you?'

Mangal was barely six years old when Tiloka had 'acquired' Rano. Rano's parents were destitute (perhaps that is why they had named their daughter dressed in tatters Rani or Rano). As Rano grew to womanhood her needs became a problem. So they sold her to Tiloka and simply disappeared from their village. This caused Rano great distress. However poor the parents' home, it is something every girl cherishes. For Rano, the past had simply ceased to exist. There come moments in a woman's married life when she seeks the security of her parental home…and if she has no home to go back to she feels she has nothing to look forward to either.

When Rano joined Tiloka's household and came to Kotla, she found new parents and a brother: her mother-in-law, Jindan, became a new mother, and her father-in-law, Hazoor Singh, a new father. But her husband's youngest brother, Mangal, was a mere baby. Once when she was giving the breast to Waddi and Mangal had wanted to feed, Rano had raised her shirt and offered him her other breast. The boy had run away....but Rano thereafter had looked upon Mangal as if he was her own son.

Mangal also looked upon Rano both as his brother's wife and as his mother. Why else would he address his real mother as 'Aunty'? And Rano treated him as she treated her other children. She boxed his ears when he was stubborn and slapped his face when he was errant. But as the years went by things began to change. Rano had other children to look after; Mangal took on the airs of an adolescent; Tiloka took to the bottle; old Jindan became the traditional nagging mother-in-law. The real cause of the trouble was their poverty. As Tiloka began to stay at home two to three days of the week, they had less money coming in. Then old Hazoor Singh got cataracts in his eyes. He would sit on his charpai trying to see with his ears and hear with his frosted eyes. His eyelids fluttered like those of the pigeons bathing in the village pond.

One evening, Tiloka took a tomato from the pocket of his long shirt and ordered his wife: 'Here, Rano, slice it up with an onion.'

Rano was busy cooking vegetables. She put the ladle on the pot and stood up. 'You've brought your other wife into the house?' she demanded.

Tiloka faltered in his speech. 'I don't do it very often, do I, Rano?'

'Often or not, I am not going to let you drink here,' replied Rano tartly. 'Where is the bottle? I'd like to see what she has that I don't.'

Tiloka did not want a scene. But Rano was obviously spoiling for a fight. He ground his teeth and hissed as angrily as he could, hoping in vain to silence her: 'Bitch! Whore! I try to hold my horses but you go full gallop with your foul tongue.'

'Sure!' spat out Rano. 'I suppose no one else but you is entitled to give rein to the tongue! I am going to settle this business once and for all. Either I stay in this house or your bottle does.'

Rano ran inside to look for the 'second wife'. Tiloka ran after her. He caught Rano by her hair and flung her to the ground. The oil lamp flickered...it almost went out but came up again...the starlings in the neem tree flew away in alarm... Dabboo stood up and, being unable to comprehend the goings on, began to bark... Waddi cried out in alarm, 'Bapu!' The little ones were terrified and tried to hide themselves in the dark: one ran out of the house, the other shook with fright and began to wail—not 'Ma...Ma..' but just 'Aaa...aa...'. Hazoor Singh stumbled from his charpai and pleaded as he swore, 'Oi, you son of fornication! Oi, you evil, shameless, mannerless brute!' He stumbled and fell on to the oven, scorching himself on the embers.

Rano put up a good fight. She dug her teeth into Tiloka's hands. This enraged Tiloka all the more and he hammered Rano's head against the wall. And he used language that he had never used even to an animal. 'Help! Murder!' screamed Waddi. 'He's killing my mother!' By the time her grandmother came in, Waddi had wet her salwar. Granny saw the fight and exclaimed: 'I knew things would come to a head one day; one day this moon of evil would shine in our courtyard. What did we do to have this vagrant seed take root in our home?'

'Why do you stick your nose in this affair?' snapped Mangal at his mother. He did not think it was right to interfere in a quarrel between husband and wife and was doing his utmost to keep out of the brawl.

'Why shouldn't I stick my nose in wherever I like?' shrieked the old woman. 'He earns, he drinks. He does not go begging at the door of that pimp who's gone to hell himself and left this sluttish daughter with us!'

His mother's words made Tiloka more violent. He tore off Rano's clothes till she had nothing left on her. And he yelled as loud as he could, 'Get out! Get out of my house at once!'

Rano was out of breath. She started to moan, 'I won't live here. I'll leave.'

A line of faces appeared over the mud wall. A crowd collected on the neighbouring rooftops. 'He's killed her! The devil, he's murdered her! Hai, this ogre!' they cried from all sides. But not one had the courage to come down and help Rano. Jehlum Arain heard the racket and came across the roof. With her were her daughters, the Brahmin woman, Puran Dei, Nawab's wife Ayesha, Channo and Sarupa. They all came up, but only Channo dared to cry for help: 'Help! Someone separate them!'

'Keep out of this!' shouted Rano from where she lay, hardly able to breathe. 'Go away! Haven't you ever had a thrashing? Let what is destined be fulfilled. Today the Devi is going to have her great offering. I am to be sacrificed by this man. I'll go to heaven. My children will wail for me today,' cried Rano, trying to send away the women, and beckoning them at the same time.

Mangal had been restraining himself for all he was worth. Suddenly it became too much for him. He yelled full-mouthed abuse at his mother and sprang at his brother. He grabbed his brother's hand as it was raised to strike. 'Let me see you bring this hand down!' he roared. 'I'll show you the dung you are made of...you who show off your strength on a weak woman! Try and move your hand if you are the son of your father! You just try!'

Tiloka did his best to wrench his arm free from Mangal's iron grip. It was of no avail. He turned to abuse him. He saw the murderous look in his younger brother's eyes and thought better of it. Mangal took full advantage of his triumph. He kicked the bottle of liquor. It crashed to the floor and the liquor spilled on to the courtyard. The women drew their veils across their nostrils to save themselves from the stench. Mangal let go his brother's hand after he had thoroughly humiliated him. Tiloka went indoors, mumbling angrily to himself. His foul words had lost their sting; they seemed to roll off his tongue like a passage from a book.

Rano also went indoors and began to pack her things in her little steel trunk. She was going away. Where could she go to? 'O God, do not even burden an enemy with the curse of a daughter! She is hardly grown up when her parents throw her out to live among strangers; and if the parents-in-law don't like her, they kick her back to her parents' home. She's like a ball made of cast-off rags. Only when she becomes heavy with her own tears is she incapable of being bounced to and fro.'

Rano did not have much to pack. In a few moments all her belongings were in the steel trunk. She came out of the room carrying her load. She resumed her wailing louder than before. It was meant to bring tears to the eyes of the other women. 'Here, keep your home; may it ever be prosperous! I was the only unwanted outsider...I will relieve you of my burden.' She turned towards the room into which Tiloka had gone. 'Get yourself another woman who'll be your slave...who will love to have her bones broken...' Her eyes fell on her children: in her rage and sorrow she had forgotten their existence. 'Children!' she exclaimed, 'I'll say I never had; I'll say they died at birth.'

Waddi caught the hem of her mother's dupatta and cried, 'Ma!'

Rano snatched her dupatta from her daughter's grip. 'Get away with you, you accursed one! When your time comes, you too will have to put up with this kind of treatment!'

Rano strode out into the great, big, limitless world. It was pitch-dark. She could see nothing but the stars in the sky. Each of these stars was as large as her world, some even larger. And there they were, twinkling before her eyes. A small cloud floated across and cut the crescent moon in two...

Mangal followed Rano. He took her by the arm and asked, 'Sister-in-law, where are you going?' Then Mangal turned to his mother and pleaded, 'Aunty, why don't you stop her?'

Jindan brushed her hands against the hem of her shirt and exclaimed, 'Where can the wretch go? She has nothing to fall back on; no one to go to.'

Hazoor Singh shouted from where he was, 'Daughter....Rano...' and then began to walk towards her. When he got closer, he raised his shirt and showed her the burns on his back. 'Daughter, see what I have suffered.'

Rano broke down. She covered her face with her dupatta; she could utter only one word, 'Bapu!' By then Tiloka's temper had cooled. He stood like an unwanted orphan in a corner of his courtyard. His threats lacked conviction. 'Go! Let me see where you can go.'

'I'll go where I like! What's that to you?' retorted Rano, wailing louder. 'I'll take a job somewhere; I'll earn enough to fill my belly. I am not going to be a burden on anyone for the sake of a couple of chapatis. If there is no other place for me in the village, I will go to the temple.'

'The temple!' roared Tiloka, somewhat startled. He stepped before her, snatched the trunk out of Rano's hand and said, 'Follow me... Then you go to hell!'

To go forward into the wide world or go back?

Rano's self-esteem required some more protestation. And protest she did. But her recriminations, like her husband's abuse, had lost their punch. All she wanted was an excuse to save face as well as be able to come back. And what was the point of leaving? The bottle of liquor had been smashed.

A PASSION
FOR
POETRY

Khushwant Singh began translating Urdu, Hindi and Punjabi poetry from the earliest days of his writing career, and his novels and non-fiction are liberally sprinkled with his translations. In the following pages, the reader will find a sampling of his translations of the poems of Kabir (1440-1518), Ghalib (1797-1869), Akbar Illahabadi (1846-1921) and the contemporary Pakistani poet, Feza Azmi, that appeared in his newspaper columns.

℗℘

91

TRANSLATING URDU POETRY

In my humble opinion, the best translations of Urdu poetry into English were done by Victor Kiernan of the works of Faiz Ahmed Faiz. It was a joint effort. Kiernan was teaching English at Lahore's Chiefs College. Faiz was teaching English in an Indian college. Kiernan had an Indian wife and was fluent in Hindustani. They became friends and together worked on the translations. They are a joy to read.

In my not-so-humble opinion my translations come next in merit. I have done a better job than any other Indian, Pakistani or foreign scholar in giving Urdu poetry good readability. My method is to first memorize the original and keep repeating it in my mind. I do this many times in bed as I retire for the night. The translation emerges bit by bit as I doze off. My translations have been well received. My rendering of Iqbal's 'Shikwa' and 'Jawab-i-Shikwa' published by the Oxford University Press has gone into more than fourteen editions. It goes on selling. So do my compilations made jointly with Kamna Prasad, but translated entirely by me: *Celebrating the Best of Urdu Poetry* (Penguin). I will quote one of the poems I have most enjoyed translating. It is by Meer Taqi Meer (1723-1810), a great favourite among fans of Urdu poetry. Though born in a village close to Agra, he spent most of his life in Delhi. This is his well-known eulogy to drunkenness.

Main nashey main hoon
Yaaro mujhey muaaf rakho main nashey main hoon
Ab do to jam khaali hee do main nashey mein hoon

401

Masti sey barhamee hai meree guftagoo key beech
Jo chaaho tum bhee mujh ko kaho main nashey mein hoon
Maazur hoon, jo paaon mera betarah padey
Tum sargiraan to mujh sey naa ho main nashey mein hoon
Bhaagee namaaz-e-jumma to jaatee nahee hain kuchh
Chalta hoon main bhee, tum to raho main nashey mein hoon
Naazuk mizaaj aap qayaamat hain Meer jee
Joon sheesha merey munh na lago main nashey mein hoon

I am somewhat drunk
Friends, you should forgive me, for I am somewhat drunk
And, if you must, give me an empty cup, for I am somewhat drunk
This is intoxication you hear, not malice in my talk
You too may curse and call me names, for I am somewhat drunk
You can see that I am helpless, when I try to walk I stumble
Don't be cross with me, please don't grumble, for I am somewhat drunk
The Friday prayer is always there; it won't run away
I will come along too if you stay a while, for I am somewhat drunk.
Meer can be touchy as hell, he's made of fragile glass
Watch what you say to him tonight, for he is somewhat drunk.

If you want to know what the greatest figure in Urdu literature, Mirza Asadullah Khan Ghalib (1797-1869), looked like and how he lived in the Delhi of his times, you will not find it in his poetry, which is often difficult to comprehend. You will, however, find it in the letters he wrote to his friends and admirers. An inveterate letter-writer, he wrote four to five letters a day and even posted them himself. Most of his correspondents were aspiring poets who sent him their compositions to correct; he did so with great care. In his replies, he invariably put in a couplet or two of his own and gave a detailed account of how he was faring.

Asadullah Khan was a handsome man—tall, light-skinned and with an imperious martial bearing. His forefathers, Seljuk Turks, were professional soldiers. Asad was a man of peace and, even as a boy, liked to study Arabic, Persian and Urdu. He was convinced that he was not going to be a soldier but a poet. He took on the pseudonym Ghalib. He was married off in his teens. His wife bore him seven sons and daughters, all of whom died in their infancy. He moved to Delhi to gain access to Mughal King Bahadur Shah Zafar, a poet of substance, and the nobility which patronized poets. His wife proved to be a poor companion. For companionship and pleasure, Ghalib sought the company of dancing girls and prostitutes. He never earned enough to maintain his household in comfort and was always in debt to moneylenders.

When the Sepoy Mutiny broke out in 1857, Ghalib had no sympathy with the mutineers and stopped calling on King Bahadur Shah Zafar, who had become a puppet in their hands. During the months the fighting lasted, he did not go out of his house. Evidently, families of Muslim hakims, who lived in Ballimaran, which was where Ghalib had his residence, also did not support the mutineers. Consequently, when the British and their Indian allies re-occupied Delhi, they drove out Muslims whom they suspected of supporting the mutineers but allowed Ballimaran Muslims to stay on. Raja Mohinder Singh of Patiala put his troops at both ends of the bazaar to ensure their safety.

Ghalib mentions his daily routine in many letters to his friends and patrons. He was not an early riser because his nights were disturbed by the malfunctioning of his bladder; he had to get up to urinate every hour. He had a frugal breakfast of peeled almonds and syrups; mutton broth at midday; and four kababs and an ounce of wine mixed with rose water made up his dinner. During the mango season, he consumed up to twelve mangoes in one sitting every afternoon. His bowels were often out of order and boils would erupt all over his body. He was full of remorse: 'I am old, idiotic, sinful, sensual, profligate and withal, a man lost to shame.' He describes himself as 'sattra-bahattra'. Before he was seventy, he started losing his memory, vision and hearing.

Ghalib did not take religious injunctions too seriously. He had his own version of Roza during Ramadan. He wrote: 'I observe fasts, but keep my fasts well-humoured with occasional sips of water, and a few puffs of the hookah. Now and then I eat a few morsels of bread also. People here have a strange sense of things and a strange disposition. I am just whiling away the fast, but they accuse me of non-observance of this holy ritual. They should understand that skipping the fasts is one thing, and whiling them away is quite another.'

He never spared himself from self-criticism. 'I have learnt to enjoy even my griefs and insults. I imagine myself as a different entity, separate from myself. When a fresh misfortune befalls me, I say, "Well-served. Ghalib receives another slap in his face. How proud he was. How he used to brag that he was a great poet and a Persian scholar, without a peer far and near. Well, deal with the moneylenders now.

"But how can this shameless fellow speak? He borrowed money left and right—wine from the cellar, flowers from the florist, clothes from the draper, mangoes from the fruit seller, and money from the creditors. He should have realized that he had no means to repay the debts."'

He had occasional outbursts of temper. When his publisher inserted some other poets' lines in his collection, he exploded: 'I do not know the b.....d who has inserted into my diwan the verses that you have sent me. May this scoundrel, his father, his grandfather, and his great-grandfather, right back to his seven adulterous generations, be damned.'

Ghalib also knew his worth. When somebody asked him for his postal address, he cut him down to size: 'Asadullah Ghalib, Delhi, will be enough.' So it was. And is today. Delhi is known as the city where Ghalib lived and died.

93

FAIZ AHMED FAIZ

Faiz Ahmed Faiz (1911-1984) was a few years senior to me in Government College, Lahore, but I did not get to know him as I was not admitted to the select coterie of Urdu savants at the time. It was during 1939-1945, when he was a lieutenant colonel in the British Indian Army, that I was able to persuade him to come to my home.

He was a kindly, soft-spoken man and a heavy drinker. I have not known another man drink from sunrise to sunset without showing the slightest sign of drunkenness. After Partition, I saw a lot more of him when I visited Rawalpindi. When he happened to be in Delhi I managed to get him to spend an evening in my home. By then, I had read quite a bit of his poetry in the original and the excellent translations by Victor Kiernan.

He had been put in prison many times for his trenchant criticism of dictatorial regimes and wrote some of his most moving poetry in prison. He had ardent admirers who included his jailers and their wives. I have no doubt they took good care of him. Another enigma about him was while he lived in princely comfort himself, most of his poetry was devoted to highlighting the abysmal poverty of the downtrodden masses exhorting them to revolt and claim their God-given right to a better life. A line of doggerel about him went somewhat like this: 'Faiz ik baraa shair hai, chaman mein reh kar maarey veeraney kee gaand.' (Faiz is a great poet, he lives in a garden and buggers the wild wastes.) As in the case of many other great poets, so too in Faiz's, it was after his verses were put to music and sung that they gained popularity. My friend, the late Kingsley Martin, editor of the *New Statesman and Nation*, told me that once when he was visiting Lahore, Faiz took him to the prostitutes' quarters, Heera Mandi. There the girls sang Faiz's ghazals and instead of asking for money loaded Faiz with gifts as they chucked him under his chin. The most famous lines of Faiz which appear first in all his compositions run as follows:

Raat yoon dil mein teyree khoee huee yaad aayee
Jaisey veeraaney mein chupkey say bahaar aa jaaye;
Jaisey sehraaon mein hauley sey chaley baad-e-naseem
Jaisey beemaar ko bewajeh qaraar aa jaaye

Last night your memory stole into my mind

As stealthily as spring steals into a deserted wilderness
As in desert wastes a gentle breeze begins to blow,
As in the sick beyond hope, hope begins to grow.

94

SHIKWA AND JAWAB-I-SHIKWA
MOHAMMAD IQBAL

Mohammad Iqbal (1877-1938) is widely regarded as the second greatest poet in Urdu after Ghalib and 'Shikwa' (The Mortal's Complaint to Allah), and its sequel 'Jawab-i-Shikwa' are regarded as one of his finest creative achievements. The Complaint was first recited by Iqbal in 1909 and created an immediate sensation and controversy. Lamenting Allah's unfairness towards the Muslim community, the poet beseeches the Lord to raise his followers once again to their former glory. Four years later, Iqbal composed 'Jawab-i-Shikwa', Allah's Response to the Poet's Complaint. The response ends with the promise that if Muslims continue to place their faith in Muhammad, God will place 'the destiny of the world in their hands once more'. This excerpt from Iqbal's remarkable poem reproduces twelve verses from 'Shikwa' and twelve verses from 'Jawab-i-Shikwa'.

SHIKWA

Why must I forever lose, forever forgo profit that is my due,
Sunk in the gloom of evenings past, no plans for the morrow pursue.
Why must I all attentive be to the nightingale's lament,
Friend, am I as dumb as a flower? Must I remain silent?
My theme makes me bold, makes my tongue more eloquent.
Dust be in my mouth, against Allah I make complaint.

We won renown for submitting to Your will—and it is so;
We speak out now, we are condemned to repeat our tale of woe.
We are like the silent lute whose chords are full of voice;
When grief wells up to our lips, we speak; we have no choice.
Lord God! We are Your faithful servants, for a while with us bear,
It is in our nature to always praise You, a small plaint also hear.

That Your Presence was primal from the beginning of time is true;
The rose also adorned the garden but of its fragrance no one knew.
Justice is all we ask for: You are perfect, You are benevolent.
If there were no breeze, how could the rose have spread its scent?
We Your people were dispersed, no solace could we find,
Or, would Your Beloved's following have gone out of its mind?

Before our time, a strange sight was the world You had made:
Some worshipped stone idols, others bowed to trees and prayed.
Accustomed to believing what they saw, the people's vision wasn't free,
How then couldn't anyone believe in a God he couldn't see?
Do you know of anyone, Lord, who then took Your Name? I ask.
It was the muscle in the Muslim's arms that did Your task.

Of all the brave warriors, there were none but only we.
We fought Your battles on land and often on the sea.
Our calls to prayer rang out from the churches of European lands
And floated across Africa's scorching desert sands.
We ruled the world, but regal glories our eyes disdained.
Under the shades of glittering sabres Your creed we proclaimed.

We blotted out the smear of falsehood from the pages of history,
We freed mankind from the chains of slavery.
The floors of Your Kaaba with our foreheads we swept.
The Quran You sent us we clasped to our breast.
Even so You accuse us of lack of faith on our part:
If we lacked faith, You did little to win our heart.

There are people of other faiths, some of them transgressors.
Some are humble; drunk with the spirit of arrogance are others.
Some are indolent, some ignorant and some endowed with brain,
Hundreds of others there are who even despair Your Name.
Your blessings are showered on homes of unbelievers, strangers all.
Only on the poor Muslim, Your wrath like lightning falls.

Our complaint is not that they are rich, that their coffers overflow;
They who have no manners and of polite speech nothing know.
What injustice! Here and now are houris and palaces to infidels given;
While the poor Muslim is promised houris only after he goes to heaven
Neither favour nor kindness is shown towards us any more;
Where is the affection You showed us in the days of yore?

Your mehfil is dissolved, those who loved You are also gone:
No sighs through the nights of longing, no lamenting at dawn.
We gave our hearts to You, took the wages You did not bestow;
But hardly had we taken our seats, You ordered us to go.
As lovers we came, as lovers departed with promise for tomorrow.
Now search for us with the light that on Your radiant face does glow

Leila's love is as intense, Qais desires her evermore,
On Nejd's hills and dales, the deer swift-footed as before.
The same love beats in the heart, beauty is as bewitching and magical,
Your messenger Ahmed's following still abides, Your presence is eternal.
Neither rhyme nor reason has Your displeasure, what does it mean?
On the faithful is Your angry eye of censure! What does it mean?

Our love may not be what it was, nor told with the same blandishments;
We may not tread the same path of submission, nor the same way give consent.
Our hearts are troubled, their compass needles from Mecca may have swerved,
Perhaps the old laws of faithfulness we may not have fully observed.
But sometimes towards us, at times to others You have affection shown,
It's not something one should say, You too have not been true to Your own.

Let the lament of this lonely bulbul pierce the hearts of all,
Arouse the hearts of the sleeping, with this my clarion call.
Transfused with fresh blood, a new compact of faith we'll sign.
Let our hearts thirst again for a sip of the vintage wine.
What if the pitcher be Persian, from Hejaz is the wine I serve.
What if the song be Indian, it is Hejazi in its verve.

JAWAB-I-SHIKWA

Words spoken from the heart never fail to have effect;
Sacred and pure their origin, on lofty heights their sights are set.
They have no wings and yet they have power to fly;
They rise from the dust and pierce through the sky.
So headstrong and insolent was my love, so much on mischief bent,
So outspoken my plaint, it tore through the firmament.

The aged vault of heaven heard. 'There is someone somewhere,' said he.
The planets spoke, 'Here on these ancient heights someone must be.'
'Not here,' said the moon, 'it must be someone from the earth below.'
Spoke the Milky Way, 'It must be someone hidden here we do not know.'
Only the gatekeeper of Eden did some of my plaint recognize
And understood that I was the man thrown out of paradise.

Spoke the Voice: 'Your tale is indeed full of sorrow;
Your tears tremble at the brim and are ready to flow.
Your cry of lament the sky has rung;

What cunning your impassioned heart has lent your tongue!
So eloquently did you word your plaint, you made it sound like praise.
To talk on equal terms with Us, man to celestial heights did raise.'

'Limitless is Our bounty, but none for it will pray.
There's no one on the seeker's path; to whom do We point the way?
Not one proved worthy of the care with which they were raised;
You are not the clay of which another Adam could be made.
If there were one deserving, We'd raise him to regal splendour,
To those who seek, We would unveil a new world of wonder.'

'The new age is like lightning; inflammatory is every haystack,
Neither wilderness nor garden is immune from its attack.
To this new flame old nations are like faggots on a pyre;
Followers of the last Messenger are consumed in its fire.
Even today if Abraham's faith could be made to glow;
Out of Nimrod's fire a garden of flowers would grow.'

'Let not the sorry plight of the garden upset the gardener;
Soon buds will sprout on the branches and like stars glitter.
Weeds and brambles will be swept out of the garden with a broom;
And where martyrs' blood was shed red roses shall bloom.
Look, how russet hues have tinged the eastern skies!
The horizon heralds the birth of a new sun about to rise.'

'Your garments are not soiled by the dust of any single native land,
You are the Joseph who sees his Canaan in every Egyptian sand.
Never will your caravan be plundered or laid waste,
You have no baggage save the starting bell. Make haste!
A tree of candles are you, your wick-like roots pierce the light;
Your thoughts are flames that dispel tomorrow's shades and make them bright.'

'You will not be destroyed even if Iran went into decline;
The shape of a goblet bears not on the headiness of the wine.
From the tales of the Tartar hordes we can clearly see
That Kaaba got its caretakers from the temples of idolatry.
The bark of truth is launched on the sea of time; its helmsman are you;
In the darkness of the new age, the faint glimmer of your star comes through.'

'The tumult caused by the Bulgar onslaught and aggression
Is to rouse you out of complacency and gird your loins for action.

Presume not that to hurt your feelings, it is a sinister device;
It is a challenge to your self-respect, it is a call to sacrifice.
Why tremble at the snorting of the chargers of your foes?
The flame of truth is not snuffed out by the breath the enemy blows.'

'Your real worth is hid, other people are yet to see what's true;
The Lord of the world's assembly has yet much need of you.
By your breath lives the world and is kept animate;
You are its destined leader, you the star of fate.
There is no time to relax, much still remains to be done;
You have yet to fully spread the light of God, the only one.'

'You are the bud's captive fragrance; burst forth and gain release;
Hoist your pack on your shoulder; scatter incense like the garden breeze
You are but a tiny speck; to infinite vastness let it increase;
You are only the wave's murmur; turn it to the roar of the raging sea.
With the power of love raise the lowest to triumphant heights
With the name of Muhammad turn the world's darkness to light.'

'He is on arid wastes and on mountain sides and on endless steppes;
He dwells by the ocean's swell that's tossed by the stormy seas.
He is in the cities of Cathay and in wildernesses Moroccan
And he lies hidden in the faith of every Muslim man.
May every eye see this spectacle to the very end of time
And testify to our saying, "We have made your name sublime."''

95

THE WICK IS DRY, THE OIL RUNS OUT

KABIR

The wick is dry, the oil runs out,
The drum is silent, the dancer sleeps,
The fire burnt out, no smoke ensues.
He is immortal, no other the vigil keeps.

The string has snapped, the lute is mute,
The player plays not, his art is gone.
It is all sermons, speeches, talk and idle gossip.
When knowledge comes, he forgets his song.
O Kabir, he who has conquered the five sins,
(Lust, anger, greed, attachment and the ego)
To reach the highest seat, he has not far to go.

96

DEATH

GHALIB

You wrote all over the pages of life and all came to an end:
You had no equal in poetry and all came to an end;
In old age wine was your consolation, Ghalib,
But you were deprived of it also, and all came to an end.

97

MANGOES
AKBAR ILLAHABADI

Neither letter nor message from my beloved send to me,
If you must send something this season, mangoes let them be.
Make sure there are some that I can keep to eat another day,
If twenty are ripe add another ten that can stay.
Your slave's address you know, it remains the same
Dispatch them to Allahabad in a parcel in my name.
Whatever you do, in your reply please be not so brash
'Order for mangoes received: First send the cash.'

98

THE AGONY TRAIL
FEZA AZMI

Prayer of love we offer to you
With your idols we will hold converse;
We will prostrate ourselves where we like
Hymns of love we will chant everywhere
How long will we remain torn apart?
Let us sew some pieces together for a start
Far too long has the tavern been deserted
Let us fill our goblets with fresh wine
We know your heart still bears scars
So do our hearts; but with every breath
It is up to us to heal them or bleed to death
We will grasp your hand of friendship when you extend it
We will take up arms and fight to our last breath
We are willing to be your friends as we are to be your foes
Will grasp your hand of friendship as the saying goes
If it is war you want, we will be ready to fight
If it is love you offer, we'll take it with delight.

99

MY OWN EPITAPH

Here lies one who spared neither man nor God
Waste not your tears on him, he was a sod
Writing nasty things he regarded as great fun
Thank the Lord he is dead, this son of a gun.

AFTERWORD

MALA DAYAL

Khushwant Singh passed away on 20 March 2014. He died as he would have liked to, at home, peacefully, but holding a bowl of soup not a glass of whisky. Within ten minutes of his death, TV channels were flashing the news and people began arriving—those whose lives he had touched in many ways.

Journalists, writers and poets came. Painters, academics and politicians arrived. He had been generous in his encouragement to fledgling writers and had co-authored books to boost the confidence and purses of many. His endorsement of good writing gave him the friendship of several of the younger generation of acclaimed novelists. Among those who flocked to his home were those who had importuned him for a favourable write-up in his widely syndicated columns or a recommendation for a national award. He knew that they came with a matlab but gave in gracefully to their bullying. Then there were those who cultivated him to bask in his reflected glory. He hated name-droppers and was unaware that his was a name to drop. He was never pompous and abhorred pomposity. He repeatedly said that one should take one's work seriously and oneself lightly.

Strangers rang his doorbell despite the stricture on the board outside his flat: '*Please do not ring the bell unless you are expected.*' They came because they admired and respected his writing and outspokenness. *The Economist,* in its obituary, called him 'the most unbuttoned voice in the whole English-language press'.

He hated fundamentalists, 'fundoos' as he referred to them, whether Sikh, Muslim or Hindu. One of his passions was furthering Indo-Pak friendship. He was probably the most loved Indian in Pakistan and, upon his death, Pakistani newspapers, both English and Urdu, paid him handsome tributes.

He had cultivated an image of himself as a womanizer, boozer, bon vivant. Beneath that image was a man of strict discipline, waking up before the break of dawn to start work on his columns. As he boasted, he 'never missed a deadline'. And without this discipline and hard work, apart from his two weekly columns, he would not have produced six novels, an autobiography, collections of short stories and essays, translations of novels and poetry, an authoritative two-volume history of the Sikhs and several popular joke books. He often quoted Hilaire Belloc, 'When I am dead I hope it will be said, "His sins were scarlet, but his books were read."'

He would have loved the attention he received at his death when it came ten months short of a century. But perhaps what would have pleased him most is that his ashes were taken by train to Pakistan to be buried in Hadali, the village where he was born.

NOTES AND ACKNOWLEDGEMENTS

The editors and the publisher would like to thank all the publishers and rights holders listed below for permission to use exclusive copyright material in this anthology. Besides the material that has been extracted from the twenty or so books that Khushwant Singh wrote and published, most of the other pieces in this volume first appeared as columns or articles in the *Hindustan Times*, *The Illustrated Weekly of India*, the *Tribune*, the *Telegraph* and *Outlook*. All columns and articles have been used with permission from the author's estate.

If a piece appeared in a publication other than the foregoing, the information is recorded in the Notes section below. A few of the pieces have been edited with the approval of the author's estate. All such editorial interventions are recorded in the Notes.

Every effort has been made to trace copyright holders and obtain permission to reproduce copyright material included in the book. In the event of any inadvertent omission, the publisher should be informed and formal acknowledgement will be included in all future editions of this book.

Thanks to Penguin Books India for granting permission to use extracts from *Train to Pakistan*, *I Shall Not Hear the Nightingale*, *Delhi*, *The Company of Women*, *Burial at Sea*, *The Sunset Club*, *The Portrait of a Lady: Collected Stories*, *Truth, Love & a Little Malice* and *Ranjit Singh: Maharaja of the Punjab*; Orient Blackswan for 'Bara Mah' from *Hymns of Guru Nanak* and an excerpt from *Umrao Jan Ada*; Vision Books for 'Exchange of Lunatics', 'Stench of Kerosene', 'The Death of Shaikh Burhanuddin', 'The Night of the Full Moon' from *Land of Five Rivers* and an excerpt from *I Take this Woman* by Rajinder Singh Bedi; excerpts from *A History of the Sikhs* (Vol 1 & 2) and *Shikwa and Jawab-i-Shikwa* reproduced with permission of Oxford University Press India © Oxford University Press; HarperCollins India for excerpts from *Nature Watch*; Rupa Publications India for excerpts from *The Good, the Bad and the Ridiculous*, *On Love and Sex* and *On Women*.

◆

NOTES TO INDIVIDUAL SELECTIONS
Village in the Desert: Extracted from *Truth, Love & a Little Malice*.
Winning My Father's Approval: Extracted from *Truth, Love & a Little Malice*. The title is new.

A Good Way to Go: Extracted from *Truth, Love & a Little Malice.* The title is new.

Death of a Lady: Extracted from *Truth, Love & a Little Malice.* The title is new.

Simba: Extracted from *Truth, Love & a Little Malice.*

Billo: Originally published in the *Hindustan Times.*

Family Matters: The author wrote often about his family in his newspaper columns. This piece has been adapted from columns in the *Hindustan Times* and the *Tribune.*

My Beloved Country

Why I am An Indian: Originally published in *The Illustrated Weekly of India.*

The Ghosts of Kasauli: Originally published in *Seminar.*

The Romance of New Delhi: Originally published in *The Statesman,* Calcutta. This piece has been updated. Teja Singh Malik, who is mentioned in this piece, was Khushwant Singh's father-in-law.

Bombay Rhapsody: Extracted from *Truth, Love & a Little Malice.* The title is new.

The Venus of Churchgate: There is more than one version of this encounter. This piece has been reproduced from *On Women.*

In Madras: This piece was originally published in *The Illustrated Weekly of India.* It has been edited.

Blowing Up Calcutta: Originally published in the *The Illustrated Weekly of India.*

The Magic of Sikkim: This piece was originally published as 'Sikkim: The Twenty Second State' in an anthology entitled *Around the World with Khushwant Singh* (Orient Paperbacks). It has been edited but not updated.

Ganga Mai: Originally published as 'Prayer to Ganga' in the *Hindustan Times.*

The Haunted Simla Road: Originally published in *The Observer,* London.

The Sikhs

Writing Sikh History: Originally published in *Seminar.*

The Sikh Homeland: Extract from *A History of the Sikhs,* Vol. 1.

Ranjit Singh, Maharaja of the Punjab: Extract from *Ranjit Singh: Maharaja of the Punjab.*

The Sikhs: Originally published as 'The Poets of Enterprise' in *Outlook.*

A Riot of Passage: Originally published as 'Oh, That Other Hindu Riot of Passage' in *Outlook.* This piece has been lightly edited.

Bara Mah: Extract from *Hymns of Guru Nanak.* © UNESCO 1969

p 89 **in flower:** In Chet the *Salvadora persica* (pee lo) is in blossom in the Punjab countryside.

p 92 **papeeha:** Common hawk-cuckoo (*Hierococcyx varius*) popularly known as 'brain-fever/ brainfever' bird because of its call. To Indian ears, the same call sounds like *pee-kahan* (where is my husband?) or *papeeha*.

The Uses & Abuses of Religion

On Religion: Extract from *The Freethinker's Prayer Book* (Aleph).

Gurus and Godmen: This piece originally appeared in an anthology entitled *Gurus, Godmen and Good People* (Orient Longman). It has been edited.

The Boy God: Extracted from *Gurus, Godmen and Good People*. Originally titled 'Balyogeshwar'.

Carnage in Gujarat: Khushwant Singh wrote several pieces on the Gujarat communal riots. This is an edited version of a piece that appeared in the *Hindustan Times*.

A Fundamental Problem: Khushwant Singh was unsparing in his condemnation of religious fundamentalism, and wrote often about the problem in his columns and articles. This piece is adapted from columns that appeared in the *Hindustan Times*.

Passage to Pakistan

Muhammad Ali Jinnah: Taken from *The Good, the Bad and the Ridiculous*.

Last Days in Lahore: Originally published in *Outlook*. This piece has been lightly edited.

General Tikka Khan: Taken from *The Good, the Bad and the Ridiculous*. This piece has been lightly edited.

Some Truths about Pakistan: First published in *The Illustrated Weekly of India*. This piece has been edited but not updated to retain the flavour of the country the author visited in the 1970s. The title is new.

The Hanging of Bhutto: Originally published in *New Delhi* magazine.

Singular People

All the profiles in this section are from *The Good, the Bad and the Ridiculous* except the following:

Indira Gandhi: Extracted from *Indira Gandhi Returns* (Vision Books). It describes Mrs Gandhi when she was in her sixties.

Nirad C. Chaudhuri: Originally published in the *Tribune*.

Pandit Nehru: Originally published as 'Like A Storm in A Gandhi Cap' in *Outlook*

R. K. Narayan: Originally published as 'Blue Hawaii Yoghurt' in *Outlook*.

Sir Vidia: Originally published as 'Nobelity, At Last' in *Outlook*.

The Ferocity & Flamboyance of Nature

The Monsoon: Extracted from Khushwant Singh's *India Without Humbug* (India Book House).

Nature's Festival of Colours: Extracted from *Nature Watch*. The title is new.

In the Heat of the Summer: Extracted from *Nature Watch*. The title is new.

Sex on My Mind

In the Land of the *Kamasutra*: An edited version of a *Weekly* piece.

Sex on My Mind: Khushwant Singh was very forthright in his views on sex. He wrote extensively on the subject and this piece is adapted from two articles that originally appeared in *The Illustrated Weekly of India* and the *Hindustan Times*.

On Kissing: Originally published in the *Telegraph*.

The Rajneesh Approach to Sex: First appeared in *On Love and Sex*.

To the Victor Go the Spoils: First appeared in *On Love and Sex*.

A Merry Heart

Humour in Indian Life: Khushwant Singh was exasperated by the fact that Indians lacked a sense of humour. This piece is adapted from the introduction to one of his joke books (No. 4).

The Joker: The edited introduction to Joke Book No. 9.

All the jokes in this section were originally published in various newspaper columns.

Enthusiasms, Rants & Soliloquies

Why I Supported the Emergency: Originally published in *Outlook*.

Angrezi Hatao: From *India Without Humbug*.

Seeing Oneself: One of Khushwant Singh's most famous essays, this has appeared in more than one anthology. It was first published in the *Hindustan Times*.

The Joys of Farting: Extract from *Delhi: A Novel*.

How to Live, How to Die

How to Live a Long and Happy Life: Originally published as 'Eight Clues to Happiness' in the *Telegraph*.

Dealing With Adversity: Extracted from *Truth, Love & a Little Malice*.

Advice to Would-be Writers: Originally published in the *Tribune*. It has been edited.

The Preoccupations of Middle Age: Originally published as 'Idle Thoughts' in the *Hindustan Times*.

Old Age: Originally published as 'Old Men's Tale' in the *Tribune*.

The Death of Loved Ones: Originally published in the *Telegraph*.

Death and Dying: Originally published as 'Have You Ever Thought of Death?' in the *Tribune*.

Some Codes to Live By: Extract from *The Freethinker's Prayer Book*.

How I Would Like to Be Remembered: This quote appeared in several obituaries. Sunil Sethi, the journalist and book reviewer, remembers Khushwant Singh saying this to him during one of their interviews.

FICTION & POETRY
The Novels

Dacoity/Kalyug: Extracted from *Train to Pakistan*.

Shooting the Crane: Extracted from *I Shall Not Hear the Nightingale*. The title is new.

Delhi: Extracted from *Delhi: A Novel*.

Dhanno: Extracted from *The Company of Women*.

Victor Jai Bhagwan: Extracted from *Burial at Sea*.

Lodi Gardens: Extracted from *The Sunset Club*.

All the **Stories** are from *The Portrait of a Lady: Collected Stories*.

Toba Tek Singh: Fiction in Translation

Umrao Jan Ada: Extracted from *Umrao Jan Ada*.

Toba Tek Singh: From *Land of Five Rivers*. Originally titled 'Exchange of Lunatics'.

Stench of Kerosene: From *Land of Five Rivers*.

The Death of Shaikh Burhanuddin: From *Land of Five Rivers*.

The Night of the Full Moon: From *Land of Five Rivers*.

I Take this Woman: Extracted from *I Take this Woman.*

A Passion for Poetry

Translating Urdu Poetry: Originally published as 'Urdu Poetry and the Peerless Art of Translation' in the *Hindustan Times.*

Ghalib: Originally published as 'Ghalib Knew His Worth' in the *Tribune.*

Faiz Ahmed Faiz: Extracted from 'Translating Faiz' in the *Hindustan Times.*

Shikwa and Jawab-i-Shikwa: Extracted from *Shikwa and Jawab-i-Shikwa: Iqbal's Dialogue with Allah.* This excerpt has twelve verses from 'Shikwa' and twelve verses from 'Jawab-i-Shikwa'.

p 407 **Your Beloved's:** The Beloved refers to Prophet Muhammad.

p 409 **Leila:** This refers to the famous love classic of Leila and Majnun (also known as Qais).

p 410 **Tartar hordes:** The Tartars who after ravaging Muslim lands accepted conversion to Islam and became zealous guardians of Mecca.

p 410 **Bulgar:** This refers to the Bulgarian invasion of Turkey in the autumn of 1912.

The Wick is Dry, The Oil Runs Out: From a column in the *Hindustan Times.*

Death: From the *Tribune.*

Mangoes: From *Nature Watch.*

The Agony Trail: From the *Tribune.*

◆

All photographs in the photo section are published courtesy Mala Dayal.

◆

A note on style: While most proper nouns, dates and words from various Indian languages have been standardized for this edition (Aleph house style), the following words and phrases have more than one variation in the text where it was important to maintain the author's original style—Shimla and Simla; Jumna and Yamuna; Wahe Guru, Wah Guru and Wahi-i-Guru; the 1857 Mutiny and War of Independence.

ABOUT THE AUTHOR

Born in Punjab's Hadali village (now in Pakistan) in 1915, Khushwant Singh was among India's best-known and most widely read authors and journalists. He was founder-editor of *Yojana*, and editor of *The Illustrated Weekly of India*, *National Herald* and the *Hindustan Times*. He published six novels—*Train to Pakistan*, *I Shall Not Hear the Nightingale*, *Delhi: A Novel*, *The Company of Women*, *Burial at Sea* and *The Sunset Club* as well as several books of short stories which were published together as *The Portrait of a Lady*. His other books are the two-volume *A History of the Sikhs*; an autobiography, *Truth, Love & a Little Malice*; a biography, *Ranjit Singh: Maharaja of the Punjab*; and a book of non-fiction, *The Return of Indira Gandhi*. In addition, he published translations of Hindi and Urdu novels, short stories and poetry, notably *Umrao Jan Ada* by Mirza Mohammad Hadi Ruswa, Rajinder Singh Bedi's *I Take This Woman* and Iqbal's 'Shikwa' and 'Jawab-i-Shikwa'.

Khushwant Singh was a member of the Rajya Sabha from 1980 to 1986. He was awarded the Padma Bhushan in 1974; he returned the award in 1984 to protest the siege of the Golden Temple by the Indian Army. In 2007, he was awarded India's second highest civilian honour, the Padma Vibhushan.

Khushwant Singh died on 20 March 2014. He is survived by his daughter, Mala Dayal, granddaughter, Naina Dayal, and his son, Rahul Singh.